# The Decline of the Left Wing in Israel

# The Decline of the Left Wing in Israel

*Yossi Beilin and the Politics of the Peace Process*

Avi Shilon

**I.B. TAURIS**

LONDON • NEW YORK • OXFORD • NEW DELHI • SYDNEY

I.B. TAURIS
Bloomsbury Publishing Plc
50 Bedford Square, London, WC1B 3DP, UK
1385 Broadway, New York, NY 10018, USA
29 Earlsfort Terrace, Dublin 2, Ireland

BLOOMSBURY, I.B. TAURIS and the I.B. Tauris logo are trademarks
of Bloomsbury Publishing Plc

First published in Great Britain 2020
Paperback edition published 2021

A catalogue record for this book is available from the British Library.

A catalog record for this book is available from the Library of Congress.

ISBN: HB: 978-1-8386-0112-6
PB: 978-0-7556-4505-3
eISBN: 978-1-8386-0114-0
ePDF: 978-1-8386-0115-7

Typeset by Deanta Global Publishing Services, Chennai, India

To find out more about our authors and books visit www.bloomsbury.com
and sign up for our newsletters.

*To my parents,*
*Sima and Haim*

# Contents

# Acknowledgments

I think very few people would be willing to place their archives in the hands of a historian unconditionally and without any involvement in what is subsequently written, and for this I hold Yossi Beilin in high esteem and owe him a debt of gratitude. It goes without saying that the book reflects my view of Beilin and the processes in which he participated, and not his view.

During the course of the research, I drew from the work of scholars from various disciplines pertaining to Israel studies—an academic field that is growing in the world (and hopefully in Israel, too). There is no space to acknowledge everyone here, but I would like to note in particular Dr. Dimitry Chomsky, Dr. Seth Anziska, Dr. Nissim Leon, Prof. Ian Lustick, Prof. Ruth Gavizon, and Dr. Ephraim Lavie. Many thanks to Ira Moskowitz for his meticulous and wonderful translation.

I also learned a lot from participating in Prof. Anita Shapira's forum of Zionist scholars and in the "Living Together" group of Tel Aviv University's Minerva Center, led by Dr. Raef Zreik. The many hours I spent at the Yad Tabenkin Archives were pleasant and fruitful, thanks to its director, Dr. Aharon Azati. I wrote most of the book during my stay as a postdoctoral fellow at NYU and at Tsinghua University in Beijing. My thanks to Prof. Ron Zweig, who hosted me in New York and to Prof. Itamar Rabinovich, president of the Israel Institute, who helped me to attain the experience in China. The book includes ideas I published in various professional journals and in articles that appeared in the *Haaretz* daily. I would like to thank *Haaretz* editors Alon Idan and Ravit Hecht, who helped me to hone my ideas.

I also owe thanks to Gadi Baltiansky and Boaz Karni, who played a key role in initiating the project and in obtaining the grant for writing the book, and I thank S. Daniel Abraham for the grant. I'm also happy to thank Daniela, Yossi's wife for her nice hospitality and advices during our meetings. I finished writing the book in a pleasant room in Shalom Tower; for this, I thank the Tel Aviv Municipality's Department of Culture.

Thank you to my Israeli publisher Yoram Roz and my editor Shmuel Rosner, who immediately embraced the idea of writing the book and welcomed me at the Kinneret, Zmora-Bitan, Dvir publishing house. The editor of the Hebrew manuscript, Yuval Elazari, contributed with advice and his ability to make the text clearer. It is my pleasure to thank Sophie Rudland, the editor of I.B. Tauris, who believed in this project and guided me smartly and kindly throughout the process of publication. If there are mistakes, they remain my sole responsibility.

Without my wife Lior and my sons Itamar and Roee, there would be no purpose in my writing.

# Introduction: The Left Wing Sorrow

## 1

The State of Israel was established through days of battle and blood. Israel's War of Independence included two spheres of warfare: a civil war between Jews and Palestinians that erupted in November 1947 immediately upon approval of the United Nations plan to partition the land into two states, Jewish and Arab; and a broader war between Israel and Arab states, whose armies invaded Israel after it declared independence on May 14, 1948.

The State of Israel was acquired in blood. About 1 percent of the 600,000 Jews in the country when the state was born were killed during the war. Against this background, the clause in Israel's Declaration of Independence that addresses its neighbors is particularly striking: "We extend our hand to all neighboring states and their peoples in an offer of peace and good neighborliness, and appeal to them to establish bonds of cooperation and mutual help with the sovereign Jewish people settled in its own land. The State of Israel is prepared to do its share in a common effort for the advancement of the entire Middle East." The call for peace was not a flowery cliché required by the historic occasion. In comparison, the US Declaration of Independence, from which Israel's founders drew inspiration, makes no mention of the aspiration for peace.

To what extent have Israel's leaders over the generations actually extended a hand of peace? More precisely, to what extent have they done this since the 1980s? This book centers on these questions. Indeed, the salient reference in the Declaration of Independence to the need for "good neighborliness" indicates that the state's founders clearly realized that the Zionist project would not be complete until Israel was peacefully integrated into the Middle East. More than seventy years after the declaration, this goal has yet to be achieved and remains, as always, a central issue on Israel's political and public agenda.

Israel's foreign and defense relations have known ups and downs. In 1979, after five wars—the War of Independence, the Sinai Campaign, the Six-Day War, the War of Attrition, and the Yom Kippur War—Israel, under Menachem Begin's right-wing government, signed a peace accord with Egypt. It was the first peace treaty between Israel and an Arab state, and included an agreement to launch negotiations aimed at establishing autonomy for the Palestinians in the West Bank and Gaza Strip. Fourteen years later, Israel—this time under Yitzhak Rabin's left-wing government—signed an agreement with the Palestinian Liberation Organization (PLO), representing the Palestinian national movement. The Declaration of Principles of the "Oslo Accords," signed in September 1993, aimed to establish Palestinian autonomy in the territories conquered by Israel in the Six-Day War. Autonomy was designed as an interim solution, slated to last no longer than five years, pending a final status accord between the two peoples. The Oslo Accords paved the way for Israel's second peace treaty with an Arab state—an agreement signed with Jordan in October 1994.

It is difficult to overstate the importance of the Oslo Accords as a historic breakthrough in the relations between the two national movements fighting for control of the Land of Israel/Palestine. The process of reconciliation with the Palestinians was also designed to transform Israel's relations with Arab states. Both the vision of "the new Middle East" of Shimon Peres and the more moderate strategy of Rabin, who sought to take advantage of the window of opportunity that opened in the Middle East with the collapse of the Soviet Union, promised a new future in the early 1990s. On September 23, 1993, when the Knesset approved the Oslo Accords, it was almost impossible to imagine how the process would deteriorate and how deeply the peace camp in Israel would decline. Even two Knesset members who were then considered future leaders of the Likud—Roni Milo, a scion of a Revisionist family, and Meir Sheetrit, who represented the young Mizrahi generation—preferred not to oppose the agreement and abstained in the voting, wishing to be on the right side of history. The press wrote that the dream of the Greater Land of Israel was over. But in 2018, a quarter of a century later, there are still Likud members of Knesset who advocate annexing the occupied territories, without granting voting rights to the Palestinians—that is, partial apartheid.[1]

Through the political biography of Yossi Beilin—who, as deputy foreign minister in the second Rabin government was responsible for leading the most important effort to reach an agreement between Israel and the Palestinians, the Oslo process, and in my view was among the politicians who made the greatest impact on Israel in the late twentieth century—I sought to examine the rise and fall of the peace process and the peace camp in recent decades.

This topic, of course, also has a global context, which since the 1990s has featured the rise of radical Islamic organizations and counter-reactions in the Western world (for example, the victory of Donald Trump in the US elections in November 2016, the British decision to exit the European Union, and the surge of populist right-wing parties throughout Europe). Nonetheless, the book focuses on the Israeli angle. That is, this book comprises historical research on the peace process in recent decades, and seeks to examine its connection to economic, social, and cultural issues in Israeli society.

This research has the unique advantage of drawing from archives kept by Beilin, who allowed me exclusive and unrestricted access to the archives' thousands of artifacts—documents, protocols, letters, diaries, and more. Some were written by Beilin himself, and many are from people he encountered during his work. Most of the material pertains to the period starting with the political upheaval of 1977, when Beilin began to work as an adviser and spokesman for Shimon Peres, and culminating at the end of the first decade of the twenty-first century, when Beilin left politics. I will elaborate later in the Introduction on the research methodology and its reasons. In any case, the result is a political biography of Beilin, and a monograph on the peace process and the sociopolitical changes that have occurred in Israel during the past four decades.

## 2

The Oslo Accords were based on a simple plan to divide the land in two stages. The first stage was designed to last about five years, during which time an autonomous Palestinian Authority (PA) would administer most of the territories Israel captured in 1967. During this initial stage, in which the two peoples were supposed to learn that coexistence is possible, Israel and the PA were expected to conclude the final status accord.

The PA was, indeed, established after the signing of the accords and the Israel Defense Forces (IDF) withdrew from a significant part of the territories. But the attempt to reach a final status accord never reached fruition—in part, because Prime Minister Rabin was murdered two years after the accords were signed and his successor, Peres, lost in the May 1996 elections to Benjamin Netanyahu of the Likud, who was skeptical about the peace process. Only in 2000, a year after Ehud Barak of the Labor Party was elected prime minister, representatives of Israel and the Palestinians tried to reach a final status agreement. This occurred at the Camp David summit in July of that year. However, even though both sides agreed in principle to establish a Palestinian state, the talks failed and exposed irresolvable disagreements on a range of topics. One of the issues in dispute was the size of the prospective Palestinian state. Israel began the talks by presenting a map of a Palestinian state on 77 percent of the West Bank and Gaza Strip. The Palestinians rejected it. In the next round of talks, held in Taba in January 2011, the Israelis presented a map offering 93–94 percent of the territories, but the Palestinians agreed to compromise only on a map that promised 98 percent, with full compensation in lands they would receive from Israel in exchange for land they agreed to cede in the West Bank.[2]

The second intifada, which erupted in October 2000 following the failed Camp David summit, was marked by suicide bombings and aggressive Israeli military responses, climaxing in the IDF's Defensive Shield operation in March 2002 and its redeployment in cities and towns in the West Bank. The IDF's actions against the Palestinian Authority, together with the fact that the PLO institutions in the territories disappointed the Palestinian public (because the autonomy did not develop into an independent state, and because of rampant corruption), weakened the PLO's standing among residents of the territories. This weakening of the PLO contributed to the Hamas victory in elections to the Palestinian legislature in 2006 and the subsequent takeover of the Gaza Strip by Hamas in 2007, following Israel's unilateral withdrawal two years earlier. The West Bank and Gaza Strip have since been under separate Palestinian regimes. Against the background of these events, and in the context of significant Jewish settlement growth (during the decade since the initial Oslo agreement in 1993, the settlement population, not including East Jerusalem, grew from about 100,000 to more than 350,000,[3] according to Israel's Central Bureau of Statistics), the principle of partitioning the land as the logical solution for peace lost much of its appeal. Even former supporters of this solution became disillusioned about the prospects of peace in the second decade of the twenty-first century.[4]

Why did the process collapse? Prof. Asher Susser represents many scholars in claiming that the pursuit of a final ("end of conflict") accord—as attempted at the Camp David summit—was in itself detrimental to the process.[5] In Susser's view, the Oslo process was wise precisely because it mapped out a gradual solution. The Palestinians cannot accommodate the Israeli aspiration for a final status accord that includes "an end of [Palestinian] demands" from Israel, while demanding Palestinian recognition of Israel as a Jewish state—and without recognition of the Palestinian right of return and Palestinian sovereignty in Jerusalem. Under such conditions, the Palestinians would be obliged to surrender not only their political demands, but also their fundamental beliefs about their right to the land and the injustice the Zionist movement inflicted on them in 1948. In Susser's view, we must give up the dream of completely ending the conflict and suffice with arrangements that would allow the fundamental disagreements to exist in a reality of de facto coexistence. Those who seek an "end of conflict" in the current generation will experience disappointment that will lead them to look for new and dangerous formulas, including a single democratic state, which would mean denying the Jews' right of self-determination and igniting a civil war, or an apartheid state that would obliterate the democratic dimension of Israel. That is, Israel should push for a nonfinal accord of two states, even if the Palestinians do not reciprocate by agreeing to drop additional demands, and even if Israel does not agree to all of their demands.

Was the aspiration to end the conflict—an aspiration that drove the Oslo process and the Barak government's Camp David venture—premature and precipitous? Should we conclude that we must wait patiently (just as the rabbinic tradition instructed Jews to wait patiently for Divine Providence to bring them back to the Land of Israel[6]) because in the foreseeable future, and perhaps for many generations, the conflict will remain irresolvable? Or is the current situation attributable to mistakes made during the Oslo process and the worldview of its leaders?

In this context, it is interesting to consider the humorous proposal of the Slovenian philosopher Slavoj Žižek, who suggested imagining an apocalyptic announcement about a meteor that is about to strike the region: at that moment, wouldn't it become apparent to both Israelis and Palestinians that their ostensibly irresolvable conflict is not so deep and complex, and is, in fact, almost ridiculous? However, on second thought, Žižek's proposal is not so helpful. It seems that he raised a hypothetical question without considering a factor that was likewise accorded insufficient weight by the proponents of the Oslo process: the religious factor. That is, after hearing that a meteor is about to hit the region and will wipe out all its holy sites and inhabitants, Jewish and Muslims might still cling to their particularistic claims to the land until the very moment they ascend to heaven. Indeed, an analysis of the peace process and its collapse indicates that religion played and continues to play a huge role, which was not taken into account by the leaders of the process, as the documents from Beilin's archive confirm.

The peace process conducted by Israel and the PLO drew from the optimistic "liberal peace" paradigm, which is based on the assumption that as regimes and economies become more advanced, secular, and free, they also become more averse to war.[7] Indeed, the PA was designed not only to provide the foundation for a state, but also to serve as a secular alternative, with a liberal and free economy, countering the threat posed since the 1980s by the growing strength of Hamas and religion in the territories. At the same time, adherents of the Oslo Accords in Israel sought to influence the nature of Israeli society, to present an alternative to those who proposed a blend of national and religious dimensions, and to shape Israel as a secular and liberal society.

Advocates of the liberal peace theory view adherence to religious principles and values as archaic, and offer, instead, an optimistic promise of economic cooperation that would raise the standard of living of the two peoples and ensure a reality of peace. This worldview is anchored in the notion of "progress," as it developed in Western philosophy since the Enlightenment era; this notion of progress sees human society advancing in a linear path toward a better future, in part thanks to science and rationalism.

The clash between the idea of progress and alternative ways of conceptualizing history—for example, the alternative of "what was will be" (as in *Ecclesiastes*), which sees history moving in circles; or even a view of history as a process of decline—was saliently expressed in the confrontation between President Bill Clinton, a devotee of the idea of progress, and Palestinian Chairman Yasser Arafat during the Camp David summit. A description of the confrontation was recorded in the diary of Akram Hanieh, a member of the Palestinian delegation at the summit. (A copy of the diary is in Beilin's archives.) The confrontation, on July 24, 2000, is an instructive example of how different and opposing patterns of historical perceptions—which can be defined as Western versus Eastern, rational versus mythological, or secular versus traditional—played a key role in the failure of the effort to achieve a final status agreement.

"Why didn't you accept my proposals?" Clinton asked in anger, after justifying Barak's refusal to give up Israeli sovereignty on the Temple Mount. Clinton scolded Arafat:

Barak offered solutions and concessions, and you refuse to present anything. The discussion is about policy, not religion. You couldn't have dreamt of sovereignty over the Muslim and Christian quarters and authority over the Haram [al-Sharif], all in the framework of a sovereign state. You couldn't have dreamt of this! You missed an opportunity in '47 when you opposed the partition . . . and now again!? You won't have a state. Our relations are over. You won't find anyone in the Middle East who will give you the time of day. You could receive the support of the churches—you brought everyone to Bethlehem 2000—and you could return as a hero to Gaza. But on the morning after, you'll be alone and you'll deprive your people of everything being offered to it. But your people will judge you. And the Muslims will also say that Clinton offered you a state and control of the

Haram. . . . You'll be the reason the Haram will remain under Israeli sovereignty. Barak made a lot of concessions—you didn't budge. You just want to pocket what Barak already gave you.

Clinton tried to persuade Arafat to suffice with receiving responsibility for the Temple Mount under Israeli sovereignty, under the ostensibly logical assumption that Arafat would accept an offer that gave him more than he currently had in hand. That is, even if a Palestinian state did not include all of the territory, he should still prefer a state to autonomy. But Arafat responded from a different perspective:

> I'm the leader of the Palestinian people and I represent the Arabs, Muslims, and Christians, in all matters concerning the Haram and the Church of the Holy Sepulcher. I will not betray their faith in me. Even if you offer me a state, and Haifa and Jaffa—without full sovereignty on the Haram, it won't happen! . . . I won't betray my people. You want to come to my funeral? I'd rather die than agree to Israeli sovereignty over the Haram. I also won't sell out the Armenians; they're part of the Palestinian people. I won't be recorded in Arab and Muslim history as a traitor. As I promised my people—We'll liberate Jerusalem! If not now, perhaps in another thousand years.[8]

The confrontation between the American president and the Palestinian chairman exposed the gaping differences in their perceptions of the dimension of time, the significance of their place in history, and the complex relations between religion and nationhood. While Clinton highlighted the immediate benefits for the Palestinians, Arafat emphasized that he was ready to wait another millennium for a full achievement. While Clinton treated Arafat like the leader of a secular organization, who weights the pros and cons in accordance with the possibilities, Arafat insisted that without full sovereignty over the site held sacred by Muslims, he would also turn down an offer of Haifa and Jaffa (as if they were offered to him). Arafat saw himself not only as representing the Palestinian interest, but also as representing the Muslim attachment to the holy places. That explains the paradox of his rejection of Israel's proposal: Arafat felt more comfortable leaving the Temple Mount under Israeli sovereignty and staking his claim to it, than compromising with Israel and gaining partial sovereignty. He did not want to be remembered as the first Muslim leader to accord de jure recognition of the Jews' claim to the Temple Mount.

Thus, while Clinton's approach offered optimism in the near term, Arafat's eyes looked beyond contemporary times—to the distant past and to the history that remains to be written in the distant future. In his worldview, the mythological, theological, and rational dwell together. But what is more surprising is that Ehud Barak, the secularized kibbutznik known for his "analytical mind," harbored similar sentiments. How else can we understand his declaration at the end of the Camp David summit that he refused to surrender sovereignty on the Temple Mount because it would mean giving up the "holy of holies"[9] —a theological concept in the Jewish tradition referring to the specific place in the Temple where the Ark of the Covenant was kept. The question is not whether Barak really believed this, but why he chose this terminology at these crucial moments.

The religious dimension, therefore, played a key role in the process, even when the process was led by secular people.

Clinton, faithful to the liberal paradigm of peace, did not understand why Arafat rejected the net gain offered to him. After all, a state—even if only on about 90 percent of the West Bank and Gaza Strip (that is, the 22 percent that remained for the Palestinians from Mandatory Palestine)—is definitely preferable to limited autonomy.

In this context, another dominant element in the peace process should be noted: the process was conducted under American auspices. The United States is not only Israel's foremost ally (at least since 1967); it is also a country inclined toward a "triumphant" and prosperous nationalism that "celebrates the positive" and has "little empathy for the whining of aggrieved nationalists whose formative experience consisted of a succession of national humiliations and defeats."[10] Therefore, the Palestinians had little chance of winning American sympathy from the outset. Palestinian nationalism was, indeed, shaped by a sense of deprivation and exploitation, having emerged in the shadow of Zionism and the European imperialism that came in the wake of the Ottoman Empire's collapse.[11] The Americans thus had less patience for the Palestinians' complaints and the latter faced an uphill battle. Proponents of reconciliation saw this US predilection as an impediment to the building of peace.

Another example of the basic differences between the Western/liberal view of the peace process and the Palestinian view is evident in Beilin's description of his first meeting with Arafat, held in the latter's office in Tunis soon after the signing of the Oslo Declaration of Principles in September 1993. Arafat asked Beilin to help secure the release of Ahmed Yassin, the Hamas leader in the territories, from an Israeli prison. He wanted to show Hamas supporters the power he could wield vis-à-vis the Israelis thanks to the agreement he had signed; Arafat also sought to reinforce his image as the leader of all Palestinians. Beilin, on his part, asked Arafat to stop wearing a military uniform in his meetings with Israelis so that it would be easier to persuade the Israeli public that the Palestinian leader was, indeed, committed to peace. Arafat responded to Beilin's request in a way that is not customary in dialogues between Western leaders: prolonged silence. The silence was broken only when Hanan Ashrawi (the spokesperson of the Palestinian delegation to talks in Washington, who was present at the meeting) intervened and said that Arafat dresses in the way his people understand him. Without his uniform, he would be a different person in their eyes.[12]

The political philosopher Frantz Fanon noted that Fidel Castro irked the West by wearing military garb during his visits to the UN because it was interpreted as an effort to demonstrate "the consciousness he has of the continuing existence of the rule of violence." In fact, Fanon claimed, Castro appeared in military uniform to express his readiness to defend himself from what he perceived as the West's violence toward him.[13] Similarly, Arafat continued to don a uniform not only as a threat to renew violence if the process failed (and this was definitely part of his message), but also to say that in his historical outlook, Israel is threatening him with violence. From Arafat's perspective, wearing a uniform was designed to emphasize Western-Zionist-imperialist injustice, still unrectified. Whether we choose to accept or reject Arafat's narrative, Beilin's demand that Arafat switch from military to civilian dress—a reasonable demand in the eyes of most Israelis—was tantamount to demanding that he ignore his national and historical feelings.

These anecdotes are not intended to say who was right. Instead, they seek to highlight the fact that the gap between Israelis and Palestinians is not only about demarcating borders. It runs much deeper.

## 3

The political scientist Michael Barnett asserts that Rabin, after winning the elections in 1992 and becoming prime minister, chose to negotiate with the PLO, contrary to his previous stance, primarily because of a window of opportunity he perceived in the wake of the Soviet Union's collapse.[14] Rabin believed there would be no better opportunity for a compromise with the Palestinians and the Arab states, because the Arabs could no longer turn to the Soviet Union for support. Thus, his view was grounded in global developments and was detached from religious influence.

Rabin's opponent in 1992 was the incumbent prime minister and Likud leader, Yitzhak Shamir, whose worldview was also clearly secular.[15] Like Rabin, Shamir recognized the strategic significance of the United States as the sole superpower in the region following the demise of the Soviet Union. But he refused to internalize the impact of the changes in the international map on Israel, and continued to insist that Israel retain control over the territories and refrain from any negotiations with the PLO. As noted, Shamir was not a religiously observant Jew, but his refusal to adapt his views to the strategic changes in the global arena unwittingly reflected a theological worldview that sees the Jews in constant peril, regardless of historical circumstances. Against this background, we can understand his well-known statement: "The sea is the same sea, and the Arabs are the same Arabs." In this view, the Arabs are the latest incarnation of the Jew haters that appear throughout Jewish history. Rabin's victory over Shamir in the 1992 elections was the last resounding political victory of the secular outlook over the religious worldview in Israel.

To understand the significance of the religious dimension in a peace process conducted by secularists, I adopt in this book a more complex approach to the relations between religion and secularity. This approach challenges the "secularization thesis" that prevailed in academia in the West until the 1960s. According to this thesis, the world of religion and its concepts are in an evolutionary process of decline dating back to the beginning of the modern era, while secular life is developing and spreading.[16] However, it is clear that even today, the dichotomy between the religious and secular worlds is very blurred, and critics of the secularization thesis point to religious phenomena, old and new, that are flourishing in the modern era, and even appropriate cultural, economic, and technological elements from it.[17] For example, Islamic State is a religious phenomenon that looks toward the ancient Islamic past, while at the same time a modern and secular phenomenon in its use of technology and ambition to change the political system in the Middle East through the power of human action.

My intention here is not simply to reject the paradigm that distinguishes between, and contrasts, religion and secularity, or religion and nationalism. Rejection of this paradigm is nothing new. Nationalism is often described as a secularized and new alternative to the religious ethos of the ancient world (and thus nationalism replaced religion, but is similar to it in its particularistic values). My intention is to argue (as Talal Asad explained in his book *Formations of the Secular: Christianity, Islam, Modernity*) that the religious world, from the outset, was not a coalesced and uniform phenomenon; it also included secular elements such as arguments and confrontations with God, as exemplified in the stories of the biblical patriarchs. This anthropomorphic approach essentially denies the unique transcendental dimension of God that is central to classic religious faith. Therefore, there is no precise division between the secular era and the religious era. Just as the liberal notion of equality draws from the monotheistic idea of a single God for all humanity,[18] secularity itself does not necessarily stand in contradiction to the religious world. In fact, secularity is "nurtured by the theological and conducts dialogues of various sorts with it."[19]

However, it is evident that the leaders of the peace process on the Western side—that is, Israel and the United States—did not recognize this complexity. Their view was steeped in the secularization thesis that sees the religious world as an outdated phenomenon that will fade into oblivion as we advance toward a future dominated by science and reason, and their refusal to recognize the phenomena clearly described in the critique of this thesis diminished their ability to facilitate rapprochement between the Israelis and the Palestinians.

# 4

The unique contribution of this book in comparison to other studies on the peace process lies in the initial and critical use of documents from Yossi Beilin's archives. In this context, I would like to explain why I chose to focus on Beilin as a key figure for understanding the peace process and the predicament of the left in Israel.

First of all, I chose Beilin because of the central role he played in the political processes in Israel since joining Peres as his spokesperson after the upheaval of 1977. Though he was never in the top leadership position, Beilin was involved in all of the contacts Peres conducted, from the time of Peres' election as Labor Party chairman through the first years of the twenty-first century. Beilin was not only Peres' confidante and adviser; he also influenced Peres and was partly responsible for the changes that occurred in Peres' views. Until the late 1970s, for example, Peres was considered sympathetic to the settlement enterprise and more hawkish than Rabin. (The archive documents indicate that as late as August 1993, just days before the Oslo talks were revealed, Peres still rejected public recognition of the PLO.) Of course, the responsibility falls on the shoulders of the leader, and Peres—as party chairman, foreign minister and prime minister—chose when to accept Beilin's ideas and when to reject them. And it is clear that other factors also contributed to Peres' transition from a hawk to a dove, including his growing ties with leaders of socialist parties in Europe, changes in the global and regional strategic map, and political considerations. Nonetheless, it is no coincidence that the American historian Guy Ziv found in his research that the change in Peres' position on the peace process occurred during the years he worked with Beilin.[20]

A well-known irony is that the greatest joint project of Peres and Rabin was, in fact, orchestrated by Beilin as deputy foreign minister in the second Rabin government. He oversaw the preliminary talks that Yair Hirschfeld and Ron Pundak conducted with their interlocutors from the PLO, starting in late 1992, while Rabin and Peres were only brought into the picture later. Even after they took over the reins, Beilin continued to be one of the leaders of the process. Moreover, immediately after the Declaration of Principles (Oslo I Accord) was signed between the PLO and Israel in September 1993, Beilin embarked on new secret negotiations, this time with Mahmoud Abbas (Abu Mazen), who since 1980 was seen as responsible for the PLO's "foreign affairs portfolio" and was elected as Arafat's successor following the latter's death in 2004. The talks with Abu Mazen and his advisers were also initially conducted behind the backs of Rabin and Peres. Beilin, fearing that the eagerness of the two peoples to advance toward a final status accord would wane during the interim period, sought to build upon the momentum of Oslo to draft an agreement with Abbas that they would present to their respective leaderships. The "Beilin-Abu Mazen" agreement was completed on October 4, 1995, a month before the assassination of Rabin. Although the leaders failed to embrace the document, its principles became the basis for the talks at the Camp David summit in 2000 and the parameters that President Clinton proposed for resolving the conflict after the summit failed.

Beilin was also a member of the Israeli delegation at the Taba negotiations in January 2001, which achieved some progress. Later, when his party was no longer in power, he signed the Geneva Initiative agreement with Yasser Abed Rabbo in 2003. Although Beilin no longer officially represented Israel, the Geneva agreement made significant waves. According to then-Prime Minister Ariel Sharon and his bureau chief Dov Weisglass, the Geneva Initiative proved there was still a chance for peace. Consequently, to avoid public and diplomatic pressure, Sharon launched an initiative of his own, the plan to disengage from the Gaza Strip in 2005. The basic ideas Beilin discussed with the Palestinians—for example, land swaps and some form of Israeli recognition of responsibility for the plight of Palestinian refugees—also served as the foundation for subsequent diplomatic efforts between Israel and the Palestinians, including the talks conducted by Ehud Olmert's government at Annapolis in 2006 and Olmert's conversations with Abbas in 2008–09. Beilin's influence on the peace process is thus indisputable, and his private archives substantially help to convey a more complete historical picture of the events.

Beilin is also important as a major player in helping to analyze the rise of the left in Israel in the 1990s and its subsequent decline. His biography and worldview—as reflected in his public image as a "Tel Aviv leftist"—clearly represent what the sociologist Baruch Kimmerling termed "*ahusalim*"[21] (a Hebrew acronym for Ashkenazi, secular, Israeli-born, socialist, nationalist). It should be noted, however, that Beilin is not exactly a socialist. At most, we can say that the habitat of Labor Party leaders in those years was not Revisionist. The book will, indeed, show how Beilin and other Labor Party leaders acted from a broad liberal economic outlook that also affected the status and identity of the left in Israel.

In any case, Beilin's image is important for analyzing the political and social developments because the peace process was not only a struggle over Israel's diplomatic path; it was also a battle over its identity and values. The Oslo process, with all its cultural, economic, and social implications, can be seen as the first shot fired in the battle over the image of the society and state, while the shots that Yigal Amir later fired at Rabin, in the name of the religious-Mizrahi dimension of the Israeli identity, were a reaction to the "Beilinish" character—liberal, secular, and cosmopolitan—the peace process sought to confer upon Israel. While this character is ostensibly more Israeli than Jewish, a closer look at Beilin's biography indicates a more complex picture. (Beilin himself says that his activities were essentially driven by his Jewishness rather than his Israeliness.) To a great extent, the subtext of the Oslo process was the conflict over the identity of Israeli society. The return of the "ethnic genie" to the public discourse in Israel in recent years and the government's decision in 2016 to publish the protocols of investigatory committees on the "abducted Yemenite children" are not coincidental. (It is interesting to wonder whether Amir's murder of Rabin would be described today as the murder of an "Ashkenazi" by a "Yemenite." Few, if any, spoke in those terms at the time.) It is impossible to understand the recurring discourse on Mizrahi-Ashkenazi relations without seeing it as a late repercussion of the confrontation that began in the 1990s.

Another reason to focus on Beilin as a key figure pertains to the research methodology. From my experience writing political biographies of the "great ones," Begin and Ben-Gurion, I know that exposure to their archives and writings can sometimes actually blur the historical picture. Major leaders tend to attribute importance to their future place in history and thus often write in a way that is designed to influence the historian who will pore over their archives in the future. In comparison, the archives of a supporting actor can be more fruitful in the effort to understand the events and the motives of the other heroes in the story.

In regard to the methodology, it should be noted that I focused on the documents in Beilin's archives—protocols, letters, maps, diaries, newspaper clippings, and so on—not only because I was given exclusive access to this material. It was also because Beilin's archives contain documentation on all of the leading figures involved in the major political developments and events in Israel during the past four decades. In all of his roles, Beilin kept meticulous documentation, the likes of which I have only encountered in Ben-Gurion's comprehensive archives at Sde Boker. I have no doubt that Beilin's archives, housed at the Yad Tabenkin Archives, will also serve many scholars in the future.

Although various figures were actively involved in the peace process in its different tracks—and were often unaware of each other's activity—I almost entirely refrained from personal interviews with them, relying when necessary on their writings and published accounts. Despite my appreciation for the genre of oral history, in order to separate the wheat from the chaff and get as close as possible to the historical truth, I preferred to rely primarily on written documents rather than personal recollections. I had long conversations with Beilin himself, but used his comments in accordance with the story as I understand it, and he holds no responsibility for what is written in this book. Any mistakes are solely my responsibility.

5

The pictures of Rabin, Arafat, and Peres shaking hands on the White House lawn on September 13, 1993, will forever be recorded in the chronicles of the modern Middle East. However, the historical importance of the agreement was not in its details, but in the mutual recognition by the respective leaders of the Zionist movement and the Palestinian national movement, and in their joint adoption of the idea of partitioning the land. In terms of the details of the agreement, they were nothing more than the implementation of the autonomy plan established in 1979 in the framework of the peace treaty between Israel and Egypt.[22] The principal difference between the Oslo agreement and Begin's autonomy plan, which was also designed to serve as a first stage toward a final status accord, is that Begin believed that the Palestinians should live under administrative/functional autonomy only;[23] he rejected the possibility that the final accord would grant them a state. The autonomy plan—which was established, absurdly, by Israel and Egypt, with the latter serving as the representative of the Palestinian cause, and without including the Palestinians themselves—did, in fact, recognize the Palestinians as a distinct Arab nation de facto, but Begin officially continued to refuse to recognize their legitimate rights to a state. Moreover, in the Hebrew version of the autonomy agreement, the Palestinians are referred to as "the Arabs of the Land of Israel."[24]

The Oslo Accords also did not include a promise of a Palestinian state in the framework of a final status agreement. However, the accords pointed toward this possibility, certainly from the perspective of Beilin, who even came to terms with Abbas on this in the agreement they drafted in October 1995. Rabin, on the other hand, agreed in his last Knesset speech to something that would be a bit less than a state—a "state minus." And Peres publicly declared his support for a Palestinian state only in 1996, after Rabin's assassination. In fact, Golda Meir's famous assertion in the 1970s that "there is no Palestinian people" (and therefore they do not deserve a separate state) was the basic view of the two main streams in Zionism and in Israeli politics—Revisionism and the Labor movement—through the late 1980s. Against this background, we can better appreciate the magnitude of the change of consciousness that Beilin introduced in the Israeli public by insisting that the conflict could only be resolved by establishing a Palestinian state. (Beilin was certainly not the only one to hold this view, but he was among the first in the Labor Party to dare support negotiating with the PLO and press to implement his ideas.)

In this context, it is interesting to examine Beilin's location on the right-left political axis. Did he represent a radical-alternative view that entered the Zionist mainstream during the days of Oslo (as the political right in Israel claims), or was the Oslo process nothing more than an Israeli diplomatic maneuver that was never intended to fulfill the Palestinians' rights and was designed to leave the territories under Israeli control in the guise of self-administration (as Beilin's critics on the left claim)?

To try to answer this question, it is instructive to check Beilin's stance vis-à-vis the two central schools of foreign policy in Israel's formative years. The first of these schools is associated with the dovish views of Moshe Sharett, the first foreign minister of Israel. During the Yishuv (pre-state) period, Sharett maintained many contacts with Palestinian and other Arab leaders and supported the UN partition plan. Following the victory in the War of Independence, he sought to understand the views of the Arabs and Palestinians in order to integrate Israel into the Middle East with their consent. In Israel's formative years, he also considered the possibility of establishing a Palestinian state alongside Israel.[25] The second school is identified with Israel's first prime minister, David Ben-Gurion, who declared his readiness for compromise, but in practice based Israel's existence on developing its military power and deterrence. He pursued this course after concluding that the Arabs were not yet ready to accept Israel.

Gabi Sheffer, Sharett's biographer,[26] depicts Ben-Gurion and Sharett as embodying opposing worldviews on the Zionist-Arab conflict, dating back to the 1920s.[27] In my opinion, the discussion should start at a different point in time, because the two originally had a common ideology, and the differences between them developed later, primarily after the founding of the state.[28] The "dovish" Sharett and the "activist" Ben-Gurion shared the same worldview regarding the justice of Zionism, and they continued to see eye to eye on the core issues after the creation of the state. Like Ben-Gurion, Sharett recognized Israel's need to remain vigilant in the face of the Arab states' hostility; he opposed Egypt's demands for Israeli withdrawals, including a demand to surrender the Negev, and rejected the return of Palestinian refugees.[29] It would also be correct to emphasize that before the creation of the state, Sharett was no less hawkish than Ben-Gurion on many issues. In 1948, he encouraged the efforts of Yosef Weitz, a top official at the Jewish National Fund, to propose solutions for the "transfer" of Palestinians and is quoted on the need to drive them out of the Negev and the villages of the Little Triangle.[30] But Sharett had an advantage over other Zionist leaders: he was familiar with the Palestinians and their culture, and learned Arabic at the age of twelve while living in the village of Ein Siniya near Ramallah, on a farm his family rented from the al-Husseini family. Sharett and his family were sad to leave the village, a move dictated by economic constraints, and Sharett kept a picture of Ein Siniya and its residents in his office for years.[31]

The crucial difference between Ben-Gurion and Sharett vis-à-vis the conflict stemmed from Sharett's belief that after completing the critical stage of Zionism by establishing a Jewish state, Israel should recognize the magnitude of the psychological blow the Arabs suffered in the Nakba (the "tragedy"—the Arabic term used in reference to the events surrounding Israel's creation). Influenced by his experience as head of the Jewish Agency's Political Department during the pre-state period, Sharett believed that precisely because Israel was the victor and the Arabs were defeated, Israel should adopt a moderate and cautious stance, and in particular, one that takes into account Arab public opinion. In his view, only a conciliatory approach, one that considers the natural aspirations of the Palestinians and the Arabs, could enable Israel to mitigate the enmity that understandably arose toward it. As we know, Ben-Gurion rejected Sharett's view. Only decades later, in light of the collapse of the peace process in the early years of the twenty-first century, scholars came to realize that there, in the days of 1948, lies the crux of the conflict from the Palestinian perspective. This is the primary reason why the liberal paradigm, which seeks to divide the land and reach an accord based only on what occurred since 1967, is incapable of resolving the conflict.[32]

Sharett understood that in light of Zionism's victory, a victory that could only be achieved at the expense of the Palestinians, Israel should adopt an inclusive and empathetic viewpoint. Thus, he contended that Ben-Gurion's "security activism"—that is, the belief that Israel must flex its military power in order to secure its existence— is an illusion that is destined to collapse. Sharett argued that the more Israel flaunts its power, the more it will fan the fires of hatred in the Arab world and alienate the Western powers. This will limit Israel's ability to integrate into the Middle East and harm its international standing in general. This viewpoint led Sharett to oppose Ben-Gurion's demand in December 1949 to transfer government ministries to Jerusalem and establish the state's capital there, as long as the UN opposed this.[33]

However, the main difference between the schools of Sharett and Ben-Gurion was expressed in their arguments over how to respond to the problem of infiltration, which plagued Israel since the end of the War of Independence and through the 1950s, and especially in light of the acts of terror committed by some of the infiltrators. As Benny Morris rightly claimed in his book *Israel's Border Wars 1949–1956*, the argument about how to respond to these acts of terror reflected fundamental differences between the way Sharett and his loyalists in the Foreign Ministry and Mapai (including Yosef Sprinzak, Zalman Aran, and Pinhas Rosen) viewed the Arab–Israeli arena and the way this arena was viewed by Ben-Gurion and his activist adherents in the Defense Ministry (led by Moshe Dayan, then IDF chief of staff; Peres, then deputy defense minister and the ministry's director-general; and Pinhas Lavon, who served as defense minister until his ouster in 1954).

Sharett himself clearly described this difference of opinion, and his words are still relevant today:

One approach [the "security-oriented" approach] says that the Arabs only understand the language of force. . . . Israel must, from time to time, clearly demonstrate that it is strong, and is able and willing to use force in a very overwhelming and efficient way. If it fails to demonstrate this, they will swallow it up; it is liable to be erased from the face of the earth. Regarding the matter of peace, this approach says—it is dubious anyway; in any case, it is very distance. If peace comes, it will come only if they are convinced that it is impossible to defeat this state. . . . The other approach says that the matter of peace must never disappear from our reckoning for even a moment. It is not only a diplomatic- political reckoning: In the long run, it is a decisive security reckoning. Without diminishing the importance of ongoing security considerations, we must always bring the matter of peace into our system of calculations. We must restrain our responses. . . . And there is always the question: Has it really been proven that acts of retaliation solve the security problem they were intended to address? . . . We have become so imbued with the recognition of our historical justice, we have not considered the relative nature of this justice of ours from the viewpoint of the other side. We have also been deficient in our psychological understanding of the problem; we have not paid sufficient attention to the depth of the Arab world's national consciousness and feeling.[34]

Ben-Gurion, on the other hand, claimed that Sharett lacked "the strength of spirit, foresight and real understanding of complex political situations."[35]

Sharett was imprecise in the accusations he made against Ben-Gurion. The "old man" was not oblivious to the mood in the Arab world. But he analyzed Israel's situation differently. In his view (and in this context, it is consistent in many ways with the view of the current prime minister, Benjamin Netanyahu), after Israel's victory in the War of Independence, it was impossible in any case to find common ground on which Israel could exist in security and peace with the consent of the Palestinians and the Arab world. In addition, Ben-Gurion assessed Israel's relations with the Western powers in light of shared interests, against the background of the Cold War. Therefore, he did not agree that a conciliatory policy would strengthen Israel's standing in the region and in the world. On the contrary, he believed it would weaken Israel.

The Arab–Israeli conflict (including the Palestinian-Israeli conflict) was waged in the 1950s over the very existence of Israel. Ben-Gurion and his supporters thus believed that conciliation and compromise would be of no avail, and that strong reprisals would not fan the flames of hatred. The fire would burn in any case, until the Arabs come to understand that they cannot defeat the Jews who returned to their homeland. There is a historical irony here that the historian Avi Shlaim noted in his book *The Iron Wall: Israel and the Arab World*: The school Ben-Gurion led, with the backing of other top Mapai leaders, adopted the "iron wall" worldview of the Revisionist leader Ze'ev Jabotinsky.[36] The essence of Jabotinsky's "iron wall" idea was to recognize that Zionism could not reach a compromise with the Arabs based on concessions, smooth talk, or all sorts of proposed economic benefits. It was also impossible to find common moral ground, because both sides believe that justice is on their side. The optimistic dimension in the "iron wall" approach is the dimension of time: the Arabs' sense of injustice would fade in time and, ultimately, they would be forced to understand that it is best to compromise with Zionism, and come to recognize its moral justice. At this later stage, Jabotinsky believed, the sides would agree to a mutual compromise. He did not specify the compromise the Zionists should make, other than to grant equal rights to the "Arabs of Palestine."[37]

Ben-Gurion rejected Jabotinsky's path and modes of operation during the days of the Yishuv. As prime minister, however, Ben-Gurion's security policy of aggressive reprisals against infiltrators and his declarations about the need to build Israel's deterrent power (a view that all subsequent prime ministers largely adopted) drew heavily from his rival's "iron wall" idea. Ben-Gurion even extolled the use of force as a vital element in establishing Jewish nationalism: "We would be rejecting the Jewish history of Joshua Ben Nun's time – and also from the time of Moses – and up until the IDF and in general, if we dismissed the value of physical strength. The rejection of physical strength is also the rejection of this world. It is the rejection of life."[38]

Sharett, on the other hand, saw the aggressive element as a fundamental mistake. He believed that if Israel continued to pound the Arabs with tactically successful military operations, it would defeat itself strategically because the use of force would only deepen Arab enmity. As foreign minister, he fought against a number of proposals for military conquests (for example, he was one of the opponents of Ben-Gurion's proposal to conquer the West Bank in 1948), and as prime minister, he opposed calls by Ben-Gurion, Lavon, and Dayan for aggressive reprisal operations.[39] Sharett believed that the Arab defeat in 1948 was an event with enormous psychological implications, and that Israel should recognize its need to create an "emotional background conducive to peace" among the Arabs. Israel should work toward "removing from the emotional background the elements that bedevil the path to peace. . . . As long as the generation that underwent this trauma as a direct personal experience continues to live, act, decide and influence, there is almost no chance, or there is little chance, of the emotional compromise that is essential for peace."[40] Thus, even though he too rejected the Arabs' conditions for a political accord and emphasized his support for "the general national stance, which opposes the return of the refugees,"[41] Sharett understood that Israel bears just as much responsibility as the Arabs for reaching a political accord; he was convinced that given the right "political climate," the Arabs could make peace.[42]

# 6

Did Beilin's views draw from those of Sharett? If asked this question, Beilin says he is a "Ben-Gurionist." He points to Ben-Gurion's readiness in principle to divide the land, dating back to the Peel Commission recommendations in 1937, as the foundation for the idea of two states for two peoples, a central element in Beilin's worldview. Beilin is convinced that Ben-Gurion's pragmatism, together with his call to return the territories after the Six-Day War (except for the Golan Heights, Jerusalem, and Hebron),[43] would have also developed into recognition of the right of self-determination for the Palestinians in an independent state (though, until his dying day, Ben-Gurion viewed the Palestinians as an indistinct part of the Arab nation and denied the existence of a Palestinian nation).

Indeed, the common label and image of Beilin in the Israeli public as the "ultimate leftist" misses the fact that Beilin never ventured beyond the boundaries of the classic Zionist outlook and never questioned the justice of Zionism. His goal was, and remains, to ensure the existence of Israel as a Jewish and democratic state. He opposes the right of return for Palestinians (except for humanitarian cases), and territorial compromise for him is a security need and not only a moral imperative, based on his assessment that Israel cannot live by its sword alone. In this context, we can say that Beilin has more in common with Ben-Gurion than with Sharett. Unlike the latter, Beilin did not base his view on understanding "the psychology of the Arab side" or immerse himself in Arab culture. His drive to divide the land stems primarily from considerations of realpolitik, which examines moral elements in accordance with political needs.

Perhaps herein lie some of the seeds of the missed opportunities in the Oslo process and subsequent peace efforts. The Oslo Accords were intended to lift the burden of "the Palestinian problem" from the Jewish state via territorial compromise, but nothing more. Israel would keep its unique place in the region and maintain its supremacy over its neighbors. In this context, the leaders of the Oslo process sought to continue the vision of Theodor Herzl, who wrote that the Jewish state would serve as part of "a rampart of Europe against Asia, an outpost of civilization as opposed to barbarism."[44] This gave rise to a central motif characterizing the Oslo process— the motif of separation between Israel and Palestine, a buffer between East and West. This was expressed in the statement by Ehud Barak, the last prime minister from the left: "We are here and they are there." It is no coincidence, therefore, that this formula of the Zionist left was implemented in a decision by the Likud government headed by Ariel Sharon in 2003 to build a barrier along the (pre-1967) Green Line border. Indeed, in contrast to the fierce political debate, the substantive difference between the moderate right and Zionist left on the Palestinian question is not profound. Both seek, above all, a separation between the Jewish and Palestinian societies. This is the essential reason why Beilin is, indeed, closer to the foreign policy doctrine of the "founding father" than to Sharett's approach. Beilin is not Sharett's successor, and certainly not the successor of the small minority of Zionists—including Asher Ginzberg (Ahad Ha'am), the educator Isaac Epstein,[45] and the members of Brit Shalom—who in the early stages of the Zionist enterprise sought to turn attention to the question of relations with the Palestinians, including on the cultural level. That is, unlike those Zionist outliers who wished to pursue the possibility of living in coexistence based on shared values, Beilin regarded peace as a vital security interest for Israel.

Beilin's worldview evolved over the years. Prior to the Yom Kippur War, he rarely questioned the actions of Israel's leadership. In the wake of the Six-Day War, in which he served as a wireless operator in the Signals Corps, he was swept up in the euphoria of victory, like most Israelis. Since his youth, he had strictly observed religious traditions—not out of belief in God, but because of his desire to maintain the customs that reflect the continuity of the Jewish people's historical existence. The capture of the holy sites in 1967 reinforced the already complex connection between religion and nation from his perspective.

Beilin's "Sharett-ization" (when he also stopped observing Jewish religious commandments) came in the wake of the trauma of the Yom Kippur War. Disappointment with the political and military echelons led to a deep disillusionment with Israel's actions in the region. He regarded Golda Meir's rejection of the Rogers Plan, which championed the principle of "land for peace," as an expression of political blindness.[46] Though he identified with the extra-parliamentary protest movements that arose after the war, Beilin, then working as a journalist at the *Davar* daily, decided to join the Young Guard of the Labor Party and to try to influence policy from within. This move was consistent with another characteristic of Beilin: the inclination to work within the establishment, with the goal of changing its ways. He was never a revolutionary who sought to upend the entire establishment from the outside. However, though he operated from within the establishment, the position he advocated—dividing the land and recognizing Palestinian nationalism—was considered radical in the 1970s.

On June 19, 1967, about two weeks after the war, the government of Levi Eshkol approved a decision to hold most of the territories as a bargaining chip.[47] However, the prevailing view in the political system and in the public (both left and right) rejected the Palestinians' right to self-determination and was skeptical about the benefits of a full Israeli withdrawal to the lines of June 4th. The PLO, in parallel, refused to recognize

Israel's right to exist as a Jewish state. Israel regarded the PLO as an enemy and saw no common ground for negotiations with it. The few Israelis who called for dividing the land into two states were emphatically rejected by the consensus:

> Ministers Victor Shem-Tov and Aharon Yariv drafted (separately, but based on a similar idea) the "Yariv–Shem-Tov Formula" that proposed direct negotiations with a Palestinian leadership to be elected among the residents of the territories. (This leadership would be required to recognize Israel and adopt UN Security Council Resolution 242, which called for an Israeli withdrawal from the territories and establishment of a "just and lasting peace" in the Middle East.) But Rabin himself, in his first term as prime minister (1974–77), rejected their proposal, stating that "the Palestinian problem is not the central problem and its resolution should be found in the framework of an accord between Israel and Jordan."[48] Yigal Allon, the foreign minister in the first Rabin government, also opposed granting independence to the Palestinians. The vision he proposed, the Allon Plan, included an Israeli withdrawal from much of the West Bank (except for Jerusalem, the Jordan Valley, the mountain ridges, and the Jordan River),[49] but identified Jordan as the partner in a future accord; in Allon's eyes, Jordan was already sitting on two-thirds of the historical Land of Israel. Right-wing Zionists were far from supportive of territorial concessions, of course. In fact, during the period of 1967–77, largely under the impact of the wars in 1967 and 1973, the political right in Israel took on a new hue, more religious and nationalistic, which is still evident today. A new political camp arose—the "national camp"—based on an alliance of secular, religious, and ultra-Orthodox parties that adopted a maximalist approach to the "Greater Land of Israel."[50]

Beilin was not a radical like Uri Avnery, Shulamit Aloni, Yossi Sarid, and others, who in many ways paved his path. However, he was the only one who succeeded in promoting the two-state vision—at least in part—while still operating from within the establishment. Avnery, who had some affinity for the Canaanite movement, placed himself outside of the classic Zionist camp. Aloni and Sarid found themselves, not by coincidence, outside of the Labor Party. Precisely because he worked from within the establishment party, and in the 1990s succeeded in leading (even if not from a top leadership role) the first significant effort to divide the land, an examination of Beilin's role is invaluable for an understanding of Israel's short history. To appreciate the magnitude of the change the Oslo agreement engendered in the Israeli public, we can perhaps imagine the idea of a binational state becoming the consensus view in another twenty years. This is comparable to what happened in the wake of Oslo. Even today, despite the decline of the peace process, over 55 percent of the Jewish public believes in dividing the land.[51]

# 7

In 1989, less than four years before Oslo and against the background of US secretary of state James Baker's attempts to persuade Shamir to support his plan to hold autonomy talks between Israel and Palestinian representatives (from the territories and abroad),[52] Beilin, then serving as Peres' deputy at the Finance Ministry, declared that Israel was deluding itself in purporting to seek peace without direct negotiations with the PLO. His remarks stirred a political firestorm and Shamir demanded Beilin's dismissal, contending that the latter's views did not conform to the guidelines of the national unity government. At that stage, it was also difficult for the Labor Party leadership to support Beilin's statement. In the end, Shamir was unable to fire Beilin because the law required Peres' consent to dismiss his deputy.

A central part of this book traces the political and historical developments that convinced a majority of Israelis to support an idea—mutual recognition of Israel and the PLO—that had been taboo prior to the signing of the Declaration of Principles in 1993. (Surveys found that 61 percent of the Israeli public supported the Oslo agreement when it was announced.)[53] Recognition of the PLO was the result of a long process that included demographic, sociological, and cultural changes in Israeli society, as well as economic aspects. Naturally, the changes in the map of international interests in the world and in the Middle East following the collapse of the Soviet Union and the dismantlement of the Soviet bloc also had an impact.

In regard to the Israeli angle, the documents in Beilin's archives reveal how a combination of low and high politics set the stage for the Oslo Accords. First, the low politics: ironically, Prime Minister Rabin's personal aversion to Peres and his lack of trust in him played a key role in paving the way to Oslo. After the Labor Party's election victory in June 1992, Rabin appointed Peres as foreign minister but limited his ministerial purview. Peres was assigned responsibility for the multilateral negotiations with Arab states conducted in accordance with the 1991 Madrid Conference. The multilateral talks were low-level negotiations aimed at promoting cooperation among Middle Eastern states in areas in which cooperation was unfeasible in the absence of peace accords between Israel and its neighbors. In this way, Rabin intended to prevent the foreign minister from becoming involved in substantial peace efforts. This was Rabin's intention when he famously declared at the Labor Party's victory rally in 1992: "I will navigate." Rabin assumed full responsibility for relations with the United States and for talks with Syria, Jordan, and the Palestinians.

The fact that the foreign minister was not supposed to be involved in critical negotiations enabled his deputy, Beilin, to examine possible alternatives to the official negotiations taking place in Washington between an Israeli delegation and a Jordanian-Palestinian delegation. (The Palestinians in the Jordanian-Palestinian delegation were residents of the territories and not members of the PLO leadership, then based in Tunis.) The fact that the negotiations with the Jordanian-Palestinian delegation reached an impasse accelerated Beilin's efforts to find another way. Peres gave him free rein and when Ron Pundak and Yair Hirschfeld, two Israeli academics acting on behalf of Beilin, began unofficial and direct talks in London with PLO representatives in December 1992, Beilin kept Peres in the dark. The PLO team was led by Abu Ala (Ahmed Qurei), who updated Chairman Arafat on the contacts. The first conversation between Hirschfeld and Abu Ala was on December 4th, prior to the revocation of an Israeli law prohibiting contacts with the PLO (although a bill to overturn the law had already passed an initial reading in the Knesset). Hirschfeld did not inform Beilin about the meeting in order to avoid implicating him in violating the law. The first meeting in Oslo took place on January 20, 1993, after the law was revoked. Beilin refrained from joining the interlocutors in Norway at that stage because he thought it was premature to inform Peres and did not want to take responsibility for the Oslo process without reporting to the foreign minister. Beilin updated Peres only after Pundak and Hirschfeld achieved an initial draft of an interim autonomy agreement with the PLO. The foreign minister was not overly impressed. He did not know Abu Ala and asked about his standing in the Palestinian leadership. Nonetheless, he gave Beilin the green light to continue the talks.

When Peres realized that the PLO was ready for progress that could not be achieved with the Palestinian delegation in Washington, he immediately informed Rabin. Like Peres, Rabin was not particularly impressed by the report about the talks in Oslo, but did not dismiss them out of hand. He seemed pleased that Foreign Ministry officials were working on alternative and nonbinding tracks, because he believed those tracks were unrealistic in any case. In early 1993, Rabin still believed that the only important diplomatic action was happening in the Washington talks. Thus, Rabin's interest in keeping Peres away from the "real" negotiations, actually landed Peres in the midst of the only feasible path toward advancing Israeli-Palestinian relations. Even when Rabin recognized the impasse in Washington and began to support the direct talks in Oslo, he still hoped to leverage the Oslo talks to convince Arafat to allow the Jordanian-Palestinian delegation in Washington, which also took its orders from him, to be more forthcoming in its talks with Israel. Rabin was also willing to allow Faisal al-Husseini, a resident of East Jerusalem, to participate in the Washington talks in order to boost the negotiations. (Both major parties had until then refused to negotiate with Palestinian residents of East Jerusalem, claiming that this would call into question Israel's sovereignty in its capital city.)

Only after the tenth round of talks in Washington failed—in June 1993, just three months before the signing of the Oslo agreement—Rabin fully understood that it was best to change the rules of the game. Instead of conducting negotiations with Palestinians who were not PLO members and then waiting for the PLO's approval of any agreements reached with them, Israel should negotiate with Arafat and his staff directly and formally. The PLO negotiators turned out to be more moderate than the Washington delegation of Palestinians from the territories, who operated under the daunting shadow of the PLO. Rabin thus decided to conduct direct negotiations with the Tunis-based PLO leadership. However, as we have seen, were it not for Rabin's desire to keep Peres and his staff away from the official peace talks, the whole series of events leading to the Oslo Accords may not have occurred. In this way, low politics contributed to the Oslo process.

In regard to high politics, the collapse of the Soviet Union in late 1991 provided the major impetus toward negotiations with the PLO because it left the Middle East in the sphere of influence of just one superpower. For Israel, this offered a rare opportunity to conduct negotiations with all of the Arab states, and the Palestinians, under the umbrella of its ally; the political weight of Russia, which represented the Arab interest, had largely eroded.

The Arab world, especially the Sunnis, also realized that it was in their interest to cultivate close relations with the United States. The harbinger of this trend was President Anwar Sadat's decision in the early 1970s (even before the Yom Kippur War) to reorient Egypt toward the United States instead of the Soviet Union. The First Gulf War also contributed to this trend. Launched in January 1991, this war was waged by the Americans on behalf of an Arab state (Kuwait) against an Arab state (Iraq), with the support of most of the Sunni states.

The coalition assembled by President George H. W. Bush for the battle against Saddam Hussein strengthened the US administration's ties with Arab states and obligated Washington to serve as a more balanced intermediary in the Arab–Israeli conflict. The Arabs were rewarded after the war when the United States pressed the Shamir government to participate in an international conference in Madrid, convened in October 1991. Shamir was opposed to the idea of an international conference, viewing it as an instrument for pressuring Israel, but he acceded to the American request—in part, because he regarded the mere fact that most of the Arab states were ready to engage in negotiations with Israel as an achievement in itself. He was also assured that the international conference would be nothing more than a festive ceremony, to be followed by direct bilateral negotiations between Israel and each of its neighbors-rivals.[54] Even more importantly, the United States assured Shamir that the PLO would not be involved in the process. In this context, Arafat's support for Saddam Hussein's regime turned out to be a mistake that weakened his international standing. In parallel, Arafat was struggling to contend with two main threats in the West Bank and Gaza Strip: local Palestinian leadership that began to develop in the territories during the years of the first intifada, and the burgeoning power of Hamas. These factors led Arafat to adopt a more flexible stance vis-à-vis Israel and to propose direct negotiations after Rabin was elected to replace Shamir in June 1992.

Although the PLO was not allowed to participate in the Madrid Conference, it became clear that its involvement was essential for progress on the Palestinian track; the Palestinian representatives in the Jordanian-Palestinian delegation refused to take any stand without receiving instructions from the PLO leadership. Following the US elections in November 1992, Bill Clinton, a Democrat, entered the White House and expressed a desire to devote special efforts toward achieving peace. The fact that about five months earlier a left-wing coalition was elected in Israel—for the first time since the upheaval of 1977—contributed to Clinton's optimism. Despite their very different personalities and backgrounds, Rabin and Clinton found a common language as both saw the window of opportunity for peace and had a shared interest in achieving this goal. During the election campaign, Rabin had promised an agreement with the Palestinians within nine months. His plan was to reach an accord with the Palestinian leadership in the territories and not with the PLO, but he was determined to fulfill his promise in one way or another.

The mood of the Israeli public, tired of the conflict (and of the inertia of the national unity governments of the 1980s and Shamir's government vis-à-vis the conflict), also contributed to the Israeli leadership's readiness for a groundbreaking move. In 1992, the first intifada waned as a mass uprising in the territories, but there was an upsurge in attacks against Israelis by individual infiltrators from the territories, often armed only with knives. Paradoxically, it became clear that Israelis were ready to struggle and suffer together when faced with a general threat to the state, as during the intifada, but when faced with a "privatized" threat of personal danger from a random knife-wielding assailant, most Israelis preferred to compromise and avert risks. (Perhaps this was related to the onset of an era of privatization and neoliberation that instilled individualization in Israeli society, and the widening of class disparities, which had been relatively small until the 1980s.) When Rabin came to power in 1992, most Israelis supported a nonbelligerent solution for the Palestinian question and a path of compromise.

## 8

Let's return to the discussion of the "liberal peace" paradigm. Proponents of this outlook not only assume that the more open, secular, and advanced a regime or economy, the more inclined it will be to avoid a situation of war; they also believe it is possible to achieve reconciliation between rival national movements through economic benefits one grants to the other.

There is a thread here connecting all of the proposals the Zionist movement has offered the Palestinians to foster coexistence. From the time of Herzl, who believed that the economic and technological benefits the Jews would bring to Palestine would induce the Arabs to accept the Jews in Palestine, to the "economic peace"[55] plans of Benjamin Netanyahu, the Zionist concept has not substantially changed. In the late 1920s and early 1930s, Ben-Gurion offered several leaders of the Palestinian national movement (including Musa Alami and George Antonius) a compromise based on economic benefits the Jews would bring to all of the residents of the land. This effort by Ben-Gurion, like the Oslo process in the late twentieth century, were based on the same liberal logic, which assumes that a compromise offering immediate benefits will yield an agreement acceptable to both national movements.

Adherents of the "liberal peace" model are convinced that the more two states (or national movements) in conflict base their relations on economic cooperation that improves their people's standard of living, the less inclined they will be to adopt measures that harm ongoing economic activity.

The global era, in which national economies are tied to each other, has heightened the need to examine the connection between conflict resolution and economic benefits. The big question, of course, is whether this paradigm, which seems almost obvious at first glance, is, indeed, correct.

Many studies have found a correlation between the ability to resolve conflict and economic benefits, but as Nitzan Feldman noted: "Economic growth or cooperation between states reduced the probability of them waging war against each other, but do not indicate that these economic factors can lead to the signing of a peace accord between them."[56] Moreover, in the context of the Israeli-Palestinian conflict, economic growth and the spread of higher education during the years of Israeli occupation have actually led many Palestinians to adopt a less favorable view of Israel and its peace proposals. It is important to note, for example, that prior to the second intifada, the PA enjoyed a high rate of economic growth, about 9 percent. But this growth did not prevent the intifada because growth often widens disparities in a society, which, in turn, stir turmoil; and a more comfortable life is not necessarily a formula for conflict resolution, as long as questions of justice and morality remain unresolved. Furthermore, a rise in the standard of living and levels of education can provide more free time for focusing on national aspirations and ways to achieve them.

The peace process with the Palestinians was largely based on the assumption that Palestinian society (and the PA established under the Oslo Accords) needed to institute democratic reforms and develop a free market economy. Beilin is the foremost representative of this view, which sees democracy and liberalism as advantageous and even necessary characteristics of regimes when it comes to establishing peace accords. He was therefore horrified in one of his meetings, during the days of the Barak government, when Arafat's adviser Muhammad Dahlan proposed that Israel grant clemency to Aryeh Deri (of the Mizrahi ultra-Orthodox Shas party), who was then serving a prison sentence on corruption charges.[57] Dahlan argued that the peace process needed the support of the Mizrahi religious camp, and Deri could supply the goods. Beilin emphatically rejected the proposal because Deri was in prison after receiving due process under the law. In Beilin's eyes, Dahlan was proposing that Israel violate the rule of law instead of focusing on reforming the system in the PA. But what Dahlan proposed was more profound than mere contempt for the rule of law. He sought to bolster the peace process with elements from different cultures, including some that are not accepted in the liberal-democratic culture. The question is how far Liberals could go to accommodate the culture of "the other" when it is incongruent with values they perceive as enlightened.

In any case, this book analyzes peace processes that were clearly grounded in the liberal paradigm. Adherents of this approach assume that the problem impeding resolution of the Israeli-Palestinian conflict is a structural problem—that is, the structural impediments should be dismantled by dividing the land and separating the populations—and tend to blur the historical and religious dimensions of the conflict that hinder its resolution. The liberal peace paradigm is prepared to grant the Palestinians a state, but has difficulty contending with the religious and historical components of the conflict. Therefore, it deprives the Palestinians of a central element—preservation of their past and their national story.[58] That is why the Palestinians are so insistent on recognition of the right of return, if only on the declarative level. The Palestinians would undoubtedly have a better future in a state of their own instead of remaining under Israeli occupation; but without recognition of the right of return, their sense of injustice would continue to simmer, preventing true and complete reconciliation.

The problem with the liberal peace is not its promise of "a better future."[59] After all, everyone seeks a good and prosperous life. The problem lies in the notion that national identities, anchored in ancient narratives that include a connection to land and holy sites, can easily be converted in a "progressive" approach that sees all of us as consumers and producers who seek tangible gain. However, partitioning this land—without regard for its historical and theological significance, including meaningful connections to the past (whether imagined or real)—is not enough. It is true that there is a positive aspect to partitioning the land—I do not see a more effective solution. However, it also has a negative connotation in the collective subconscious of the Palestinians in that it expresses the colonialist mindset of the Sykes-Picot agreement that divided the Middle East into states under French or British influence in 1916. That is, although logic would dictate the partition of the land for the good of both sides, this logic is colored by a neocolonialist way of thinking. The Palestinians feel this deep in their hearts.

The liberal peace paradigm has another side effect: the leaders and supporters of the peace process in the liberal version, most of whom tend to come from a strong socioeconomic background, perceive themselves as enlightened (and are portrayed as such in prominent circles in the West). And those who have reservations about their approach to achieving peace (by simply partitioning the land into two states) are looked upon as backward people who resist progress and impede peace. The Palestinians who insist on recognition of the right of return and sovereignty over the holy places (like the right-wing Israelis who refuse to relinquish the settlements and control over the territories) are seen as outdated and nonprogressive. In the eyes of the extremists, the Palestinians' unbending stance is actually more enlightened because it is anchored in principles of justice and of commitment to their familial, communal, and national past.

The critique of liberalism is laced throughout this book. The fact that the Oslo process was conducted on the Israeli side by a homogeneous group—representatives of the Israeli elite (*ahusalim*)—underlines the connection between the sociology of the conflict and its history. Indeed, what appears in retrospect as the collapse of the peace camp and of the liberal camp in Israel is closely linked to the liberal ideology in economics that characterized Beilin and the left. Since the Likud rose to power in 1977, the right in Israel has accelerated and deepened a neoliberal policy whose main criterion of economic success is growth (and not the narrowing of disparities in society, for example). In parallel, however, the left jettisoned its social values and thus significantly contributed to the adoption of neoliberal policy in Israel. This trend ultimately helped to entrench the rule of the right wing in Israel, because as neoliberalism continued to widen the gaps in society, there was a growing need for the national-religious "glue" that reduced support for the peace process and leftist camp.

Another reason for adopting a critical perspective in examining the peace process is the simple fact that the goal was not achieved; Beilin failed to fulfill his plans and the efforts of his successors were likewise unsuccessful. In the epilogue, I try to suggest alternative ideas in light of the lessons we can draw from the history of the Israeli left in recent decades.

Still, it is appropriate to note at the end of this introduction that Beilin's years of political activity were characterized by the courage to promote his vision, almost to the point where we could see the Promised Land in a partitioned and secure future. Developments that occurred after he left politics, climaxing in Prime Minister Ehud Olmert's proposal to Abu Mazen in September 2008 (which included a Palestinian state on nearly 95 percent of the territories plus additional territory in land swaps with Israel),[60] drew from various formulas in the Geneva Initiative and from various proposals presented in negotiations Beilin conducted over the years.

The fact that the most "Beilinist" proposal by an Israeli prime minister came from someone like Olmert, who was suckled on the doctrine of Jabotinsky and the Revisionist movement, only underlines the magnitude of Beilin's influence on Israeli policy. Therefore, while the book is full of attempts to understand why the liberal camp in Israel failed in its efforts to achieve peace and shape Israeli society in the spirit of its values (and thus the book's critical tone), it is important to note that it is written with great appreciation for Beilin's activity. He was one of the only Israeli politicians at the end of the twentieth century who tried, with considerable success, to change the reality of our lives.

# Part A

# 1

# A Broken Dream

## 1

When he was only seven years old, Yossi Beilin took a pen and paper, and wrote the following lines:

> I'm tired
> So tired
> Too exhausted to sing
> My dreams are over
> My melodies are done
> Oh, I've grown old
> So old
> My hand too weak to write
> I won't be able to sing any more
> I've grown old
> I've grown old, so old
> So old.

Surrounded by the photographs of Zionist titans that adorned his parents' living room, perhaps the boy could only feel exhausted. The weight of Jewish history was piled onto his shoulders at home, almost from the day he was born.

Yossi Beilin was born on June 12, 1948, during the first ceasefire of the War of Independence, at the Beilinson Hospital in Petah Tikva. His father fought in the war, so he was not present for the birth. Beilin is named after his maternal grandfather, Yosef Bregman. The grandfather died two years earlier, but Beilin felt his presence throughout his childhood; the dominant shadow of his grandfather continued to hover in the family's home.

Bregman was born in 1880 in Pinsk, Belarus, to a devout family. Like many in his generation, he grew distant from religion during his teenage years; he turned away from the yeshiva and Jewish law, and developed a growing interest in the principles of economics, which he learned on his own. He began working as a banker when still a young man, while also keeping close tabs on the developments in the Zionist movement. Inspired by his hero Theodor (Benjamin Ze'ev) Herzl, Bregman decided to engage in political activity. At age 22, he was a delegate at the 5th Zionist Congress in 1902. He also participated in the sixth congress the following year, known as the Uganda Congress or "Congress of Tears," and this experience left an indelible impact on his life.

The connection to the Land of Israel stood at the center of Bregman's understanding of the modern Jewish national movement. Consequently, Herzl's famous proposal to consider the option of settling persecuted Jews in East Africa (the "Uganda Plan") as a "nighttime refuge" (as his deputy Max Nordau termed it) was a source of deep disappointment for Bregman, who had placed his personal and national hopes in Herzl. Many considerations led Herzl—who had already weighed the possibility of settlement in Argentina as an alternative to Palestine in his book *The Jewish State*—to pursue Britain's offer and propose sending a delegation on an expedition to East Africa. As an astute statesman (even if naïve in believing that his plans could succeed through a diplomatic campaign he waged almost on his own), Herzl hoped that assembling a large Jewish community in Africa would not only provide a temporary solution for the Jews' distress, but also establish them as a formidable political force. He saw great political importance in Britain's patronage of Jewish settlement in Uganda, believing it would serve as a catalyst for recognition of the Jews as a nation deserving and capable of sovereignty. Although from Herzl's perspective the Uganda option was largely designed to serve as a sort of dress rehearsal for settlement in the Land of Israel,[1] many Zionists, including Bregman, rejected the proposal, and did so with high drama that included rites of mourning.

It is important to briefly discuss the Uganda proposal in the context of our story because Herzl's array of rational calculations ignored one basic element to which Bregman's grandson, Yossi Beilin, was also indifferent: the power of the primordial religious myths that influenced the modern Jewish national movement since its inception. To an important extent, Zionism was a product of Judaism's encounter with modernity. In this sense, one of Herzl's objectives was to stir a revolution in the history of the Jewish people. The aim of this revolution, in part, was to create an alternative culture to the traditional-rabbinical culture that developed in the Diaspora. That is, nationalism was designed to replace and inherit the role of religion.[2] However, from the vantage point of the early twenty-first century, it is clear that religion and nationhood have been entangled in a complex and symbiotic relationship in Zionism from the outset. Zionism, indeed, drew from the values of the Enlightenment era, which shaped the worldview of the state's visionary. However, Zionism also was driven by concepts from the religious past and it filled them with new meaning.[3]

The "secularization thesis" that prevailed in the Western world through the 1960s related to modernity as an evolutionary process in which the religious world, its institutions and concepts would fade into oblivion,[4] while recent studies critiquing this thesis emphasize the salient role of religious phenomena, old and new, that are flourishing in modernity, and even draw from it.[5] Therefore, the distinction between religion and secularization is complex, and secularism in itself does not stand in contradiction to the religious world. Indeed, secularism is "nurtured by the theological and conducts dialogues of various sorts with it."[6] This is not only true vis-à-vis the Zionist movement. Most national movements—despite emerging from the Enlightenment and its values, and constituting a chapter in the global secularization process—have reflected a mixed approach to religion: On the one hand, they look toward a future of progress and present a system of rational and universal concepts that oppose placing God and "His representatives" at the center of human existence. On the other hand, nationalism has flourished precisely because it offers a narrative that preserves, in different hues and forms, religious concepts that reinforce the old particularistic identity of human beings. In many ways, therefore, nationalism can be seen as a religious phenomenon in its own right.

The modern Jewish national movement, which has never differentiated between religion and nationhood, is a more acute and distinct example of this ambivalence. Even those who interpret Zionism as a break in Jewish historical continuity, as a new secular phenomenon in Jewish history, will find it difficult to deny that the idea of returning to Zion and the aspiration for an ingathering of exiles are anchored in the religious discourse.[7] Amnon Raz-Krakotzkin correctly noted:

> [Although] the theological dimension is not exclusive to Zionism and is found at the core of many national consciousnesses, in Europe and elsewhere, Zionism was unique in that the national consciousness included an interpretation of the religious myth from the outset, and not an alternative to the story that stood at the core of the previous identity. The trend of the secularization of religious consciousness was not expressed in neutralizing it or in breaking away from the myth, but in the national interpretation applied to the myth. The secularization was expressed in nationalizing the religion, on the one hand, and in according theological meaning to political activity, on the other hand.[8]

The delegates at the 6th Zionist Congress supported Herzl's Uganda proposal by a vote of 295–178. The supporters included representatives of the religious faction, Hamizrahi, who ironically were more moderate than the secularists, as their faith distinguished between compromise in "this world" and maximalist aspirations that looked toward messianic times. Indeed, in presenting the proposal to settle in Uganda and to bypass—at least for a while—the Land of Israel, the sacred myth, Herzl failed to appreciate the power of the religious dimension among secular Jews and did not anticipate how deeply it would shock many delegates at the congress. The lamentations of the Uganda proposal's opponents (primarily Russian Jews), who demonstratively left the hall after losing the vote, made a powerful impression.

One of those who exited the hall was Yosef Bregman, who never forgave Herzl for advocating this proposal. His hero suddenly became the embodiment of Shabtai Zvi, the false prophet. Though Herzl died about a year after the 6th Zionist Congress, and the Uganda proposal was removed from the agenda in 1905 at the next congress (and had become irrelevant in any case, because the fact-finding expedition to Uganda found it unsuitable for Jewish settlement), the Uganda episode was etched deeply in Bregman's consciousness and his attitude toward the Land of Israel figured prominently in the discussions of his offspring. Bregman could not have imagined, of course, that the Land of Israel would also be a focus of the political activity of his grandson—as one of the architects of the plan to divide it between Jews and Palestinians in the 1990s—or that the religious dimension in the Zionist movement would play a considerable role in the failure of the process his grandson helped to lead.

## 2

Menahem Ussishkin, who had opposed the Uganda plan, succeeded Herzl as president of the Zionist Congress. Bregman was personally acquainted with Ussishkin even before the confrontation over the Uganda proposal, and they had a relationship of mutual respect. In particular, Ussishkin was impressed by Bregman's financial talents. In 1913, Ussishkin asked Bregman to postpone his planned emigration to Palestine in order to manage a Zionist bank in Russia. The First World Wa disrupted this plan and Bregman was forced to relocate several times during the course of the war.

In 1923, Bregman finally fulfilled his Zionist vision and left for Palestine with his wife Rivka and their two children, Baruch and Zehava. The family lived at 24 Kalischer Street in the first Hebrew city, Tel Aviv. Bregman raised his children to observe religious tradition (the house was strictly kosher), but the trappings of religion were intended to express a unique and transcendental Jewish national identity, supplanting devotion to God. The Zionist fervor of the family members was unquestionable, but their party affiliation was less clear. Under Ussishkin's influence, and like most Zionists of that period, the Bregmans belonged to a stream called "synthetic Zionism," which sought to combine the diplomatic activity of political Zionism with the land settlement activity of practical Zionism. The goal for them was to be "just a Zionist"—that is, they were ideologically nonpartisan.

After arriving in Palestine, Bregman received a prestigious job: he was appointed manager of a savings and loan bank on Herzl Street in Tel Aviv, a position he held until his death in 1946. It was a well-paying job and the Bregman family lived comfortably as members of the upper-middle class. During the time of the Yishuv, it was one of the few families to have a private telephone line, electric refrigerator, and radio.

Zehava Bregman married a bank employee named Zvi Beilin. After their wedding, the couple lived with Zehava's parents. Their son Yinon was born in 1937, followed eleven years later by a second son, Yossi. (Despite the large age gap, the two became close friends. Yinon served as director of the Israel Philatelic Service.) Kalischer Street was adjacent to one of the command centers of the Haganah (the precursor of the IDF) and the Bregman's home itself became a Haganah post. It became dangerous to live there, and Yossi spent the first few months of his life at his uncle's home in Petah Tikva, which was considered a safer locale.

Those were inspiring days in the Beilin family: the dream of independence came true and the atmosphere of "from destruction to rebirth" was strongly palpable. In other areas, however, matters were less uplifting. Since the grandfather's death, the family's standard of living significantly declined. The telephone was disconnected and the electric refrigerator was replaced by an icebox. (The family members brought ice from the Carmel Market, walking at a brisk, yet careful pace, fearing that the ice might fall or melt in the blazing heat of the summer months.) They kindled wood to fire the water heater for the bathtub, and cut off the tips of the children's shoes to allow their feet room for growth, thus postponing the need to buy new shoes for a while. Nonetheless, the number of books on the shelves in the living room—primarily books on Jewish history and Zionism—continued to grow. It was important for the family to preserve its cultural wealth even in times of economic distress. And the grandfather's spirit continued to hover over everything.

His study, which the family referred to as "the cabinet," remained as it was during his lifetime. No one dared to take possession of it, or even rearrange the room. The grandfather's walking stick still hung proudly next to his books. Outside the room, the walls of the home were decked with numerous portraits of Zionist leaders. Especially prominent were portraits of Ussishkin and Weizmann—a sort of alternative to the picture of Herzl routinely displayed in other Zionist homes. But the home was not only adorned with portraits of Zionist leaders. Beilin's childhood habitat also included photographs of victims of the pogroms in Russia in the early 1900s. He had never spoken publicly about the impact of these photographs, but they may shed light on the poem he wrote about how utterly exhausting his life was as a seven-year-old. When already a politician, looking at his childhood in retrospect, Beilin defined himself in those years as "a serious child who took big national tasks upon himself. I grew up in an intimidating home in that respect."[9] In fact, until he reached first grade, no one told him that his grandfather was deceased; the family's cover story was that he had traveled to America. In many ways, during Beilin's early years he felt like "the grandson of." His grandfather was not widely known to the public, but he was one of the founders of the banking system in Israel. Only in retrospect did Beilin realize how difficult it was for his mother, who worshipped her father, to cope with his death.

# 3

Zvi Beilin, Yossi's father, grew up in Warsaw in a less privileged and more religious family than that of his mother. In 1926, when Zvi was 16, he arrived in Palestine with his family as part of the fourth major wave of Jewish immigration, the Fourth Aliyah. The immigrants in this wave came for a variety of reasons. Beilin's family immigrated primarily because of the desire to fulfill the connection to the Land of Israel, in accordance with the national dimension in the Jewish tradition. It was a sort of intuitive Zionism, without profound familiarity with the philosophers of the Zionist movement and their writings. Zvi's mother, Rachel, found it difficult to adjust to a new language and never learned to read and write in Hebrew. She continued to conduct her life in Yiddish, a language she later imparted to her grandson Yossi. Zvi's father, Ze'ev, was a carpenter according to his immigration certificate, but he worked as a low-ranking bank official after arriving in Palestine. When his wife died, he moved into the home of his son Zvi and daughter-in-law Zehava.

Zvi completed his studies at the Geula High School and volunteered for the Haganah. His religiousness was moderate, not unlike the approach that most of the Jews from Islamic countries brought with them to Israel in the 1950s.[10] Like them, his connection to Zionism did not develop by studying the writings of Zionist thinkers. He identified the national movement as a modern link in a Jewish historical continuum, anchored in the religious culture, and not as a revolutionary idea inspired by the nationalism that stirred the peoples of eastern and central Europe.[11] Thus, he put on a yarmulke on Friday evenings and recited the blessing over the wine, but did not visit the synagogue on a daily basis—only on the Sabbath and holidays. After prayers on Saturday morning, he would go straight from the synagogue to watch soccer games, usually at Basa Stadium in Jaffa (today the site of Bloomfield Stadium).

Zvi wanted his son Yossi to adopt his moderate approach to religion. But Yossi, who still today defines his identity first and foremost as "Jewish,"[12] did not easily accept his father's ways, like many young people. He saw an irreconcilable contradiction between synagogue and soccer on the Sabbath, and sought to decide between the two: religious or secular. Like many Israelis whose formative teenage years were in the sixties, the social and cultural revolutions of that decade had little effect on him. He remained engrossed in the inner world of Zionism and Judaism. And even though the question of God's existence did not burn within him, he chose to express his Jewishness through strict observance of the tradition. From the time of his bar mitzvah through his mid-twenties, Beilin regularly put on *tefillin*, ate only kosher food, observed the Sabbath, and prayed at the neighborhood synagogue. The interest he showed in the commandments and principles of the Jewish religion continued to deepen in high school, and his Talmud teacher, recognizing Beilin's potential, tried to convince him to study at a yeshiva. Beilin's father opposed this idea.

Beilin would later say that he never regarded himself as a "repenting" Jew (*hozer b'tshuva* in Hebrew parlance). Still, his interest in religion was not a fleeting episode. When he was conscripted into the IDF, he carried two mess kits—one for dairy and one for meat—in keeping with the religious prohibition on mixing milk and meat. Beilin's father did not hide his dissatisfaction with his son's path, but refrained from arguing with him. Zvi Beilin was an amiable person, hungry for knowledge and a book lover, who failed to realize his dream of becoming a writer or journalist, and had to continue working at a bank. He was very close to his two sons and tried not to show that he was racked by a sense of missed opportunities in his life. But it was difficult not to notice. After the War of Independence, Zvi continued to regularly report for reserve duty in the IDF and served as a reservist in the Sinai Campaign in 1956.

After realizing that he could not afford to leave his job at the bank, Zvi prepared himself for retirement, so that at least then he could devote himself to writing as "a full-time job"—in the spirit of "better late than never." Until then, he occasionally found ways to combine his banking profession and his hobby. He managed to secure a part-time position at the *Hador* newspaper, but unfortunately, it went out of business soon afterward. Another opportunity to combine his banking work and his dream of journalism materialized when he became the accountant for the Israel Press Association. He also edited two internal publications for Bank Leumi (*Igeret* and *Beiteinu*). On Friday evenings, he would take his son Yossi to Mughrabi Square in Tel Aviv to hear journalists interviewing each other in a sort of roundtable discussion open to the public. Later, he and his Yossi also started going to similar events at the Beit Sokolow press center in Tel Aviv.

Zvi was an autodidact par excellence. Though he did not find time to acquire an academic education, he studied various languages: he knew Arabic, English, French, German, Polish and Russian, and had a rudimentary knowledge of Latin. He died in 1972 when he was only 62 years old.

Looking back at his father's death, Beilin feels sad that his father did not fulfill his potential. He appreciates how his father sought to avoid burdening his sons by trying not to let his frustration show. With the passage of time, this appreciation has only grown.

The life story of Beilin's mother Zehava is different. She also observed some religious traditions, including *kashrut* (the Jewish dietary laws), though she did this from a sense of *Yiddishkeit* (Jewishness) and respect for tradition, rather than faith in the words of a living God. She chose to study literary Arabic at Hebrew University, but her decision did not stem from a clear ideology about the need to understand the "other" or a prescient perception of the explosiveness of the Arab-Zionist conflict in the Middle East. Instead, it reflected her practical recognition of the need to communicate with the country's Arab residents.

She realized the importance of such communication one summer day in the 1930s, when she was on her way home and began to feel ill. An Arab wagon driver stopped to help and brought her to the hospital. The fact that the two of them were unable to converse during the trip struck her as absurd, and she decided to learn Arabic. After acquiring some facility in the language, Zehava began working at the *Davar* daily as a reporter on Arab affairs. But she did not continue in this line of work or with her Arabic studies. Instead, she completed a degree in Bible studies and archaeology. Here too, she found a way to connect her academic studies and journalism: she contributed to a daily feature on Bible stories, broadcast on Israel Radio. Thanks to this work, she was also invited to participate in the famous Bible study group of David Ben-Gurion and President Yitzhak Ben-Zvi. She died in 1994 at age 84.

The Zionist ethos was a central feature of the Beilin family's life, reflected in the historical references in birthday greetings—for example: "11 years since our liberation" (or "redemption") or "[x] years since the Balfour Declaration." Naturally, the most important holiday on the calendar was Independence Day, when Beilin's parents would light candles and invite guests to their home. This atmosphere shaped the worldview of Beilin as a boy and teenager. When his teacher asked the pupils to bring an object of art from their home, the enthusiastic Beilin brought a picture of Ahad Ha'am. (The teacher refused to consider the portrait a work of art.)

However, the Beilin home was not clearly affiliated with any particular political party. Though Zvi had served in the Haganah and was a member of the Histadrut labor federation, he refused to join the Mapai party. He admired Ze'ev Jabotinsky, though he later had reservations about Menachem Begin and his Herut party. His parents usually thought alike, though not always. The murder of Haim Arlosoroff in 1933 was a subject of contention in the home. Zvi argued that the Revisionists were being falsely accused of the murder, and suspected that the Arabs were involved. Zehava believed that it was the work of Jabotinsky's supporters, and pointed to fascist motifs in the Revisionist camp. When they failed to reach agreement, and to prevent further flare-ups, they decided not to discuss this subject any more. After the establishment of the state, they shared an admiration for the virtues of the first prime minister, David Ben-Gurion.

In 1953, the "old man" made the surprise announcement that he was resigning as prime minister and relocating to Kibbutz Sde Boker in the Negev. Many Israelis were fearful about the future. Zalman Aran, a senior Mapai leader and education minister in the 1950s and 1960s, reflected the public mood when he wrote to Ben-Gurion: "I implore you, don't do it. This unfortunate people and tragic state do not have the strength to bear it."[13] Beilin's parents were also alarmed. Yossi was only five years old, but he sensed this. When the kindergarten teacher informed the children of the prime minister's resignation, he found this news difficult to accept. He went and sat alone in a corner to brood over the news. As a pupil in elementary school, he was still captivated by Ben-Gurion when the "old man" returned to politics in 1955. Beilin often took walks on Keren Kayemet Boulevard (later renamed Ben-Gurion Boulevard) hoping to see the "old man" entering or leaving his home.

Like his parents, and despite his strong interest in politics, Yossi did not clearly identify with a particular political party in his youth. He saw Ben-Gurion as the father of the nation, as a prime minister representing the state's interests, and not as a Mapai leader embroiled in disputes with various factions in the society and in the political system. During election campaigns, Beilin's father tried to expose him to the platforms and election rallies of most of the parties. In general, his relationship with his father peaked during election campaigns: they would go together to rallies held by various candidates. Etched in Beilin's memory are speeches by Begin in Mughrabi Square and by Moshe Dayan at the Carmel Market. Together with his father, he also watched Sharett and Ben-Gurion deliver speeches, and listened to the words of Ben-Gurion's antagonist, Nahum Goldmann, the chairman of the World Zionist Organization from 1956 to 1968. Nonetheless, their politics had clear boundaries. Moshe Sneh, who joined the Communist Party, was beyond the pale. Beilin's father regarded communism as the primary threat to Zionism. As noted, he was a member of the Histadrut, but he defiantly went to work on May 1, International Workers' Day.

Beilin also learned his love of reading from his father, and immersed himself in books from the moment he learned to read and write. Books on history and Zionism were his favorites, but he also read world literature and in his youth enjoyed D. H. Lawrence's *Lady Chatterley's Lover* as much as he enjoyed Tolstoy's *War and Peace*. His discipline and diligence were not typical of boys his age, and even his father sometimes complained about his habit of cloistering himself in his room and reading, and encouraged him to spend more time playing games with his friends. Yossi, indeed, tried to develop athletic skills and played a little soccer, but usually refrained from the frivolities and pastimes of youth. His personal archives, meticulously organized, includes certificates of excellence from elementary school and the Herzliya Hebrew High School.

Like many families during Israel's first decade,[14] the members of the Beilin family averted their attention from the horrors of the Holocaust. Zvi boycotted German products, but did not elaborate on this topic or present his position as part of a coherent ideology. Yossi, like other children of his time, sometimes encountered mentally disturbed survivors in the streets. There was a woman who constantly screamed that she was being hunted, and a man who sat at the corner of the street frantically sewing pieces of cloth. But Yossi and his friends saw them as part of the Tel Aviv landscape, and not as a reminder of the disaster that had befallen the Jewish people. They were viewed as insane and regarded with astonishment at best, and often with ridicule. When Beilin grew a bit older, he took an interest in the "Searching for Relatives" section that was popular in newspapers at the time, reconnecting relatives and friends separated during the Holocaust. But he did not devote much attention to this issue. The image of the Jewish people as victims was not a dominant element in his view of history.

The experience that shaped his Zionist worldview was the heroism and victory in the War of Independence. His father's participation in the war was a source of pride, and memorial days for the fallen soldiers touched his heart more deeply than Holocaust memorial days. Like many other Israelis, it was the Eichmann trial in 1961, and its repercussions in the public and in the media, that deepened his interest in the Holocaust. He wanted to look into the complaints that were sounded—albeit outside the mainstream—about the feebleness of the Zionist leadership when it came to rescuing European Jewry. But after reading about this subject, he concluded that the Zionists were simply incapable of fathoming the dimensions and significance of the catastrophe. He still maintains that opinion today.

During his childhood, the Holocaust was like a story that was impossible to grasp and assimilate into everyday reality. Thus, it was easier to look at the mentally troubled Holocaust survivors as crazy vagrants. When he was older and had read widely on the Holocaust, he concluded that it is important to understand the Holocaust and teach the next generations about it as an integral part of human history, and not as a foreign or anomalous event. The lesson is that it could happen again to some extent or another. The circumstances that led to the Holocaust were not unique. In Beilin's eyes, the Holocaust is a universal lesson that teaches Jews to take responsibility for their fate, yet also to ensure the fate of other peoples in distress.

# 4

Despite the teenage Yossi Beilin's strong interest in the fate of the Jewish people and in Zionism, he did not dream of a political future; he wanted to be an actor on the stage. At the age of ten, he joined Menachem Golan's acting studio on Sholem Aleichem Street in Tel Aviv. Later, he signed up for the Habima Youth Theater, which mainly involved analyzing plays and listening to lectures by actors, directors, and playwrights. True to character, he approached the world of acting with complete seriousness. He did not show extraordinary talent as an actor, but he memorized his lines well and rarely missed a rehearsal. Beilin participated in the Habima program for five years. What fascinated him about theater was the ability to play different roles and create new worlds; he had no aspiration to become famous and part of the bohemian scene.

Beilin was cognizant of the dissonance between his introverted personality and the extroverted dimension of the world of acting, but did not dwell on this. He also recognized his limitations as an actor. While in high school, he also decided to invest his energy in another direction—journalism. An advertisement offering a job as a reporter at *Maariv L'Noar*, a teen weekly with very high circulation at the time, caught his attention. After proving his writing skills, he won the job and, in parallel, began occasionally broadcasting a program for teenagers on Israel Radio. Beilin also edited his high school newspaper. He again brought his earnest approach to these endeavors;

when his friends called him to join in their games, he often responded that he was too busy with his important tasks.

Beilin met Helena Einhorn in high school and took a liking to her. Her father had headed the Revisionist Party at the displaced persons camp in Kassel, Germany, at the end of the Second World War. Yossi and Helena became a couple toward the end of their high school days.

Beilin did not only engage in journalistic writing. At age 17, he read *Where the Jackals Howl*, the first book published by Amos Oz, and rushed to tell the radio audience that it was "the book of the year" of 1965. Oz was moved by Beilin's book review and sent a letter to him at Israel Radio, inviting him to meet at his home in Kibbutz Hulda. After corresponding on postcards to arrange the date, the two met at the kibbutz. In the course of the friendship that developed, Beilin showed Oz a text he had written: a romantic novel about a teenager who falls in love with his literature teacher. After reading the manuscript, Oz suggested that more work was needed to improve the text before trying to publish it, but he encouraged Beilin to persist in his literary efforts and they continued to correspond. In 1968, when Beilin was a soldier and still uncertain about his talents as a writer, Oz wrote to him: "Don't wake and don't stir your writing, and certainly don't eulogize it. Perhaps it will suddenly awaken with renewed strength. (I, for example, didn't write anything during my army service except for letters to girls.)" Beilin, in any case, concluded that writing prose was not his purpose in life. However, he went on to write eleven works of nonfiction and essays.

5

On May 15, 1967, Israel's nineteenth Independence Day, the Egyptian army moved large forces into the Sinai Peninsula. IDF chief of staff Yitzhak Rabin and Prime Minister Eshkol were informed as they attended a military parade. Eight days later, the Egyptians, upon the directive of President Gamal Abdel Nasser, blocked the Straits of Tiran.

The actions of the Egyptian army exacerbated tensions that had been simmering for several months between Israel and its neighbors Egypt and Syria. A consensus emerged among the IDF's general staff that war was inevitable and that Israel should launch a surprise attack if it wanted to win. But there was a sense of anxiety in the Israeli public and in the political system, and fears intensified, in part because of the public image of Eshkol, who was seen as a weak and hesitant leader. Booklets entitled "All the Eshkol Jokes" and "More Eshkol Jokes" were published in Israel in 1966 and 1967, ridiculing his personality and limitations. The top IDF brass felt they should assume responsibility.[15]

The economic situation did nothing to boost the general mood. The Israeli economy had not yet completely recovered from the recession that began in 1966. About 12 percent of the workforce was unemployed—about 108,000 people in a state with a population of 2.6 million. (Historians only later discovered that the recession was, in part, a result of policy charted by Finance Minister Pinhas Sapir, with Eshkol's backing, designed to slow economic activity in a controlled way. This came as the flow of reparation payments from Germany came to a halt, and was aimed at reducing the deficit and stemming inflation.)[16]

The public in Israel was also influenced by the threats of Arab leaders and the Arab media: "We'll hang the last imperialist soldier on the innards of the last Zionist soldier," Radio Damascus declared in late May, and the Voice of the Arabs radio station in Cairo swore that the world was at the threshold of "the day of Israel's annihilation."[17] Some politicians in Israel also felt panic. The feeling was that without the founding father, David Ben-Gurion, Israel had lost the leadership required for times of crisis. One of those who contributed to this feeling was Ben-Gurion himself. In 1967, the "old man" became the leader of Rafi—the first centrist party in Israel. Rafi was formed after Ben-Gurion quit Mapai in anger and sought to instigate a rebellion against the establishment that he himself had created; he believed the leaders of Mapai had acted improperly in what became known as the Lavon Affair. Even though Rafi won only ten Knesset seats in the 1965 elections and remained in the opposition, Ben-Gurion's critique of Mapai and its leaders began to make waves in the public. After the elections, Ben-Gurion often complained about Eshkol's "security and moral failings" and though he provided no specifics, his remarks reinforced the sense that Israel was suffering from weak leadership.[18] An attempt (led by Shimon Peres, then a member of Knesset representing Rafi) to restore Ben-Gurion to a position of leadership failed, but the contacts conducted among the various parties led in early June to the formation of a national unity government. Gahal (the precursor of the Likud) joined the government for the first time in Israel's history and its leader Menachem Begin became a minister without portfolio. Eshkol remained prime minister, but was pressured to yield the defense portfolio to Moshe Dayan, the former IDF chief of staff and a Rafi member at the time.[19] The national unity government prepared to order the IDF to carry out a preemptive strike.[20]

It later became clear that the Six-Day War did not erupt only because the Arab states wanted to annihilate the "Zionist entity," as their leaders bombastically declared. It was also the result of misconceptions and complex assessments, including Israel's interests. However, for the soldiers waiting in the field for developments, the situation was black and white. One of those soldiers was Yossi Beilin, who had been conscripted about a year earlier and now served as a wireless operator in the Signal Corps. Like many in the public and in the IDF, he was fed up with the nerve-racking waiting and hoped for a decisive war that would put an end to it. In his youthful eyes, war was also a chance to participate in making history. He felt unfortunate in having missed the opportunity to be part of the generation that experienced the two wars that shaped Israel and the IDF—the War of Independence and the Sinai Campaign.

Beilin brought to his military role the same earnestness and devotion that had characterized him as a pupil, actor in the theater group, and young journalist, and received the rank of staff sergeant ahead of schedule. His handle on the military radio network was "soap." For Beilin, the national had always blended with the personal; thus, it was fitting that he began to write a journal as a historical memento during the days of waiting. "Death," he wrote a day before IDF aircraft destroyed the Egyptian and Syrian air forces, "is possible and plausible, but I'm not afraid."

On the eve of the battles, Beilin was attached to the 8th Armored Division, which operated in the Sinai Peninsula. Beilin's primary job was to call for aerial support for ground troops. Like most of the soldiers, Beilin could not imagine the historical repercussions of the IDF offensive on June 5, 1967, and was mainly concerned with the number of IDF casualties. Only on June 7, when the 55th Paratroopers Brigade captured the Old City in Jerusalem and Beilin listened on a transistor radio to Motta Gur announce that "the Temple Mount is in our hands," he began to realize this was not just another war. He was moved to tears by the capture of the Old City. From the Sinai Peninsula, he was sent to the Golan Heights and participated in the last day of battles to capture this territory from Syria.

The horrific sights of the war only hit him after it was all over. He later recalled how during one of the lulls in fighting, he made his way to the canteen to buy a candy bar, nonchalantly walking among the corpses of Egyptian soldiers. During the war itself, a body that was still lying under the food truck, with no one bothering to remove it, did not spoil his appetite. He was mainly upset by the looting incidents he witnessed during the fighting. Such incidents received scant attention in the Israeli media, which was swept up in the euphoria of victory (and contributed to whipping up this euphoria). One time, he gathered his courage and asked a soldier not to steal an expensive watch from the body of a Syrian soldier. Toward the end of the war, he tried to speak with Syrian captives, using the Arabic he had learned in high school, but no real conversations developed. After the war, Beilin was sent with his unit to Ramallah and spent several weeks there. He remembers the city as impressive in beauty, but he did not take interest in the Arab culture he found there. Next, his unit was transferred to the northern sector of the Suez Canal, to El-Qantara. Shelling continued there from time to time. Beilin completed his period of compulsory army service in 1969, and due to his reputation as an efficient and dutiful soldier, he was assigned reserve duty as a wireless operator at the IDF general staff.

At that stage, Beilin did not participate in discussions about war and morality. Nor was he particularly concerned with the question of the status and rights of the Palestinians and the occupied territories. On the contrary, the results of the war strengthened his faith in the Zionist path and the Israeli establishment. Like many other Israelis, the conquest of the territories also strengthened the religious dimension in his identity. There were various reasons for this: the days of waiting were accompanied by a sense of existential threat, echoing the themes of persecution and redemption in the Jewish tradition; in the consciousness of Israelis, the pre-war threats by Arab leaders resonated with historical anti-Semitism; and after the victory, the territories that were captured evoked the biblical era. The return to Jewish holy sites stirred religious sentiments, implicit and explicit.[21]

The war had an enormous impact on Israeli society and its political system. Among national-religious Jews, the worldview championed by Rabbi Zvi Yehuda Kook gained prominence. According to this worldview, the creation of the State of Israel marked the beginning of redemption, which should now be hastened by settling in the newly captured territories. It is no coincidence that seven years after the war, national-religious Jews formed the Gush Emunim movement, which became the vanguard of the settlement enterprise. An awakening of the religious connection also characterized some of the traditional-minded representatives of the socialist Zionist camp. The Movement for Greater Israel, established in November 1967, based its arguments against withdrawal from the territories on security and historical grounds, but due to the difficulty in separating Jewish national history from the religious dimension, theological motifs were intertwined in their arguments. There were ideological differences within the movement, and many of its first members had roots in the left. After the Yom Kippur War, however, the movement joined the Likud under Menachem Begin, who cited God's biblical promise as the basis for his connection to the Land of Israel.[22]

The Six-Day War also strengthened the "Jewish" dimension of Israel because of its impact on world Jewry. The IDF's achievement was a source of pride in Jewish communities, and was expressed in financial assistance and other types of support—and in a new wave of immigration.[23] Between 1967 and 1973, about 260,000 Jews immigrated to Israel, most of them from the West and the Soviet Union. The closer ties with Diaspora Jews illustrated the idea of Israel as the state of the entire Jewish people. This placed the religious-ethnic motif in an advantageous position in Israel, as opposed to the possibility of building a civil nationalism disconnected from world Jewry.

These processes were still embryonic at the end of the war, and not yet discernible. Beilin was not exceptional in being swept along in the enthusiasm in Israel. Nor was he exceptional in feeling that the war was not only the product of political processes driven by realpolitik, and from assessments and counter-assessments, but a formative chapter in Jewish history and even proof of Divine Providence. He went with his family on exciting trips in the territories and visited Jewish holy sites. The question of the future of the territories and their residents was not of primary concern to him. From his perspective, Israel had won a just war of defense. He was part of the broad consensus in Israel that stretched from the right and national-religious Jews to members of the Labor movement on the left. On June 19, 1967, nine days after the war ended, the government of Israel expressed readiness, in principle, to concede territory in the framework of a future accord. However, the prevailing view, even among the Zionist left, was that the Arabs were not yet ready for a peace accord. This perception effectively narrowed the disparity between the views of Begin and those of Eshkol and Golda Meir, who replaced Eshkol after his death in early 1969.[24]

During the last week of his military service, Beilin married Helena. The army rabbi of the Signal Corps conducted the wedding. The marriage lasted 32 years. After leaving the army, Beilin continued to strictly observe Jewish tradition—he refrained from travel and work on the Sabbath, and kept kosher. He even exhorted his family to adopt his ways, refused to eat in homes that were not strictly kosher, and surprised Helena's parents by threatening not to come to the Passover *seder* at their home if they did not make their kitchen kosher for Passover. (They bowed to his demand.) However, unlike most of those drawn to religion in their youth, Beilin was not interested in the question of God's existence. He never believed in a Supreme Being that drives the world, and did not turn to God in times of distress. His fastidious observance of religious trappings stemmed entirely from a national worldview, and primarily from his desire to ensure the continued existence of the Jewish people. His approach was consistent with the spirit of Judaism, which requires the strict performance of commandments and is less concerned with Orthodox belief.

6

The young couple rented an apartment on Arba Arazot Street in Tel Aviv and applied to study at Tel Aviv University. Helena studied law and became an attorney. Beilin chose to study Hebrew literature and political science. Prominent teachers in the Department of Hebrew Literature included Dan Miron and Uzi Shavit; Beilin studied political science with Asher Arian, Yonathan Shapiro, and Shevach Weiss.

At the time, the political science departments at Tel Aviv University and the Hebrew University of Jerusalem competed over the proper way to teach political science. The faculty in Jerusalem emphasized political philosophy, while the department in Tel Aviv was more inclined toward the school of quantitative research, which was also Beilin's inclination. He liked the technical dimension, using equations and tables as methodological tools for understanding and analyzing political processes.

The positivism that Beilin embraced led him to aspire to specialize in survey theory. However, like his father, he loved to read and write, and the temptation to be a journalist competed with his ambition to engage in academic research. Thus, while still a student, Beilin applied for a job as an economics reporter at the *Davar* daily after noticing a want ad for the position.

Beilin had four years of experience as a writer at *Ma'ariv L'Noar*, and six years of experience as a reporter at Israel Radio. Two talented young journalists were also vying for the job—Eli Mohar and Doron Rosenblum. The editor of the *Davar Hashavua* magazine, Ohad Zmora, set a condition for the candidates: they had to commit to a full-time position. He did not like the fact that many of the young reporters worked part-time while pursuing university studies. Rosenblum won the job, but Beilin and Mohar were also offered an opportunity to work as freelancers. (In 1972, Beilin was promoted to a regular position as a reporter.)

Beilin's first article was ahead of its time: a farewell to the old central bus station in Tel Aviv. (In the end, a new central bus station would only be built in the 1990s.) Besides writing magazine articles, Beilin primarily covered economic issues, including the activity of the Histadrut labor federation. Though the Histadrut actually owned *Davar*, and though the newspaper served as a central platform for Mapai and was clearly partisan, Beilin did not encounter explicit attempts to influence his reporting. In part, there was no need for such intervention because most of the newspaper's reporters identified with the party line. There was also an unspoken understanding at the newspaper that certain figures were beyond criticism, namely, Yitzhak Ben-Aharon, the secretary-general of the Histadrut from 1969-1973, and Yaakov Levinson, the CEO of Bank Hapoalim from the late 1960s. Nonetheless, under the editorial leadership of Yehuda Gotthelf and his successor as editor-in-chief, Hannah Zemer, the newspaper maintained a high level of quality. The weekend magazine, *Davar Hashavua*, featured promising young journalists, including Nahum Barnea, Doron Rosenblum, Michael

Handelzalts, Eli Mohar, Dani Kerman, Yair Garboz, and Yehonatan Gefen; the holiday supplements included pieces by such writers as Amos Oz, Yoram Kaniuk, Haim Be'er, Nissim Aloni, Dan Zalka, S. Yizhar, Haim Gouri, and Moshe Shamir. The newspaper represented the Ashkenazi elite in the fields of culture and literature.

Print journalism was then the main field of journalism in Israel. (Television broadcasts began sparingly only after the Six-Day War.) The status of journalists as the intermediaries between the public and the political arena was at its peak. Contributing to this was the fact that journalists were employed under collective bargaining agreements that made it difficult to fire them. However, the 1970s were also the years when party-affiliated newspapers, which depended primarily on party funding, began to decline. As parties reduced their funding of newspapers, the first signs of the problematic connection between the business world and journalistic content emerged. Beilin was surprised to hear about gifts from corporations in exchange for favorable coverage. For example, a day before he was slated to attend a press conference convened by a large watch company, a special messenger came to him and offered a gift: an expensive watch. Beilin gave the watch to the editor, who complimented him on his integrity, though some of Beilin's colleagues ridiculed his naivety. When Zemer was editor-in-chief, Beilin was told to scrap a critical article he had written about the credit terms offered to customers when purchasing Contessa automobiles. No reason was stated, but it was obvious: the automobile company was investing in giant advertisements in the newspaper. Beilin's efforts to fight the decision to quash his article were to no avail.

Another important area that Beilin came to know during his time as a journalist concerns the relations between journalists and their sources. It was not hard to see that many politicians leaked information in exchange for favorable coverage. But Beilin realized that the politicians who earned greater respect from journalists were those who collaborated in a more sophisticated and less submissive way. On the other hand, those who completely shut themselves off from journalists lost the chance to influence the media on the issues they sought to promote. When he later became a politician, Beilin developed his system of constructive relations with the press based on this realization: he maintained cordial relations with quite a few journalists, but usually preferred to give off-the-record commentary rather than directly leaking information. In this way, he fostered close relations of mutual benefit, while still guarding his reputation as someone who does not leak the information he receives.

At this stage, in the early 1970s, Beilin had not yet decided on a professional path. During his work at *Davar*, he developed relationships with Pinhas Sapir (the finance minister at the time), Yitzhak Ben-Aharon, and Yosef Almogi. Almogi, the mayor of Haifa, who wielded enormous clout in Mapai, asked Beilin to serve as his spokesperson in 1972, in part out of respect for Beilin's grandfather. But Beilin chose not to enter the political world at that time. However, he did accept Yossi Sarid's invitation to become a member of Yehoshua Rabinovich's brain trust for the Tel Aviv municipal elections in 1973. He did not believe this political involvement compromised his integrity as a journalist. Just as IDF officers, especially those who sought to climb the ranks, were not deterred (at least until the early 1960s) from membership in a political party (Mapai), it was not considered unethical or a violation of the unwritten covenant between the journalist and the public for a journalist to serve as an adviser to a party.

The sociologist Yonathan Shapiro, one of Beilin's teachers in the Department of Political Science, took note of not only Beilin's analytical skills—but also his inclination not to fully commit himself to the world of academia. One day, he summoned his student for a conversation and suggested that he make a decision about his future: a researcher, journalist, or politician. Beilin was sure he would choose one of these paths, but was not ready to commit yet; of the three choices, politics seemed the least likely. Meanwhile, he continued his academic studies and completed his doctorate. His dissertation topic was "Intergenerational Friction in Three Parties in Israel." His central thesis focused on how the generational transition places limitations on the young generation in large parties and prevents the injection of new ideas. His study explained, for example, the failure of Ben-Gurion's attempt to institute regional elections in Israel[25] due to resistance from the Mapai party's old guard. "The party apparatus, led by a group from the Third Aliyah and Fourth Aliyah, strongly opposed regional elections—because it would naturally weaken the center and the central apparatus, or because most of them were not built for competing in that kind of system," Beilin wrote.[26] The dissertation was approved in 1981—eleven years after he began his academic studies. It took him a while because he was not in a hurry, and also because in the elitist atmosphere that prevailed in Israeli universities in the 1970s, and especially in the Department of Political Science at Hebrew University, the feeling was that a scholar should complete at least twenty years of study before being deemed worthy of the title of doctor.

Is the study of political science beneficial for a politician? Beilin, who lectured for thirteen years in the Department of Political Science at Tel Aviv University, believes that his academic training indeed helped him make his way in politics, contributed to his understanding of the rules of the political game, and gave him the broad perspective that a politician needs. In retrospect, however, he believes that the study of economics and law can provide an even better understanding of the forces at work in politics. In any case, he says that experience rather than theoretical studies is the essential ingredient for a politician's success. Experience is something no theory can replace.

## 7

In September 1970, the president of Egypt, Gamal Abdel Nasser, died and his deputy, Anwar Sadat, replaced him. The Israeli establishment saw Sadat as weak and believed he would refrain from renewing the war effort against Israel. After Israel rejected several proposals from Sadat to renew diplomatic talks, he declared that 1971 would be a "year of decision." The fact that the year passed without event only strengthened the conviction of Israel's leaders that Egypt did not pose a threat. The IDF, in any case, was seen as invincible after the Six-Day War and War of Attrition.

In fact, from the end of the Six-Day War through 1973, there was a flurry of diplomatic activity, with mediators trying to promote all sorts of peace initiatives—including the mission of UN special envoy Gunnar Jarring, the efforts of US secretary of state William Rogers, Nahum Goldmann's attempt to establish a direct channel between Israel and Egypt, and the Four Power talks at the UN. Under American pressure, Israel accepted the Rogers Plan, which included partial adoption of UN Security Council Resolution 242 (land for peace), but this was essentially lip service. In fact, new research shows that in 1971 Golda Meir came to secret understandings with Henry Kissinger, then President Nixon's national security adviser, on the advantages of a diplomatic standstill.[27]

The voice of Ben-Gurion, who feared another round of bloodshed and believed that Israel should aim to enter into negotiations, even at the price of withdrawal from the territories, remained almost solitary. The assessment of the founding father that now, at the beginning of Israel's third decade, the conditions were ripe for peace (primarily due to the economic and political needs of Egypt), was viewed as nothing more than delusional.[28] When Sadat recognized Israel's obstructionism, he turned to the alternative of breaking the stalemate through a military initiative. Although the IDF identified unusual military activity, Israeli intelligence was convinced that it only involved training maneuvers at this stage.[29] Israel regarded Sadat's diplomat feelers and military threats as expressions of distress, and believed that Egypt would not go to war before rebuilding its air force and that Syria would refrain from waging war on its own. In May 1973, Israel's intelligence services suspected that Egypt was about to launch a war, but then concluded that this was unlikely. The fact that war did not erupt reinforced the Israeli leadership's confidence in the intelligence assessment.

On September 13, there was a dogfight between Israeli and Syrian aircraft. The Israeli Air Force downed twelve Syrian planes and lost only one of its own aircraft. The IDF saw this as another sign of Syria's weakness. On September 25, in a secret meeting held in Israel, Jordan's King Hussein warned Golda Meir that Egypt and Syria were prepared to attack in the near future. But Israel was so confident in its ability to respond quickly and ward off any Arab attack that it paid no heed to the king's warning. Concerns about the diplomatic repercussions of launching a preemptive strike—which the American administration warned against—influenced Israel's leaders to prefer a policy of waiting passively. At the beginning of October, when Israel learned that Egypt was concentrating troops near the Suez Canal, it was therefore comfortable for the Israeli leadership to adopt the intelligence assessment that Egypt was engaged in training exercises. It was only on October 4 that Prime Minister Meir and Defense Minister Dayan became convinced that Israel was about to come under attack. Still, the IDF was placed on only partial readiness. Questions about what transpired among the top political and defense echelons in Israel still occupy scholars in Israel and the world.

On October 6, 1973, during the morning of Yom Kippur, the most sacred day on the Jewish calendar, the decision was made to call up IDF reserves in anticipation of an attack expected to be launched that evening. But the decision came too late. Around 2 p.m. sirens pierced the silence of Yom Kippur, signaling the onset of a horrific war.

Beilin was also caught by surprise, having believed—as the prime minister famously declared—that Israel's situation had never been better. As usual on Yom Kippur, he fasted and prayed in a synagogue. Though as a journalist he had access to sources and assessments, he was oblivious to the possibility of war. He had just written an article arguing that the order to shut down Abie Natan's Peace Ship was illegal. In an earlier article, he had focused on developments at the Yamit settlement in Sinai. He was in favor of Jewish settlement in the Sinai, considering it an integral part of the Zionist enterprise. At this stage, he saw a straight line connecting the labor movement's Zionist settlement activity in the pre-state period and the settlement activity in the territories captured in the Six-Day War (though he was primarily sympathetic to the outposts set up by the Nahal Brigade).

When he heard the sirens, he had no time to reflect on his articles. He was mobilized for reserve duty and rushed to the IDF general staff, where he served as a wireless operator. He had no idea that this reserve duty would last about six months, and that a completely different Yossi Beilin would emerge at the end of this period. In fact, it is impossible to understand Beilin as perceived by the public since the 1980s without understanding how the war affected him and reshaped his consciousness.

As a wireless operator at the general staff, Beilin was among the first and few in Israel to be exposed in real time to the crisis among the leadership, its sense of helplessness, and the terrified cries of the wounded, and to the infighting among the generals and senior officers he had so greatly admired.

The first days of the war, when it seemed that Israel was on the brink of destruction (and Dayan spoke about the impending fall of "the Third Kingdom of Israel"), were eye-opening for Beilin. Suddenly, the foundations of his confidence in the Israeli establishment and in the justness of Israel's path were shaken. The abandonment of soldiers in the outposts along the Suez Canal, the violation of orders, and the tragedies visited upon thousands of families—all tore the mask from Israel's face and exposed its shame and weakness. Even after the IDF survived the fierce battles in the south and north, pushed back the Egyptian and Syrian forces, and even crossed the Suez Canal and advanced to within 100 kilometers of Cairo—his thoughts were focused on the terrible price. About 2,600 Israeli soldiers had fallen, nearly three times as many were wounded, and hundreds were in captivity or missing in action. In Beilin's view, the leadership's ineptitude and shortsighted vision of Israel's situation in the Middle East were to blame for this tragedy.

The profound transformation that took root in him also affected his attitude toward religion. He suddenly felt it was absurd to continue observing the commandments. His immediate alienation from religion was not a result of theological reasoning; it expressed his profound disappointment and desire to free himself from the beliefs that had shaped his worldview. It was a sort of private rebellion through which he sought to resolve the national crisis he had experienced. And so, after completing that period of reserve duty, Beilin stopped putting on tefillin, no longer kept kosher, and rarely attended synagogue services.

What started as a rebellion, became a search for a significant Jewish essence separate from the Orthodox dimension. Beilin challenged the binary distinction between religious and secular Jews, and proposed a full secular Jewishness. In 2006, as chairman of Meretz, he formed the "secular lobby" in the Knesset, which, in the spirit of Jewish renewal organizations, sought to promote topics such as secular conversion, civil marriage, separation of religion and state, and funding of secular Jewish education. All these were aimed at creating a secular Jewish identity as an alternative to the religion, and not only as a retreat from it.[30] However, this development came later in his worldview. At this stage, in the wake of the Yom Kippur War, he primarily felt frustration and disappointment that he wished to dispel by turning away from the religious practices he had observed.

8

The trauma of the war did not affect Beilin's view of the fundamental justice of Zionism. He had no misgivings about the idea of ensuring a national home for the Jewish people in the Land of Israel, but was angry at the leadership's lack of readiness and wisdom to explore new ways of ensuring the survival of the Jewish state in the Middle East. The almost mythical faith that had accompanied him since childhood, faith in the abilities of the state's leaders to guide the Zionist enterprise to safe shores, collapsed and was gone. His confidence in the power of Israel's military to ensure its existence gave way to concerns about the state's ability to achieve what should have been central to its security strategy: peace accords.

At this stage, Beilin did not seek to reexamine the roots of the Zionist view or its original approach to the "Arab question." He emphasized the current importance of a diplomatic agreement and directed his anger primarily at what he began to see as a blindness that had afflicted the leadership since 1967. When roaming the streets of Tel Aviv in the months following the war, Beilin saw posters for the Alignment (the alliance of Labor and Mapam) here and there, in the lead-up to the eight Knesset elections. (The elections, originally scheduled for October 1973, were postponed for two months because of the war.) He saw these posters, which ironically promised "quiet" on all fronts "thanks to our policies," as signaling that he should change his way of thinking. After the initial shock wore off, the rapid transition from the euphoria ushered in by the Six-Day War to the depression that came in the wake of the Yom Kippur War began to express itself in a desire for action, reform, and the charting of a different way. However, he did not yet think seriously of engaging in political activity.

The public also needed time to digest what had occurred and to look for an alternative political path. Even though Meir and Dayan, who were already perceived as the ones who bore primary responsibility for the *mehdal* (blunder), continued to lead the Alignment, the party won the elections for the 8th Knesset, garnering fifty-one seats. (The Likud, formed at the beginning of 1973 in a merger of Gahal and other right-wing parties, had to settle for thirty-nine seats.) Thus, like many traumas, personal and collective, the post-1973 trauma simmered under the surface and came to the fore only later. It took nearly four more years to generate the first political turnabout in Israel, which brought to power the contemporary incarnation of the Revisionist Party, the Likud, in the 9th Knesset elections. It seems that the public was primarily interested in maintaining some stability when it went to the polls in December 1973. The time was not ripe for another upheaval so soon after the shock of the Yom Kippur War.

Beilin, too, despite his disappointment in Meir and Dayan, did not lament over the election results. He wanted to change the system—not to break or replace it. Beilin sought to find the solution within the establishment. In his eyes, the solution required Israel's recognition of the fact that the Zionist enterprise would only survive if it reached a compromise agreement with the Arabs.

Beilin concluded after the war that Israel's policy since 1967 (as in the twenty-first century under Netanyahu) was flawed in preferring interim agreements rather than bold efforts that could bring lasting benefit but required painful compromise. In Zionist perspective, the leadership thus continued to rely on the same sort of "tower and stockade" approach of the early twentieth century, hoping that gradual progress would someday lead to complete fulfillment of the vision. In this view, time was on Israel's side.

This was the primary mistake, in Beilin's view. The gradual approach may have been appropriate in the early days of Zionism, but no longer. He saw a significant difference between Israel's situation after the Six-Day War as a stable state, with international weight, and the status of the Zionist project in its infancy. In his eyes, the preference for interim accords with Egypt, instead of a bold effort to achieve a comprehensive agreement, was not only a tactical error, which enabled Egypt to build up its military might and prepare for war, but primarily a strategic error. The Middle East was not static: the Arabs were advancing and developing, and diplomatic inaction was stoking the fires of war.

His solution drew from initiatives that were already on the international shelf—first and foremost, the Rogers Plan. He saw the "land for peace" formula as the only option. In retrospect, he concluded that adoption of the plan could have led to an earlier peace treaty with Egypt. Meir's argument against the plan—that it was dangerous because it would also require Israel to withdraw from the West Bank—was unconvincing to Beilin. He now believed that withdrawal from the territories was in Israel's interest, and preferred to coordinate this move with Jordan, in the framework of a possible confederation.

Although Beilin attributed responsibility for the war to Meir's approach, which he saw as a failed model of leadership—stuck in the past, fixated on traditional Jewish paradigms of persecution and redemption—he refrained from joining the protests mounted by demobilized reservists, who demanded the leadership's resignation.

The protest movement, initially led by Motti Ashkenazi, commander of the Budapest outpost during the war, was conducted at the same time as the hearings of the Agranat Commission, assigned to study the blunders and events leading to the war and the first days of battle. The commission's decision to blame the military echelon and exempt the political echelon only intensified public anger, and led to the spread of demonstrations and protest in the media. In April 1974, Meir bowed to pressure and resigned. A new government was formed by Yitzhak Rabin, who had not served in an official role during the war, having just completed his term as Israeli ambassador in Washington. Rabin did not choose Dayan to continue as defense minister in his new government. Thus, belatedly, the top Israeli leaders—Meir and Dayan—paid a price for the war.

Beilin was glad that Meir resigned. Besides his opposition to her policies, her political biography exemplified in his eyes the destructive nature of internal politics in ruling parties, which tend to become corrupt after years in power. In this case, the party had chosen Meir as its candidate for prime minister mainly to avoid being forced to choose between Moshe Dayan and Yigal Allon, both of whom were more worthy to lead the country, in Beilin's opinion. He had a more positive view of Dayan than of Meir, and more empathy for him. Dayan was more pragmatic—for example, he had been ready to consider redeploying IDF forces in the Sinai prior to the war. Beilin could not have imagined that he would soon walk beside Dayan's successor at the Defense Ministry, Shimon Peres.

2

# First Political Steps

1

In 1975, less than a year after his release from reserve duty, Yossi Beilin, twenty-seven years old, joined the Young Guard of the Labor Party, the main venue for young party members. Although his belief in the Israeli establishment had been shaken, he preferred to try to reform it from within rather than work to create a new entity, outside the establishment. (This was also his political strategy in later stages of his career.) In this sense, Beilin's approach contains a conservative and clearly anti-revolutionary element. At the same time, it is characterized by commitment and courage to fight for his beliefs in a more compelling and significant way.

The Labor Party, formed in 1968 in a merger of Mapai, Ahdut Ha'avoda, and Rafi, was attempting to revamp its leadership following the Yom Kippur War. This was not an ideological upheaval, but mainly an effort to place different people in the top ranks. Meir's resignation from the Knesset in June 1974, the selection of Rabin to replace her as the head of the party, and Pinhas Sapir's death in May 1975 marked a turnover of generations.

In fact, this process occurred belatedly due to the selection of Meir as Eshkol's successor following his death in 1969. Two young candidates were then expected to compete for the leadership: Moshe Dayan and Yigal Allon.

However, as charismatic and promising as they were, both were considered outsiders in the party. In the 1950s, Dayan was regarded as one of "Ben-Gurion's boys" and joined the "old man" when he quit Mapai in anger and formed Rafi. Even though Rafi reunited with Mapai in 1968 (much to Ben-Gurion's chagrin), Dayan was still seen as an outsider. Dayan's inclination to stake out independent positions, detached from considerations of loyalty, did not contribute to his candidacy in the party. An example of his detachment, even from those close to him, was evident in his attitude toward his patron, one of the only leaders he greatly admired: In early 1961, after Ben-Gurion resigned as prime minister in order to form a new coalition, Mapam, the Liberals and Ahdut Ha'avoda sought to exploit the circumstances and form a government without the "old man." This was still unthinkable for Mapai leaders, but surprisingly, during a meeting of the Mapai secretariat, Dayan was the only one who declared that a government without Ben-Gurion should not be ruled out "as long as its path is Ben-Gurionist." Haim Yisraeli, Ben-Gurion's aide, thought this would cause a rift between the "old man" and Dayan. But Ben-Gurion, who forgave Dayan on many other matters too, said after reading the minutes of the meeting: "Dayan spoke the truth. He's wise. What is Ben-Gurion? Only flesh and blood. The main thing is the path, the policy, and not the man."[1] In any case, without the backing of Ben-Gurion, who quit Rafi in response to its merger with Mapai, Dayan was left without a significant political camp in the Labor Party, despite his strong public aura.

Dayan's potential rival suffered from a similar weakness. Yigal Allon was considered an outsider because he originally belonged to Ahdut Ha'avoda, and was often critical of Ben-Gurion during the latter's long tenure as prime minister. Though Allon temporarily served as prime minister (for 19 days) after Eshkol's death, he continued to be looked upon as an outsider within the Labor Party. In addition, his glory from the days of the Palmach had also dimmed in the Israeli public; most of the public was unfamiliar with the heroes of the pre-state era and, instead, venerated the heroes of the Six-Day War. He also faced opposition from Rafi members, in part because of his tense relations with Ben-Gurion, who regarded Allon as a worthy commander but a controversial figure. Allon confronted Ben-Gurion on two central issues. Allon opposed Ben-Gurion's readiness to suffice with the armistice lines of 1949 and rejected the doctrine of *mamlachtiyut* ("statism"—placing the state above partisan interests). In Allon's view, *mamlachtiyut* stifled the pioneering, voluntary, and independent dimension in the emerging Israeli society. He thought that Ben-Gurion's efforts to impose authority and a monolithic social view, as expressed in the dismantling of the Palmach and the State Education Law (which eliminated the different streams in the education system), created a society that was "indifferent to vital political and social questions." He accused Ben-Gurion, in various ways, of preventing the development of initiative and the uniqueness of individuals and groups that did not conform to his line.[2] These past rivalries, both ideological and personal, made it difficult for Allon to establish political power in the Labor Party.

Thus, Meir was selected as Eshkol's successor, as a compromise. When she resigned, however, it was again evident that there is no vacuum in politics; when you stand in place, you are in effect taking a step backward. That is, although Allon and Dayan continued to see themselves as candidates for the leadership in 1974, the fact that they had not established a following in the party, along with their involvement in the Yom Kippur War—Dayan as defense minister and Allon, who served as education minister but also played a dominant role in war consultations—made Rabin the leading contender, despite his limited political experience. (He became a Knesset member only in January 1974 and served for several months as labor minister.)

After being sworn in as prime minister, Rabin appointed Allon as foreign minister and Peres as defense minister. Thus, the changes in the party were cautious and hampered by personal considerations. In broad perspective, the ruling party remained exclusivist, closed to external figures, ideas, and forces. Allon, Dayan, Rabin, and Peres (who failed in his first attempt to defeat Rabin for the party's leadership) were all molded in the same ideological and social milieu of the labor movement in its various facets. Someone different, who promised deep and dramatic change, had no chance of winning a leadership role in the party, even in the shock engendered by the war. Veterans of the Palmach and Haganah continued to constitute the core from which the movement's leaders sprouted, and the Ashkenazi origin was conspicuous at all levels of the party, even in the 1970s, when Israeli society was a completely different mosaic than the society of the pre-state Yishuv.

By contrast, a deeper process of change in the social fabric began in the rival Likud party, formed in 1973 when Gahal merged with the Free Center faction and with members of the Movement for Greater Israel (most of whom came from the labor movement). This was largely thanks to the leadership of Yitzhak Shamir, a former head of the pre-state Lehi underground organization who resigned from his position at the Mossad in the early 1970s and joined the Herut party, the leading faction in Gahal. Shamir opened the ranks of Herut to local activists and leaders from among the second generation of Mizrahi Jews in Israel. This occurred beneath the surface and escaped the notice of journalists and scholars, as the Likud leadership in the 1970s remained clearly Ashkenazi. However, the fruits of Shamir's efforts to open the party's ranks to Mizrahi Jews became evident in the next decade, the 1980s,[3] and helped the Likud gain power in subsequent decades, while the Alignment remained closed to the changes that occurred in Israeli society.

This stagnation was also expressed in a lack of real differences among Labor's leaders on issues of defense and foreign affairs (and it is ironic that this was the primary focus of a party that was supposed to champion social and economic issues). Here, it seems that Meir Avizohar was correct in his assessment, in the context of the rivalry for party leadership between Rabin and Peres in the 1970s, that the difference between them was "a difference of style."[4] This distinction can also be applied to Allon and Dayan. Despite the different nuances in their approach to the Arab–Israeli conflict, all four Labor leaders—Allon, Dayan, Rabin, and Peres—drew from the same doctrine: Ben-Gurion's "security activism." This included a readiness for territorial compromise, in principle, with the aim of leaving most of the geographical assets considered vital for security in Israel's hands. However, none of them examined the Palestinian issue in a more profound way, including the ethical, postcolonial, and theological layers of the Arab-Zionist struggle. Those with other viewpoints were pushed aside. One of the exceptions was Aryeh Lova Eliav, who immediately after the Six-Day War tried to convince the party to address the plight of Palestinian refugees. He quit the party in 1975 because of what he called an "ideological narrowing." In economics, the party abandoned the socialist scaffolding on which it was built—scaffolding that had served largely as a mobilizing myth for national ambitions back in the days of Mapai. That is, socialism was a historical necessity for creating the "new Jew" who returned to manual labor, instead of continuing to engage in the "exilic" vocations of commerce and in pedantic Torah study. Since the 1950s, however, the Israeli left has generally not regarded socialism as an end in itself, but as a means of strengthening the national enterprises.

When Beilin joined the party, while still working as a journalist at *Davar*, he was one cog in a machine that continued to fossilize, despite the new parts added to it. On a personal level, as is customary in social systems, and certainly in politics, he needed a patron. Beilin found one in Micha Harish, who was elected to the Knesset for the first time in 1973. The star of the party's Young Guard was Haim Ramon, who had started his political path as a Rafi supporter and entered politics while maintaining a partnership in a restaurant. The energetic Ramon was the Young Guard's information director and was known for the new propaganda methods he instituted, which included less weighty wording, reflecting the spirit of the new generation of native-born Israelis.

Despite their different temperaments, Ramon and Beilin became friends. Beilin, who sought to challenge the party with new ideas, complemented Ramon in many ways. Ramon tended to focus less on ideology, but was eager to engage in political battles. And though Beilin did not permit himself to make long-term plans, he, like Ramon, was ambitious and confident in his abilities. Early in their friendship, and in light of the paralyzing rivalry between Dayan and Allon, and the emerging rivalry between Peres and Rabin, they vowed never to run against each other. When Ramon later became the secretary of the Young Guard, Ramon appointed Beilin to serve as its international secretary. In this role, Beilin was responsible for relations with the foreign press and with socialist parties overseas. Ramon also chose Beilin to chair the Young Guard's political-diplomatic committee.

Their view on the Arab–Israeli conflict was considered bold and outside the consensus in the party, so they preferred not to accentuate it. The model they advocated was close to what was called in those days the Yariv–Shem-Tov Formula, a plan whose contours were similar to those adopted in the Olso Accords in the 1990s. This indicates the pace at which marginal ideas are assimilated into the political mainstream.

The Yariv–Shem-Tov Formula bore the names of Victor Shem-Tov, a Mapam leader who served as health minister in Meir's government and later in Rabin's government, and Aharon Yariv, the head of military intelligence during the Six-Day War and information minister in the Rabin government. Shem-Tov and Yariv separately formulated plans based on a similar idea: direct negotiations with a Palestinian leadership to be elected among residents of the territories. This leadership would commit to recognize Israel and agree to UN Security Council Resolution 242 (which called for Israel to withdraw from territories captured in the Six-Day War in exchange for a just peace)[5] and a two-state solution.

To be historically precise, it should be noted that there were earlier proposals to create a Palestinian state. Interestingly, one such proposal came from Rehavam Ze'evi, who later founded the Moledet party that advocated the transfer of Palestinians from the territories. After the Six-Day War, he argued that Israel should help to establish a State of Ishmael in the territories, which would be a sort of protectorate of Israel. But Yariv and Shem-Tov proposed recognizing the Palestinian people and its right to a state while serving as government ministers. On July 12, 1974, during an interview on Army Radio, Yariv declared that "negotiating with those who reject our existence is inconceivable," but added that "if the Palestinian Liberation Organization declared that its National Charter is null and void, and that it recognizes the sovereign existence of Israel—then, and only then, it would be a new situation in which we could consider a new stance in regard to negotiation." However, this statement, which embodies one of the pillars of the Oslo Accords, was strongly rejected by Rabin, who was still closer to Meir's stance of denying the existence of an independent Palestinian people. Yisrael Galili—a government minister who remained faithful to the maximalist approach of Ahdut Ha'avoda's leader Yitzhak Tabenkin in regard to the state's borders[6]—asked for a clarification of the government's position. In response, Rabin firmly stated: "In Israel's aspiration for peace, it gives first priority to accords between Arab states and Israel, and first of all to Egypt, and that the Palestinian problem is not the central problem and its solution should be found in the framework of an accord between Israel and Jordan."[7]

The rigidness of the Alignment's leaders on the Palestinian question was also evident in the views of Allon, then serving as foreign minister. Though he changed his original maximalist stance and proposed the Allon Plan that called for relinquishing parts of the West Bank (not including the Jordan Valley, mountain ridges, and Jordan River),[8] he was opposed to transferring these territories to a Palestinian state. The accord he proposed would be implemented via Jordan, which in his view already occupied two-thirds of the Land of Israel.

The exceptionality of Beilin's views on the Arab–Israeli conflict comes into sharper focus when comparing them to those of other Labor Party figures at the time, and in light of Allon's ideological roots in Ahdut Ha'avoda.

Yitzhak Tabenkin, the leader of Ahdut Ha'avoda and a leader of socialist Zionism since the days of the Yishuv, placed the Greater Land of Israel at the center of his national perspective. In his memoirs, he noted that the Uganda episode was a seminal event in his life[9] (as it was for Beilin's grandfather). While this is not the place for an in-depth exposition of Tabenkin's complex view of the Land of Israel,[10] we can briefly state that the land was more important than the state in his eyes, and his attitude toward territory was characterized by a mix of socialist and revolutionary values and objectives. For Tabenkin, there was no moral validity in acquiring the right to the land through diplomatic or political arrangements. Pioneering settlement activity throughout the land was the decisive factor in establishing the right and expressing its acquisition. "Our central interest is the Land of Israel as a land of settlement. . . . That is the content of our movement and the land is given to us for that purpose only. There is a value to the historical rights of the Jewish people to the land, but our grounds are first of all settlement-based."[11]

Tabenkin's pupils, led by Allon, were imbued with the value he attributed to the land: during and after the War of Independence, Allon advocated capturing the Gaza area and the West Bank, and settling the border along the Jordan River. For him, the war was an opportunity to acquire parts of the homeland and prepare them for settlement. According to Allon, this would ensure Israel's military security and bolster its strategic standing, thus improving its ability to conclude peace agreements.[12] "If we don't take control of this important piece of land, then in addition to the ongoing military dangers, we lose the crucially valuable possibilities of developing the land in the future," Allon wrote to Ben-Gurion on March 27, 1949, in regard to the West Bank.[13] Ben-Gurion, who identified the future demographic problem, replied that Israel required "an effort for peace that is not necessarily based on the option of our power."[14] Unlike Ben-Gurion, Allon made no account for the Palestinians at this stage. In another letter to Ben-Gurion, which he labeled "private and top secret," Allon argued that there was no need for concern about the demographic problem because the Arabs would flee or agree to live under Israeli rule, and that the War of Independence offered a rare opportunity to achieve secure borders. "There is no stronger border imaginable than the line of the Jordan along the length of the entire country. . . . We should not ignore the heavy burden that might fall on our shoulders when assuming responsibility for a large piece of land with a relatively dense population of local Arabs and refugees, and there are two answers for this: a large number, especially the refugees, will retreat eastward because of the military operations. As for those who remain, we'll surely find a solution that allows them to live in dignity and enables us to prevent military dangers."[15]

When Beilin came to know Allon, the latter was already ready to accept territorial compromise. In one of their conversations, Allon even said that he regarded the Allon Plan as an interim solution. However, as noted, he firmly insisted that an independent Palestinian state was incongruent with the compromise he proposed. While Beilin initially looked toward Allon as a future leader of the party, he did not become a devotee of Allon—a man who was seen as the ultimate *sabra* in the days of the Palmach.

Beilin's attitude toward Rabin was ambivalent at first. (Rabin, like Allon, was raised on the values of Ahdut Ha'avoda—the party of Rabin's parents Rosa and Nehemiah.) He met Rabin for the first time as a soldier in the Six-Day War, when Rabin came to visit the troops as the revered IDF chief of staff. Beilin was favorably impressed by the speech Rabin delivered at Mount Scopus after the war ended. The speech—written by Mordechai Bar-On, then chief education officer in the IDF and later a historian and leader of the Peace Now movement—emphasized the uniqueness of the IDF as a moral army. The fact that Rabin was not involved in the Yom Kippur War debacle also stood to his credit. On the other hand, their first conversation—in the summer of 1973, when Beilin was asked to interview the outgoing ambassador for the Histadrut's youth publication—did not go well. Rabin was rigid and demanded to see the questions in advance. After looking at the questions, he handed them back to Beilin in disappointment and emphatically stated: "The questions aren't good." Only after Beilin remarked that he had yet to encounter an interviewee who dictates the questions to the interviewer, Rabin consented to respond. Beilin remembers feeling astonished to hear Rabin speak almost like a Republican, emphasizing the importance of the free market. Therefore, though Rabin sometimes spoke with surprising moderation as prime minister—he said he was "ready to come to Gush Etzion with a visa," and in a private conversation spoke disparagingly of the settlement built at the Kadum camp[16]—Beilin was not surprised when Rabin refrained from proposing a dramatic change in Israeli policy at the end of the Meir era. The fact that most of his friends in the party came from Ahdut Ha'avoda also had an impact.

At that stage, however, Beilin also had qualms about Defense Minister Peres, who was then more hardline than Rabin. In particular, Beilin did not look kindly upon Peres's close relations with the leaders of Gush Emunim. Peres's remarks at a party meeting in November 1972 reflect the rigidity of his views at that time. The party members were discussing the demographic burden on Israel and its repercussions on the democratic component of the Jewish state in the absence of territorial compromise or without granting equal rights to residents of the territories. Peres protested: "Since when have we taken a statistical approach to the problems of the Jewish people? And when did the Zionist movement ever have a statistical advantage . . . ? The future of Israel and the future of the Jewish people are a matter of faith, of fundamental assumptions and of energetic action."[17] Peres later scoffed at the contention that economic relations with the Palestinians since the Six-Day War were based on exploiting them as "hewers of wood and drawers of water" (a biblical allusion). "What are they capable of doing? Can they be computer operators? Department heads at Beilinson [Hospital]? What alternative do they have: either unemployment or work they are capable of doing."[18] Peres was then a strong advocate of security activism in the spirit of his mentor, Ben-Gurion. (As noted, despite Ben-Gurion's call immediately after the Six-Day War to withdraw from most of the territories conquered in the war, he also advised that Jerusalem, the Golan Heights, and Hebron remain in Israel's hands.)[19] Ben-Gurion did not reject the settlement enterprise (though he did not know, of course, how it would develop in the future) because he believed that in the framework of what he called "true peace"—that is, peace based on cultural relations and economic cooperation between the peoples—it would be possible to maintain Jewish settlement under foreign sovereignty, in the same way that Palestinians live in Israel. Against this background, Peres tried to moderate Rabin's opposition to Gush Emunim and was the guiding spirit behind the compromise reached in late 1975 between the settlers and the government—a compromise in which settlers agreed to evacuate an illegal settlement at Sebastia in exchange for permitting them to settle at the Kadum camp. "Since when has it become such a crime to listen to the feelings of the public?" was Peres's public explanation. "I'm glad we concluded this affair as we did, without deepening the rift in the nation."[20]

Disappointed in both Rabin and Peres, Beilin tried to avoid taking a side in the complicated relation between the two until 1976. (And at that stage, Beilin did not yet have an influential voice in the party in any case.) When Micha Harish asked all of the members of the Young Guard to declare their explicit support for Peres, Beilin argued that it was not right to expect all Young Guard members to make a uniform choice between Peres and Rabin. But Harish insisted, and offered to arrange a meeting between Peres and Beilin.

Even after meeting with Peres, Beilin harbored reservations about the defense minister's hawkish line and attitude toward the settlements. Nonetheless, Beilin was influenced by Peres's personal charm, broad horizons, love of books, and the optimism he radiated. He was also impressed by Peres's conviction that he would be able to lead the Israeli public to a peace accord in due time—though Peres did not specify the details of the future accord during their conversation. Perhaps this indicates that Peres was maintaining good relations with Gush Emunim in order to win broader public support before running for prime minister. In retrospect, it, indeed, seems safe to say that the run-up to the battle for party leadership contributed to the different approaches of Peres and Rabin vis-à-vis the settlers.

In any case, the special relationship between Beilin and Peres developed only after the political upheaval in May 1977, when for the first time in the chronicles of the Zionist movement, a political incarnation of the original Revisionist Party rose to power—the Likud.

2

There were many reasons for the upheaval. Some of them rose from deep currents that had long existed in Israeli society; these currents surged in the wake of the Yom Kippur War and were finally channeled into a groundswell of support for political reform in the 1977 elections. Other reasons stemmed from the corruption of the ruling party and internal changes in the political system.

In this context, it is important to emphasize the role of the centrist Dash party, formed prior to the elections and led by the archaeologist and former IDF chief of staff Yigael Yadin. Dash expressed the public's disgust with the old political frameworks and won the support of many Alignment voters. Dash was not the first attempt to establish a centrist party in Israel. It was preceded by Ben-Gurion's Rafi party, formed in 1965 in the wake of the Lavon Affair. Dash, like Rafi, demanded government reform, but had greater potential: the public was not convinced that Rafi, a party led by Ben-Gurion, who built the establishment, was the address for anti-establishment sentiment. The Dash party was seen as fresher and more legitimate.

The election campaign was expected to focus on the battle between Begin, the Likud candidate, and Rabin, the incumbent prime minister and Alignment candidate. However, in April 1977, Rabin announced his resignation after the journalist Dan Margalit reported that Leah Rabin, the prime minister's wife, had failed to close a dollar account in the United States after his ambassadorship ended, as required by Israeli law at the time. Peres was selected, for the first time, as the party's candidate in place of Rabin.

The election campaign featured innovations imported from the United States, including a television debate between the two main candidates to head the government. The journalist Shaike Ben-Porat served as moderator in the debate. Peres presented himself as a young man, in contrast to the older Begin, and emphasized that he had been party chairman for only four weeks (compared to Begin's twenty-nine years at the helm of his party). Peres promised to bring a new and forward-looking spirit, and to create government ministries of science and technology, social welfare, and environmental protection.

Begin also made promises: he declared that his government would number only twelve ministers and he vowed to reduce bureaucracy, which was identified with the Mapai establishment. On the Arab–Israeli conflict, he explained that he was opposed to withdrawing from the territories, but would work to maintain the alliance with the United States because a strong Israel is a strategic asset in light of the Soviet Union's threat to take over the Middle East. Peres emphasized that he was also in no hurry to relinquish territories, and that the Jordan River should be Israel's eastern security border in any accord. However, unlike Begin, Peres also emphasized that he would not rush to make declarations that undermine the chances of reaching an accord. Though Begin's forte was in delivering speeches in town squares, his theatrical skills also served him well in the television medium. At the end of the debate, Begin was in high spirits. After the cameras were turned off, and as Peres was removing his makeup, Begin approached Peres and exclaimed, "Wow, look how beautiful he is," to the delight of his entourage.[21] Indeed, Begin had the last laugh.

Of course, the upheaval cannot only be understood in the context of the personalities competing for the post of prime minister. It should also be seen against the background of the repercussions of the 1967 war, which turned Begin's maximalist ideology—which previously seemed anachronistic and detached from reality—into a realistic plan. The historical irony is that Labor's opposition to relinquishing the territories and partial support for the settlement enterprise paved the way for the Likud's ascension to power. The differences between the parties became less striking and the Likud was no longer seen as a party with an extremist ideology. Furthermore, since Begin based his connection to the territories on historical and theological grounds, while the Labor leaders took a similar stance on security grounds, the Likud's position was perceived as more authentic and profound.

The decline of the left and the ascension of the right can also be understood in the context of changes that occurred in the attitudes of Israelis toward the state's original values—changes engendered by demographic trends and the turnover of generations. The Labor Party's values of socialism and collectivism lost their allure, superseded by liberal aspirations. This also resulted from changes that occurred within the labor movement itself. An interesting expression of this can be seen in Peres's decision to omit the term "socialism" when drafting the platform for Ben-Gurion's Rafi party. Instead, the platform emphasized the "scientization of the state" and economic renewal. Thus, in the third decade of Israel's existence, laborers wanted to become contractors, craftsmen aspired to own factories, and peddlers dreamed of becoming business owners. The labor movement's original vision of "the new Jew" faded as Jews in Israel returned to primarily engage in commercial activity.

From a demographic perspective, the first and second generations of the mass immigration from Islamic lands comprised nearly 40 percent of Israel's residents at this stage. The heads of the two major parties were clearly aware of the importance of the ethnic question. Although the Likud had fewer Knesset members of Mizrahi origin than the Alignment, and only two in the top eleven spots (Moshe Nissim, born in Iraq, and David Levy, from Morocco) compared to three in the Alignment (Shlomo Hillel and Shoshana Arbeli-Almozlino, both born in Iraq, and Yitzhak Navon, of Sephardi heritage)—most Mizrahi voters identified with the Likud. They were less concerned about the ethnic composition of the parties' respective Knesset factions; their support for Begin and the Likud stemmed from deeper reasons. First, although Mizrahi Jews were still a minority among the Likud's leadership, their presence was growing in the party's central committee and branches. Thus, contrary to the impression that the Likud had included a few Mizrahi Jews in its Knesset slate merely as window dressing, they became integrated into the Likud's institutions and influenced the party's character, even though the top leadership remained Ashkenazi.

It is also possible to discern a different type of "Mizrahiness" in the two parties. For example, the resume of David Levy—a construction worker who began his political career in the Mapai branch in Beit Shean, but felt his path was blocked and turned, instead, to the local Herut branch—was perceived as an authentic expression of the difficulties Mizrahi Jews faced vis-à-vis the establishment. By contrast, the prominent Mizrahi members of Knesset (MKs) in the Labor Party—including Hillel, Arbeli-Almozlino, and Moshe Shahal, all three from Iraq—came from a higher socioeconomic class in their country of origin, found their place in the party of the Israeli establishment, and thus were perceived as more elitist. The data shows that Mizrahi Jews comprised about 60 percent of Herut voters since the 1955 elections, but only about 30 percent of all Mizrahi voters cast their ballot for Herut. The electoral change occurred in 1973, when the second generation became the dominant component of this population and the

Likud garnered 50 percent of Mizrahi votes.[22] This percentage rose to 53 percent in the 1977 elections, when 44 percent of native-born Israelis (primarily second-generation Mizrahi Jews) voted Likud, compared to only 20 percent of Ashkenazi voters.[23] This data on the impact of Mizrahi support for the Likud speaks for itself and this voting pattern continues to influence Israel's political system in the twenty-first century.

In voting for Begin, Mizrahi voters were not looking to start a revolution—they were seeking recognition and equal opportunities. Therefore, they were not inclined to pursue the revolutionary agenda proposed by the local Black Panthers, for example. The path Begin offered for creating justice and social equality—solidarity based on a shared Judaism—suited their worldview, which rejected the Ben-Gurionist attempt to establish solidarity based on the state and through participation in the melting pot designed to forge a "new Jew," divorced from religion tradition.

Yonathan Shapiro, Beilin's teacher, stated in his impressive study on the Revisionist movement, that Begin's rhetoric employed emotional manipulation that helped to create a false consciousness among Mizrahi Jews, which led them to support the Likud without any direct connection to their views on the Arab–Israeli conflict.[24] Indeed, the Likud's hawkish positions on foreign affairs and security issues did not account for its support among Mizrahi voters. In fact, when Begin decided in 1979 to withdraw from the Sinai Peninsula, and when Sharon (then the Likud leader) pulled out of the Gaza Strip in 2005, opposition to the withdrawals did not come from the Likud's Mizrahi voter base; it came primarily from national-religious Jews of Ashkenazi descent. Still, the claim of manipulation that deceives Mizrahi Likud supporters—a claim that is common even today to explain Mizrahi support for Netanyahu—also illustrates the condescension that is still popular in the media and in academic discourse vis-à-vis Mizrahi Jews. After all, emotional manipulation does not work its wonders only on people from one particular ethnic origin, and political leaders, in any case, act in a manipulative way to influence public opinion. If this is the case, what can explain the Mizrahi connection to the Likud?

The political scientist Dani Filc defined Begin's Likud as an "inclusive populist movement"—that is, a movement with populist views that also includes marginalized groups within its ranks.[25] Thus, the secret of the connection between Mizrahi Jews and the Likud is that the party treated them as an integral and natural part of the movement. By contrast, the Labor Party related to Mizrahi Jews as a separate group that should be adopted only after it undergoes a process of socialization.[26]

Another explanation for the connection between Mizrahi Jews and the Likud can be suggested through the term "habitus," coined by the French sociologist Pierre Bourdieu, who used this complex term to analyze the connection between social structures and an individual's patterns of behavior. Bourdieu assumed that people do not act arbitrarily or based on independent thinking; instead, they are a product of social structuring, which in itself is a chapter in an overall model of cultural action. Habitus is thus a weave of behaviors and worldviews that are imprinted in a person's subconscious by the society's system of cultural mediation, until they become the person's view of reality and motive for action. According to Bourdieu's notion of habitus, the act of voting is not an independent and isolated action performed privately by an individual person. A person's habitus is the historical product that ensures here and now, in the present, the presence of the past, which is salient in both individual and collective practices and in ways of thinking.[27] Therefore, the trend of voting for the Likud in 1977 and onward can also be understood as an anti-establishment protest echoing the collective memory, even if this memory is not always precise. (For example, Avi Picard's research found that when the population of transit camps peaked in the years of mass immigration, 1952–53, immigrants from North Africa comprised only 6 percent of those living in these temporary quarters. Nonetheless, many of the first generation of immigrants— and even the third generation—from Morocco identify themselves with these camps due to other difficulties they faced in the immigration absorption process.)[28] In this perspective, the pro-Likud orientation can be traced to the historical and political contexts in which Mizrahi Jews assimilated into Israeli society.

The changes described above were open for all to see. What astonished the state's citizens on May 17, 1977, was only the suddenness in which they found expression at the voting stations. Leon Trotsky stated that revolution occurs when the Old Regime is no longer able to solve a society's basic problems and, at the same time, an alternative force emerges. This aptly describes Israel's situation in 1977. The shock and disillusionment caused by the Yom Kippur War were only the straw that broke the camel's back.

## 3

As much as Beilin wanted a dramatic change in the Israeli establishment, he was far from viewing the Likud's victory as a positive step. He recognized the effect of the ethnic rift on the election results and the Mapai establishment's responsibility for the condition of many of the immigrants from Islamic lands. However, in the spirit of the classic modernist perspective, he believed that the solution for class disparities was education; thus, as Mizrahi Jews climbed the ladder of higher education, the "problem" of ethnic-based voting would automatically be solved.[29]

On a personal level, Beilin is aware that he is "an Ashkenazi icon" and says: "I didn't try to fight this." He does not like Mizrahi music, just as he is not fond of ballet, and has never bothered to make a populist pretense of this. Beilin was raised on the idea of the blending of exiles, and continues to hold this view. He says he will never forget the disappointment his mother expressed when he told her that his future wife, Helena, is not Sephardi—because his mother had hoped that her son would fulfill the idea of the melting pot. (Beilin's brother Yinon "surpassed" him in this respect and married a woman of Greek descent.) He did not feel ethnic tensions in his childhood. Immigrants from Romania were the main target of ridicule at his school, not those of Mizrahi heritage. He remembers everyone striving to be Israeli.

Beilin does not deny a history of discrimination but attributes it to mistakes that stemmed from Zionist praxis and not from the basic ideology itself, since the ideology called for equality for all ethnic groups via the melting pot. He believes that in principle both tribes—Ashkenazi and Mizrahi—were required to accept compromises and changes in light of the need to fulfill the Zionist idea, which demanded the creation of a single nation from various communities: just as the Ashkenazi Jews were required to give up their traditions, including the Yiddish culture, Mizrahi Jews were compelled to shed the cultures they brought with them. In the course of his political activity, it was not difficult for him to recognize that the division between hawks and doves largely overlapped the Mizrahi-Ashkenazi divide. However, he does not believe that the "Mizrahi option"—selecting a Mizrahi Jew as the leader of the left, or leveraging "Mizrahiness" to foster Arab–Israeli coexistence—is the formula for strengthening the peace process. These views of Beilin, which deny or fail to fully appreciate the deep power of identity politics, accompanied him throughout his career.

In any case, Beilin considered Begin a rabid demagogue and saw his rise to power as a real threat to democracy. Though he realized the public needed a change, it had chosen the wrong route in his eyes. It so happened that Beilin was sent by *Davar*—where, as noted, he continued to work after joining Labor's Young Guard—to conduct the newspaper's first interview with Begin after his victory. En route to the interview, he pictured the Likud leader as described for years by Ben-Gurion. In a famous letter Ben-Gurion sent to Haim Gouri a month before stepping down as prime minister in 1963, he described Begin as follows:

a saliently Hitler-like type, racist, ready to annihilate all of the Arabs for the sake of Greater Israel, justifying any means for the sake of the holy objective—absolute power, and I see him as a serious threat to Israel's internal and external situation . . . all these [Begin's actions] are not isolated actions. They reveal a method, a character, and an aspiration. Begin will replace the command of the army and the police with his hooligans and will rule like Hitler ruled in Germany—he will forcibly and violently suppress the workers' movement—he will entangle the state in adventures that will bring about its destruction.[30]

This is, indeed, how Beilin imagined Begin while preparing the questions for the interview. He recalled an incident that occurred during the election campaign in 1959: Begin moved through the streets of Tel Aviv accompanied by a convoy of motorcycles—an action that evoked a whiff of fascism. Beilin did not know then what he knows now: the excited motorcyclists happened upon Begin by chance; the convoy was not planned. Herut's campaign staff had decided to assign two motorcyclists to guide Begin's car to an election rally. But while driving through the Hatikvah neighborhood, some admirers of Begin hopped on their motorcycles and joined them. Thus, by the time they passed through the bourgeois Dizengoff Street, it took on the appearance of a raucous and ostentatious motorcade.

However, Beilin was surprised in the first conversation he ever conducted with Begin. He met a leader who answered pertinently and thoughtfully. This interview taught Beilin something about images and truth in the political system, though he stopped short of becoming an admirer of the newly elected prime minister.

On the other hand, Beilin was deeply disappointed to learn that Dayan had decided to quit the Labor Party and accept an appointment as foreign minister in the new government. Begin needed Dayan because immediately upon his election he received indirect messages from Washington indicating that the United States was already preparing to revise its relations with Israel.[31] Dayan was important to Begin as a means of gaining international legitimacy, while joining Begin's government was important to Dayan as a means of rehabilitating his public image in Israel by facilitating a diplomatic turning point. Zionist and Israeli politics had already known schisms and politicians who jumped from one party to another—including Ben-Gurion's rebellion against Mapai and the creation of Rafi. However, Dayan's collaboration with the leader of the Revisionist stream seemed to Beilin an extreme ploy, too extreme. "Excuse us Rahamim Kalanter," Hannah Zemer wrote in *Davar*, referring to the Jerusalem city council member who changed parties in exchange for a job (and whose name became a generic term in Israeli political parlance for this type of self-interested party hopping: Kalanterism).[32] Beilin concurred with Zemer's disdainful view of Dayan. In Beilin's eyes, when it came to disloyalty, Dayan remained Dayan his entire life.

In any case, the upheaval also had an enormous impact on Beilin's own life path. Many Labor Party members reacted to Begin's victory with despair, and Yitzhak Ben-Aharon suggested on a television broadcast that the people who voted for Likud were blameworthy. One of the first to recover was Peres. On the day after the elections, he declared in a radio broadcast that the losing side should accept the results "like men" and he telephoned Begin to congratulate him on his victory. "On the personal level, we'll remain friends. And in politics—rivals," Peres said. His telephone conversation became a gentlemanly precedent in Israeli politics. About a month later, when Ezer Weizman replaced Peres at the Defense Ministry, Peres was already hard at work on plans for the next elections. One of his first steps was to offer Beilin the position of his spokesperson and personal adviser. He regarded Beilin as an energetic and educated young man who could inject new ideas and give a fresh image to the party and to Peres personally. Faithful as usual to the Ben-Gurion model, in both his ideology and his political conduct, Peres wanted Beilin to fill a role that he himself had filled for the "old man"—a young man with original ideas, who could get things done.

But Beilin was less enthusiastic about the role. He was increasingly captivated by political activity and the need to restore the party to power was vital in his view, but he was uncomfortable with the idea of engaging in political marketing and spokesmanship, rather than content. He was flattered by the offer, and at this stage already believed in Peres's ability to lead, but he had a different path in mind: he preferred to limit his involvement in the party, concentrate on writing his dissertation and pursue an academic career. And, if the opportunity arose, he would enter the world of politics from the position of a more experienced and esteemed person.

David Libai, who completed his doctorate in law prior to entering politics, and Shevach Weiss, who was a political science professor before turning to politics, were his role models. Unlike the political field in Israel in the early twenty-first century, which is not particularly kind to intellectuals and academics, on the eve of the 1980s the status of a political scientist could serve as a springboard for political activity. (Most of the leading political activists at that time were still members of an elite club, and ideas such as open primaries were a distant vision.) After all, the rising star of the 1977 elections was Dash's leader Yigael Yadin, who was not only known as the IDF's second chief of staff, but primarily as the leading archaeologist in Israeli academia.

Beilin's desire to complete his doctorate before entering politics reflected his chosen path and the fact that he had no aspirations of reaching the top leadership position. His study of political science led him to conclude that the struggle for first place could be fruitless and frustrating for someone who sought to make a difference, and that his electoral abilities were not outstanding. Beilin preferred to invest his energy in assisting and influencing the party leader, rather than trying to take the helm himself. Perhaps this nonthreatening stance contributed to the success of the growing partnership between Beilin and the ambitious Peres.

In any case, Beilin did not accept Peres's offer. At the end of their conversation, they loosely agreed that if Peres did not find another suitable candidate for the position within two months, he would call upon Beilin again. Indeed, before long, Peres repeated his offer. This time, Beilin consulted with Micha Harish and Gad Yaakobi, who both encouraged him to accept the offer. But then Beilin presented Peres with another obstacle: Helena, his wife, who thought he should pursue an academic track.

Vigorous and confident in his powers of persuasion, Peres invited Helena for a conversation in which he explained the significance of the position and its potential for influencing Israel's future. Although she was raised in a Revisionist home, Helena was captivated by Peres and the two became friends, a friendship that continued after the divorce of the Beilin couple.

Thus, after receiving a green light from Helena, Beilin told Peres he was ready to accept the job, which marked the start of his political career. Still, he harbored some doubts and, just to be sure, he arranged with *Davar*'s editor to go on unpaid leave for one year so that he could return to the newspaper if his work alongside Peres did not pan out.

# 4

For the next four decades, the paths of Peres and Beilin were intertwined, and they developed a close rapport—but never a deep friendship.

There was some distance between the two at the beginning of their collaboration. Peres never scolded his spokesperson and adviser, but was also not inclined to praise him. Beilin became accustomed to this pattern of behavior, even if he did not enjoy it. Their primary focus in the years of opposition was to reinvigorate the Labor Party's branches and instill a new spirit in the party. Peres and Beilin traveled the length and breadth of Israel—from branch to branch, from one gathering to another, sometimes from one party member to another—to energize the party following its fall from power. Beilin was quick to see that political activity was a total commitment for Peres, and that family demands took a back seat to the needs of the party. Still, he was impressed by the fact that Peres's children and wife did their best to surround him with warmth, and noted that Peres always preferred to be in the company of someone rather than to be alone. Despite working together in close proximity on a daily basis, Peres was not quick to share his feelings at this stage. Beilin saw that Peres was surrounded by activists, but did not have a real friend. Despite Dayan's participation in the Begin government, Peres still liked and admired him (he seemed to have also "inherited" this attitude toward Dayan from Ben-Gurion). But Dayan was also not a soul mate. Peres liked to converse with people and deliver lectures, but his innermost thoughts he kept to himself.

As he came to know Peres and his personality, Beilin found a completely different character than the one depicted by his rivals—both those on the opposite side of the political map and those in the Rabin camp. Beilin categorically rejected the description of Peres as an "indefatigable schemer"—the pejorative attached to Peres in Rabin's memoirs (*Pinkas Sherut*) published in 1979. (Rabin gladly adopted this phrase, suggested by the book's ghostwriter, Dov Goldstein.) In Beilin's eyes, Peres was not a schemer, but an ambitious and optimistic person who always looked for new alternatives. What others regarded as an obsession to become prime minister, Beilin interpreted as a sincere and profound interest in Israel's fate. Beilin also appreciated the fact that Peres, unlike most of the politicians he knew, was concerned with issues that affect the entire Jewish world and not only Israel.

For Peres, the transition to the opposition was not only a painful landmark in his political career. In retrospect, we can also see the harbingers of the "dovization" process he underwent. Peres gradually began to shift from the position of "security activism" he learned from Ben-Gurion to a more moderate stance.[33] Beilin certainly had a hand in this. Nonetheless, even when Peres adopted territorial compromise as a solution for the conflict, he remained fundamentally alienated from the "left." It was not difficult for Beilin to sense this. Peres never thought of the conflict in terms of post-colonialism; he looked at the conflict from the perspective of Israel's needs and the Zionist project. His view of the Arab world was somewhat Orientalist in nature. (In a documentary aired in the final days of his presidency, Peres characterized the Arab leaders he had met in his life by the aftershave they lavished upon themselves.[34])

Despite his grandiose and flowery speeches during the Oslo process, peace was primarily a security imperative for Peres rather than a moral vision. On one of his trips abroad to attend an event celebrating the signing of the Oslo Accords, Peres told the *Yedioth Ahronoth* daily: "I'm not a peacenik shmuck" and this clearly expressed his basic position. He worked for a peace agreement as one component of a strategic worldview: as a means, and not as an end in itself. In this sense, too, Peres was the quintessential protégé of Ben-Gurion, who as prime minister placed Israel's security needs above other values and declared: "The right to life comes before other rights." During the election campaign in 2015, Netanyahu tried to paraphrase this declaration when he stated: "When we speak about housing prices, about the cost of living, I don't forget for a moment the matter of life itself."[35] Unlike the original declaration by the founding father in the early years of the state, Netanyahu's statement was not well received—and this also reflects the changes that have occurred over the years in Israeli society.

# Statecraft and Politics

## 1

Although Peres hired Beilin as his spokesperson and adviser to help revive the party, the importance of their relationship stems primarily from the role they played in the peace process, which is the focus of this book. From the late 1970s, Beilin participated in most of the political-diplomatic meetings Peres conducted as opposition leader, and later as prime minister. In the 1990s, Beilin began to concoct peace initiatives on his own, occasionally mobilizing Peres's support only after the fact. However, in the most dramatic event in Israel's foreign relations in the twentieth century, Peres and Beilin were not privy to the initial details. They had to watch from the sidelines, though excitedly, as the Begin government conducted talks with Egypt and ultimately signed a peace treaty in 1979, which also outlined an autonomy plan for the Palestinians.

The negotiations between Israel and Egypt began in a secret meeting on September 16, 1977, in Morocco between Foreign Minister Moshe Dayan and Egypt's Deputy Prime Minister Hassan Tuhami. The meeting, held in the royal palace in Rabat, was also attended by King Hassan II and Morocco's prime minister and foreign minister. Dayan asked Tuhami whether a commitment to a full withdrawal from the Sinai Peninsula was a prerequisite for arranging a meeting between Begin and Sadat, or if "Egypt would agree to a meeting even if Begin could not fully agree on the issue of evacuation."[1] When Tuhami demanded an explicit commitment, King Hassan intervened, having previously discussed the matter with Sadat. The king explained that he "would give his word of honor that Sadat would meet Begin and shake his hand if Begin could personally commit that the bilateral talks would be conducted based on an understanding about evacuating the territories." Dayan responded with a vague promise whose basic intention was clear: "We'll work out an arrangement with you."[2]

Thus, Sadat received a promise, before his meeting with Begin, that Israel would agree to withdraw from the Sinai in exchange for peace, though the extent and details of the withdrawal were not specified.

Since the contacts were initially in secret channels, hidden from the eyes of the public and the political system, the impression was that Sadat took the first step. On November 9, 1977, in a surprising speech before the Egyptian People's Assembly, Sadat announced that he was "ready to travel to the ends of the earth if this will prevent the wounding, let alone the killing, of one of my boys, the soldiers. Israel will surely be surprised to hear me say this: I'm ready to come to them, to their home, to the Knesset itself, to argue with them."[3] Begin responded to the speech by inviting Sadat to come to Jerusalem and, on November 19, the president of Egypt arrived in Israel on a bold and groundbreaking visit.

The minutes of cabinet meetings released in recent years reveal how Begin chose to conduct himself vis-à-vis the ministers in his government to avoid being seen as playing second fiddle to Sadat. In a meeting convened after Sadat's speech at the Knesset, Begin told the ministers that he was responsible for the initiative that brought Sadat to Jerusalem, and emphasized that the personal dimension was one of the reasons why negotiations were launched when the Likud was in power. That is, both the American administration and the Egyptian leadership understood that it was best to conduct negotiations when a dominant leader of the political right was serving as prime minister. According to Begin:

> We didn't let up on the initiative from the first moment, and the government should know that we were the ones who proposed the idea of this type of meeting, about a week after the government was formed. We sent signals in various ways. When Secretary of State [Cyrus] Vance visited the Middle East, he told me that he said to Sadat: "Today, there's a government in Israel you can rely on. When it says yes—it means yes. When it says no—it means no." Sadat's response was: "I know." When I said to Vance that I'd like to see Sadat, he told me: "Sadat would also like to see you."[4]

As noted, Peres and Beilin watched the developments from the side. But Peres did not suffice with this and presented an original idea to Beilin. Since as opposition leader he was entitled to speak during Sadat's Knesset visit, he would include a surprise proposal in his remarks: He would ask to be appointed as Israel's first ambassador in Egypt after the conclusion of the process and signing of the peace treaty. This proposal was typical of Peres: On the one hand, it was clever and innovative, and expressed readiness to put his political career on hold for several years. On the other hand, it placed him at the center of events, when it was not yet clear if negotiations would result in a peace accord and how Peres's presence in Cairo could help Israeli-Egyptian relations.

Peres's idea was one of the first significant challenges Beilin faced in his role as adviser. He opposed the idea; he did not see how it would benefit the peace process and feared it would be detrimental to Peres's political career. Peres remained unconvinced, insisting that it would be his contribution to peace and that he would return to politics after his term as ambassador. The author S. Yizhar and Hannah Zemer came to Beilin's assistance, both advising Peres that the idea was unnecessary. The scene in Peres's office that day would have appeared a bit strange to an onlooker: While public opinion in Israel and in the Middle East identified the historic developments with Begin and Sadat, the discussions in the office might have given the impression that Peres was at the center of these developments. In the end, Peres agreed to drop the idea.

In any case, it quickly became evident that the dramatic opening of the peace process did not bode well for the negotiations. Despite the general agreement to withdraw from the Sinai (the central element in the accord), many issues remained in dispute, including the depth of the withdrawal, the future of the Israeli settlements in the Sinai, security arrangements, the question of the Israeli military bases in the Sinai, and Sadat's demand for linkage between the Israeli-Egyptian accord and progress in negotiations on the Palestinian issue.[5] As the negotiations continued to experience ups and downs, Peres began to play a role in it, albeit a secondary one, by virtue of his position as opposition leader.

In July 1978, as Beilin's wife was about to deliver their second son, Peres prepared to travel to Austria for a meeting with Sadat. He invited Beilin to accompany him, and despite Beilin's excitement about the impending birth, he found it hard to refuse the invitation to participate in what would be his first involvement in the peace process.

There were two interesting aspects to the meeting. The first was an exchange of assessments between Peres and Sadat on the situation of Shah Mohammad Reza Pahlavi, less than six months before the Islamic Revolution in Iran. Peres and Sadat were both confident that despite the emerging opposition to the shah's rule, he would not be deposed. Their joint assessment was that the shah would continue to rule thanks to international support from the United States and Western countries, and in light of the power of his security apparatus. This shows—nearly four decades before the Arab Spring—how Middle Eastern leaders underestimated the importance of the longings of the simple and oppressed masses.

The second interesting aspect was a surprising proposal by Sadat concerning negotiations with Israel: In exchange for an Israeli announcement that Security Council Resolution 242 also applied to the West Bank, he would be willing to lease Israel the airfields it held in the Sinai—a demand Begin had made and which Egypt had rejected until then. Was this, indeed, a serious proposal? Could Israel have achieved better conditions in the Sinai in exchange for compromise in the West Bank? Or did Sadat, knowing that Begin would reject territorial compromise in "Judea and Samaria" draw intellectual pleasure from his assumption that Peres would convey the message to Begin? The transcript of the conversation provides no answers to these questions. In any case, from this conversation, and of course from hundreds of other conversations Beilin subsequently conducted (on his own and alongside others) with Arab and Israeli leaders, he learned an interesting methodological lesson: When the archives open, historians will uncover many surprising oral statements, but in the Middle East, and in general, the historical "truth" is ultimately found on the surface—because leaders are bound by their public declarations, which are dictated by broader considerations, beyond their own personal views.

Peres and Beilin had planned to continue from Vienna to London for a meeting with King Hussein of Jordan, but their plan was nixed by Begin after he got wind of it. Peres, disappointed, managed to arrange another meeting, this one with King Hassan in Rabat. Meanwhile, Beilin called Israel to check on his wife's condition and to inform her that he would be away a bit longer. Helena told him that she was still waiting to give birth. He asked for her okay to extend his travel, though he did not reveal the secret of his next destination.

While a fondness for alcohol is primarily attributed to Rabin in the media, Beilin learned that Peres was also sometimes inclined to indulge in a bit of alcohol—mainly wine, cognac, or good whiskey. Beilin, less familiar with the ways of the world, had to deal with Peres's teasing: Every time they were offered alcoholic drinks, Peres would kindly ask whether Beilin would prefer "tea or coffee." Peres told Beilin that he learned to appreciate good wine during his visits in France in the 1950s, and explained that the way to drink and avoid inebriation is to eat bread and butter together with the drinks. Beilin rose to the challenge, but one time was enough for him, and for Peres, to understand that he would not become a connoisseur of alcohol. Over the years, he learned to adapt.

During the visit, Beilin was impressed by King Hassan. He was less impressed by Morocco: The country's beauty was marred by the flagrant disparity between the enormous wealth in the palace and the poverty in the streets. When he went out for a short walk, he shuddered at the sight of butchered animals on display in shop windows and the legions of flies hovering over the filth in the streets. The East was a necessity for him, because it was in Israel's interest to integrate into it. But in cultural contexts, Beilin undoubtedly felt more at home in Europe.

2

At the end of the process, on March 26, 1979, Begin and Sadat met on the White House lawn in Washington and signed the first peace treaty between Israel and an Arab state. Israel committed to fully withdraw from the Sinai Peninsula and to evacuate the Israeli settlements and IDF bases from the peninsula. In a letter appended to the treaty, Begin and Sadat also committed to begin negotiations aimed at establishing a "self-governing authority" for the Palestinians in the West Bank and Gaza Strip, in accordance with the Camp David Accords.[6] The Israeli version of the document, reflecting Begin's outlook, still called the Palestinians the "Arabs of the Land of Israel"[7] and used the biblical names Judea and Samaria to refer to the West Bank. The stated aim was "to provide full autonomy to the inhabitants" of these territories, but, absurdly, the details were to be ironed out between Israel and Egypt and not with the Palestinians themselves. Nonetheless, the autonomy framework outlined at Camp David was a significant milestone in the history of the conflict, marking the first time that the State of Israel (under a Revisionist leadership!) recognized de jure the legitimate rights of the Palestinians. Though the autonomy talks between Israel and Egypt ultimately failed, the Oslo Accords in the early 1990s drew heavily from the framework agreement of the 1978 Camp David Accords.

From Begin's perspective, the agreement with Egypt was designed to ensure that Judea, Samaria, and the Gaza Strip remained under Israeli sovereignty, even if the Palestinians enjoyed autonomy within these territories. Therefore, he insisted that the Palestinians were not a distinct nation, but Arabs of the Land of Israel. They would receive civil, cultural, and religious rights (in accordance with the status that Jabotinsky planned to grant to the Arab minority in the Land of Israel, on both sides of the Jordan River) —but only under the sovereignty of the Jewish state. In this context, Begin emphasized that the Palestinians would receive rights "in the land" and not "to the land."

In fact, one of the reasons Begin agreed to withdraw from the Sinai was that he distinguished between the peninsula—which is not considered part of the Land of

Israel held sacred by the Jewish people—and Judea and Samaria. He even cited a commentary on the Book of Exodus (verse 19:13) to prove that Mount Sinai was not a holy site.[8] Thus, the Sinai Peninsula had only strategic importance, which could be exchanged for a strategic card of greater significance for the security of Israel—a peace treaty with Egypt, backed by the United States. That is, from Begin's viewpoint, the withdrawal from Sinai was not meant to create a precedent for applying the "land for peace" formula in future peace accords. On the contrary, it was intended to show that only what is not part of the Land of Israel could be relinquished (out of considerations of realpolitik).

In any case, besides support in principle for the agreement, Peres's role as head of the opposition included many informal contacts with the Egyptian leadership—contacts that sometimes served as an additional channel for conveying messages, and sometimes an outlet for the Egyptians to express their views and share their frustration with candor that surprised Beilin.

For example, in November 1980, a senior Labor Party delegation—including Peres, Abba Eban, and Haim Bar-Lev—held a series of meetings with the Egyptian leadership in Cairo. These meetings were documented by Beilin and his notes are kept in his archives. Their publication here for the first time helps to shed light on the views of the Middle Eastern leaders and their authentic approach to the conflict.

In one of the meetings, Egypt's minister of state for foreign affairs, Boutros Boutros-Ghali, asked how extensive the Israeli withdrawal would be if the left returned to power.

Eban responded that "no [Israeli] government would return to 1967" and explained that the governments of Eshkol and Meir had consented to Security Council Resolution 242 only after the United States and Britain had agreed that Israel would not be forced to return to the pre-1967 lines.

Peres preferred to respond with a graphic metaphor: "Israel's problem is like a modern young woman who has various broad features, but narrow hips. It's nice for a young woman, but dangerous for a state."

Boutros-Ghali answered with a chauvinistic quip of his own: "It turns out that we have different taste here."

On the question of bringing the PLO into the negotiations, Peres explained why his party would also oppose this: "The PLO solution is not possible because they won't agree to demilitarize their state. And there are too many armies here."

The Egyptian foreign minister later raised another grievance: "Your special relations with South Africa create a difficult problem for us in the Third World because they criticize us for supporting you in spite of those relations."

Peres: "But you yourselves have relations with South Africa."

"That's not important," concluded Boutros-Ghali. "The main thing is the image."[9]

The Labor delegation met the following day with Sadat. Beilin's notes include the president's comments on the US elections held on November 4, when Jimmy Carter lost to Ronald Reagan. According to Sadat, "Carter fell from power because of his lack of intelligence and his indecisiveness."[10] On November 9, the delegation met with Hosni Mubarak, who was then serving as vice president. The conversation took place against the background of reports that the Likud government was planning, with the support of some top Labor figures, to apply Israeli sovereignty in the Golan

Heights. Mubarak tried to convince the Israelis to refrain from annexing the Golan, claiming that this move would actually benefit Hafez al-Assad, the Syrian president. Mubarak explained that the Golan was not particularly essential for Assad, but the ongoing struggle against Israel's occupation of this territory helped him to legitimize his regime. "Why do you need the Golan Heights Law? That's excellent material for perpetuating Assad's Ba'ath regime. It's vital for him and for the Russians."[11] Concerning the Palestinian issue, Peres argued—just as he later argued regarding the Oslo Accords—that the time was ripe for progress because of the PLO's weakness. He suggested starting negotiations with an agreed solution for the Gaza Strip and later trying to transfer the territories of Judea and Samaria to Jordan in a confederation framework. "We should start with Gaza and only afterwards deal with the West Bank. The PLO is weak. We need to continually remind the Jordanians that they're invited to join the negotiations."[12]

It is understandable why Israel pinned its hopes on negotiating with a more moderate Palestinian leadership from the territories rather than the PLO, which at this stage still refused to recognize Israel and renounce terrorism. But this was actually another case of blindness afflicting the Israeli leadership, which finally realized, over a decade later, that it was not Israel's prerogative to choose the Palestinians' leaders. The Oslo Accords also demonstrated that a weak PLO is not in Israel's interest, because the PLO was and remains the only Palestinian entity with which it is possible to reach and implement agreements.

In his conversation with the Labor Party leaders, Mubarak seemed primarily concerned about the growing power of the Soviet Union in the Middle East. (This came in the context of the Egyptian regime's strategic shift in the early 1970s, when Sadat adopted a pro-American orientation.) Mubarak also expressed his dislike for King Hussein and his regime. Peres took note of the rifts in the Arab world, though he interpreted these divisions a bit differently than Mubarak. A few days later, in a speech at the Socialist International assembly on November 13, Peres asserted that Israel should seek to achieve its next accord with Jordan, but postpone pursuing agreements with Syria and Iraq. He believed that the regimes in Syria and Iraq were unlikely to survive, because "Syria is led by an ethnic minority, a new state in a problematic situation. . . . Iraq too is led by a national minority."[13] While it took about two decades for Peres's forecast to materialize, it proved to be correct after the collapse of Saddam Hussein's Iraq and Syria's plunge into civil war in the wake of the Arab Spring. Though the Middle East has its own timeframe, it is still impossible to stop the inevitable from occurring.

## 3

The first time that Peres shared with Beilin his long-term vision for the Middle East was in 1981, during another visit to Morocco.

In one of their conversations at night, Peres said what he dared to state publicly only after another decade had passed: Israel should engage in dialogue with the PLO because it is the authentic representative of the Palestinian people and because only with the PLO would it be possible to make and implement agreements. Beilin later wondered whether the years that passed between the time of this conversation and the Oslo Accords expressed the time required to instill new ideas in Israeli politics, or the time required for girding political courage. Indeed, when Beilin asked Peres during that conversation what he planned to do about the need to talk with the PLO, Peres responded that it was "a tragedy" that Israeli public opinion was not ready for a bold move. Beilin did not question Peres on the leader's responsibility to shape public opinion—in part, because he thought that perhaps Peres knew best about the "wisdom of timing" when it comes to historic decisions. It did become clear to Beilin, however, that Peres's approach to the Arab–Israeli conflict was changing.

As noted, the transformation that began in Peres's thinking was inseparable from the labor movement's fall from power for the first time in Israel's history. The ascension of the Likud, something that had seemed unimaginable to Peres just a few years earlier, also proved that the Israeli public was open to changes and alternative options, and this encouraged him to examine new ideas and reconsider formulas that had become entrenched in the left.

Another reason for the change was Peres's exposure to the ideology and personalities of social-democratic leaders who led Europe in the 1970s and early 1980s—Adolfo Suárez González, who led Spain from 1976 to 1981; Mário Soares, who served as prime minister of Portugal (1976–78, 1983–85) and later as president (1986–96); Helmut Schmidt, the chancellor of West Germany (1974–82); Bruno Kreisky, the chancellor of Austria (1970–83); and especially François Mitterand, who was elected president of France in 1981. Peres formed a relationship with each of them, and they contributed to shaping his new perspective on the Palestinian national movement and its leaders. Beilin also changed during those years. He wrote in 1977 that if Israel did not find a suitable partner for negotiations on the territories, it should consider a unilateral withdrawal to defensible borders. But as he learned more about Arab leaders, he began to realize there was no alternative to direct talks with Palestinians who identify with the PLO. Starting in 1981, he developed a circle of contacts and relations with Palestinian figures from East Jerusalem, including the Palestinian national poet Raymonda Tawil (the mother of Suha Arafat), though these contacts were sporadic and produced no tangible results. Beilin was also still a political lightweight at the time, despite his proximity to Peres.

Meanwhile, the Knesset elections were approaching, scheduled for June 1981. There was optimism in the Alignment about the chances of returning to power. However, the sour relations between Rabin and Peres cast a shadow over the election preparations. The competition between the two dated back to the days of Ben-Gurion, when Rabin was a promising young officer and Peres was an aide to the "old man" in the Defense Ministry and later the ministry's director-general. Peres believed that his work to procure weapons during the War of Independence and his involvement in creating military industries (including the reactor in Dimona) placed him in a position of precedence. On the other side, Rabin, who commanded the Harel Brigade in the Palmach, looked upon Peres with suspicion—the type of suspicion a man of the field often harbors toward politicians. In Beilin's view, without understanding the depths of the enmity between Rabin and Peres, it is impossible to explain the way the Oslo

Accords developed from the Israeli side. To understand the roots of this enmity, it is helpful to examine their respective relations with the founding father, Ben-Gurion.

The connection between Ben-Gurion and Rabin was complex. The "old man" was friendly with Rabin's parents—Rosa and Nehemiah Rabin, who came to Palestine in the Third Aliyah and were members of Ahdut Ha'avoda—and appreciated their son's choice to pursue a military career.[14] However, he thought that Rabin was "a little too cautious" as a person and as a commander.[15] The seeds of this assessment were in the War of Independence, when Ben-Gurion wanted to ensure that Jerusalem would not fall into the hands of the Arab Legion, and demanded that the IDF complete Operation Yoram and capture the police fort at Latrun, which the Legion was using to block the road to Jerusalem. Rabin, as commander of the Harel Brigade, believed that this operation was a mistake and unnecessary. He and Palmach commander Allon believed that the battle for Latrun—which had already cost the lives of many soldiers, including Holocaust survivors sent into battle immediately upon arriving in Israel—would exact an unbearable price. They proposed an alternative: to accelerate work on the makeshift Burma Road so that it could serve as a bypass route instead of the Nachshon-Sha'ar Hagai road that was blocked by the Legion, and thus lift the siege of Jerusalem. Allon dispatched Rabin to persuade Ben-Gurion. "Only after a stormy argument, Ben-Gurion agreed to the alternative. According to Rabin's account, Ben-Gurion shouted during the argument, "Yigal Allon should be shot!" because his stance bordered on insubordination.[16]

Rabin and Ben-Gurion had another confrontation at the end of the war, this time over the latter's decision in October 1948 to dismantle the Palmach and integrate its fighters in other IDF units. Ben-Gurion feared that keeping the Palmach fighters in a separate unit would subject them to undue political influence by Mapam. Rabin thought these fears were exaggerated, but did not oppose Ben-Gurion's decision because he agreed with the principle of *mamlachtiyut* (statism)—that there should be only one military body in Israel, subordinate to the Israeli government.[17] There was just one, symbolic, demand that Rabin could not accept: to absent himself from a farewell gathering of Palmach veterans held in October 1949. If he refrained from attending this event, Rabin argued, it would be a blow to the value of comradeship; he was guided in this matter by "a deep emotional need,"[18] he explained. Ben-Gurion, stubborn as usual, saw the Palmach gathering as an act of defiance. In the end, Rabin insisted on attending, and a reprimand was filed in his military record.

Nonetheless, and though Ben-Gurion never expressed understanding for Rabin's motives for participating in the Palmach event, one of his last requests from Eshkol, before vacating the prime minister's office and Defense Ministry, was to appoint Rabin as the next IDF chief of staff. Eshkol agreed, and Rabin became chief of staff in January 1964. In his later years, Ben-Gurion continued to refer to him as "General Rabin" in his diary.[19]

Therefore, Rabin had reasons to believe that despite the disagreements with the founder of the state, and despite his association with Ahdut Ha'avoda, Ben-Gurion held him in high esteem. This assumption was expressed on the eve of the Six-Day War, when Rabin initiated a meeting with Ben-Gurion in order to draw encouragement and confidence from his insights. His hopes were dashed. Much to Rabin's surprise, Ben-

Gurion reproached him for dragging Israel into a dangerous war. The meeting was apparently one of the factors leading to Rabin's collapse soon afterward. At the end of the war, Ben-Gurion hurried to meet Rabin and displayed uncharacteristic excitement.

The depth of Peres's connection with Ben-Gurion is also difficult to exaggerate. Ben-Gurion had cultivated Peres since the time the latter served as his aide in the Defense Ministry during the War of Independence, and Peres maintained complete loyalty to Ben-Gurion—at least until January 1968, when he and other Rafi members decided to join the Labor Party, despite Ben-Gurion's objection. Although the "old man" was aware of the antagonism that Peres stirred among many top Mapai officials in the 1950s,[20] he saw him as a political asset: a young man with original ideas and an ability to get things done. Ben-Gurion's primary criterion for judging his staff was the benefit they brought, and Peres made an important contribution to developing the military industries and forging relations with France that facilitated the construction of the reactor in Dimona. Peres also identified with Ben-Gurion's security activism and worked against the conciliatory policy that Moshe Sharett advocated. Thus, Ben-Gurion continued to back Peres, even when Golda Meir, then serving as foreign minister, repeatedly complained that as deputy defense minister Peres did not report accurately and undermined her authority.

Both Peres and Rabin saw themselves, therefore, as protégés of the founding father and, as such, anointed for leadership. However, it should be noted that Ben-Gurion never designated Rabin or Peres as his future successor, and this was not because he ignored this question. In the 1950s, he designated Yigael Yadin for this role, and spoke on many occasions about Yadin's leadership qualities. There were times when he also singled out Haim Zadok, minister of development in Eshkol's government, as having leadership potential. Late in his life, he lamented that if Enzo Sereni had not been captured by the Nazis while on a mission in Hungary, he could have been a leader."[21]

The roots of the battle for primacy waged between Rabin and Peres from the 1970s through the early 1990s thus stretch back to Israel's early and formative years, and their grudge match only intensified over the years. In fact, two years after Beilin began working as Peres's spokesperson, following the publication of Rabin's memoirs in 1979, the two rivals were unable to directly converse. The mutual aversion, especially from Rabin's side, was evident in his efforts to skip party activities whenever possible, just to avoid having to talk to Peres and his aides. For Beilin, this was further proof of Rabin's weakness as a politician, because a politician should build bridges between people.

As the 1981 elections approached, Rabin opposed Peres's leadership, but initially decided not to run for party chairman and to support Allon, instead. On January 20, 1980, the party's central committee cast their votes and Peres defeated Allon handily, 457 to 220. Allon, with Rabin's support, did not give up, despite this clear expression of support for his opponent. He demanded that the leadership contest be brought to the party's convention for a vote. However, Allon's plans were suddenly cut short as he suffered a fatal heart attack on February 29, 1980. The enmity between the Peres camp and the Allon-Rabin camp even surfaced during Allon's funeral, when Allon's widow Ruth turned to Rabin and dramatically asked him to continue her husband's path. Rabin acceded to the call and the party convention met on December 17, 1980, to choose between Peres and Rabin. The hard work that Peres and Beilin had invested among party members over the previous three years proved itself. Peres defeated Rabin with a majority of 7 percent.[22]

As often occurs in politics, Peres's salient victory led to a turning point in the relations between the two. Rabin concluded that he no longer had a chance in a head-to-head confrontation, and that the circumstances required him to cooperate with Peres. With the mediation of various party activists, it was agreed that after winning the Knesset elections, Peres would appoint Rabin to serve as defense minister, instead of Haim Bar-Lev, who was previously slated for the position. After this was agreed, Rabin decided to make a goodwill gesture and did this in his awkward-charming way: He walked unannounced into Peres's office at the party headquarters and offered a cigarette to Peres, a man he had demonstratively avoided for a long time.

At this stage, about half a year before the elections, there was great optimism in the party about the chances of winning the elections and returning to power. The polls forecast a lead of 25 percent over the Likud.

The main reason was the economy. During the two years leading up to the elections, the excitement over the peace treaty with Egypt had waned and was replaced by disappointment on the economic front: The inflation rate reached 133 percent in 1980. The frequent turnover at the Finance Ministry also reflected an inability to control the economic situation. Following the resignation of Simcha Erlich, a member of the Liberal Party, Yigal Horowitz was appointed to serve as finance minister. He tried to pursue an unpopular policy of budget cuts, but encountered difficulties in implementing his plan.

Horowitz resigned in January 1981 after failing to receive Begin's support, and was replaced by Yoram Aridor, who favored a completely different economic policy. Begin's new finance minister proposed a mix of neoliberalism with Begin's simplistic economic vision of "bringing benefit to the people"—and this helped to close the gap in the polls. (Begin's model of leadership, dating back to the days of the Irgun, was to outline principles and leave the details to "experts.")[23] On the one hand, the government lowered customs duties and taxes on consumer products without cutting government spending. On the other hand, the government stepped up efforts to privatize factories, retreating from the responsibility of saving Histadrut enterprises that employed tens of thousands of workers. In the short term, members of the middle class and lower-middle class were the main beneficiaries of this change in policy. The state was flooded with Subaru vehicles made in Japan, which were now more affordable, and electronic products like televisions also became less expensive (and restrictions on color broadcasts were lifted). At the same time, Israel's foreign currency reserves were dwindling and, consequently, the government was compelled to print more shekels and inflation rose. But the public began to fully understand the negative economic impact of the government's economic policy only after the elections.

This is one of the reasons that many Israelis from the middle and lower-middle classes, who enjoyed the improvement in their economic situation since Aridor's appointment, decided to vote for the Likud again. This was contrary to earlier polls that predicted an optimistic outcome for the Labor Party. Thus, the votes for Begin can be clearly attributed to rational motives, rather than to emotional manipulations in the fiery stump speeches Begin delivered in the summer of 1981, as commonly assumed in analyses published in the late twentieth century.[24]

Another factor that eroded the chances of the Labor Party is evident when examining the list of candidates of the major parties. The Likud offered a list that saliently featured young, second-generation Israelis of Mizrahi heritage—including Moshe Katsav, Meir Sheetrit, David Levy, and David Magen—along with the children of Lehi and Herut veterans, who were labeled "the princes." Thus, the Likud was more relevant to the Israeli society of the 1980s. By contrast, both the Mizrahi and Ashkenazi candidates on the Alignment's list represented the original elites of the founding generation, veterans of the Haganah and Palmach, activists from the heyday of the labor movement, who had grown old and lost their luster. Furthermore, many of these candidates belonged to the activist stream of the labor movement. Therefore, besides their sociopolitical affiliation and the original socialist context (which lost its relevance as a worldview in Israel), their views on foreign affairs and defense actually matched those of the Likud. Thus, for example, when the Camp David Accords were ratified in the Knesset—by a vote of 84 to 19 with 17 abstentions—two senior members of the party, Shlomo Hillel and Shoshana Arbeli-Almozlino, joined the hawkish wing of the Likud that opposed the accords. Allon, who was then a candidate to lead the party, abstained. He explained that he was not opposed to peace, but believed a better agreement was possible. In this way, the alternative the party could have offered became less distinctive.

Beilin, a member of the new generation of the left, which had yet to receive real expression in the Labor Party, felt the generation gap and the party's disconnection from the spirit of the times. His meetings with Galili, head of the party's settlement department, usually ended in frustration—from both his personal style and the content of the discussion. Galili was responsible for the wording of the party's decisions, a task that was still accorded great importance. He tended to use archaic language, devoid of nuance, much to the chagrin of the young party members. From an ideological perspective, he not only opposed the withdrawal from the Sinai Peninsula, but he also strongly rejected proposals that Beilin tried to promote, such as the need to give up Gaza because of the demographic burden it posed.

For Galili, the settlement enterprise in the territories was a direct continuation of the pre-state settlement project. He was proud that seventy-six new settlements were established under his chairmanship of the ministerial committee on settlement in the governments of Eshkol, Meir, and Rabin, including thirty-three settlements during Rabin's term.[25] Galili was also the only senior party figure to prompt Beilin to consider quitting his job. This occurred in December 1981, when Begin introduced the Golan Heights Law, which applied Israeli law in the territory captured from Syria in 1967. One of Begin's motives in promoting this legislation was to embarrass the Labor Party, whose leaders had accused the Likud of favoring Judea and Samaria at the expense of the Negev, Galilee, and Golan. Begin believed that his initiative would force Labor's leaders to support the new law, and that if they opposed it, he would win points domestically—in part, because most of the settlers in the Golan were affiliated with the labor movement.

The prime minister, who was then recovering from a knee injury, chose to submit the legislation personally. On December 14, 1981, he rolled up to the Knesset podium in a wheel chair. In his speech, Begin declared a holiday, explaining that the Golan Heights has been part of the Land of Israel for many generations, and was "arbitrarily" severed from the mandate allotted to the British after the First World War. He could not ignore the argument that he was undermining the chance of peace with Syria, and noted that if the Syrians at "the end of days" wish to conduct negotiations, "the transfer of territory to a civil administration would not prevent negotiations."[26] The Golan Heights Law was formulated in a clever way to apply Israeli law without formally annexing the territory.

From the moment the Likud's intention to propose this legislation became known, ideological turmoil and confusion prevailed in the Labor Party. In a meeting of the party's leadership on September 29, 1980, Peres emphasized the need to promptly pursue territorial compromise, explaining that Israel's policy should be based on "concern that the nuclear advantage will disappear at the end of the decade." (He believed that "the first [Muslim] state to [acquire] a nuclear bomb will be Pakistan.") On the other hand, Peres declared at another party gathering: "It is impossible to defend Israel without the Golan Heights. The settlements were built as our mission, and no one questions this mission."[27] It is no surprise, therefore, that Peres was in a bind when it came to deciding how the party should vote on the new legislation. He explained his stance in the spirit of the classic school of the labor movement: The Golan should be kept by reinforcing settlement there and establishing facts on the ground, without a formal declaration of annexation or applying sovereignty, which would only complicate Israel's international relations. Beilin supported this view and was glad that Peres opposed the law. But he was forced to contend with Galili's efforts to persuade the party's Knesset members to vote in favor of Begin's initiative. Beilin, who felt he had established a solid footing in the party, decided that if Galili's efforts were successful and Labor supported the law, he would resign. In the end, it was decided not to impose party discipline, leaving the MKs to vote as they pleased. Most of them chose to be absent from the Knesset plenum when the voting took place; eight voted in favor and 13 against. As Begin savored his achievement in passing this legislation, Beilin became more convinced that the party needed to be revamped on both the personal and ideological levels.

# 4

The election campaign for the tenth Knesset was undoubtedly the most violent and stormy of Israel's history. It seemed reasonable to expect that after the Likud's rise to power, the flames of anger between supporters of the two major parties would subside—if only because the Labor Party, representing the historical Mapai, had already lost its mythical power. According to this view, the excitement over the defeat of the establishment should give way to a more measured assessment of the alternatives. But the opposite occurred.

Despite the disagreements in the present, and contrary to the Labor Party's intention of focusing on the future, the Likud turned the election campaign into an indictment of Mapai for the injustices of the past. The Likud's television commercials featured impoverished neighborhoods that had yet to be renovated under the Project Renewal program, with the narrator attributing the situation to "thirty years of neglect by Mapai." One of the Likud's main posters stated: "You have to decide—continuing forward or turning back."

Consequently, the ethnic divide also received prominent attention. We briefly discussed this issue in the context of the 1977 elections, but there was an additional explanation for the outburst of ethnic tensions in the June 1981 elections: In the wake of the political upheaval in 1977, there was entrenchment around the Ashkenazi identity. Motta Gur's response to a crowd of Likud supporters—"We'll screw you, just like we screwed the Arabs," and the way Peres chastised hecklers during a campaign rally in Petah Tikva—"Great, so that's how the people will look, the people of Begin, a people of Mizrahi movements,"[28] were interpreted in the media primarily as tactical errors that exacerbated the Mizrahi alienation toward Labor's leaders. In retrospect, however, it seems that these statements, though spontaneous, reflected a deeper layer: a sort of counter-reaction to the emerging loss of hegemony of the *ahusalim* (Ashkenazi, secular, Israeli-born, socialist, nationalist Israelis), to borrow the successful acronym of Baruch Kimmerling.[29] Yitzhak Ben-Aharon's famous statement in the wake of the upheaval ("if that's the people's decision, I don't honor it") is an example of a flare-up of Ashkenazi anger against Mizrahi Jews, This anger peaked a few days before the elections when the entertainer Dudu Topaz, speaking at a Labor election rally, referred to Likud voters as *tchachachim* (Mizrahi riffraff) who skirt army duty or at most serve as sentries at army bases.[30] In a demagogic but politically brilliant response, Begin delivered one of the most dramatic speeches in Israel's history. He presented the Revisionist movement as an alternative to the labor movement—not only in the fields of economy and diplomacy, but also in offering a different formula for social equality, based on Jewish solidarity.

It is difficult to assess the electoral impact of Begin's speech. And the successful operation to destroy the Iraqi nuclear reactor three weeks before the elections certainly contributed to the Likud's success (especially after Begin publicized a secret letter Peres had sent to him, urging him not to attack the reactor "at this time and in the current conditions"). In any case, when the polling stations closed on June 30, 1981, two days after Begin's speech, he was the winner again. Only four months earlier, Begin had come to terms with his impending defeat and had asked to appoint a successor (Ya'akov Meridor). His victory was a narrow one—forty-eight seats for the Likud, versus forty-seven for the Alignment—but it was enough for him to form his second government.

5

The election results were very frustrating for Beilin. He believed that the main reason for the loss was that Labor had failed to create a clear ideological alternative to the Likud. In December 1981, he set out to address the situation by creating a forum in the party to discuss new ideas. The forum, called Mashov ("feedback"), was based on members and graduates of the party's Young Guard. It widened and by 1985 was already the core of a broader caucus group operating under the name Hakfar Hayarok and led by Nissim Zvili. One of the motives for establishing the Mashov group was the feeling among young members of the party that when they submitted proposals as individuals—primarily on issues pertaining to territorial compromise, recognition of the Palestinians' right to self-determination, and separating the Histadrut labor federation from its economic arm (Hevrat HaOvdim) and from the Clalit HMO—they were easily rebuffed by the party's old guard. Beilin realized that it would be best to repackage these ideas and submit them as a unified group.

Although the Mashov group operated within the party, it had an overarching objective that extended beyond internal reform. It aimed to set in motion a process that would lead to the creation of two main blocs in Israeli politics—a social-liberal party and the Likud, which would represent the conservative camp. According to Beilin's post-election analysis, the cardinal error of the Labor Party in its various incarnations was that it abandoned the original alliance that Ben-Gurion had formed between Mapai and the General Zionist stream. The latter was initially represented in the Knesset by the General Zionist Party and the Progressive Party, which merged in 1961 to form the Liberal Party. In Beilin's eyes, Gahal—the alliance Begin initiated in 1965 between Herut and the Liberal Party[31]—was the Likud's source of power and gradually paved its way to power. Beilin envisioned a renewal of the partnership with the Liberal Party; he was convinced that, ideologically, the common ground the Liberals shared with the young generation in the Labor Party outweighed their differences—especially in the post-socialist era.[32]

Historically, Beilin was right. Ben-Gurion formed his first and second governments in collaboration with the Progressive Party; the General Zionist Party, which demonstrated its strength by winning twenty seats in the second Knesset, joined his fourth government. In general, until the early 1950s, the political centers of power in Israel were Mapai and the General Zionist stream, and this was a natural development of the early political map in the Zionist movement. The General Zionists controlled the World Zionist Organization—even if not in a party format—from the first Zionist Congress in 1897 until the 1920s. Only later did socialist Zionism rise to leadership, when leftist parties headed by Ben-Gurion replaced the General Zionist stream, whose leaders included Chaim Weizmann,[33] president of the WZO from 1921 to 1931.

The political partnership forged between Mapai and the Progressive faction in the General Zionist stream collapsed after the Progressive Party and the General Zionist Party joined to form the Liberal Party in 1961. Menachem Begin identified the potential of a united bloc of Herut and the Liberal Party,[34] and was prepared to meet the Liberals' demand and remove the call for conquering both banks of the Jordan River from Gahal's platform. Gahal's contribution to Begin's rise to power is indisputable. With the formation of Gahal, Begin became the unchallenged leader of Israel's second largest party. More importantly, the union with the Liberals gave him the political legitimacy that Ben-Gurion had sought to deny him as the leader of Herut, which was seen as a fundamentally radical opposition party.

Beilin thought that the political objective of the left should be to renew the connection between the Labor Party, whose affiliation with socialism had weakened in any case in the 1980s, and the Liberals, who admittedly supported a freer economy, but were not committed to a rigid ideology and generally showed flexibility in matters of security and foreign affairs. This partnership, Beilin believed, could change the face of the political system in Israel.

In fact, this plan nearly materialized. Few recall that Eshkol had already signed a coalition agreement with the Liberals before Begin managed to unite them with Herut, but Mapai's central committee rejected this agreement, preferring a coalition pact with Ahdut Ha'avoda.[35] Beilin sought to rectify this mistake, which in his view pulled the party in a more hawkish direction and blurred its distinctiveness. We should not forget that Beilin's vision also drew inspiration from his family biography: His grandfather defined himself politically as a General Zionist.

Beilin's view is interesting, and perhaps the realization of his vision of a left-liberal bloc would have prevented the continual failure of the Labor Party for nearly the past four decades. Most of the centrist parties formed since 1977 largely echoed the perspective of the General Zionists —Dash in the elections that produced the upheaval, Yahad in the 1984 elections, Tsomet in 1992, The Third Way and the Center Party in 1996, Tommy Lapid's Shinui in 1999, Yair Lapid's Yesh Atid in 2013, and Moshe Kahlon's Kulanu in 2015—and most of them joined a coalition led by the Likud, though there was no ideological imperative for this. Of course, the partnerships between the Likud and the centrist parties were a function of the numerical advantage enjoyed by the right-religious bloc. However, an alliance formed, in principle and in advance, between the left and the Liberals might have, indeed, led to a change in the political map.

Beilin's thesis is also interesting because of an element missing from it, which perhaps better explains the decline of the Zionist left in recent decades: the attitude toward religion. What fortifies the right's hold on power in Israel—more than its economic or diplomatic stance—is the alliance Begin formed with the religious camp. Since the Ben-Gurion era, the absence of a salient pro-Jewish identity in the left (in image or in practice) has contributed to its difficulty in renewing the alliance the "old man" formed with the religious camp. There are many reasons for the Israeli public's shift to the right since 1977, and especially since the second intifada in 2001—but it cannot be attributed to the public's political fixation or clear-cut views on issues of state. On the contrary, the election results in the 1980s indicate near parity between the blocs, and the election results in the 1990s—until the outbreak of the second intifada, which, indeed, caused a fundamental shift rightward—actually demonstrated how open Israelis are to change: In 1992, Rabin defeated Shamir, but preferred Netanyahu to Peres in the next elections. In 1999, the public lurched leftward again, when Ehud Barak defeated Netanyahu. But two years later, the right returned to power, as the Likud's candidate Ariel Sharon handily defeated Barak.

These were not real upheavals. Netanyahu was elected after the assassination of Rabin, when it seemed that the left's hold on power was certain; Barak, who promised a withdrawal from Lebanon and a final status accord with the Palestinians, won by a huge margin only three years after the public had ostensibly rejected Oslo; the election of Sharon, previously perceived as an extremist who had even challenged a hard-liner like Shamir, was inconceivable before 2001.

If the Israeli public is so fickle, why has it consistently rejected the left for nearly two decades? A study by the Molad institute in 2013 indicates that in principle the public supports the views of the left on the two-state solution and a more social-oriented economy, [36] but still recoils from voting for the left and identifying with it.

It is an open secret: The left's main problem is not its views, but its public image. Israeli politicians are aware of this. To counter the public's negative perception of the left, numerous efforts have been made in the last two decades to rebrand its image. For example, Amir Peretz sought to build an ethnic-Mizrahi left, Eldad Yaniv championed the National Left, and when Shelly Yachimovich headed the Labor Party, she advocated a more radical social-economic left. Only one combination was never tried: a Jewish left. Surveys by the Guttman Center and others[37] indicate that while most Israelis are not religiously observant, about 90 percent see importance in maintaining central Jewish ceremonies and identify themselves, first and foremost, as Jews. Accordingly, the left's problem stems primarily from its lack of identification with the Jewish dimension and the perception that it is not committed to Jewish heritage. When Netanyahu said to Rabbi Kedourie on the eve of the 1999 elections—"the left has forgotten what it means to be a Jew," it was, of course, a wily political maneuver. However, in the uproar it provoked, the raw nerve the comment struck was overlooked: Has any leader of the left accorded central importance to his or her Jewishness?

In this sense, the left has, indeed, gradually cut itself off from its roots. A. D. Gordon and Berl Katznelson were not Orthodox Jews, but they wrestled a lot with their Jewish identity. Ben-Gurion opposed the traditional Jewish lifestyle, but engaged with the Bible and its characters throughout his life. His successors, however, did not show interest in the Jewish identity, and refrained from any involvement with tradition—except for donning a yarmulke when meeting with the rabbis of ultra-Orthodox parties (which only underlined their alienation from religion). The left aspires to reform Israeli society according to the European model and yearns for peace in order to live in tranquility like in North America. This does not mean the solutions it seeks are necessarily "non-Jewish." But they are not conveyed to the public as anchored in Jewish sources and driven by a concern for maintaining Jewish existence and identity. And this concern, or anxiety, does, indeed, trouble most Israelis, consciously or unconsciously.

A "Jewish left" does not mean support for religious coercion; it means recognizing the importance of the tradition and placing greater emphasis on the Jewish dimension of Israeliness.

The Israeli left has not forgotten to be Jewish. However, if it wishes to survive, it should remind the public more emphatically that it represents a central part of the diverse range in Jewishness. In this sense, Beilin represents a missed opportunity—he was close to religion in his youth, is familiar with the liturgy, and is one of the only Israeli politicians who have invested efforts (described below) to develop programs designed to preserve the unity of the Jewish people and build modern cultural frameworks that can sustain Jewish values in Israel and in the Diaspora. Nonetheless, as noted, he identified the key to empowering the left in its connection to the liberal camp, and not to the religious-traditional camp.

Beilin and his colleagues in the Mashov group brought fresh thinking on social and diplomatic issues, and differed in their young style from the generation of the party's titans. But they were secular and blatantly indifferent to Jewish religious affairs. The Mashov circle included Ramon, Zvili, and later Ron Pundak, Yair Hirschfeld, Amir Peretz, Boaz Karni, Nimrod Novik, and Amnon Neubach. Yael Dayan also joined later. The only religious person in the group was Avrum Burg.

Although Beilin was the moving force and ideologue in Mashov's early days, and though one of the group's objectives was to groom an heir for Rabin and Peres, Beilin did not try to establish himself as number one. In this context, the political model he followed was quite similar to that of someone he loathed for jumping from the Labor Party to the Likud—Moshe Dayan. Just as Dayan was involved and influential, and significantly shaped many stations in Israel's political path and culture from the time of Ben-Gurion through the days of Begin, Beilin also saw himself as a mover and shaker working alongside the top leader. At this stage, as he became more deeply involved in politics, he also became more convinced that he was not prime ministerial material. The Mashov member designated for leadership was Ramon. Over time, more and more party members joined the group (which began, as noted, as an ideological platform), as well as public figures who were not involved in politics but supported Mashov's ideas. From the mid-1980s, a group coalesced that the media referred to as the Octet: Beilin, Ramon, Peretz, Zvili, Dayan, Burg, Hagai Merom (who represented the kibbutz movement), and Nawaf Massalha (who represented the Arabs of Israel). In retrospect, Beilin stated: "We were the most influential group in Israeli politics"[38] from the 1980s through the beginning of the twenty-first century. Indeed, many of the group's ideas, which were considered radical at the time, eventually became the mainstream views of the Labor Party and the political center in Israel. The Octet members sought to avoid taking sides in the fight between the rival camps in the Labor Party, but most of them were identified with Peres, who liked their ideas but refrained from publicly embracing them. Rabin, who was suspicious of them in the 1980s, referred to them as "the Liquidators, Inc." because he feared they would pull the party too far to the left. However, after Rabin defeated Peres in the run-up to the 1992 elections, Ramon became one of Rabin's favorites.

On the Palestinian question, the Mashov members advocated negotiating with the PLO and dividing the land—though they did not outline a specific map. Their primary and more original innovations were expressed in the economic and social reforms they proposed, and in their ideas for revitalizing the political arena: instituting primaries to select the party's representatives; severing the connection between the Histadrut and the Clalit HMO, and between the party and the Histadrut; promoting legislation on personal liberty; lobbying to liberalize the economy; reducing government intervention in the economy; and separating religion and state. For Beilin, the revolution in the relations with the Histadrut was the most important achievement in the social-economic field because of the corruption that had infected the labor federation over the years and because the Histadrut's traditional role was incongruent with the economic model he sought for Israel. In retrospect, some of the members of the group, Zvili in particular, concluded that this weakening of the Histadrut in the 1990s, when the Rabin government came to power, also weakened one of the party's bases of support and harmed its ability to remain in power.

In any case, in the 1980s, when the group's ideas were being formulated, Beilin and his colleagues still had a long path ahead of them in the opposition and in national unity governments. Finally, with Rabin's election in 1992, they had a chance to implement many of their ideas.

4

# From Opposition to Unity

## 1

As the Mashov group was drafting plans for a new ideological platform, the Begin government was busy preparing for Operation Peace for the Galilee. The IDF's incursion into Lebanon was launched on June 6, 1982, in what was officially billed as a move to drive the PLO forty kilometers north of the border and thus prevent Katyusha rockets from reaching Israel. This original objective was achieved in two days, but the operation devolved into the First Lebanon War, which played an important part in Begin's decision to resign in late August 1983.

At first, there was a consensus of support for the war among both the right and left in Israel. As usual, criticism was muted while the cannons still roared. It was the first war waged under the Likud's leadership, and the general support during the initial days illustrated how small the differences were within the Zionist camp. In fact, nearly all of the Labor Party's MKs supported the operation. On the eve of the incursion, Begin invited senior Labor leaders to his office for a briefing—Rabin, Peres, and Bar-Lev—and emphasized that the final objective was forty kilometers. The three did not express opposition in principle, though Bar-Lev warned against a confrontation with the Syrians and against entering Beirut. Begin explained that Beirut was not a target;[1] he caustically alluded to unplanned developments in wars conducted under leftist governments (he was referring to the Six-Day War) and assured the Labor leaders that the operation would not get out of control.[2] At the end of the meeting, it was agreed that the leaders of the Labor Party would vote in the Knesset to approve the operation. There was no disagreement about the need to ensure the security of northern Israel by striking against the PLO. Even earlier, Rabin had asked to tour the border with General Yanush Ben-Gal, then serving as commander of Corps 446 in the Northern Command,[3] and was concerned about Israeli entanglement in Lebanon's civil war. However, Rabin was the most enthusiastic supporter of the government's decision among opposition MKs—as long as the operation did not extend beyond forty kilometers.

The Lebanon War in its various aspects has spawned dozens of books and articles, both academic and popular. In our context, the war had special significance for the evolution of the Labor Party. As the operation bogged down, some vocal criticism surfaced in the Labor Party and Operation Peace for the Galilee became the first war in Israel's history waged without a political consensus about its objectives. The war marked a watershed vis-à-vis one of the most defining characteristics of Israeli society: political solidarity in times of national crisis.

As noted, the Labor Party's opposition to the war was belated and developed gradually. On June 16, Beilin published an article calling for the IDF to pull out of Lebanon and warning against expanding the war aims to include finishing off the PLO and striking a blow against the Syrian forces deployed in Lebanon. The article stirred a fury,[4] even though Beilin wrote cautiously—affirming Israel's right to protect its citizens—and personally reported for reserve duty in the IDF. Criticism of government actions in wartime was seen as a challenge to Zionism itself.

The Labor Party's leaders—at least Rabin and Peres—were aware of the more grandiose plan that sought to expel the PLO from all of Lebanon and not suffice with pushing the PLO back forty kilometers, out of Katyusha range.[5] But one of the reasons the party did not dare to publicly oppose the operation, despite reservations expressed by party members from the outset, was the fact that the Rakah communist party was the sole dissenter in the Knesset vote that approved the operation. The Labor Party feared being identified with a non-Zionist party. Even Yossi Sarid, the only Alignment MK to abstain in the vote (and, in retrospect, Beilin regards this as one of the most important decisions in Sarid's career) volunteered for reserve duty in Lebanon in order to underline his distinction between opposition to the government's plans and refusal to serve in the IDF.

The change only occurred in late June when Rabin—who until then had refused to publicly express his reservations about how the war was being conducted, as long as IDF troops were still on the ground in Lebanon—published an article in the *Yedioth Ahronoth* daily entitled "Opposed to Capturing West Beirut."[6] Only then, the party adopted a sharply critical stance. From that stage, and despite the unity governments that ruled from 1984 to 1990, the Labor Party began a gradual process of embracing an alternative approach on issues of defense and foreign affairs, an approach that substantially differed from that of the Likud and peaked in the 1990s under the second Rabin government. It was also a period of generational change in the party, which found expression primarily in the 1990s, when members of the Mashov group rose to senior positions in the party.

The difficulty in parting with fixed political principles was evident in the arguments among party leaders on the question of whether to participate in the protest demonstration in Kings of Israel Square in Tel Aviv in the wake of the massacre in the Sabra and Shatila refugee camps.

The massacre was preceded by a chain of bloody events: on September 14, Bashir Gemayel, the commander of the Phalangists and president-elect of Lebanon, was assassinated. Gemayel, Israel's ally, was killed at the Phalangists' headquarters in East Beirut by a bomb that was likely planted by a Syrian intelligence agent. Ariel Sharon had met with Gemayel the previous day and the two had agreed that any PLO personnel still in West Beirut should be expelled.[7] Following the assassination, the IDF invaded West Beirut and, on September 16, Phalangists entered Sabra and Shatila and murdered hundreds of Palestinians. The camps were in an area under Israeli control and the fact that the IDF allowed the Phalangists to enter the camps, despite the reasonable fear that they would take revenge against the Palestinians, led many people in Israel, and certainly in the world, to hold the Israeli government responsible for the massacre.

The demonstration on September 25 was organized by Peace Now with the aim of pressing the demand for a commission of inquiry. Although this was the specific objective, it was clear that the demonstrators sought to express broader opposition to the war objectives and to the almost imperial mission the government had assigned the IDF in its attempt to shape the regime in Lebanon. However, many in the Labor Party were concerned about being associated with the Black Panthers and leftist organizations that were planning to participate in the demonstration. The Labor Party would need to undergo paradigmatic change in order to join the demonstration. Beilin was in favor of participating in the event. In his eyes, the fact that some of the demonstrators did not subscribe to the Zionist narrative did not detract from the moral importance of the demonstration. Moreover, he also regarded Labor's participation in the demonstration as a political opportunity to break the taboo on expressing criticism during wartime, even when such criticism could save lives and prevent unnecessary entanglement. Together with other young party members, with the support of their patron at the time, Uzi Baram, Beilin set out to convince Peres and Rabin. The latter argued that the demonstration could be interpreted as a protest against the IDF rather than against the government. Yisrael Galili raised another argument against participating: the Labor Party was not intended to be a party of public protests. In his view, the party's role was to chart the state's path through governing. The party leaders struggled to make a decision.[8] Beilin thought that the underlying question was whether Israeli society had become mature enough to distinguish between criticism of the war and opposition to the army. He believed that the public that opposed the conduct of the war was capable of making this distinction.[9] After further deliberation, and in light of public opinion surveys presented by Tzali Reshef and others, Peres decided in favor of participating in the demonstration. However, he waited to receive Rabin's consent. Rabin, too, was persuaded and even agreed to speak at the demonstration, though his reluctance was evident.

Rabin's participation in the demonstration indicates, like the Oslo Accords a decade later, the special role he played in Israeli history: he was a leader who was loath to initiate change, but whose support made change possible. In any case, this famous "demonstration of the 400,000"[10] (though the actual number of demonstrators was closer to 150,000) contributed to the government's decision to appoint a state commission of inquiry. (The public intervention of President Yitzhak Navon also played a part.) The demonstration also shook Prime Minister Begin's confidence in continuing to conduct the war.[11]

After the demonstration, the IDF continued to operate deep in Lebanese territory and the internal debate in Israel intensified, with an increasing number of reservists refusing to serve. This vocal wartime debate and refusal to serve were unprecedented phenomena; this had never happened during Israel's previous wars. Clearly, a key element in this dissension was the fact that the Lebanon War was the first in Israel to be perceived as a war of choice, and was even described as such by Begin. (Israel's previous wars were considered wars of "no choice," though it is doubtful that the Sinai Campaign was different from the Lebanon War in this respect.)[12]

But there also may be some truth in what the right claimed: the consensus on the war collapsed sooner than expected because it was difficult for members of the labor movement to accept a war led by a party that represented the Revisionist movement. It is no coincidence that nearly two decades passed before a right-wing government (albeit a national unity government led by the right) again launched a major military initiative—Operation Defensive Shield in March 2002, which followed a series of suicide bombings culminating in the Park Hotel attack in Netanya. The irony is that Ariel Sharon, who was forced to step down as defense minister in the wake of the commission that investigated the Sabra and Shatila massacre, was now the prime minister. Sharon had clearly internalized the lessons of Lebanon: he launched Operation Defensive Shield only after securing a broad consensus of support.[13]

In August 1983, Begin made the surprise announcement that he was "no longer able" and resigned. Many have interpreted this laconic declaration as an admission of Begin's loss of emotional strength to continue as prime minister. Indeed, Begin was in a mentally weakened condition, but few noted that Begin was following the example of Ben-Gurion, who announced his resignation in 1963 in a similarly terse statement. It was not the only time that Begin echoed Ben-Gurion. In his victory speech in 1977, Begin cited a verse from Jeremiah (2:2) to thank his wife Aliza ("how you followed me in the wilderness"). Ben-Gurion cited the same verse in 1968 in his eulogy for his wife Paula. In fact, there was also an earlier precedent: Jabotinsky quoted the same passage from Jeremiah in reference to his wife Yohana during a Beitar conference in the 1930s. Perhaps this reflects the similar mindsets of the leaders of Zionism, both in nuances and in their approach to fundamental questions.

The Lebanon War further deepened Beilin's disappointment with the political leadership in Israel. From close observation of Begin during his second term as prime minister, Beilin concluded that already in the early stages of the war, and not only when things went awry, Begin suffered a mental breakdown and was no longer the same person. He also knew that many people in the political system, including in the Likud, shared his perception of Begin's condition. Beilin was disappointed to discover that not a single politician of stature dared to say that the prime minister was unfit. His familiarity with the timid side of politicians influenced his actions in the 1990s.

## 2

Begin's resignation marked the end of an era in the Likud. People tend to stick with what is familiar in turbulent and distressful times, and that is what the Likud central committee did when faced with choosing between Yitzhak Shamir and David Levy as Begin's successor. Levy failed in his attempt to offer an alternative leadership to supplant the generation of pre-state underground leaders. In parallel to selecting Shamir as party chairman, it was decided to move up the elections for the 11th Knesset to June 23, 1984.

Meanwhile, inflation continued to skyrocket, reaching nearly 400 percent; bank shares crashed, taking the stock exchange with it; and Begin and Sharon's hopes for a peace accord with Lebanon after expelling the PLO proved to be a pipe dream. The IDF, which had prepared to wage war against the PLO, achieved its mission and the PLO was expelled from Beirut and exiled to Tunis. However, the army now found itself battling against terror organizations, old and new, including the Shiite Hezbollah organization. Against this background, the Labor Party grew convinced that the moment of truth was approaching. Peres again prepared for victory in the elections and his appointment as prime minister.

Beilin advised Peres to form a team to prepare programs for the first 100 days of his government. Peres enthusiastically embraced this idea and appointed Beilin to lead what became known as "The 100 Days" team—a group of experts from various fields, including Nimrod Novik, Amnon Neubach, Shimshon Zelniker, and Ehud Kaufman. The team prepared detailed plans of action for changing Israel's economic, diplomatic, and military situation. Plans were drafted for a full withdrawal from Lebanon, the continued privatization of government corporations, and further economic liberalization, while ensuring protection for employees. The team recommended initiating an accord with Jordan and resolving the question of the territories through a confederation with Jordan and broad autonomy for the Palestinians.

On a personal level, Beilin felt ready for the next stage. He asked to leave his position as Peres's adviser and spokesperson, and to compete for a spot on the Labor Party's Knesset list. At that time, the list was still determined by a committee of several senior party members. Peres wielded influence over the committee, but was not sympathetic to his adviser's Knesset ambition. He explained to Beilin that he had committed to securing spots for David Libai and Simcha Dinitz, who needed his help. Peres promised Beilin that his time would come, but that he was last in line this time because of his young age. This was an interesting argument by Peres because he generally saw youth as an advantage. At this stage, Peres apparently preferred to keep Beilin at his side, in a nonpublic role. Beilin decided to compete nonetheless and requested the support of Rabin and Bar-Lev. The two said they would not oppose his candidacy, but also would not lobby on his behalf.

Beilin hoped to be No. 40 on the party's Knesset slate—a modest, yet secure spot—but the committee placed him in the fifty-fourth spot. Beilin expressed his disappointment to Peres, who responded that this was the best he could do for him. At least he was assigned to a spot reserved for "optimistic people," Beilin quipped, in a mix of sarcasm and submission.

This time, Peres and Rabin did not directly lock horns over the party leadership. Both were concerned that Yitzhak Navon, who had completed his term as president, would decide to compete against them. Navon, like all presidents of Israel, enjoyed great popularity during his presidency, and polls augured well for his chances to win the public's trust. Other factors in his favor included his close association with Ben-Gurion (Navon was director-general of the Prime Minister's Office from 1952 to 1963) and his Sephardi origin. But Navon was not made of prime ministerial material and decided not to compete after Peres promised him the No. 2 spot on the list. Rabin called upon Peres to honor their agreement from the previous elections—that Peres would appoint Rabin as defense minister in any government he led.

The list of candidates did not yet reflect a turnover of generations. Ramon was the only representative of the Young Guard to win a Knesset seat. The optimism Beilin needed as No. 54 in the list was not enough. While the Likud dropped to forty-four seats, the Alignment won just forty-four, and Beilin remained outside the Knesset.

The election results reflected additional changes in Israeli society. Since 1977, when the political system transitioned from an era of one dominant party to a two-bloc era, the Likud and the Alignment accounted for the majority of Knesset seats.[14] However, Begin's departure from the political arena led to the fragmentation of the political right. This was expressed in the formation of parties with a traditional, religious and/ or ultra-Orthodox orientation, combined with a connection to the Greater Land of Israel. These parties drew from voters who had regarded Begin, with his pro-tradition approach, as their representative. For example, the Tami party, formed by Aharon Abuhatzeira, targeted the national-religious and traditional-Mizrahi communities; and Shas was created as a Mizrahi ultra-Orthodox party, though many of its voters were traditional and not ultra-Orthodox. The widening rifts in Israeli society after the Lebanon War also spawned new parties. Thus, Ezer Weizman's Yahad party, Amnon Rubinstein's Shinui, and Yigal Horowitz's Ometz party all competed for centrist voters, hoping to fill the void left by the now defunct Dash party.

The ill winds of Israeli ultra-nationalism swept Rabbi Meir Kahane into the Knesset at the head of the Kach party, which advocated expelling the Arab population. At the same time, the Palestinian identity of Arab society in Israel grew stronger in the wake of the Lebanon War, which brought defeat to the PLO and greater distress to the Palestinian refugees in Lebanon. The Progressive List for Peace (PLP), which was led by Mohammed Miari and drew most of its support from Arab voters, entered the Knesset for the first time, winning two seats.[15] (Although the PLP had a joint Arab–Jewish Knesset list, the ideological orientation of the party was perceived as more radical than that of Rakah, a communist party. The PLP supported the recognition of the PLO as the representative of the Palestinians and the two-state solution, while criticizing the Jewish character of Israel.)

The social rifts were evident not only in the proliferation of parties, but also in the fact that neither of the two major parties was able to form a government. The Likud, which was down seven seats compared to the previous elections, could not put together a right-religious government without Kahane's support, and his racist views were still considered beyond the pale by members of the Revisionist movement. The Alignment needed the support of the Progressive List for Peace and Hadash. (The latter was a union of the communist Rakah party and other leftist organizations.) However, the Alignment's Zionist ethos prevented it from seeking a coalition with Arab parties. Thus, although Israeli society became more diverse and decentralized in its ideas and characteristics, the two major parties marginalized the sectors that were outside the consensus by choosing the path of national unity governments. Peres, the eternal optimist, still tried to form a left-leaning government by forging an alliance with the religious and ultra-Orthodox camps that were already identified with the right. But this attempt failed.

Beilin, participating for the first time in coalition negotiations, was surprised to learn how far removed the religious camp was from the traditional alliance it had maintained with Mapai and its successors until 1977. The main reason for this was the Six-Day War; the Greater Land of Israel became the defining criterion for a pro-Jewish identity. Another reason was that the Israeli left defined itself and its views without reference to Jewish values, even though it could have cited principles from the

Jewish tradition to justify its positions. Against this background, the representatives of the ultra-Orthodox Agudat Yisrael party told Beilin that they felt a more natural partnership with the Likud.

During the discussions, the Agudat Yisrael members referred the Labor Party's negotiators to their platform, which included a call for the separation of religion and state. Surprisingly, most of the negotiating team, including Peres, had never read this section of the platform. It turned out that Shlomo Hillel had composed this section of the platform on his own and none of the party's leaders had bothered to read it carefully. (Hillel actually hoped to strengthen the status of religion in Israel by severing it from politics.) The dissonance between the ultra-Orthodox worldview, which attributed supreme importance to the written word, and the Labor politicians' casual disdain for their own platform made it harder for Peres to persuade the ultra-Orthodox parties that his government's policy would not follow its platform.

On the contrary, even though Peres promised the ultra-Orthodox benefits and budget allocations the Likud did not dare to offer, it seems that the distinction Rabbi Elazar Shach made between Likud and Alignment members played, and continues to play, a central role in the ultra-Orthodox community's relations with the left. In his view, which represented the prevailing intuition in the ultra-Orthodox camp, Likud supporters possess an "innocent faith" in tradition, even if they do not strictly observe it, while leftists are hostile toward religion. Rabbi Shach was more inclined toward the Likud even though he supported the left's stance on issues of diplomacy (primarily to avoid "provoking" the world's nations) and even though it was clear to him that there was no significant difference in religiousness between the supporters of the two camps.[16] Of course, the fact that many of the Likud's voters were Mizrahi Jews, whose Zionism was grounded in an attachment to tradition, also played a part.

This distinction between the Likud's ostensibly deep ties to Judaism and the left's weak connection to Judaism also helps to explain how Ariel Sharon—whose worldview and lifestyle were far from traditional Judaism, and in many ways closer to the Canaanite movement[17]—was able to find paths to the hearts of ultra-Orthodox leaders during the coalition talks and persuade them not to join Peres, despite the far-reaching promises he offered.

However, as noted, the Likud was also unable to form a firm coalition; it only had enough power to block a left-leaning government. Thus, from this deadlock, the idea arose of creating a national unity government with Peres and Shamir taking turns as prime minister.

When Peres told Beilin about this possibility, Beilin found himself in a dilemma. In his view, a national unity government was a formula for paralysis. It meant that Israel would continue to be mired in a vague consensus that would not lead it on a new course. On the other hand, the plans of the "100 Days" team could be implemented, at least in part, only if Peres finally became prime minister. From a personal perspective, a unity government would also enable him to participate in the executive side of political life for the first time.

After the Likud agreed that Peres would serve first as prime minister—in part, because the Alignment won three seats more than the Likud—the Labor Party convened to approve the agreement. Beilin abstained, but after an overwhelming majority voted in favor of the arrangement, he joined Peres's preparation team for the new government.

The unity government was supported by a very broad coalition of 97 MKs. Rabin was appointed defense minister (and continued to serve in this position after Shamir took over from Peres under the rotation arrangement). Shamir became foreign minister and Yitzhak Moda'i was appointed finance minister. Besides the Likud and Labor Party, the coalition partners included the National Religious Party (NRP), Agudat Yisrael, Shas, Shinui, Moreshet led by Haim Druckman, Horowitz's Ometz faction, and Weizman's Yahad. In response to the formation of the unity government, Mapam quit the Alignment and was replaced by Yahad.

For Peres, the burning issues were stabilizing the economy, withdrawing from Lebanon, and finding a new formula for promoting the peace process. The Labor Party expected to enjoy an advantage in the government, which included twenty-five ministers, because the NRP's Yosef Burg was inclined toward its views on issues concerning defense and the economy. In order to offset this advantage, the Likud demanded the formation of a ten-person cabinet, divided evenly between the two major parties. Beilin regarded the cabinet as a mechanism designed to stymie the changes he planned to propose to Peres. But he was buoyed by the optimism of Peres, who promised to make the best of the situation.

## 3

Shimon Peres finally realized his great dream—but not fully. His term was limited to two years, and he was eager to squeeze as much as he could into that period. Cognizant of Beilin's disappointment in failing to win a Knesset seat, Peres offered Beilin the choice between two positions he described as influential: director-general of the Prime Minister's Office or cabinet secretary. He emphasized that these positions involve substantial media exposure, which would boost his political fortunes. Beilin chose the job of cabinet secretary, seeing it as an opportunity to influence government deliberations. He also saw the position as more *mamlachti*—more focused on issues of state. The fact that his predecessors, Dan Meridor and Arye Naor, rose to public prominence also influenced his decision. At this stage, it was already clear that his political career took precedence over his academic work. As a doctoral student, he had already begun teaching in the Department of Political Science, and he now turned down an offer of a postdoctoral fellowship at Harvard. Beilin saw himself as a representative of the new generation in politics, and one of his main goals as cabinet secretary was to effect a technical-methodological reform of the civil service. Indeed, during his period, it was decided to computerize the government bureaucracy.

Beilin was the senior member of the young group Peres assembled, which the media referred to as "the blazers" in reference to their well-tailored appearance (by Israeli standards—this did not mean elegant three-piece suits). The group included Amnon Neubach, Uri Savir, Israel Peleg, and Nimrod Novik. The "blazers" nickname was meant to be derisive, suggesting a non-Israeli style. In particular, it highlighted the stark difference between the current generation and the labor movement's founding fathers, whose modest dress expressed the Jews' return to manual labor and agriculture. Beilin, in any case, did not see "the blazers" as an insulting epithet. He was not raised in a home that identified with a particular party and was not committed to the trappings of the working class and its representatives. But he was also unaccustomed to dressing elegantly and began wearing suits upon the advice of his wife, Helena, perhaps influenced by her Revisionist home, which placed a greater emphasis on grandeur. She felt it was inappropriate for someone with a PhD to lecture at the university while dressed like a student. Beilin also brought this approach—which attributes importance to dress as an expression of professional status—to his public role. His only reservation was about wearing suits in the summer months. Most of "the blazers" decided to leave their suit jackets in the closet in July and August, but Beilin decided that summer or winter, it was never appropriate for the cabinet secretary to go around in a short-sleeved shirt.

One of Beilin's tasks was to formulate official announcements. One of the most dramatic of these concerned the Jonathan Pollard affair, involving an American Jew who spied in the United States for Israel (via the Lekem Bureau of Scientific Relations). His capture in November 1985 stirred an uproar in top Israeli circles, primarily due to concerns about damaging the alliance with the United States and harming the status of the American Jewish community. Peres asked Beilin to read a carefully worded public statement and Beilin did so, his eyes glued to the paper: "If the allegations are confirmed, those responsible will be brought to account, the unit involved in this activity will be completely and permanently dismantled. . . . Spying on the United States stands in total contradiction to our policy." This was the first time that Beilin stood alone in the international spotlight, though many of the newspapers, apparently due to the mix of espionage and international politics, chose to print a picture of Beilin reading the statement with the caption: "The head of the Israeli Shin Bet delivering a statement to the press."

In any case, the most critical issue facing the government was the IDF's entanglement in Lebanon. During the election campaign, Rabin had already proposed a plan for a partial withdrawal that included a buffer zone in southern Lebanon. The guidelines of the unity government also stated that it would endeavor to withdraw the IDF from Lebanon, while ensuring quiet for Israel's northern communities. As defense minister, Rabin initially proposed negotiating with Lebanon, and talks were held in the Lebanese town of Nakura. Israel sought to withdraw its forces and ensure security for northern Israel by establishing two buffer zones. The first would be based on South Lebanon Army (SLA) forces. The SLA was actually an Israeli-controlled militia manned primarily by Lebanese Christians, as well as local Druze and Shiite residents. The plan called for SLA forces to deploy in the area stretching from the international border to the Zahrani River. The second buffer zone would be based on UNIFIL forces and replace the IDF in the territory between the Zahrani River in the south and the Awali River in the north, and from the Mediterranean in the west to the Syrian border in the east.

The plan had many advantages for Israel, which sought to indirectly control southern Lebanon and provide security for northern Israel via an army of mercenaries—an approach with an imperial dimension, even if only on a small scale. But the complexity of the Lebanese state defeated Israel's aspirations. The government of Lebanon, under the influence and guidance of the Syrians, rejected Israel's proposals and, ironically, accused Israel of violating its sovereignty. Based on UN Security Council Resolution 425, the Lebanese demanded that their army, with UNIFIL's backing, receive exclusive control of the areas evacuated by the IDF, and that Israel withdraw from all of Lebanon's sovereign territory.

Consequently, the Israeli government had to present a different plan, based on a unilateral withdrawal to a single security zone in southern Lebanon in which the IDF and SLA would jointly operate. The plan was also the initial test of the government's ability to make decisions. It was approved on January 14, 1985, with the support of the Alignment ministers and the religious parties. Beilin was impressed with the determination of Housing Minister David Levy, who pressed for answers from security officials. In the end, Levy joined the Alignment ministers in voting for the withdrawal.

The security zone left about 10 percent of Lebanon's territory under Israel's control. About 150,000 people lived in this area, most of them Shiites. At this stage of planning, Israel believed that the Shiites, led by the Amal organization since the 1970s, would help keep PLO forces out of the area. This assessment lost its validity after Amal was eclipsed by the rise of a new Shiite organization, Hezbollah, established in 1982 and primarily backed by Iran. Thus, Israel found itself contending with an enemy that was more dangerous and radical than the PLO, and which enjoyed the support of many residents of the security zone.

This was another chapter in the long book of irony in the Middle East, because the Shiites had been regarded as friends of the Zionist movement in its early days. For this reason, when France and Britain drew the borders in the region following the First World War, and the Zionist movement submitted a map of the area it deemed essential for a national home, the demarcation of the northern border in close proximity to Shiite villages in southern Lebanon was not perceived as a source of concern. Ben-Gurion even asked to include part of southern Lebanon within the bounds of the national home because of the need for the sources of the Litani River.[18] The Sunnis in Lebanon were actually the source of concern, because of their hostility to the Zionist idea.[19]

Now, however, the situation was completely different.

In early 1985, when Rabin admitted in a Knesset discussion that "no one imagined there would be a Shiite problem," Yossi Sarid asked: "What are you saying? No one knew that there's a dynamic of occupation, which would also operate on Shiites and lead to expressions of resistance?"[20] But now it was already too late. Even after the partial withdrawal and redeployment in the security zone, the IDF continued to bleed in Lebanon. During the subsequent fifteen years, the IDF presence in Lebanon cost the lives of hundreds of people. Thousands were injured.

The IDF redeployed in the security zone in the summer of 1985. Though it was the least-bad option, Beilin felt frustrated with the way the decision was made. In his view, it epitomized the ills of the unity government, which derived from the constant need to please both sides, Labor and Likud. The vague wording of the government's decision to create the security zone was one of the reasons Israel remained there until the year 2000, according to Beilin. The government decision in 1985 did not specify the type of support the IDF would provide to the SLA, or the number of IDF forces in the security zone. The decision was formulated in a way that portrayed the security zone as a temporary need, limited in scope and duration, without deadlines. Beilin believed that in many ways the government adopted the same tactic that Sharon had used as defense minister during the Lebanon War. The lack of clarity was designed to manipulate the ministers while establishing facts on the ground. As cabinet secretary, his impression was that many ministers believed that the government had decided in principle that the IDF would withdraw to the international border, and that the security zone with the SLA was supposed to serve only as a temporary solution.[21] Withdrawal from Lebanon became almost a personal project for Beilin, even when it was far from the national consensus—a consensus that began to erode only after the helicopter crash in 1997 that claimed the lives of seventy-three soldiers en route to southern Lebanon.

4

The second central issue on the agenda was the economy. Like most of Israel's prime ministers —except for Eshkol and Netanyahu—Peres had little expertise in economics. However, he was a fast learner and the precarious condition of the Israeli economy required his urgent attention. In late 1984, the inflation rate was nearly 450 percent and continued to climb during the first half of 1985. Peres, who was responsible for erasing the word "socialism" from Labor's platform in 1968, sought to combat the economic crisis by promoting a process of liberalization. However, while aiming to adapt the Israeli economy to the Western market, Peres was still imbued with basic Zionist ideas such as favoring "blue and white" [Israeli] production. For example, when he entered office, he was convinced that the rampant inflation stemmed in part from excessive imports. He asked customs officials to prepare a list of imported products; after studying the list, he proposed blocking the import of water from South Africa and complained about other import products. However, Finance Ministry officials were able to persuade Peres that some of the imported products were vital for Israel's exports, and that it would be best to open the Israeli economy to external markets.

Beilin examined the situation from a different vantage point. Like his father, he had no sentiments for the labor movement's basic socialist principles, and from the outset was inclined toward an expansive liberal economic worldview. He was one of the leading proponents of the economic stabilization plan submitted in 1985, which charted Israel's future economic path. The plan also reflected a change in ideological approach among the elites and labor movement leaders on economic and social issues.

The main elements in the plan included a drastic cut in government spending, lowering real wages, boosting export competition, capping unemployment, freezing prices, a major devaluation, and exchange rate stabilization. Due to pressure from the Histadrut, the government refrained from instituting emergency regulations designed to trim the public sector; in exchange, the Histadrut agreed to wage erosion.

The plan continued a process the Begin government had initiated, designed to reduce state intervention in the economy and redistribute its revenues. The historian

Danny Gutwein traces the change in the labor movement's economic perspective to the fact that growth had become a primary objective in itself, rather than an instrument for achieving social objectives. The Begin government gave prominent expression to this trend, though the Labor Party had already begun to abandon socialist values in the 1960s. Moshe Dayan was one of the first party members to do so, publicly arguing that the values of the labor movement were not consistent with the privatization needs of a modern national economy.

Nonetheless, the economic plan presented by the unity government was a more significant milestone in Israel's economic path than the process initiated under Begin's government, which had to contend with opposition from the Histadrut and the Labor Party. The Peres government's plan was able to institute changes that were more systemic. Furthermore, in light of its success in stabilizing the economy, subsequent Israeli governments continued in the same direction and even accelerated the process. In the 1990s, again under a prime minister from the labor movement, Rabin this time, an economic regime of monetary policy and globalization of capital was introduced. With Netanyahu serving as finance minister in the Sharon government in 2003, this approach morphed into a policy of predatory neoliberal policy.

While the Peres government's plan received the consent of the Histadrut (without this consent, the government would have refrained from assisting it and the Histadrut's coffers would have continued to dwindle), and though it did not have a distinctly neoliberal character (this would develop only later, under Likud rule, Beilin emphasizes), the plan clearly signaled the path Israel had embarked upon.

The economy, indeed, began to quickly recover. However, along with the advantages of freeing the economy from government monopolies, the plan contributed to widening the disparities in society. It helped to create a capitalist economic system that was contrary to the labor movement's original vision. The irony is that the plan approved by the government was opposed by several Herut ministers. Thus, the right-wing party, which was ostensibly supposed to represent a liberal economic policy, strengthened its identification with poorer populations. At the same time, the socialist left became more closely tied to business tycoons.

Beilin prefers to emphasize the positive impact of the stabilization program. The plan—prepared by senior treasury officials with an academic team led by Prof. Michael Bruno, and instituted by Peres in collaboration with Finance Minister Yitzhak Moda'i, a member of the Likud's liberal faction—saved the Israeli economy from collapsing under outdated economic principles that would have left Israel lagging behind the countries of the West.

Indeed, the recovery plan was a clear success in the short term. Inflation plunged to 20 percent, the government's budget deficit was drastically reduced and the economy began to move toward growth. The decline in oil prices in the world market and a $1.5 billion assistance grant from the United States contributed to the plan's success. In fact, American economists (including Stanley Fischer, the future governor of the Bank of Israel) oversaw the implementation of the plan, in part because most of Israel's national debt was owed to the United States, which thus had a special interest in steering Israel toward a more capitalistic market.

5

Along with the economic and security issues, there was also the question of the peace process, which continued to be a primary concern of Peres and his cabinet secretary, who still served unofficially as his adviser. In the early days of the unity government, Beilin had already proposed that Peres make a dramatic move, something akin to Sadat's visit to Jerusalem: meet with Arafat.[22] Peres, who had already spoken with Beilin about the need to involve the PLO in the peace process, did not argue, but rejected the proposal for the same reason he had expressed in 1981: public opinion would not bear it. Therefore, unlike Sadat's trip to Israel, a meeting with Arafat would not have a positive impact, Peres contended.

Moreover, in 1986, during Peres's tenure as prime minister, the government and Knesset approved legislation (an amendment to the Prohibition of Terrorism Ordinance) prohibiting Israelis from meeting with representatives of terror organizations (that is, with PLO members). Peres justified the legislation by emphasizing the security risk entailed in such meetings and argued that contacts between Israelis and PLO members could hinder the peace policy he sought to promote: the Jordanian channel, which would make Jordan responsible for the fate of the Palestinians.

Although the PLO officially rejected Israel's existence and carried out acts of terrorism, the absurdity of the legislation was evident from the outset. One of those who recognized its problematic nature was Michael Eitan, a Likud MK, who sought to limit the prohibition on meetings with PLO members. Eitan noted that not every PLO member is a terrorist and wondered about the situation of a law-abiding Arab citizen of Israel whose relative was a PLO activist. Labor MK David Libai pointed out another problem: in the law's current format, an Israeli medic could not "come into contact with" a wounded PLO member, and a politician was forbidden from being interviewed in the same studio with a PLO representative.[23] The legislation was eventually revised to exclude family meetings and medical treatment. Beilin was also opposed to the legislation, and the fact that he knew Peres's real position on this subject again exposed him to the hypocrisy in the political arena. Labor MKs supported the legislation primarily to placate public opinion, which was then enraged over the murder of two teachers in Afula in an act of terrorism. Here a question arose that repeatedly resurfaced throughout the peace process: Should public opinion surveys be treated as expressing views that the leader must take into consideration, or as reflecting public moods that the leader can change by offering a different path? It is noteworthy, for example, that less than a decade after the law prohibiting meetings with the PLO was enacted with broad public support, over 60 percent of Israelis not only favored contacts with the PLO, but also an agreement with them, as expressed in the Oslo Accords.

In any case, Peres's goal was to circumvent the PLO and reach an accord through negotiations with Jordan on a confederative framework.

Indeed, during Peres's term as prime minister, contacts with King Hussein intensified. From the beginning of 1985 to April 1987, when the London Agreement was concluded, Peres and Hussein met at various places about every two months. Except for the first meeting, Beilin (in addition to Rabin and Shamir) was one of the few who were privy to the secret negotiations and he participated in most of the meetings. After Hussein came to the first meeting with the prime minister of Jordan, Peres chose to bring Beilin to the talks as "his adviser."

The meetings remained a secret and Beilin did not even share the information with his wife. The basic idea was to reach an agreement between Israel and Jordan—with the latter assuming responsibility for the territories, the Palestinians, and the holy sites—and to create a sort of confederation that would free Israel from administering the territories and from the demographic burden, without compelling it to relinquish its military presence along the Jordan River. The Jordanians believed that in light of the severe blow to the PLO's status, with its leadership languishing in exile in Tunisia, it would be possible to mobilize PLO support for a deal that would grant the Jordanians control over the West Bank.

The PLO was formed in 1964 by the Arab League to pursue independence for the Palestinians and as an instrument of the Arab states to contest the very existence of Israel. It was initially controlled by Egypt through Palestinian "notables" from "the generation of the Nakba." After the Six-Day War, however, Fatah became the dominant group in the PLO[24] and the organization's independent standing strengthened as the legitimate and principal representative of the Palestinians. This process occurred much to the chagrin of the leaders of Arab states.

Although the king's Hashemite regime pretended to support the PLO's ambitions, Jordan was fearful that an independent Palestinian state in the West Bank might undermine the kingdom's stability. Thus, Hussein sought to take advantage of the PLO's weakness in the wake of the Lebanon War to convince the organization to join in forming a confederation. Talks between Jordan and the PLO commenced in late 1982 and the two sides signed an agreement on February 11, 1985, that ensured the Palestinians' independent right of self-determination in the occupied territories, while forming a joint political entity and resolving the refugee problem via an international conference.[25] However, tactical disagreements over how to conduct the negotiations led to a rift between Jordan and Arafat. In a speech on February 19, 1986, Hussein announced a suspension of the agreement with the PLO. Consequently, he sought to fulfill the idea of a confederation through an agreement with Israel.

From Israel's perspective, a confederation was one of the basic ideas in Zionist history in regard to the Jewish state's relations with its neighbors. Ben-Gurion pursued the idea of an Arab–Jewish federation in the 1920s and early 1930s, envisioning Jewish settlement in the Land of Israel on both sides of the Jordan River as part of a national Jewish home within a federation of Arab states. This idea gained currency in the wake of the Arab riots of 1929, when the British government seemed poised to reassess its policy, limit Jewish immigration, and regulate the transfer of lands to Jews due to Arab opposition.[26] Ben-Gurion hoped the federation idea would help mitigate Arab fears of a Jewish majority. That is, if the Jews were part of an Arab–Jewish federation that stretched over a large territory, there would be no reason to restrict immigration and Jewish settlement, because in the expansive territory of the federation they would remain a minority, albeit an independent minority. Ben-Gurion conveyed a proposal in this spirit to Musa Alami, one of the representatives of the Higher Arab Committee and a leader of the Palestinian national movement, during talks they conducted in 1933 and 1934, and again in 1935 after Ben-Gurion became chairman of the Jewish Agency's executive committee.[27]

Ben-Gurion made a similar proposal in 1936 in conversations with George Antonious, who, like Alami, was a member of the Higher Arab Committee.[28] "I told him that I reject the assumption that the aspirations of the Jews and the Arabs are incompatible," Ben-Gurion wrote. He asserted:

> There is no necessary and unavoidable contradiction. . . . As a starting point, we should assume that the question is not between the Jews of the Land of Israel and the Arabs of the Land of Israel. In this limited territory, there is indeed a conflict that is difficult to overcome—unless we see the Jews as a global group and the Arabs as a global group. And I believe that there is no necessary contradiction between the national aspiration of the Jewish people and the national aspiration of the Arab nation.[29]

At this stage, we see that Ben-Gurion believed the struggle between Jews and Arabs over the limited territory of Palestine/Land of Israel could be resolved—but not through partition or by separating the two peoples. He proposed the opposite: enlarging the area earmarked for Jewish settlement, with the aim of including the Jewish national home within a broader political framework—an Arab–Jewish federation. After the Arab revolt began in 1936 and the Peel Commission published its recommendations the following year, Ben-Gurion shifted to supporting partition as a solution for the conflict.

In any case, in the mid-1980s, in light of the Israeli attempt to find a solution to the Palestinian question without agreeing to an actual Palestinian state, and with the failure of the negotiations between the PLO and Jordan, the different interests of Peres and King Hussein led them to support a similar solution for the territories: the formation of a confederation of Israel and Jordan, which would accord the Palestinians a state-like entity under Jordanian patronage.

Shamir and Rabin knew about the talks Peres held with Hussein, though they were not always updated immediately. Thus, one time Peres set out to meet Hussein on a Saturday, leaving Beilin behind as his contact person for urgent matters. Meanwhile, a suspicious ship was reported and Rabin called the prime minister's military secretary and then tried to reach Peres, but was referred to Beilin. "Where's Shimon?" Beilin can still remember Rabin asking in his dry, matter-of-fact voice. Beilin did not reveal Peres's whereabouts and asked Rabin why he was calling. Rabin explained, and because Beilin knew that it would be difficult to reach Peres in the short time required for a decision, he took it upon himself to call Rabin with the general message, which he had also heard from the military secretary, that the prime minister prefers to refrain from firing until all other options are exhausted. Beilin waited tensely until receiving word that it was a false alarm.

The conversations between Peres and Hussein moved forward. A meeting held in October 1985 produced the outlines of an agreement that included readiness for an international conference, joint control of the West Bank for an interim period, and an interim arrangement in Jerusalem that would include Jordanian control over Haram al-Sharif (the Temple Mount) and the flying of the Jordanian flag there. However, the two failed to conclude an accord due to disagreements on conference procedures and the composition of the Palestinian delegation: Would the Palestinian delegates be PLO officials or residents of the territories who are not PLO-affiliated? Would it be a joint delegation with the Jordanians, and if so, what would be the status of East Jerusalem Palestinians in this delegation?[30]

In February 1986, during talks between Jordan and Israel, Peres and Beilin met with Thomas Pickering, the US ambassador in Israel from 1985 to 1988, and asked for American help in improving the quality of life in the West Bank. The assistance was designed to reinforce the Palestinians' trust in a diplomatic solution. Israel and Jordan shared the assumption that the more the Palestinians' quality of life improved, the easier it would be to mobilize their support for an agreement. Indeed, according to the notes from the meeting, the Jordanian prime minister told the US ambassador in Amman that Jordan and Israel were interested in transferring additional municipal authorities to Palestinian moderates (with connections to Jordan) —but without exposing Jordan to accusations of collaboration with Israel. The Jordanian prime minister also asked for $50 million in American economic assistance for the West Bank.[31] His request was part of the effort to prepare the ground for a joint accord between Israel, Jordan, and the Palestinians; as noted, the assumption was that the likelihood of the Palestinians agreeing to an accord (that did not include an independent state led by the PLO) would increase as their situation in the territories improved.

# 6

Shamir was aware of the peacemaking efforts, but he was skeptical and his relations with Peres were characterized by ideological and personal suspicion. He was not the only Likud minister who harbored hostility toward Peres. Finance Minister Moda'i and Industry and Trade Minister Sharon also publicly lashed out against Peres.

Beilin thought that Peres should exploit these incidents to fire both Moda'i and Sharon, and thus precipitate the breakup of the unity government. He believed that in light of Peres's achievements as prime minister, the public would support him in elections and he would then be able to advance on the Jordanian track without the ball and chain that Shamir attached to his legs. But Peres rejected Beilin's suggestion. Only in April 1986, after Moda'i called him a "flighty prime minister" in a play on words referring to his frequent overseas travel and lofty dreams of peace, Peres decided to fire the finance minister. From the government's first day, the Likud feared that Peres would find an excuse for dismantling the government toward the end of his term and thus renege on his commitment to hand over the reins to Shamir in accordance with the rotation agreement. Therefore, Shamir agreed to demote Moda'i, sending him to the Justice Ministry and assigning the more prestigious Finance Ministry portfolio to the incumbent minister of justice, Moshe Nissim.

However, while Peres came under fire from some of the Likud ministers, the relations in the government were not all conducted on a partisan basis. Beilin's archive files reveal clashes, alliances, and cross-party understandings. For example, Deputy Prime Minister David Levy admitted, "Shimon Peres has made brilliant achievements." And prior to implementing the rotation agreement, which called for Peres to move to the Foreign Ministry, Levy advised him to stay away from economic issues. "What is he looking for in the economic arena? The economic situation is precarious. What will happen now? [If] he gets involved in economics, he'll clash with Nissim, and the two will bring the matter to Shamir. Why does he need this?"[32] Levy also showed surprising support for Beilin's idea of transferring the Gaza Strip to the autonomous control of the Palestinians, as an initial move in negotiations. After analyzing the expected reactions in the two parties, Levy concluded: "'Gaza First' is a good subject for both the Alignment and the Likud. You'll say that the Likud is blocking progress and that it will ease the demographic problem, and we'll say that it's the beginning of the end (even though the opposite is true)."[33] The views Beilin discovered in private conversations with Levy and others in the Likud convinced him that the chance of mobilizing public support for a peace initiative was higher than it seemed, and that there were also some people in the Likud who recognized the need to divide the land. Therefore, he continued to encourage Peres to jettison the rotation agreement and call for new elections. He was convinced that the public's appreciation of the withdrawal from Lebanon and the economic stabilization program would lead to victory. Beilin was not the only one. Many in the media and in the party urged Peres to make a bold move and dismantle the government. Roni Milo, who was considered a Shamir loyalist, already began thinking about the post-Shamir era in the Likud, taking for granted that Peres would defeat Shamir in early elections, thus ending the latter's political career. In a conversation documented by Beilin, Milo assessed the talents and chances of the Likud's leaders and did not rule out the possibility of competing himself against Peres. "Sharon—a disaster. Arens—weak. Levy is superior to both, but a demagogue. . . . If I run against Peres, I'll beat him. We have unworthy successors and an excellent young generation. If they [the old-timers] are the candidates, it would be better to go into opposition."[34] Peres, contrary to expectations, was determined to complete his term and honor the rotation agreement. In part, Peres was motivated by a desire to disprove his image as someone "untrustworthy"—an image that Rabin had helped to foster and which the Likud was glad to exploit. There was also another, more substantive reason: Peres believed he could still advance the agreements with Jordan as foreign minister and that prospects for peace would constitute a better reason for calling early elections than a confrontation with one minister or another.

Indeed, in October 1986, Peres fulfilled his part in the rotation agreement—became prime minister and Peres assumed the role of foreign minister.

## 7

As the end of Peres's term as prime minister approached, the question of Beilin's future arose because it was clear that Shamir would prefer to appoint a new cabinet secretary. Peres had already promised the job of director-general of the Foreign Ministry to Avraham (Avrasha) Tamir, who was currently serving as director-general of the Prime

Minister's Office. In part, Tamir was slated for the Foreign Ministry position because he was also in Shamir's good graces.

Peres thought it would be best to appoint Beilin as Israel's ambassador in Washington. Beilin was interested in this post, seeing it as an opportunity to stand at one of the central intersections of Israel and its principal ally. However, he fully understood that the role would place him directly subordinate to the prime minister and not only to the foreign minister; this was a cause of concern for Beilin. In any case, Shamir's consent was required. The incoming prime minister tersely responded that he would not oppose the appointment, but made it clear that he was not enthusiastic about the idea. Another difficulty was the need to obtain Rabin's consent. This requirement was part of the internal party understandings between Peres and Rabin vis-à-vis important appointments. The first discussion on this matter was conducted via notes exchanged between the two during a meeting.

Peres: "Yitzhak, in the situation that developed, I don't want to lose Yossi. I want to propose him for Washington. We'll have a loyal and reliable person there. What do you think?"

Rabin: "Yossi has outstanding skills. However, he's not the right candidate for Washington. But if you want him, do it."[35] Beilin was afraid he would fall between the cracks. He began thinking about returning to the academic world. He planned to accept an offer from the British publisher Weidenfeld to write a book on Israel's system of government, and was also considering applying for a position in the Department of Political Science at the Technion in Haifa. The more he thought about the relations between Peres and Shamir, the more convinced he was that he would not be appointed ambassador, and that this appointment would have trapped him in the thorny relations between the prime minister and foreign minister. He believed that if he devoted himself to the academic world, he could later return to politics from an independent status as a professor of political science.

In the end, Peres was again the one who charted Beilin's path. Though the position of director-general had been promised to Tamir, Peres decided to offer the job to Beilin, too. The solution Peres devised was to split the role of director-general into two: Beilin would serve as director-general for diplomatic affairs, while Tamir would be director-general for administration. In practice, Peres wanted to place Beilin in charge of the special channels he sought to develop in foreign relations, including negotiations with Jordan, while Tamir was slated to be involved in the official, open channels. Beilin accepted the offer and Peres sent a letter to the two directors-general stating that Beilin would effectively serve as deputy minister, while Tamir would be "No. 3" in the ministry. This situation naturally generated suspicions and friction between the two directors-general, but in time Tamir and Beilin learned to work with each other. Tamir, a strategic thinker, saw himself as a "public servant" and preferred to avoid power struggles as long as he was allowed to perform his work. Beilin was also "easy" in this respect. In any case, he was closer to Peres and thus knew to avoid battles of ego and prestige with Tamir.

One area on which Beilin chose to focus was South Africa. Beilin sought to cool the warm relations Israel had maintained with South Africa since the 1970s. His negative approach to the close ties with the apartheid state did not stem only from a moral imperative. Beilin never examined politics only through the eyes of morality. In the case of South Africa, his approach combined utilitarian and moral interests; according to Beilin, these interests are not mutually exclusive and often overlap. Already as cabinet secretary, he could not ignore the fact that one of the foundations of Israel's security outlook—the military and diplomatic relations with the apartheid regime—was losing its value because the Western world had begun in the late 1970s to boycott the white regime in South Africa. Beilin concluded that the damage caused by Israel's relations with South Africa outweighed the advantages.

The defense establishment presented calculations of its own: most of the countries of Africa would continue to be hostile to Israel in any case because of their dependence on Arab states. There was a large Jewish community in South Africa that prospered under the regime. (The Jewish population numbered 120,000 in the 1970s and most of them had a Zionist orientation.) Despite sporadic incidents of anti-Semitism, the philo-Semitic element in the Afrikaner culture, which accorded great weight to the Bible, the Holy Land, and "Christian Zionism," contributed to the solid status of Jews in South Africa. (Nonetheless, many Jews supported the struggle against apartheid, and about 50,000 Jews left the country because of interracial tension from the 1970s to the 1990s.) The Mossad's assessment was that Israel should continue its relations with the apartheid regime because the blacks would not be successful in their struggle. In short, it was difficult to lead a campaign against the ties with South Africa.

The question of relations with South Africa was connected to a broader issue—Israel's relations with the states of Africa since the late 1950s. Though it would be correct to describe Israel's relations with white South Africa as a dismal and gloomy chapter in the chronicles of Zionism—in part, against the background of the frequent comparison between the Israeli occupation and the apartheid regime—this view overlooks the complexity of the Zionist story. More precisely, Israel-South Africa relations are a good example of the deterioration of the Zionist dream from utopia to tragedy. Zionism is partly to blame, but not entirely. Therefore, a short historical background may help in understanding the events.

In 1982, during a Knesset debate on the Lebanon War, Begin sang the praises of Zionism and noted that one of the original goals of the Jewish fight for equality was to serve as an inspiration for the blacks in Africa. What sounded like typical Beginist hyperbole actually echoed what Herzl wrote in his utopian novel *Altneuland*, where he addressed the connection between Zionism as a national liberation movement and the emancipatory aspirations of the peoples of Africa, who sought to free themselves from the yoke of European colonialism. In this context, Herzl described a visit to the laboratory of the bacteriologist, Professor Steineck. The professor said that after helping to make the wilderness bloom in the Land of Israel, he turned to the next project: developing Africa. Contrary to the colonial attitudes of that period, shared even by writers considered enlightened, Herzl's hero emphasized that the development of Africa would not only be in the hands of the white man; the blacks themselves would be involved:

> There is still one problem of racial misfortune unsolved. The depths of that problem, in all their horror, only a Jew can fathom. I mean the Negro problem. . . . Think

of the hair-raising horrors of the slave trade. Human beings, because their skins are black, are stolen, carried off, and sold. Their descendants grow up in alien surroundings despised and hated because their skin is differently pigmented. I am not ashamed to say, though I be thought ridiculous, now that I have lived to see the restoration of the Jews, I should like to pave the way for the restoration of the Negroes.[36]

During the pre-state period, Ben-Gurion also tried to draw a parallel between the Jews' emancipatory struggle and the liberation struggle of blacks and Third World nations. He declared that Zionism was a standard-bearer of the fight against colonialism, not only in Palestine, but also in Africa and the Far East. In 1930, he participated in a "Workers of the British Empire" conference held in London and attended by socialist movements from Africa, Palestine, India, Ireland, and other lands under the rule of the British Empire. The conference was convened as a show of support for the Labor government—with the hope that it would back the aspirations of national liberation movements.[37]

Against this background, it is no wonder that starting in the 1950s, the State of Israel developed warm relations with the states of Africa and shared expertise with them, primarily in the fields of industry, health, and agriculture.

Of course, this approach also included utilitarian calculations: Israel sought close ties with Africa as a way to extract itself from its isolation in a hostile Middle East. In the late 1950s, as Israel found itself without a significant strategic ally (Charles de Gaulle cooled France's relations with Israel and the US-Israeli partnership had yet to blossom), Ben-Gurion initiated an "Alliance of the Periphery." Israel forged closer relations with Ethiopia, Turkey, and the Kurds, and Mossad agents, led by Michael Harari, were dispatched to African states to establish ties.[38] Foreign Minister Golda Meir played a key role in this project, and in her autobiography, *My Life*, she devoted a chapter to "African and Other Friendships" and vowed never to visit South Africa as long as apartheid continued.

It should be noted that the writings of Zionist leaders about Africa are colored with an Orientalist hue, and Israel's activity in Africa in the 1950s can be read as part of the postcolonial discourse. Ben-Gurion largely regarded these states as backward places that had nothing to teach Israel and could only learn from Israel's Western ways. Meir usually described her meetings in Africa in exotic colors. In general, it can be said that Israelis, who as Jews in Europe were seen as blacks, felt like enlightened white people who came to free the blacks on behalf of Western values. Nonetheless, as a young country, Israel backed the struggle of weak states in Africa for liberation and prosperity, and refrained from relations with South Africa—at a time when leading Western countries still maintained good relations with it. In 1961, Israel unhesitatingly supported sanctions against South Africa, and it was one of the few nations to recognize Biafra as an independent state. The tragedy that occurred there touched the hearts of Israelis and the word "Biafra" became part of Israeli slang for decades.

The question then arises: How did Israel become the friend of the apartheid regime since the 1970s? How did it happen that Israel grew so close to South Africa that in 1986 it was the only Western country that did not join in imposing sanctions on it?

It is tempting to suggest the Six-Day War as the turning point. But in this complex story, the occupation is not the reason. Among the range of reasons, it was actually the war that Israel refrained from initiating, the Yom Kippur War, that led most of the states of Eastern Europe and Africa to sever their relations with Israel. These states bowed to Arab pressure and the embargo that sent oil prices skyrocketing.

After that war in 1973, Israel was isolated in the international arena, and was thus pushed into deepening its ties with South Africa. This does not absolve Israel of the moral stain, but the historical truth requires stating that Israel never willingly backed apartheid, and it was far from being entirely a villain in this complex story.

Nonetheless, when Beilin and others sought to cut off relations, or at least drastically chill them, it is hard to say that the Israeli establishment responded nobly. Among the leading trio in Israel in those years (Peres, Rabin, and Shamir), it was Rabin, like many others in the defense establishment, who was the strongest opponent of Beilin's proposals. The defense minister examined the situation from a strategic viewpoint, without moral considerations, and thus saw enormous importance in maintaining relations with South Africa, which were lucrative for Israel's military industries. Rabin argued that most of the African states were hostile toward Israel in any case, and that this attitude would not change due to their connection with the Arab world. He also cited the Mossad's assessment that the whites would not relinquish the reins of power in South Africa, because that would mean their demise.

Beilin, who began working on this issue as cabinet secretary, and stepped up his efforts as director-general of the Foreign Ministry, did not give up. He asked David Kimche, a top Mossad official who had served as director-general of the Foreign Ministry under Shamir, to prepare a memo on the advantages and disadvantages of the alliance with South Africa.

On March 7, 1986, Kimche sent the document, which stated that Israel's relations with South Africa have six components:

> Diplomatic: the nature of the relations between the two states and their impact
>     on our relations with other states;
> Image: the effect of the relations on Israel's image in the world;
> Economic: the economic benefits the relations provide us;
> Security (secret, not cited);
> Moral: the significance of relations with a racist regime from the perspective of
>     our values;
> Jewish: the implications of the relations on the status of the Jewish community in
>     South Africa, and the essence of the ties between it [the South African Jewish
>     community] and Israel.

The document ended with the conclusion that "a reassessment is suggested in light of all the considerations."[39] Although Kimche's memo did not recommend severing relations, it marked the beginning of the process in which the Israeli establishment recognized that the subject required reexamination.

In July 1986, Beilin invited a group of twenty South African opponents of apartheid to tour Israel. The delegation included public and media figures, and scientists. The tour was aimed at presenting the social-cultural face of Israel so that it would not only be seen in the context of its ties with the apartheid regime, and also to promote relations with anti-apartheid forces in South Africa.

Beilin's independent activities—in relation to South Africa and in other areas—angered Rabin, who was quoted in the press as describing Beilin as "a lowly bureaucrat" who should learn his place. A note Peres passed to Rabin during a government meeting on February 1, 1987, illustrates the Peres-Rabin conflict in an entertaining way:

> Peres: "Yitzhak, I saw in the newspaper that you called Yossi 'a lowly bureaucrat.'
> I don't believe that you used such a phrase, and I'd like to tell that to Yossi."
> Rabin: "It was all in the cabinet [meeting]. I used the word 'bureaucrat.' An
> expression of a civil servant as opposed to a ministerial decision. I didn't use
> the expression 'lowly bureaucrat.'"[40]

The struggle to revise Israel's policy toward South Africa culminated in a victory of morality—a decision to cut ties with the apartheid regime. In March 1987, Israel admitted that it had violated the UN sanctions policy in its relations with South Africa and announced that it would not renew its defense contracts with the apartheid regime. The Foreign Ministry formed a committee on sanctions against South Africa and the committee decided on twelve sanctions, mainly pertaining to culture and trade. Beilin says in retrospect that the moral consideration was not the deciding factor on this issue, and that a stronger political-diplomatic interest tipped the scales: after the US Congress mandated that the president report twice a year on the relations of various countries with South Africa, Israel feared that the reports on its ties with South Africa would adversely affect its standing in Congress. At this stage, both Peres (who had not prevented Beilin from acting independently, but was reluctant to lend his support) and Rabin agreed that Israel should join the right side of history.

Shamir's position on this issue is noteworthy. Compared to the views of the Labor leadership, Shamir's stance was closer to that of Beilin. Like many former Lehi members, Shamir, as one of the organization's three leaders, based the Zionist struggle against the British not only on the needs of the modern Jewish national movement, but also on opposition to imperialism. Therefore, he was inclined to identify with the blacks' fight for national liberation.

## 8

During his term as prime minister, Peres permitted—with the knowledge of Rabin and Shamir—Shin Bet officials to conduct talks on humanitarian issues with mid-level PLO activists. But he was not ready to expand the talks into an official diplomatic channel between Israel and the PLO.[41] In any case, after Israel's air force bombed the PLO's headquarters in Tunis in October 1985, the humanitarian channel also closed. The main objective was to advance "the Jordanian option" with King Hussein, and Beilin enthusiastically supported this.

After moving to the Foreign Ministry, Peres and Beilin continued the secret talks with the king. The conversations were generally held in London, and sometimes at the magnificent country home of Lord Victor Mishcon, one of the leaders of London's Jewish community and a mover and shaker in the Labor Party. (Mishcon's daughter was a classmate of the king's sister in London, and the two men met through this connection and developed a friendship.) The meetings covered a variety of topics, ranging from theoretical thoughts on the future of the Middle East to concrete discussions on the amount of money permissible to transfer via the Allenby Bridge. Security was provided by Shin Bet operatives, who maintained a low profile. Only one meeting was held in Israel—on a Friday afternoon, on the route between Eilat and Taba. The army prepared a caravan and large generator, and an army cook prepared dinner. The Israeli navy received a directive to stop radar tracking to ensure that the king's arrival would go undetected and remain secret. Hussein personally sailed his yacht to the port of Eilat. After climbing down the narrow ladder to the dock, he saw several unfamiliar Israeli agents waiting for him. Then he spotted Beilin and he fell into the latter's arms with a sort of sigh of relief, reflecting the momentary anxiety he had experienced. Beilin accompanied him to the caravan, where Peres and Rabin were awaiting him.

As the talks progressed, Peres and Beilin were also joined by Efraim Halevy, a senior Mossad official. Halevy served as the representative of the prime minister, who feared that Peres would conclude agreements without his knowledge. Another Mossad official, Nahum Admoni, also occasionally joined the talks. On April 11, 1987, a crucial meeting was scheduled in London. Beilin and Halevy made plans to arrive together. Halevy drove and Beilin sat in the passenger's seat. They were running a bit late, so Halevy pressed hard on the gas pedal. They were pulled over by a British police officer for speeding, and Beilin was impressed by the skills of subterfuge Halevy had acquired during his Mossad service. One way or another, the police officer sent them on their way, and they managed to arrive at the meeting on time. Jordan's prime minister, Zaid al-Rifai, also attended this meeting. Peres suggested summarizing their understandings in writing and the king agreed.[42] Beilin wrote the document, according to Peres's instructions and with Halevy and Lord Mishcon helping to refine the wording.

The text of the document was terse and mainly addressed the anticipated negotiations. It stated that both sides had agreed to the convening of an international conference, to be scheduled by the UN secretary-general. Participants in the conference would include the Arab states involved in the conflict (except Iraq), the five permanent members of the UN Security Council, an Israeli delegation, and a Jordanian-Palestinian delegation whose members would be required to accept UN Resolutions 242 and 338—that is, recognition of Israel and acceptance of the land-for-peace formula. The document also stipulated that members of the Jordanian-Palestinian delegation would be required to renounce terrorism and that any accord would include recognition of the "legitimate rights" of the Palestinian people. It was agreed that the international conference would be a sort of festive umbrella leading to direct talks between the sides, without imposing any agreement unacceptable to one of the sides. That was Peres's principal achievement in the negotiation, because it eliminated the threat the Likud identified in an international conference—that it would push Israel into a corner as the recalcitrant party that was resisting the unanimous demands of the other participants.[43] The document did not mention the participation of PLO members in the Jordanian-Palestinian delegation, and thus left an opening for their participation. (The conditions the Palestinian members of the delegation were required to meet later became the conditions Israel presented to the PLO prior to signing the Oslo Accords. That is, the Palestinians were required to renounce terror and recognize Israel in exchange for Israel's readiness to recognize their legitimate rights.) The document was not signed because Peres was unauthorized to do so without government approval. But the king wanted to add an official dimension to it and asked Beilin to write at the bottom: "London, April 11, 1987." The document, which became known as the "London Agreement," stated in the final paragraph that it would be submitted to the Americans so that they could officially present it to the stakeholders and thus make it more binding.

Peres and Beilin were excited. The agreement was intended to pave the way for a confederation that was consistent with the basic Zionist aspiration to live in security as an integral part of the region and would resolve the question of the occupied territories. Peres had no doubt: It was the most important agreement in the history of Zionism since the Biltmore Conference in 1942, when the Zionist demand for a "Jewish commonwealth" in the Land of Israel was presented in public for the first time.[44] From a political perspective, the constructive ambiguity of the London Agreement was an advantage. True, Peres could have anticipated that Shamir would object to the international conference envisioned in the document. However, on the other hand, the London Agreement explicitly stated that the negotiation itself would be conducted directly between the sides, and that the conference would only open the negotiation and would not impose decisions. The fact that members of the Palestinian delegation would be required to accept Resolution 242 at a time when the PLO had yet to recognize Israel, served Peres as proof that the PLO would be excluded from the process or that it would become a changed organization. Most important of all was the triangular structure. Since Israel was slated to negotiate with a Jordanian-Palestinian delegation, and not with the Palestinians alone, the solution was designed to be confederative and would not compel the IDF to retreat from the Jordan River. Beilin and Peres believed it would be possible to obtain Shamir's consent, and Beilin expected at least a few Likud ministers to lend their support, including Moshe Nissim and David Levy.

Upon returning to Israel, Peres decided to update Shamir in a one-on-one meeting, and sent Beilin to personally brief the American ambassador. Ambassador Pickering gave his support in principle, calling the document an "achievement." He also asked to immediately inform the secretary of state, George Shultz, who was in Helsinki at the time, busy preparing for a meeting with Mikhail Gorbachev. Beilin was concerned about a "broken telephone" and, after consulting with Peres, decided to fly urgently to Helsinki, where he met Shultz's senior adviser, Charles Hill.

Hill was less enthusiastic than Pickering—not because of the content of the London Agreement, but because of how it was achieved: he felt there was a "problematic" element in the fact that Prime Minister Shamir had not been involved in the agreement reached between Peres and Hussein.[45] Nonetheless, his assessment was that Shultz would agree to promote the agreement. Hill also advised against updating the Russians in the meantime and asked for time to make preparations. Shultz has a completely different recollection. In his memoirs, he wrote that when Beilin met with him on Peres's behalf and reported a "historic breakthrough," he was taken aback by the way the two had operated behind Shamir's back. Beilin says that he never met with Shultz in Helsinki and that the latter was referring to what he heard from Hill. Indeed, there is no record of a meeting with Shultz in Beilin's archives.

In any case, the message was conveyed to the Americans that although the agreement was not signed, it had been concluded with a handshake, and the two sides wanted the UN secretary-general to convene an international conference. Shultz wrote in his memories that he understood that in Peres's view, the matter "is in your hands"— that it was now the responsibility of the United States to advance the agreement and that Peres wanted the secretary of state to come to Israel to present the plan to the government as a US-backed initiative. The idea of marketing the agreement as an American initiative was a ploy intended to weaken the anticipated opposition in Jordan and in Israel. Beilin returned to Israel with the feeling that he had received a green light from the Americans.

As noted, Peres met with Shamir immediately upon returning from London. In their one-on-one meeting, Peres gave Shamir a detailed and forthright report on the London Agreement, and tried to convince the prime minister of its advantages. The foreign minister emphasized that Hussein was taking responsibility for the Palestinian issue, that the international conference would not be able to impose anything on Israel, and that the negotiations would be conducted directly between the sides. He added that Hussein needed the international conference to receive legitimacy for establishing relations with Israel later on. Shamir expressed some reservations, but did not respond unequivocally. He asked Peres to leave him the document so he could study it and give it more thought. Peres refused to leave the document with Shamir; he would only agree to read it to him. He explained that in any case it was unsigned, and he was afraid of leaks. But this approach only reinforced the suspicion and rancor Shamir already felt toward his foreign minister.

In the following days, things continued to go awry for Peres and Beilin: Shultz chose to clarify the situation in a direct conversation with Shamir, who asked him for some time to mull it over. Shultz, as noted, suspected that the activity of Peres and Beilin was not in line with the prime minister's aspirations, and did not want to come to the region and promote the London Agreement before confirming that the Israeli government was united behind it. Indeed, before Shamir spoke again with Shultz, his cabinet secretary, Elyakim Rubinstein, telephoned Shultz and told him that the prime minister refrained from saying this directly out of respect for the secretary of state, but the agreement was unacceptable to him, so it would be best if Shultz did not come to the region to promote it.[46] In consultation with Hill (who says that he, too, suspected from the outset that Peres and Beilin were trying to force the agreement on Shamir), the secretary of state said he felt an uncomfortable sense of "dishonesty" about the conduct surrounding the agreement. Despite the positive aspects that Shultz and Hill identified in the agreement, they believed it was a nonstarter as long as it was opposed by the prime minister of Israel. In the prevailing state of affairs, the London Agreement expressed academic aspirations that lacked political backing.[47]

In retrospect, Beilin still finds Shultz's conduct difficult to understand. Like Peres, Beilin believed that the objective was much more important than the means and methods used to reach it. In any case, as soon as Shamir was informed, everything was above board, Beilin argues. He feels that the Americans should have pressured Shamir to advance the document, whose great achievement was in winning the king's consent.

There is no doubt that Shultz was angry. This was evident in an interview with his adviser three decades later. Assuming that the content of the London Agreement was worthy in the eyes of the Americans, the question is why they chose to act as they did. One theory is that Shultz had already lost his faith in Peres in the wake of the Iran-Contra affair in 1986: Peres had failed to directly inform Shultz about the affair, thus placing the secretary of state in an embarrassing situation. (Peres claimed that he was sure that Shultz had been updated by the relevant entities in the US administration.)[48]

In any case, this was not the reason that Shamir rejected the London Agreement. Shamir believed that the agreement was designed to allow PLO officials into the joint Jordanian-Palestinian delegation without stating this explicitly. He also feared that participating in the international conference would harm Israel because even if the agreement formally recognized Israel's right to oppose proposals that were inconsistent with its needs, concerted international pressure would make it difficult for Israel to resist such proposals. Peres argued that the prerequisite for inclusion in the Jordanian-Palestinian delegation—acceptance of Resolution 242—slammed the door in the face of the PLO. But Shamir, who once stated himself that "for the sake of the Land of Israel, it is permissible to lie," was afraid that PLO activists would pay lip service to qualify for inclusion in the delegation and thus win de facto acceptance.

Shamir's fear was not baseless. The prime minister of Jordan himself argued that the agreement was designed to include the PLO—if it renounced terror and recognized 242.[49] Shamir also thought there was no cause for Peres's urgency to achieve an accord. In his view (which included a mix of Jabotinsky's "Iron Wall" and an "Eastern" perception of time), it would be several decades before Israel could reach an accord with the Palestinians and, in the meantime, Zionism would continue to thrive. Shamir believed it would only be possible for Israel to reach an accord with a new generation of Palestinians in the territories, who recognize Israel's existence and are prepared for a more comfortable compromise.

Unbeknownst to Peres and Beilin, Shamir dispatched Moshe Arens (then serving as a minister without portfolio) to the United States to convince the administration of the dangers of the London Agreement, and to emphasize that Israel under Shamir's leadership would not adopt it. Shamir sent a document to the secretary of state with nineteen points, expressing his fundamental objections. He argued that the agreement would pave the way for recognition of the PLO because it mentions "sides" and not states. In addition, Shamir claimed that in light of the views of the states and sides slated to participate in the conference, it would undoubtedly culminate in an effort to force Israel to recognize the PLO and retreat to the pre-1967 lines. He also decried the fact that the Soviet Union's involvement in the process was not conditioned upon opening its gates to Jewish emigration.[50] Shamir proposed sticking with the original plan of administrative autonomy for the Palestinians as outlined in the Camp David Accords.

In parallel to this argumentation vis-à-vis the US administration, the Likud and Labor waged a battle for public opinion in Israel. The Likud often briefed the press on the circuitous means Peres was using to promote the agreement behind the prime minister's back. Shamir explained that it was not merely a question of Peres's character flaws: the foreign minister's conduct violated the "rules of the game" necessary for the sound operation of the political system. This accusation was a blow to the soft underbelly of Peres, who already had the image of an untrustworthy politician. (To Peres's disappointment, even Shulamit Aloni publicly questioned how he had dared to act in this way.)[51] The Labor Party, as part of its efforts to mobilize public support for the London Agreement, leaked the text to the *Maariv* daily in September 1987 and emphasized its historic potential. Based on private conversations they conducted, Peres and Beilin believed that some Likud ministers would support the agreement, but this did not happen. Levy and Nissim, who were expected to back the agreement, also lined up against it.

Was Shamir correct in claiming that Peres was helping to usher the PLO into the process? A meeting that Peres and Beilin held on July 30, 1986 (before the talks with King Hussein produced an agreement), with Vice President George H. W. Bush and Ambassador Pickering indicates otherwise. Although Peres had privately shared with Beilin his belief that Israel should engage in dialogue with the PLO, Peres maintained the official Israeli position on this subject in diplomatic talks.

During the meeting with Bush, the vice president wondered about Peres's vision and asked directly: "Are you willing to return all of the West Bank?"

Peres: "I don't know. Any solution has to be gradual."

Bush asked about the confederation initiative and Peres explained why a Jordanian-Palestinian delegation was preferable to direct negotiation between Israel and the PLO:

> The choice is between Hussein and Arafat. . . . King Hassan [also] asked me what we have against the PLO. "It's weak, divided, conflicted, and if you invite them, they'll disappear." I told him frankly: "If we invite them, it will be a stab in the back to King Hussein. It will sink him like a stone." There are so many Palestinians in Jordan. Dual loyalty can be detected among them. If we lift up Arafat—we'll destroy the king. Whoever brings Arafat—will bring the Soviet Union to the Jordan River.[52]

The conversation with Bush indicates the lack of any substantial difference between Peres and Shamir concerning the PLO's participation in the process and the desire to retain the Jordan River as Israel's eastern border. This fact supports the premise that the missed opportunity of the London Agreement resulted from Shamir's exaggerated suspicion of Peres and the prime minister's historical shortsightedness.

Beilin's archives also may indicate that Shamir's fear of the Arab world uniting at the international conference to demand Israel's full withdrawal from the territories captured in 1967 did not take into account their different interests and the aversion that Arab leaders felt for each other. This is evident, for example, in the transcript of a conversation that Peres and Beilin conducted with top Egyptian government officials in April 1986. Egyptian President Hosni Mubarak expressed his antipathy toward the Alawi regime in Syria. He advised Israel not to fall under the illusion that it could return the Golan Heights to Hafez Assad in exchange for a peace accord. Syria's basic interest, he argued, was to maintain the status quo vis-à-vis Israel— neither war nor peace. According to Mubarak, hostility toward Israel helped Assad to secure the legitimacy of his minority Alawi regime. Indeed, the Egyptian president emphasized, the return of the Golan and a peace accord with Israel would undermine Assad's justification for heavily investing in his security forces. The transcript of the meeting states:

> When Syria was mentioned in the course of the conversation, Mubarak commented: "Nothing will come of the Syrians. The Syrians are opposed to the peace process. If they leave Lebanon and their forces return to Damascus, the Alawi regime will be in trouble. It will be the end of the Alawi regime. For this reason, they also don't want the Golan. I told Sharon once: Offer them the Golan under the condition that it is demilitarized, and you'll see that even then they'll refuse."[53]

Of course, today it is ironic to read the remarks of Mubarak, who was deposed by his people in the Arab Spring in 2011. But perhaps he was right in his diagnosis of Syria.

In any case, in light of Shamir's opposition, Peres had to decide what to do next. Beilin pressed him to submit the agreement to a vote by the government, knowing full well that it would not be approved. The idea was to expose the advantages of the agreement and the Likud's insistence on scuttling the opportunity. Peres should then resign, Beilin advised, and go to elections that would be a sort of referendum on the London Agreement. Labor ministers Moshe Shahal and Rafi Edri backed this approach, but Peres decided there was no point in putting the agreement to a vote. He argued that in the absence of a majority in the government, the result would be an official rejection of "the Jordanian option" for generations. Beilin was disappointed.

Beilin does not remember if during the April meeting in London, when the agreement was put into writing, Peres led King Hussein to believe that he would resign if the agreement was rejected by Israel's government. Since the meeting was not documented, it is impossible to verify whether Peres made this promise. Either way, it soon became clear that Hussein was angry about Peres's inability to deliver the goods, and their relationship soured.

If there was still a change to revive the agreement by resigning from the government and going to new elections, Rabin came and tipped the scales against this move. He argued that resigning from the government would only help the Likud accelerate Jewish settlement in the territories and would not necessarily lead to implementation of the agreement, because there was no guarantee that Labor would win the elections. In the meantime, the PLO also declared its opposition to the agreement, and King Hussein officially announced that he was abandoning the process.

For Beilin, the rejection of the London Agreement was a mistake and a missed opportunity that could have changed the course of history. Moreover, in his view, the decision to refrain from breaking up the government was disastrous: the Labor

Party lost its unique political identity that might have propelled it to victory if the next elections, indeed, revolved around the agreement.

In broad perspective, one of the repercussions of thwarting the agreement was the outbreak of the first intifada—the popular Palestinian uprising that erupted in the territories in December 1987, and for which no one in Israel was prepared. Shamir saw the intifada as another chapter in the Arabs' hostility toward the Zionist enterprise and refused to recognize it as a Palestinian struggle for national liberation. Rabin, Shamir's defense minister, had a more complex view of the uprising, but the fact that he sought to suppress it with force, blurred the differences between the Likud and Labor in the general public. Beilin's fears about Labor's loss of an alternative political identity were realized in the 1988 elections. Although the Likud's victory was slim (forty to thirty-nine seats), and it again formed a unity government with Labor, the election results did not allow the Labor Party to demand a rotation arrangement this time.

Three decades later, against the background of the impasse in relations between Israel and the Palestinians, the potential of the agreement concluded between Hussein and Peres shines bright. Like the London accords of 1934 between Jabotinsky and Ben-Gurion, which aimed to mediate between the Revisionists and the workers' camp, the London Agreement of 1987 was never implemented. The agreements in the 1930s could have changed the course of internal Zionist history, while the agreement in the 1980s nearly triggered a watershed in Israel's external relations. However, it is instructive to look back at the London Agreement not only to lament what could have been. In many ways, the seeds of a future, ideal solution can still be found in the agreement.

The underlying idea was brilliant: instead of squabbling over the partitioning of the land into two states, the area of dispute could be expanded eastward to create a federation of three separate states connected by some sort of joint system of rule. In the distant, but foreseeable future, when the national movements become less salient, a confederation will be seen as a simple and natural solution for resolving everyday disputes: the Palestinians will have a state whose security also depends on Israel's military power; Jerusalem will be a shared capital de facto; some of the Jewish settlements will be able to remain in the territories; the Palestinian refugees will be permitted to return to Palestine if they so choose; and Jordan's fears of a Palestinian state undermining its regime will be mitigated. Everyone will share a mutual commitment and responsibility.

# 9

On December 8, 1987, four residents of the Jabalya refugee camp in the Gaza Strip were killed when an Israeli truck crashed into their car in the northern part of the Strip, and rumors circulated that the collision was deliberate. The next day, their funeral procession turned into a large-scale demonstration against Israel. In the following days, similar demonstrations took place throughout the Gaza Strip and West Bank, and the popular uprising was soon labeled the *intifada* (an Arabic term for insurrection or "shaking off"). It took the Israeli establishment some time to realize that this unrest was a national revolt that would not be short-lived. Two decades had passed since the Six-Day War, and only now the full extent of the curse of victory became apparent.

The intifada was not a sudden event; it was the climax of a process that had been brewing in Palestinian society for years. This process was fueled in part by the spread of higher education in the territories, which brought national aspirations to the fore. This combined with growing religious fervor to create a volatile mix of religion and nationalism in the Palestinians' demand for independence. In March 1987, the first poster signed by "the Hamas organization" appeared in Gaza, calling for a war on drugs.[54] Hamas subsequently broadened its activity from strictly religious matters to social-community activities and its influence grew. Unlike previous Palestinian struggles, the intifada was the first Palestinian battle led by the generation that grew up in the post-1967 era. On the one hand, the frustrating Israeli occupation was the only reality they knew. On the other hand, they were familiar with the Israeli system and were no longer fearful of the Zionists.

The intifada took Israelis by surprise, and there was a reason for this. On the surface, the 1970s and 1980s were largely a golden age for Palestinian-Israeli relations. For example, both peoples could travel freely and relatively safely throughout the Land of Israel/Palestine. Although the economic ties between the two sides were based primarily on Palestinians performing manual labor for Israelis inside the Green Line (in construction and services), and thus were of a postcolonial nature, the interaction helped both economies—Israeli and Palestinian. And despite occasional attacks by Palestinians against Israelis, they were mainly the word of PLO militants who infiltrated into Israel from outside the territories. In parallel, the attacks conducted by the "Jewish Underground" against Palestinians in the territories in the early 1980s were seen in Israeli society as sharply deviating from the norm. Perhaps Dr. Raef Zreik is correct in advocating a "state of all its citizens" as the best solution. According to this prognosis, the Palestinians made a historic mistake in launching the first intifada: if that uprising had not occurred, the shared fabric that had developed may have naturally led to a blurring of borders and evolved into a format of a single state.[55]

In any case, the intifada did not only erupt because of the aspirations of Palestinian residents of the territories for independence and fulfillment of their national rights. They also sought to liberate themselves from the PLO, whose exiled leaders had lost their hold on the ground over the years. The intifada was led by local committees and expressed a feeling that the Arab world had treated the Palestinians like pawns. Palestinians in the territories painfully watched the internecine warfare among the various factions in Lebanon and noted Syria's role in stoking these rivalries. By September 11, 1987, when the battles ended in Lebanon's civil war, over 3,000 Palestinians had been killed during two and a half years of fighting. These events, together with the collapse of the London Agreement and failure to implement the autonomy promised in the Israeli-Egyptian peace accord, led the Palestinians in the territories to conclude that they must look after their interests on their own.

But many Israelis were blind to these feelings and developments in Palestinian society. They had grown accustomed to a sense of superiority over the Palestinians and found it hard to understand how those submissive laborers were daring to rebel. When the intifada erupted, Rabin was on a visit to the United States. At first, he refused to cut short the visit and was photographed playing tennis to express his confidence that the violent demonstrations would be quickly suppressed. One of his directives was to equip IDF soldiers with clubs and to refrain from using firearms. During the initial months of the intifada, the public discourse in most of the popular media centered on the question of how much force Israel should exercise. Right-wingers argued that a more crushing and rapid response could have nipped the uprising in the bud. But this assessment proved wrong—harsher Israeli measures only further inflamed the situation, and the intifada developed into a national struggle characterized by low-level violence (primarily rocks, and no firearms) and popular resistance, reflected in numerous strikes by workers and shopkeepers.

There was no military solution for the intifada because it was driven by a national aspiration whose violent expressions could be quieted from time to time, but which could not be completely eradicated. In time, the defense minister also began to recognize this. Nonetheless, without a readiness to include the PLO, a diplomatic resolution was impossible because the leaders of the intifada in the territories were unwilling to completely cut themselves off from the PLO. Although they harbored anger against the PLO's leadership in exile, and although the intifada was an expression of the independence of local residents vis-à-vis the Tunis-based organization that represented them, severing ties with the PLO would have rendered a blow to national pride, so this was not an option.

While it is clear that the IDF, or any other military force, could not "eradicate" the Palestinians' national aspirations, it should be noted that in the complex reality of the Middle East, the more Israel refrained from using force, the weaker its hand became in shaping events in accordance with its interests. That is, at least some of the players in the arena viewed Israel's reluctance to exercise force as a sign of weakness. In this context, it is fascinating to examine the minutes of a secret meeting held during the intifada years between a top Israeli security official and Elie Hobeika, a Lebanese-Christian politician who served as the liaison officer between Israel and the Phalangists at the beginning of the First Lebanon War. (Hobeika, notorious for his cruelty and involvement in the massacre in Sabra and Shatila, was a government minister in Lebanon in the 1990s and was assassinated in 2002.)

According to Hobeika, the reason he decided to align himself with the Syrians during the First Lebanon War, after initially collaborating with Israel, was the change in consciousness that occurred in the Arab world regarding Israel's power after it agreed to withdraw from the Sinai Peninsula in exchange for peace with Egypt, and in light of its military entanglement in Lebanon. Hobeika explained to his interlocutor:

> There was a period when there was a mythos in Lebanon and in the entire Arab world about Israel as omnipotent. A strong state capable of doing whatever it pleased. The Israelis were heroes, like Superman, in Lebanon. This mythos no longer exists. It disappeared throughout the Arab world because of the many failures that became apparent. Even Camp David was seen as a failure, because Israel gave more than it received. In Lebanon, the Israeli mythos was replaced by

the Syrian mythos. Today the Syrians are omnipotent, even if we don't love them—we work with them. The [Lebanese] president has deep hatred for the Syrians, but he fears them. And according to Mustafa Tlass [Syria's defense minister], Syria cannot allow Lebanon to be independent because that is contrary to the conception of Greater Syria.[56]

Hobeika expressed a perception based on a belligerent worldview. But it seems that the fact that Israel has, indeed, tended to be more cautious in exercising force since the First Lebanon War, while at the same time avoiding bold compromises, has weakened its standing.[57]

In any case, the continuation of the intifada and the failure of efforts to implement the London Agreement led King Hussein to declare on July 31, 1988, that Jordan was relinquishing its ties to the West Bank, and that the matter should be resolved by the Palestinians and Israel. Thus, the curtain closed on the opportunities of Jordanian-Israeli dialogue on confederation.

Hussein's announcement also influenced the PLO's path. In late 1988, in part due to concerns about losing its standing among Palestinians in the territories and its weakened position as a player in the international arena, Arafat declared that his organization accepts UN Resolutions 242 and 338—a historic announcement that signified recognition of Israel and a renunciation of terror. In exchange, official contacts began between the PLO and the American administration. In the background, there was also recognition of the changes occurring in the Soviet Union under Gorbachev, who launched the era of *perestroika* ("restructuring") and *glasnost* ("openness"). The Arab world in the Middle East could no longer count on strong Soviet backing. The world was on the threshold of a new reality dominated by a single superpower, an ally of Israel. Meanwhile, Israel was preparing for new elections, scheduled for November 1, 1988.

# 10

Despite their differences of opinion on foreign affairs, there was one subject on which the Likud and Labor were united: ensuring the continued emigration of Jews from the Soviet Union.

At this stage, when the Soviet Union began to slowly but steadily change its policy that prevented Jews from emigrating, it was clear that the Zionist project had an opportunity for renewal. According to Israeli estimates, there were two to three million Jews living in the Soviet Union at the time. It was hard to determine a precise number because Jews were not allowed to practice their religion under the communist regime and the number of intermarriages grew. There was a consensus in Israel on the need to invest in maintaining ties with the Jewish communities in the Soviet Union in order to realize the vision of the ingathering of exiles—perhaps the noblest principle of the Zionist movement. During the 1980s, tens of thousands of Jews left the Soviet Union, but most immigrated to the United States and West Germany. Israel, under the unity government, sought to channel Soviet émigrés to Israel, especially in anticipation of a possible opening of the gates to mass emigration.

Shamir attributed such great importance to this potential stream of Jewish immigrants that he defined this opening of the Soviet gates as a condition for agreeing to an international conference. Beilin shared Shamir's feelings about the supreme importance of Jewish immigration to Israel. Peace was his top priority, but among the few times he shed tears was when he watched Jews from Ethiopia and the Soviet Union disembark from the planes that brought them to Israel. He tried to promote various initiatives to induce the Soviet Union to permit Jewish emigration and considered proposing a deal that would enable 20,000 Jews a year to leave for Israel in exchange for diplomatic progress, but the echoes of the "Kastner affair" from the Holocaust era[58] deterred him from offering proposals that included the release of Jews according to a predetermined quota.

Unlike those who saw the struggle for Jewish emigration from the Soviet Union as a humanitarian-emancipatory act aimed at rescuing Jews regardless of their destination, Shamir lobbied the American administration and West German government to tighten the conditions for allowing Soviet Jews into their countries. Shamir believed that Israel should compel the Jews to come to Israel first. He later wrote:

> The State of Israel waited for them as the homeland of the Jewish people. It was the essence of Judaism in my eyes. I heard the complaints of the non-Zionist organizations that assisted the dropouts—that the final destination of Soviet Jewry is unimportant. That it is enough that they leave the country and are saved from all of the dangers they face there, and that they should have complete freedom of choice to settle where they wish. I understood, and I couldn't accept it, and of course, I didn't accept it.[59]

Beilin too, in the spirit of the Ben-Gurion school of classical Zionism, regards living in Israel as the most significant expression of Jewish identity in the modern era. The national model that characterizes his view is "political nationalism" as defined by the historian Salo Baron. That is, a nation's cultural-ethnic identity can only be maintained under political sovereignty exercised by members of that nation.[60]

Therefore, Beilin and Shamir saw eye to eye on this issue.[61] Thus, Beilin also worked in the late 1980s to persuade Shultz to help arrange direct flights from Moscow to Israel, even before the opening of the gates to mass emigration. The hope was that when the gates finally opened, it would be easier to prevent Jews from heading toward other destinations. Indeed, in 1990, El Al aircraft began landing in Moscow and taking off from there.

# In the Eye of the Storm

1

Prior to the elections for the 12th Knesset, held on November 1, 1988, the Labor Party changed its procedure for selecting its list of candidates. Instead of placing this responsibility in the hands of a few party elders, Labor's 1,260-member central committee would now vote to select the candidates. The Likud (or more precisely, its Herut faction) had already instituted this procedure prior to the 1977 elections. The Labor Party decided to adopt this method in an effort to renew its ranks.

Indeed, the change facilitated an injection of youth into the party's slate of candidates, including Ramon, Burg, Masalha, Merom, and Eli Ben-Menachem—all affiliated with the Mashov group. They offered an alternative to the hawkish wing of the party, which included people like Emanuel Zisman and Shlomo Hillel, who supported the settlement enterprise and could have easily felt at home in the Likud.

The new method helped Beilin, who was elected to the twenty-eighth spot on the list. However, the transfer of power to the central committee hurt several illustrious politicians who lacked a power base in the party's branches. Thus, for example, Abba Eban was bypassed by the central committee and found himself outside of politics. The transfer of political power—from the proverbial smoke-filled backroom to the central committee, and since 1992, when both major parties instituted primaries, from the central committee to the entire party membership—was inspired by the US election system and marked another stage in the development of the democratic dimension of politics in Israel. The primaries opened the ranks to more authentic and broader representation of Israeli society in politics, but they also required candidates to invest considerable sums in election campaigning. This engendered many cases of corruption and a populism that swept incompetent candidates into the Knesset. Public discourse became shallower.[1]

This phenomenon is not unique to Israel; it exists throughout the democratic world. But the decline in the quality of politicians is even more salient in Israel, because political activity in the Zionist movement had always involved an elite group of intellectuals. In his book *An Elite without Successors*, Yonathan Shapiro analyzed the waning quality in the labor movement from a different perspective, focusing on the roots of this process. According to Shapiro, there was a conflict between the demand by the Second Aliyah generation for loyalty to the cultural-national collective and the parallel demand for avant-garde pioneering activity. Ultimately, the demand for collective loyalty overcame the aspiration to foster avant-garde activity. Consequently, a conformist second generation emerged that lacked the revolutionary fervor of the Zionist idea,[2] and that generation was followed by a breed of politicians who primarily viewed politics as a professional opportunity. The primaries in the late 1980s, and certainly as they developed in subsequent years, only accelerated the decline in the quality of elected officials.

The generational decline in the quality of politics also characterized the Revisionist movement, though the process was slower in the Likud compared to the Labor Party. After four decades in the opposition, Herut retained its ideological fervor in the second generation, referred to as "the princes," who became the party's elite in the 1980s and 1990s—together with the second generation of immigrants from Islamic lands, which the party had welcomed into its ranks. However, in the twenty-first century, primaries have also contributed to eroding the quality of Likud MKs, in part due to the impact of social media discourse. It is interesting to note that among the major parties in the twenty-first century, the list that included the highest quality of individuals was Kadima's list in 2006 (without regard to their political stance). This is largely attributable to the fact that the list was assembled in the old-fashioned way—by a small group of Ariel Sharon's associates. (Some changes were made to the list that lowered its quality after Sharon suffered a stroke and Ehud Olmert replaced him as party chairman.)

Therefore, Plato's famous critique of democracy's vulnerability to populism and demagogy still holds true. Incidentally, Herzl was also cognizant of this problem of opening all issues to free voting by the masses. Thus, in the constitutional profile of the liberal state he envisioned, Herzl opposed the referendum method of decision-making:

> I also hold a settling of questions by the referendum to be an unsatisfactory procedure, because there are no simple political questions which can be answered merely by "yes" and "no." The masses are also more prone even than parliaments to be led away by heterodox opinions, and to be swayed by vigorous ranting. It is impossible to formulate a wise internal or external policy in a popular assembly.[3]

The impact of the primaries era is important in Beilin's case because his weakness as a politician can be attributed to the fact that he lacked an army of followers. His strength derived from his programs and initiatives within the political system, and his subsequent work in the diplomatic sphere; but his standing in the wider public was weak. Perhaps under a Platonic model of the "philosopher king," Beilin would have found a more suitable place in politics.

Beilin is aware of how the primaries hurt his standing and lowered the quality of the entire political system. He recognizes that it is impossible to return to the previous era of smoke-filled rooms, but suggests reforms in the primaries system in light of the problematic Knesset lists of recent years. For example, voters could be allowed to rank a party's candidates when voting in general elections in order to reduce the power of "vote contractors" within the major parties. Alternatively, he proposes dividing Israel into voting regions apportioned in accordance with geographic, sectorial, ideological, and demographic criteria.

However, these are retrospective thoughts, from a post-career perspective. As the November 1988 elections approached, Beilin was happy with his new status as a realistic candidate for the Knesset, as a public figure who drew his support from party delegates and not only from his political patron.

There was relative quiet on the Peres-Rabin front this time. Peres's term as prime minister was considered successful, and his power base in the party was solid. A few surveys found that Rabin was more popular among the public, thanks largely to his military image, but Peres firmly rejected several proposals (including one by Motta Gur) that he yield to Rabin in order to boost the party's electoral chances. Rabin chose to refrain from competing for leadership of the party, sufficing with Peres's promise that he would continue to serve as defense minister.

Beilin again felt optimistic. The intifada was not only a security burden for the Shamir government; it also hurt the Israeli economy because the security situation led to a drastic reduction in the Palestinian workforce in Israel. The election campaign itself was relatively calm. After four years of shared rule, and without Begin's fiery presence, it seemed that the public was less tempestuous. The High Court of Justice's decision to ban Kahane's racist list (for rejecting the state's democratic character) was accepted with understanding among the various camps in the Jewish public.

## 2

Many in the Labor Party attributed the disappointing election results to a terror attack conducted a day before the elections. A Molotov cocktail was tossed at a bus in Jericho, killing five people—Rachel Weiss, her three children, and David Delrosa, a soldier who tried to save the Weiss family and died of his injuries. The attack inflamed the public and this may have affected the elections, but there were also deeper reasons for the results.

Prior to the elections, Rabin and Peres tried to emphasize the differences between Labor and Likud—an essential mission after four years of sitting together in national unity governments with Shamir and his colleagues. In light of the failure of the Israeli-Jordanian confederation initiative, they held a press conference to present a new plan calling for local elections in the territories that would lead to direct negotiations—if the Palestinians agreed to suspend the intifada for a period of three to six months. But in the public's eyes, the reality was that Rabin had served as defense minister in Shamir's government, Peres had refrained from dismantling the government after Shamir nixed the London Agreement, and both the Likud and Labor were opposed to negotiating with the PLO. The prohibition on contacts with the PLO eliminated any chance of launching a peace process because the Palestinian leadership in the territories refused to negotiate without the PLO. Consequently, it was hard to distinguish between the positions of the two major parties concerning the peace process. This lowered motivation to vote for the Labor Party because at least the Likud promised a tough policy that would bolster security.

The election results reflected the ongoing process of political fragmentation, at the expense of the two major parties. Parties to the left of Labor included Ratz, Shinui, Mapam (which had left the Alignment), the Progressive List for Peace, Hadash, and the Arab Democratic Party; together, these parties garnered sixteen seats. To the right of the Likud were Tsomet, Hatehiya, and Moledet, a new party led by Maj. Gen. (Ret.) Rehavam Ze'evi that called for a transfer of Arabs for security reasons. Moledet is historically important in highlighting the racist dimension underlying part of the Zionist mainstream, because the difference between the racism of Moledet (accepted in the political system because of its secular and "rational" character) and the racism of Kahane (rejected due to its religious nature) is merely aesthetic. The elections also increased the power of Shas to six seats, and the two Ashkenazi ultra-Orthodox parties, Agudat Yisrael and Degel Hatorah, won a total of seven seats. Together with the NRP (five seats), whose ideology had become more hawkish since the Six-Day War, the number of seats held by religious parties grew to eighteen. Although the Likud defeated the Alignment (as noted, by a single seat: 40 to 39), the differential between the rightist bloc and the leftist bloc was small. Consequently, the kingmakers were the religious parties, which were inclined to stick with the alliance that Begin had forged between the political right and the religious parties.

Peres reacted quite emotionally to the results. He quickly informed Beilin and Novik that after consulting with his wife Sonia he had reached the conclusion that she was right: it was time for him to exit from political life. Whether Peres truly intended to quit politics, or whether this was an emotional outburst and he secretly hoped to be pressured against quitting, Beilin and Novik strongly urged him to reconsider.[4] It apparently did not require much effort to change his mind. After recommitting himself to politics, Peres asserted that it was still possible to form a narrow government under his leadership by enlisting the support of the ultra-Orthodox parties. This would only require some creativity and conceptual flexibility—that is, a substantial payoff. Beilin agreed. He believed that the goal, the possibility of peace, was more important than exemplary political conduct, and that in any case politics was an arena of alliances—sometimes including strange bedfellows—designed to make inroads that benefit the entire society.

Beilin's approach to relations with the religious camp actually echoed the stance of Jabotinsky. In late 1934, in the context of his reconciliation talks with Ben-Gurion, the Revisionist leader wrote:

> If I came to realize that there was no way to [achieve] a state except . . . a state of the devoutly religious, where they force me to eat gefilte fish from dawn to dawn (but there was no other way)—I would agree . . . and I would leave a will for my son to foment a revolution. But I would write on the envelop: "Open five years after the creation of the Hebrew state."[5]

However, while Jabotinsky was ready to compromise on the religious character of the state (for example, in the culinary field), Beilin—with the support of Peres, who appointed him to lead the negotiations with the ultra-Orthodox parties—was prepared to agree to more substantial pro-religious legislation in exchange for ultra-Orthodox support for a left-wing coalition.

The main stumbling block was the ultra-Orthodox parties' demand to redefine "Jew" in the Law of Return in accordance with the strict Orthodox interpretation of Jewish law: a person born to a Jewish mother or converted under Orthodox auspices.

The "Who is a Jew?" issue had already shaken the political system in 1958 and 1970, but this time, in anticipation of large-scale Jewish immigration from the Soviet Union, it was no longer primarily a theoretical matter: many Soviet Jews did not meet the Orthodox criteria for Jewishness. In addition, this amendment of the Law of Return would create a rift with the non-Orthodox community in the United States because the ultra-Orthodox also demanded that Israel deny recognition of non-Orthodox conversions conducted outside of Israel. Nonetheless, in the heat of the battle to form a coalition, Beilin and Agudat Yisrael formulated an agreement that adopted the ultra-Orthodox position. Shamir—whose worldview was clearly secular and who defined modern Jewishness in purely national terms—initially rejected the ultra-Orthodox demands. However, he ultimately followed the Labor Party's lead and succumbed to those demands. In retrospect, Beilin explains that he was not emotionally torn over the proposals he presented to MK Shmuel Halpert, Agudat Yisrael's representative in the coalition talks. Beilin's plan was to find a way to block the actual implementation of the agreement. In the meantime, it would allow a Peres-led government to advance the peace process, which he regarded as the main path for creating a brighter future for Israel.

On the other hand, Rabin—realistic and a bit pessimistic, as usual—refused to believe in the feasibility of a coalition between the left and the ultra-Orthodox parties. In his analysis of the election results, it was best to aim toward forming another unity government. Knowing that Beilin was trying to pursue his patron's ambitions, Rabin publicly referred to him as "Peres' poodle." This was not the first time that Rabin coined a term that entered the Israeli political lexicon. Beilin regarded this as a cowardly act by Rabin, who preferred to "kill the messenger" rather than confront Peres head-on. On the other hand, while the term was intended as an insult, it expressed recognition of Beilin's power and influence. It was only later that Beilin began to feel angry over Rabin's demeaning slur against him—especially after the second Rabin government was established based on the same left-religious formula, and when he was still labeled "Peres' poodle," despite the independent standing he had acquired.

The main damage caused by Rabin's words was that they reinforced the public's feelings of disgust toward the political wheeling and dealing, and this made it harder for Peres and Beilin to form a coalition based on convoluted agreements with the various parties. They terminated these efforts after Rabin announced on television that he did not believe in the possibility of an Alignment government, and did not see justification for another rotation arrangement in exchange for a unity government. In the eyes of Peres and Beilin, Rabin was mainly motivated by vengeance and personal interest: in any unity scenario, he would likely continue as defense minister, and may have even preferred Shamir to Peres as prime minister. The tension that Peres and Rabin were able to conceal during the first unity government erupted again.

Rabin's statements weakened Peres's hand in negotiations with the Likud, which noted that even Rabin thought there was no reason for rotation this time, because the Likud had the option of forming a coalition, albeit a narrow one, without Labor. After it was agreed to form a unity government without rotation, the question arose: What would Peres's role be in the new government? Beilin advised Peres to continue in the Foreign Ministry. Many others in the party exhorted Peres to take the finance portfolio, in part due to fears that without government assistance for the Histadrut, and without the finance minister's help in addressing the insolvency crisis in the kibbutzim and moshavim following years of high inflation, these labor movement enterprises would collapse.[6] The shutdown of the Ata textile factory, despite a battle by the workers, was a clear reminder of the need to take action to prop up the Histadrut's factories.

Beilin, whose primary interest was the peace process, and who felt no special attachment to the Histadrut, tried to lobby the party's bureau against entering another unity government. He mounted this effort together with Uzi Baram and other former members of the Young Guard, led by Ramon, Merom, and Peretz. Peres was of a different mind, preferring to serve as finance minister in the unity government instead of leading the opposition in the Knesset. Thus, Peres and Rabin joined forces against Beilin and his colleagues. Indeed, politics makes for strange bedfellows.

In the end, the party supported joining the unity government led by Shamir, and Peres asked Beilin to serve as his deputy at the Finance Ministry. Beilin accepted the offer. Upon assuming his new post, Beilin surprisingly advocated budget increases for the ultra-Orthodox sector. Some saw this as a narrow political ploy. Beilin explained that he was adopting a more far-reaching approach: if the establishment invested more in the ultra-Orthodox sector, then ultra-Orthodox Jews would integrate more fully into Israeli society and the ultra-Orthodox parties would lose their importance and become weak. In other words, he identified an inverse correlation between socioeconomic conditions in the ultra-Orthodox sector and the strength of ultra-Orthodox parties. Thus, to weaken those parties, the government should increase funding to the sector.[7]

In retrospect, Beilin did not understand the full complexity of the ultra-Orthodox community. In the late 1980s, about 3 percent of Israelis were defined as ultra-Orthodox. By 2015, this percentage had risen to about 9 percent (800,000 people).[8] Beilin saw the ultra-Orthodox phenomenon via the "secularization thesis," the prevailing view in the Western world through the 1960s. According to this view, the world becomes increasingly secular as history advances. Thus, in the Jewish context, the ultra-Orthodox phenomenon expresses a fossilized form of Jewish Diaspora existence, and is expected to fade away as more resources are invested in ultra-Orthodox society.

However, like the peace process, the ultra-Orthodox story is not merely a matter of budget allocations and resources. Today it is clear that ultra-Orthodoxy is dynamic and hybrid in nature; even when it encounters the general society, imbibes secular Israeliness, and refashions itself, it remains ultra-Orthodox. Ultra-Orthodox society is both influenced by the general society and influences it. This creates a new ultra-Orthodoxy—certainly in the Mizrahi ultra-Orthodox sector,[9] but also in the various groups within Ashkenazi ultra-Orthodoxy.

It is interesting to consider the similarity between Beilin's approach to the ultra-Orthodox community and his approach to the Arab–Israeli conflict, and how this approach echoes Herzl's view of how the Jews should live in coexistence with the Arabs. Just as Beilin sought to encourage the ultra-Orthodox society to adopt Western values and progress, and thus "neutralize the problem," Herzl believed that Zionism would bring advancement and Western culture to the Middle East, and thus persuade the Arabs not to oppose the Zionist project. Herzl's hope—as embodied by Rashid

Bey, the Arab hero of *Altneuland*, who was educated in Germany—was that the Arabs would accept Jewish immigration to Palestine because they would wisely recognize how the prosperity and Westernization the Jews brought would also serve their own aspirations to develop. This notion was consistent with the Orientalist mindset of the time: the West would reform the traits perceived as "Eastern." In Herzl's words, Zionist would serve as a "vanguard against barbarism." This applied not only vis-à-vis the Arabs, but first and foremost in regard to the Jews of Eastern Europe. Ironically, the hero of *Altneuland* envisions the Levant as the place where Eastern European Jews will become Westerners.

Herzl's naïve-condescending view sounds detached from reality today, and it should be understood as a product of the times in which he lived, before the era of relativism and postmodernism. Nonetheless, the deep currents of the Herzlian attitude toward the East are still evident today in the liberal Zionist left's view of the Arabs' disposition—and vis-à-vis the ultra-Orthodox, who were expected to "Westernize." However, the ultra-Orthodox population is actually growing due to its high birth rate and the phenomenon of "returnees" (*baalei tshuva*); and the ultra-Orthodox parties have not weakened, despite the huge budgets lavished upon the ultra-Orthodox sector. On the contrary, ultra-Orthodoxy has sustained itself while setting new boundaries, some more flexible and some more rigid, in its relations with the secular society. Money and technological progress are not enough to change a person's national or religious identity. Such change involves many other dimensions (emotional, spiritual, mythical, and historical) that shape a person's identity. Many good Liberals fail to recognize this, and their hopes crash against reality.

## 3

As deputy finance minister, Beilin had the opportunity to influence the Histadrut and often clashed with members of the Histadrut and Labor Party of a more socialist bent. For example, the media reported on his ongoing confrontation with the Histadrut's secretary-general, Yisrael Kessar. Beilin asserted that if Israel wanted to develop and strengthen its economy, it would have to learn to live with periods of 7 percent unemployment. Kessar accused Beilin of insensitivity to the weaker population and called upon him to set a personal example by being unemployed himself.[10] Beilin was forced to apologize. He explained that he had intended to say that without the necessary economic reforms, Israelis would need to become accustomed to 7 percent unemployment. But when given an opportunity to present his position in a more detailed way, he admitted that in his view a small percentage of "frictional unemployment" is, indeed, essential for a society in the stages of developing new fields of production,[11] because until the workers from outdated industries acquire the professional training required for employment in new branches of the economy, it is unavoidable that some will be unemployed. A society that fails to recognize this exigency will find itself trailing behind the advanced economies.

These two examples—Beilin's approach to ultra-Orthodoxy and economic development—indicate that his worldview is rooted in classical economic liberalism, as expounded by philosophers such as John Stuart Mill, and completely rejects Karl Marx's doctrine. Mill argued that in order to stimulate growth it is necessary to recognize the fact that technological progress continually makes "outdated" employees redundant, but that these workers can be retrained for new jobs created through this technology-driven economic growth.

Contrary to Mill and his "compensation principle," Marx pointed to the "law of increasing poverty." According to Marx, the capitalist economy's pursuit of economic growth and ever-increasing profits inherently requires the weakening of the working class. Therefore, unemployment is not a temporary adjustment; it is the fruit of a deliberate and organized policy designed to protect the employer's profits and keep wages low. Workers—until the longed-for revolution—will accept wage erosion rather than risk losing their livelihood.

More concretely, Beilin sought to make the economy more efficient at the expense of weakening the Histadrut, which he viewed as hindering this process. The Histadrut General Federation of Labor, established in 1920 to protect salaried workers, developed into a unique entity in the Western world: it was not only a trade union that encompassed most of the workers in the economy (in 1952, 90 percent of salaried workers in Israel were Histadrut members);[12] it also established institutions in all areas of life, including health clinics, sports associations, newspapers, publishing companies, and economic ventures organized in the framework of the Hevrat Haovdim ("the Workers' Company").

The Histadrut became the principal employer in Israel, as well as its largest labor union. Thus, as the researchers Avi Bareli and Uri Cohen explain, "The government, representing the public sector, and the Manufacturers' Association, representing the private sector, did not deal with separate unions based on different professions, as is customary in most Western countries. Rather, there was a triangle of forces in which the Histadrut, through its Trade Union Division, was a central player in shaping working conditions and salary levels." Bareli and Cohen emphasize that this was not the original intention when the Histadrut was created, "and this situation did not exist in the pre-independence period. Instead, it resulted from the consent and strong encouragement of the Mapai-led government, which regarded this organization as one of the central components of the principle of statism [*mamlachtiyut*], which was identified during the first decade with the principle of sovereignty of the people."[13] Underlying the changes in the economy was the need to prepare for signing the Maastricht Treaty in 1992. The treaty stipulated that the European states would adopt a shared currency as part of becoming a united economic-political bloc on November 1, 1993. Beilin chaired a ministerial committee formed to adapt the Israeli economy to the European Union and the economic globalization it heralded. One of the committee's main recommendations was to cancel many administrative restrictions, such as the requirement to obtain a license to import many products, and to replace them with taxes and tariffs. Indeed, in September 1991, based on these recommendations, competing imports began to enter the economy. The impact of this exposure to imports was enormous. Israelis were introduced to new consumer products, and a wider range of imported products was available for purchase in Israel. But this exposure also severely hurt traditional industries—paper and textile, for example—which employed tens of thousands of workers. Attempts were made to protect them, and relatively high import duties were imposed on these products, but the fact is that by the beginning of the twenty-first century, the paper and textile industries were almost completely wiped out in Israel. Of course, this problem is not unique to the Israeli economy. However, in Israel, which was founded on the socialist ethos, the change was more drastic and economic disparities rapidly widened.

In the Labor Party, Beilin—together with Ramon and members of the Young Guard—worked to promote decisions to separate party membership from Histadrut membership, and to prepare legislation for nationalizing the Histadrut's health care array. On July 7, 1991, the Labor Party's central committee approved allowing party membership to people who were not members of the Histadrut. These were the initial steps in adopting the neoliberal ethos in Israel—a trend that gained strength during the second Rabin government and accelerated in the twenty-first century under governments led by Sharon and Netanyahu.

Beilin's role in this trend was not insignificant. The boy whose father boycotted International Workers' Day events contributed to Israel's abandonment of the original vision of the labor movement. He emphasizes in retrospect that the policy he promoted in the Finance Ministry under Peres should be distinguished from the neoliberal policy of Netanyahu as finance minister from 2003 to 2005. According to Beilin, his aim was to update the economy and free it from the bonds that would have left it behind the Western world in the era of globalization, while Netanyahu deliberately created "the new poor"[14] by systematically cutting government spending and reducing taxes for the top decile.

Israel, which in 1960 was the most egalitarian society in the Western world (according to the GINI index[15]), thus became one of the countries with the widest socioeconomic disparities in the West, a trend that continued under both leftist and rightist governments. Bareli and Cohen contend that in terms of economic policy, the much-maligned Mapai rule was better than its image in the collective memory of many Israelis: "The state (during the days of Mapai), in close collaboration with the Histadrut, fostered an economic policy aimed at reducing wage differentials between the two new classes that emerged in Israel. This policy was consistent with an ideology of general national solidarity that saw wide disparities as a source of sharp tensions that would lead to the collapse of the immigrant society." Gutwein notes a paradox. In his view, Labor Party leaders also adopted the principles of neoliberal economics for reasons of political benefit. Since the end of the 1980s, they recognized the hostility many Israelis felt toward the socialist system, and its values and symbols. This was part of a global trend—influenced by Reagan in the United States and Thatcher in Britain—of alienation from the welfare state (especially in the wake of the Soviet Union's collapse). However, by relinquishing its distinct socioeconomic worldview, the Labor Party subsequently lost its electoral power and its ability to serve as a political alternative. As Gutwein explains: "The privatization processes highlighted the contrast between the left and the lower classes, which reinforced their affiliation with the right. Therefore, as privatization continued to widen socio-economic inequality with the left's support, its political and public strength eroded and the hegemony of the right strengthened."[16]

Beilin is not convinced. He insists that he and Peres acted in good faith, without considerations of political gain. Beilin emphasizes that he had already learned of the Histadrut's corruption as a reporter for *Davar*, and that the way the labor federation was run, at least from the 1970s, was far from its original objectives. The Histadrut had become a monstrous monopoly that was used to hand out jobs, some of them superfluous, to party hacks whose abilities did not necessarily match the jobs they filled. Moreover, the dependence of Labor MKs on the leaders of the large workers' committees, who served as power brokers within the party, was fertile ground for corruption. The system rose up against its creators. Beilin defines his view as "social liberal." His encouragement of privatization processes stems from his complete rejection of state ownership of enterprises, including hospitals. From his perspective, competition is the key to providing better services to the citizenry, while restrictions on imports and trade would lead to the downfall of the Israeli economy.

He supports the right to unionize, opposes contract labor, and believes that wages should also be limited in the private sector. Beilin also recognizes the fact that the Mapai era had advantages in the context of narrowing disparities, but adds that the measures employed during the state's formative years, before the era of globalization, cannot be used today.

Beilin also recognizes the fact that in the Western world, primarily among the young generation, a trend is growing that differs from that of the Thatcher and Reagan era. Though he found it difficult to identify with phenomena like the social protest in Israel in the summer of 2011 and Bernie Sanders' campaign in the 2016 Democratic presidential primaries, he sees in them an expression of a justified protest against the flaws of the neoliberal system (even if such opponents have yet to present a serious alternative). As an example of needed reform in the neoliberal system, he says that the successful fight to eliminate the "indebtedness" of politicians to party apparatuses by instituting open primaries has created indebtedness of a different type—to tycoons and major contributors. This indebtedness is so problematic that Beilin, on second thought, is not sure that the previous system was worse. Therefore, as in every social process, economic views should be updated in accordance with contemporary needs. If he served today in a public role in the field of economics, he would work to strengthen regulation in a way that would support the rights of workers and prevent capitalistic monopolies, while recognizing the needs of the global market.

## 4

While tackling economic issues at the Finance Ministry, Beilin, like the minister he served, was still primarily interested in the peace process.

The years 1987 and 1988 were critical for the Palestinian national movement and the Middle East. Four events had the potential for changing the course of history in the Israeli-Palestinian conflict: the intifada, which transferred the center of gravity of the Palestinian struggle to the territories and expressed a revolt against the Tunis-based PLO leadership and the Arab states; Jordan's formal disengagement from the West Bank, as declared by King Hussein on July 31, 1987; the PLO's subsequent announcement in October 1988 that the Palestinian National Council adopts Resolution 242, effectively recognizing Israel and the idea of two states; and, in response, the American administration's decision to engage in dialogue with the PLO.[17]

The guidelines of the national unity government did not keep pace with these developments. The government approved a four-point initiative that called for strengthening the peace between Israel and Egypt on the basis of the Camp David Accords; noted Israel's general aspiration for peace with the Arab world; called for a solution to the refugee problem that did not include the right of return; and proposed conducting elections in the territories to choose representatives for dialogue on self-rule for an interim period, pending a permanent solution (within the autonomy framework).

However, even on these general policy guidelines, fundamental differences of opinion emerged between the Labor Party and the Likud. When Secretary of State Shultz officially announced the launch of US-PLO dialogue on December 14, Prime Minister Shamir issued a strong statement of condemnation, while Peres made do with a softer version, defining the US decision as a "sad day." Beilin, on the other hand, was one of the few members of the coalition to publicly applaud the decision, stating: "We're on the threshold of a new period."

Soon afterward, a new US president was inaugurated. In January 1989, following his victory over the Democratic candidate, Michael Dukakis, George H. W. Bush replaced Ronald Reagan in the White House and appointed James Baker to serve as secretary of state. Baker set out to promote an accord between Israel and the Palestinians, showing less patience with Shamir's policy than his predecessor, Shultz, had displayed. He also aimed to assign Egypt a central role in the negotiating process. Baker's proposal was formulated in a five-point document that called for a meeting between Israeli and Palestinian delegations in Cairo. The composition of the Palestinian delegation was to be determined with Israel's consent, but in coordination with Egypt and the United States, which were less rigid about the connection between the delegation members and the PLO. The disagreement between Baker and Shamir revolved around the secretary of state's demand to include Palestinians from East Jerusalem and from outside the territories in the delegation. The meeting in Cairo was intended to promote the plan for elections in the territories, and a meeting between Baker and the foreign ministers of Israel and Egypt was proposed as a step in facilitating the US initiative.[18] Rabin proposed an initiative of his own, which was not substantially different. Its main points included a halt to the intifada; elections in the territories monitored by the Israeli military; negotiations on autonomy; and then, after a transition period, negotiations on a final status accord. Rabin emphasized that his proposal drew from the autonomy plan outlined in the Camp David Accords.

As noted, Rabin's proposal did not include any substantial innovation. Rabin was more moderate than Shamir in that he suggested allowing Palestinians who had been expelled from the territories to return and participate as "external negotiators."[19] But his plan continued to repudiate the PLO—contrary to the general trend in the United States, and also contrary to a change that was occurring among some of the leaders of the Jewish community there, who internalized the need to include the PLO in the process.[20] Therefore, Rabin's proposal was a nonstarter.

Although the intifada had significantly empowered the local leadership in the territories, there was clearly no substantial leader in the territories willing and able to operate independently of the PLO, especially when this demand came from Israel. Consequently, the presentation of the Israeli peace plan was an illusion—self-delusion at best and an attempt to deceive the international community at worst. Beilin was fed up with this stance, and stated in the context of the various proposals (Egypt also put forward a similar plan)[21] that it was clear that the success of all the plans depends solely on a "green light" from the PLO. Beilin's position angered Shamir, who wanted to fire him, arguing that a deputy minister cannot make statements that contradict the government's basic guidelines. Beilin refused to apologize, but was ready to say that it was his personal opinion and that he would not violate the law prohibiting meetings with PLO personnel. Shamir was not reconciled, but learned that the law authorizes a prime minister to fire a minister, but not a deputy minister. (A minister could fire his deputy, but Peres refused to fire Beilin.) Left with no legal basis for firing Beilin, Shamir assigned Tsachi Hanegbi the mission of amending the law.

The stalemate in the peace process, and the fact that his party did not publicly support his position, impelled Beilin to independently search for paths to dialogue. In July 1989, he traveled to The Hague with his friend Yair Hirschfeld, a Middle East expert, to participate in talks with Palestinian representatives. One of them was Abdullah Hourani, a member of the PLO Executive Committee. Since Beilin had promised not to violate the law, the negotiation was conducted via a third party: Max van der Stoel, a former Dutch foreign minister, passed messages between the two hotels where the Israelis and Palestinians were staying.

Surprisingly, they were able to draft an agreement: Israel would commit to withdraw from most of the territories, while the Palestinians would receive a status that was not precisely defined, but was portrayed as a model of "almost a state." Incidentally, the draft did not include a commitment to recognize the PLO. Although the agreement had no official authority, Beilin was happy to verify that PLO representatives were prepared to accept an accord that entailed dividing the land, without demanding a "full" state. He planned to present the document to Peres in order to encourage the latter to launch a new diplomatic initiative. In the end, however, the parties were unable to sign even this general and unofficial draft: PLO officials in Tunis instructed the Palestinians that the document should explicitly state that Israel would withdraw from "the Palestinian lands" and not just from the territories. Beilin, while favoring a withdrawal and recognizing the Palestinians' right to self-determination, refused to refer to the territories as devoid of any connection to the Jewish people and its history.[22]

In any case, these contacts were secondary. On the official diplomatic front, the American administration had been pressing since early 1990 to launch negotiations based on the Baker Plan, and the secretary of state demanded a response from Israel on whether it agreed to the participation of Palestinians from East Jerusalem and representatives of the Palestinian Diaspora in the proposed elections in the territories. Peres wanted to respond in the affirmative, while Shamir opposed the Baker Plan (but wanted to stymie the initiative without giving a direct response), and Rabin suggested that the Knesset decide on the question in order to avoid a crisis with Shamir. The debate between the leaders of Labor and the Likud also reflected pressures and processes within the two major parties that stemmed from a turnover of generations in them.

Rabin and Peres had to take into account the views of the young generation—the "doves' camp," most of them graduates of the Young Guard—who demanded a more moderate stance and preferred dismantling the government to diplomatic futility. In the Likud, on the other hand, the pressure on Shamir was to toughen his stance. David Levy, Yitzhak Moda'i, and Ariel Sharon formed a camp, referred to in the media as the "constraints" ministers. They sought to limit Shamir's range of maneuver vis-à-vis the US administration, and demanded that he reject Baker's proposals. This ostensibly ideological fight also reflected the change in generations in the Likud. The middle-generation "constraints" ministers sensed that the end of the Shamir era was approaching, and feared that he would bypass them and designate the generation of "princes" for leadership. (Roni Milo, Tsachi Hanegbi, Ehud Olmert, Benny Begin, and Dan Meridor were prominent members of this younger generation.) Consequently, Levy, Sharon, and Moda'i preferred to dismantle the government, assuming that this would weaken Shamir and make it harder for him to "coronate" his young associates.

Under pressure from the Labor Party to accept Baker's demands, and pressure from the Likud to reject them, it was difficult for Shamir to pursue his preferred course of undermining the Baker initiative without explicitly rejecting it. The Labor Party convened to discuss whether to remain in the government after the prime minister refused to agree to Baker's initiative. In light of rumors that at least some Labor MKs intended to support a no-confidence motion in any case, Shamir chose to act preemptively. On March 11, he fired Peres, claiming that the finance minister had acted in violation of the government's basic guidelines. All of the Alignment ministers resigned in response. Rabin also resigned, though his almost habitual reluctance was evident. On March 15, 1990, the government fell in a no-confidence vote for the first time in Israeli history. Five Shas MKs absented themselves from the vote, as directed by their leader Rabbi Ovadia Yosef, and thus contributed to toppling the government. This was a clear hint of things to come.

# 5

The collapse of the government was the result of behind-the-scenes moves by Beilin and Ramon, inspired by Peres and initially opposed by Rabin. The plan was to establish an alliance between the Labor Party and the ultra-Orthodox camp, and to form a government led by Peres and supported by the ultra-Orthodox parties. However, the plan went awry and ultimately produced another phrase coined by Rabin: "the stinking maneuver." Although the struggle between the Likud and Labor centered on a diplomacy-related question that was probably inconsequential as long as the two parties refused to engage in dialogue with the PLO, the political events surrounding the government's fall and the efforts to form a government of the left and the ultra-Orthodox are still important for understanding the predicament of the left in Israel.

The plan of Peres and his associates was based on the willingness of Shas' rising star, Interior Minister Aryeh Deri, to join forces with the Labor Party. The unquestioned authority in Shas was Rabbi Yosef, who was known for his moderation in questions of war and peace. He cited the Jewish principle of *pikuah nefesh* (mandating the violation of religious commandments if necessary to save lives) to describe Israel's hold on the territories and the absence of peace, and thus supported a withdrawal and backed Deri's political moves. Deri was then a young and energetic minister, an immigrant from Morocco who was educated in Ashkenazi yeshivas. As someone closely familiar with both the Mizrahi and Ashkenazi ultra-Orthodox worlds, as well as the secular Israeli world, he had great potential for breaking the existing molds, including the customary affiliation of Mizrahi and religious Jews with the right. Although his biography was completely different from that of Ramon and Beilin, secular Ashkenazi Tel Avivians, the three were members of the new generation in Israeli politics.

Shas' absence during the no-confidence vote was designed to be the first stage in a plan to create a new coalition under the Labor Party's leadership. At this stage, it looked like Peres's plan was going to work, as Rabbi Menachem Porush of Agudat Yisrael also signaled his party's readiness to join the Labor government. Porush's stance was based on his desire to remain in the emerging coalition in order to receive government funding; it also reflected the fact that his party was more inclined to accept compromises on sovereignty because it represented an ultra-Orthodoxy that was non-Zionist and had an ahistorical worldview. That is, it viewed reality as unfolding in accordance with God's plan; as long the state is not governed by Torah law, its decisions are not sacred in any case, and its policies can be flexible. However, even if this was Porush's view and was shared by many in the ultra-Orthodox camp, it was not necessarily the view of "the ultra-Orthodox street." It seems that Peres and his team saw the ultra-Orthodox in the image of Porush and Yosef, as a moderate monolithic group, and thus ignored developments in the ultra-Orthodox community concerning the state and the connection to the Land of Israel.

Contrary to Deri and Yosef, for example, the official political leader of Shas, Rabbi Yitzhak Peretz, was a supporter of the Greater Land of Israel and considered it a religious obligation to ensure Israeli sovereignty over the territories. The Lubavitcher rebbe, who wielded influence in Agudat Yisrael, also had a right-wing worldview and was opposed in principle to any territorial compromise, though he never defined himself as "Zionist." Rabbi Elazar Shach, the leader of the non-Hasidic branch of Ashkenazi ultra-Orthodoxy in Israel, was not involved in the political machinations at this stage. Shach, who was also instrumental in creating Shas in 1984, was the most moderate of all on diplomatic matters and the most radical of all in regarding the Jewish people as existing outside of history. His absence in the current political turmoil was not taken into account by Peres and his agents, Beilin and Ramon, who were encouraged by the fall of the government. Even Rabin, who was skeptical about the success of the plan, chose to support it at this stage.

Now came the moment of truth: the actual formation of a coalition of the Labor Party and the ultra-Orthodox parties. Indeed, after the fall of the Shamir government, President Chaim Herzog tapped Peres to form a new government, since he seemed to have the best chance of success in this mission. However, while Peres was already working on the allocation of ministerial portfolios to top Labor leaders, his coalition negotiators began to realize that a large gap separated the left and the ultra-Orthodox public, and that the "Torah sages" (the rabbinical mentors of the ultra-Orthodox parties) were attentive to the sensibilities of their people, who were defined as non-Zionists but in practice had adopted right-wing Zionist views. That is, while the media and secular political system tended to understand the ultra-Orthodox world as exclusively ruled by the rabbinical leadership, the rabbis were also in fact politicians, committed to weighing the preferences of their constituents when making decisions. Thus, it became clear that it was one thing to reach agreements with a few rabbinical and political ultra-Orthodox leaders, and something entirely different to implement the agreements to form a coalition when this was contrary to the wishes of the ultra-Orthodox public.

A salient expression of this occurred on March 26, during the period allotted to Peres to form a coalition. After Yosef approved Shas' participation in the leftist government, Shach made the surprise decision to speak at a gathering of supporters at Yad Eliyahu Stadium (today called the Menora Arena) in southern Tel Aviv. Due to the importance of his speech, and its relevance to the rift between the left and the religious camp in Israel, I will discuss it here at length.

Shach was perceived in the secular public and media as having "leftist" views and, indeed, he publicly supported the return of territories in exchange for a peace accord. But this perspective failed to appreciate the complexity of his view, and stemmed from a lack of interest in studying the ultra-Orthodox worldview in depth. The rabbi was amenable to a withdrawal—not because of a conciliatory political orientation, but because he saw the Jewish people as existing outside of history. In his view, "The Jewish people lives and exists wherever it is present. The people's existence is not contingent upon an inheritance of land, but on the power of the Torah. The ground we are sitting on can be taken from under us, but the Pentateuch [*Chumash*] remains in our hands."[23]

Since he regarded faith and religious observance as the essence of the Jewish people, Shach rejected Zionism, which sought to find a remedy for the Jews' distress through nationalism, and led to a sovereign and secular state in the Land of Israel. The transformation of the Jewish people into an ordinary people, one that is like all other peoples (as one of the slogans of Zionism proclaims), was abhorrent to him. To support his view on the inherent exceptionalism of the Jewish people, as the chosen people, Shach cited an ancient commentary of the book of Genesis (*Bereishit Rabbah*) that explains why the patriarch Abraham was called "the Hebrew" (*ha'EVRi*): because the whole world was on one side (*me'EVR ehad*) while Abraham, as the representative of the Jewish people, was on the other side (*ha'EVR hashani*).[24] In the rabbi's eyes, the Jewish people's safety did not lie in its sovereignty, or in any military and diplomatic accords. "We lived in the exile for 2,000 years . . . the synagogue and study hall preserved us. They were the fortresses. The secret of the Jewish people's existence: the government, the army and territories—none of them have a part in its existence. The Torah alone sustains it."[25]

Indeed, in light of Shach's anti-Zionist worldview, it was possible to expect collaboration between him and the Zionist left because in any case the issue of the territories was not critical to him. Moreover, contrary to figures like the Lubavitcher rebbe, he saw no connection between the actual existence of the State of Israel and the Jewish people's situation. But Shach's readiness to return territories did not stem from his faith in peace accords. On the contrary. In his eyes, the Arabs, as non-Jews, were the incarnation of the Jewish people's enemies over the generations, "because from the day the Torah was given to Israel, it was decreed that the Jewish people would be hated."[26]

Shach's attitude toward non-Jews is also at the root of the paradox that affected his connection with the political right. Though he was willing to give up the territories and did not sanctify the state's borders, Shach's view of Jewish history as an ongoing ahistorical story of persecution and redemption was consistent with the rigid worldview that characterizes the right in its suspicious attitude toward the Arab world. In this light, it is easier to place the rabbi in a coalition with the Likud. Furthermore, as someone whose perspective on Zionism was shaped in the context of the fundamental conflict between Orthodox Judaism and the worldview of the Second Aliyah generation, Shach identified socialist Zionism, from which the left evolved, as the source of evil in the modern existence of the Jewish people. For him, the left was shaped in accordance with the Marxist view of religion as manipulation and as the "opium of the masses." On the other hand, he interpreted the secularity of right-wingers, including Mizrahi Jews, as deriving from the fact that they were "infants who were captured" that is, their errant ways were unintentional and the spark of their connection to tradition was still burning.

Shach's speech received unusually broad coverage by the media, which together with the public and the political system was waiting to hear whether he had decided to support joining a Peres-led government. His speech went in different directions: he described the state's condition as imperiled, in a way consistent with Shamir's pessimism, but, on the theoretical level, he rejected the Likud's stance on the strategic importance of the territories. Then he surprised by focusing his speech on vilifying the kibbutz lifestyle as an allegory for liberal life in general and as an expression of the rift that Zionist created in the continuity of generations. The rabbi declared:

> I did not cut off my fathers' inheritance. I did not sever the connection with my forefathers. I am connected to Abraham, Isaac and Jacob. . . . I'm living, and I'll continue to live if I act in the ways of my fathers. I follow my father's path. My grandfather's path. My grandmother's path. And I'm not looking for other wisdom. . . . I'll study my wisdom, my culture, and you do not study your culture. You are also a Jew, you are circumcised. But do you know your culture? What is your culture? English. That's your culture? You also know Arabic? Every idolater knows those things, every Egyptian knows Arabic. You tossed away the Pentateuch, and you cut yourself off from your father . . . you have no connection with the forefathers. If you have no connection, you'll inevitably be lost. . . . If there are kibbutzim that don't know what Yom Kippur is, don't know what the Sabbath is, don't know what the *mikveh* [ritual bath] is . . . rabbits, pigs. Do they have a connection to their father? This kibbutz universe? Can this be called having a connection with their father? Their father also ate on Yom Kippur?[27]

Shach did not explicitly announce his support for one government or another. But in the language of the ultra-Orthodox community's codes, it was clear. For the rabbi, the question of Jewish identity outweighed questions of statecraft. He poured out his rancor against the kibbutzim as a metaphor for the left, and thus expressed his opposition to forming a coalition with Peres. This indicated that if the left wanted to forge a political alliance with the ultra-Orthodox, it would have to reassess its identity.

The rabbi's resolute speech quickly made waves in the ultra-Orthodox community. In the wake of Rabbi Shach's speech, Rabbi Yosef also reneged on his promise to support a Peres-led coalition. The secular media criticized him for surrendering to Shach, attributing this to the fact that Shach was Ashkenazi and Yosef was Mizrahi. But here too the secular liberal interpretation erred in its understanding of ultra-Orthodox society. A more sensitive look at the ultra-Orthodox camp would have found that Yosef adopted Shach's stance mainly due to considerations of Jewish law. And when it came to interpreting Jewish law, his supreme concern, Yosef was prepared to challenge or accept the opinion of any rabbi, Ashkenazi or Sephardi. That is, despite his identification with the Shas slogan of "restoring the glory" of Sephardi Jewry (though, ironically, Yosef was a scion of a Babylonian rabbinic dynasty that was distant from Sephardi traditions), the ethnic affiliation was not a determining factor in his decision to accept or reject the opinions of other rabbis.[28] But Jewish law was not the only consideration that guided him: Yosef also changed his mind about joining a leftist government because he recognized that his followers had right-wing inclinations. That is, while his liberal critics presented him as an unenlightened person stuck in considerations of a bygone world, the ultra-Orthodox world, Yosef acted as a politician with rational electoral considerations.

The ultra-Orthodox newspaper *Yated Ne'eman* described Shach's speech as provocative, but also as a call for dialogue between the liberal and ultra-Orthodox communities. If this was, indeed, his intention, such dialogue, with all its potential, was not initiated. The lack of dialogue between the camps continues to characterize the relations between the left and the ultra-Orthodox even today.

Rabbi Yosef's retreat from backing a left-wing government left Peres's potential coalition with only sixty MKs. The political system was in turmoil. The parties conducted talks that included promises of personal benefits to MKs in exchange for their support for a new government. The public felt alienated from the political system in general. Beilin was not fazed by the criticism. He saw the attempt to form a government as "a legitimate political move," part of the parliamentary game. Pressure was now exerted on the Party for the Advancement of the Zionist Idea—five MKs, led by Yitzhak Moda'i, who had recently quit the Likud and formed an independent Knesset faction. After negotiations with Moda'i's faction also failed, Labor tried to reach an agreement with one of its members, Abraham Sharir. The newspapers reported that he was promised a ministerial appointment in the new government and a guaranteed slot on Labor's list for the next Knesset.

Sharir was also courted by the Likud and remained undecided. (Shamir's plea to Sharir— "Avrasha, come home"—entered Israel's political lexicon.) But this was not the only problem. On April 11, the night before the Knesset was scheduled to approve Peres's new government, it turned out that Agudat Yisrael's support was not secure. MKs Avraham Verdiger and Eliezer Mizrahi—followers of the Lubavitcher rebbe, who opposed territorial compromise—"disappeared." Attempts to contact them were to no avail. Although an agreement had already been signed with Agudat Yisrael, it was clear that the two "missing" MKs did not intend to honor it. And without them, Peres did not have the required majority. Sharon played a significant role in this: he was highly regarded in the rebbe's court and influenced the two MKs to break their party's commitment.

Thus, the plan concocted by Beilin and Ramon, with Peres's blessing, fell apart. At this stage, Peres realized that the chances of implementing the agreement were slim. Nonetheless, he was wary of acknowledging this and decided to present the list of ministers slated to serve in his government to the party's central committee. He and Beilin still hoped that Yosef would adopt a stance contrary to that of Shach. On the morning of April 12, the day of the scheduled Knesset vote, Peres visited Yosef and sounded a bit encouraged when he left. He apparently continued to believe, paradoxically in this context, that a divine miracle would occur during the confidence vote in the Knesset. He arrived at the Knesset accompanied by his wife Sonia, who usually did not attend such events. In retrospect, it seems that Sonia came to support him in his hour of distress. When he realized that he could not garner a majority of MKs, Peres announced at the last moment that he would not present his government for a vote of confidence.

That evening, exhausted and frustrated, Peres preferred to sequester himself with his family at his home in Ramat Aviv. Beilin, no less doleful, was one of the few invited to his apartment. There had been reports during those tense days about Peres bursting into tears (including in the presence of Shulamit Aloni, Moshe Shahal, and President Herzog)[29] and Beilin feared that it would be a difficult meeting. Sonia greeted him upon his entering the apartment and tried to lighten the atmosphere a bit by asking, as if nothing special had occurred that day, "Shalom Yossi, you bought new pants?" Beilin smiled. Peres smiled too, complimenting Beilin on the new pants. As he did throughout his political career, Peres demonstrated enormous will power, and began to talk with Beilin about renewing his efforts to seize the reins of power.[30] In the meantime, Shamir formed a narrow government of right-wing and ultra-Orthodox parties.

The abortive attempt to build a coalition between the left and the ultra-Orthodox demonstrates, more than any other episode, the politics of identity in Israel and the type of Jewishness that emerged in the wake of the Six-Day War and conquest of the territories. Indeed, even though Peres and Beilin were closer to Judaism than Sharon and Shamir, it was easier for the ultra-Orthodox camp to collaborate with the secular right because the maximalist stance on the Land of Israel had become identified with being pro-Jewish.

# 6

Shamir narrowly managed to cobble together a government. MK Ephraim Gur abandoned the Labor Party after being promised a position as deputy minister and a guaranteed slot on the Likud's next Knesset list. Moda'i's faction also joined the new government after a secret clause in its agreement with the Likud promised to erase its debts.

Journalists uncovered the promise to the Moda'i faction. It turned out that even earlier, when Agudat Yisrael signed the agreement with the Labor Party, one Agudat Yisrael MK had moved his pen over the paper without actually signing his name. Such reports heightened the public's disgust for the political system in Israel. Soon after the formation of the government, thousands of Israelis gathered for a demonstration in Tel Aviv and called for changing the system of government. Demonstrations followed throughout the country under the slogan "Corrupt [politicians], we're fed up with you." The protest was aimed at politicians in general and the system of government, and did not target a particular person as responsible for the situation. However, on May 12, Rabin summed up the move that Peres, Beilin, and Ramon had tried to orchestrate as "the stinking maneuver." He added: "This bluff, and all of the corruption that entered political life in Israel in an attempt to form a narrow government, was a failure not only tactically but also conceptually."[31] Rabin failed to mention that at a certain stage in this attempt to form a left-wing government, he gave his blessing and even participated in the discussions with the ultra-Orthodox, even if unenthusiastically.[32] His remarks resonated with the public's feelings of disgust, and again tainted the image of Peres and, indirectly, of Beilin.

In retrospect, Beilin still finds no fault in the effort to collaborate with the ultra-Orthodox or in the promises he was willing to make to each MK who indicated willingness to join the coalition. In his mind, he worked to exploit all possible opportunities in the political field in accordance with Israel's coalition system. "If it had succeeded, they would be calling it a brilliant maneuver and not a stinking one."[33] This viewpoint, which identifies the political field as an instrument, and allows the political system to be ridiculed and muddied for the sake of a desired outcome, was also evident in much of Beilin's subsequent political career. Although he maintained high ethical standards as a politician and as a person, he thought it was less important to conform to "the rules of the game" in politics. In this context, too, his view is completely rational. Like an attorney, his fidelity is to the letter of the law, the formal dimension only. The fact that the agreements that were almost signed with MKs and political parties included exorbitant benefits was secondary in his eyes. Similarly, he blithely disregarded the connection between the ultra-Orthodox politicians and the constituents they represented. The boundary was set in the legal dimension. As long as it was possible to move MKs from one side to another within the bounds of the law and for the sake of a worthy purpose—peace—Beilin was in favor of exploiting opportunities. Likewise, he supported the political payoffs to MKs Alex Goldfarb and Gonen Segev in 1995 to secure their votes in favor of the Oslo B Accords—despite the fact that they were elected to the Knesset as representatives of Tsomet, a right-wing party that opposed territorial compromise. In a similar context, Beilin advocated continuing negotiations with the Palestinians in Taba in 2001 under the Barak government—even though it was then a caretaker government that had lost its public support, and despite the dubious legitimacy of the government offering concessions that would obligate the next government.

This stance of Beilin echoes to some degree the famous remarks of Ben-Gurion in his speech to the Mapai central committee in 1965, against the background of the

Lavon Affair. "I don't know what the people want; I know what the people need." However, while history remembers Ben-Gurion's statement as an expression of bold leadership, it tends to forget the other side of the coin: Ben-Gurion failed in his efforts to lead the party in a direction contrary to the wishes of its members, and was in effect ousted from Mapai. At that stage, his efforts to lead in his way, without public support, were ineffectual. In fact, Ben-Gurion carried out his greatest deeds after establishing a political and public majority for his views. This naturally raises the question of whether Beilin's inclination to assign secondary importance to the public's opinions and wishes also stymied the peace project on which he labored during the Oslo period.

In any case, "the stinking maneuver" also had positive repercussions. In the wake of the public protests, several laws were passed that improved governance in Israel. Today, a majority of sixty-one MKs is required to topple a government, as opposed to the simple majority previously sufficient. In addition, there is an amendment to Basic Law: the Knesset prohibits an MK who leaves a party, without resigning from the Knesset, from competing in the next elections on the list of a party represented in the outgoing Knesset. This amendment, enacted in 1991, aims to prevent MKs from switching parties in exchange for a secure seat in the next Knesset. In the same spirit is another amendment to Basic Law: the government prevents an MK who left the party he was elected to represent from being appointed a minister or deputy minister during the same Knesset term, and withholds state funding if the MK forms a new party.

In addition, following the media's exposure of coalition agreements that included monetary benefits such as debt relief, the High Court of Justice required the parties to publish coalition agreements prior to the formation of a government. Today, coalition agreements are presented in full to the Knesset and the public before a new government assembles for a vote of confidence. Furthermore, following a petition submitted against the agreement between the Likud and the Party for the Advancement of the Zionist Idea, the court did not suffice with criticizing the content of the coalition agreement; for the first time in Israel, it invalidated a clause in a coalition agreement. (The clause involved a monetary payoff.) This precedent has guided the court ever since. The threshold percentage for Knesset representation was also gradually increased and now stands at 3.25 percent.[34]

Of course, these measures did not rectify all of the flaws in the Israeli system of government and politics, but today we are in a better situation than we were on the eve of the "brilliant" maneuver that became a "stinking" one.

## 7

Along with the political disappointment, the return to the opposition benches gave Beilin the freedom and time to work together with other Young Guard alumni (including Ramon, Burg, and Yael Dayan) in an effort to revise the Labor Party's platform in advance of the next elections. During the two years in opposition, until its victory in 1992, the party conducted discussions of historic importance that changed its profile. Labor's platform became less socialist in the economic realm and more moderate vis-à-vis the Arab–Israeli conflict.

Beilin also began meeting more intensively with Palestinians. On August 5, 1990, a meeting was held at the Notre Dame monastery in Jerusalem between Palestinian leaders from the territories who maintained a connection to PLO-Tunis, including Faisal al-Husseini, Hanan Ashrawi, and Ziad Abu Zayyad, and representatives of the dovish wing of the Labor Party and representatives of Mapam, Ratz, and Shinui, including Lova Eliav, Yossi Sarid, Dedi Zucker, and Amnon Rubinstein. The goal, contrary to previous meetings that tended to skirt the issue, was to formulate a document that could pave the way toward direct negotiation between Israel and the PLO. The Israeli participants hoped that a document of this type could win the hearts of the Israeli public, which was tired of the intifada. The Palestinian side agreed to adopt UN Resolution 242—in effect, recognizing Israel, in exchange for Israel's willingness to negotiate with "the legitimate and recognized representative of the Palestinian people."[35]

However, the PLO's response to the Iraqi invasion of Kuwait cast a shadow over the talks: on August 2, 1990, the Iraqi army captured Kuwait in a few hours. Saddam Hussein's offensive was denounced by the West and by most of the Arab states. The PLO, on the other hand, openly identified with the Iraqi regime. The Israelis were disappointed by the PLO's stance. Their Palestinian interlocutors admitted that they too were unhappy with it, but did not want to confront Arafat. Ashrawi said that the reality was more complex than it seemed from the Western perspective, which saw the Iraqi invasion as aggression by one Arab state against another. The Iraqi violation of the principle of sovereignty, she added, should not blur the fact that Kuwait was a client state of the United States and the West, whose very existence was a reminder of Western imperialism. Whoever fails to understand this, she concluded, cannot understand the complexity of the Arab situation.[36]

Her remarks were grounded in historical truth: during the Ottoman Empire, Kuwait was merely part of the Iraqi Basra Province, and from the day that Iraq became an independent state in 1932, it insisted that "Kuwait" be included within its boundaries. Kuwait was, indeed, created by the British; in 1899, Britain extended its patronage to the al-Sabah family, which still rules Kuwait, in exchange for control over its foreign affairs. Kuwait's borders were demarcated from the outset to restrict Iraqi access to the Persian Gulf and protect British troops stationed in the area. Similarly, Kuwait's independence, granted only in 1961, was designed to create a buffer between Iraq and the oil fields of Saudi Arabia, on which the US economy was largely dependent. Against this background, the PLO argued that while the West portrayed Iraq as the aggressor, as the Goliath attacking David, played by Kuwait, the opposite is true: Saddam Hussein was the one displaying courage in confronting the caprices of the Western powers.

In any case, in part due to the impact of the Soviet Union's collapse and the strengthened status of the United States as the world's only superpower, many of the Arab states (including Syria, Saudi Arabia, Bahrain, and the UAE) agreed to join the international coalition the American administration formed to fight Iraq. Other Sunni states, including Egypt, provided support for the coalition behind the scenes. The military campaign—officially named Operation Desert Storm, and known today as the First Gulf War—was launched on January 17, 1991. It ended with the defeat of the Iraqi army and the restoration of the al-Sabah family to power in Kuwait.

The PLO's continued support for Saddam Hussein during the war, and the fact that Scud missiles launched by Iraq against Israel were cheered and celebrated by Palestinians in the territories, prompted Yossi Sarid to publish his well-known "Don't Look to Me" article in the *Haaretz* daily. In his article, Sarid informed the Palestinians that in light of his disappointment in their stance, he would no longer bother to try to promote their national rights. This article is important for understanding the flaws of the Zionist left, which refused to consider the complexity of the Palestinian issue and Palestinian consciousness, even as it strived for peace with the Palestinians. It seems in this context that the publicist Yitzhak Laor was correct in arguing that "Yossi Sarid's 'Don't Look to Me' was the most succinct summary of the Zionist left's connection with the Palestinians: You need us, we don't need you."[37] Beilin also was disappointed by the PLO's stance, but in this case was more sensitive to the Palestinian plight. Responding to Sarid, he wrote about the complexity of the Palestinians' situation, which commits them to positions that are difficult for Israel and the West to understand from an instinctive perspective. Incidentally, Sarid later apologized about his article.

However, the Gulf War not only created a rift between the Zionist left and the Palestinians. The American success in defeating the Iraqi army also triggered important developments. On the one hand, the PLO lost status in the Arab world because of its support for Saddam Hussein and now had to be more solicitous of the Arab states. On the other hand, Israel's expectation of enjoying stronger standing in the American administration proved false. During the war, Iraq fired Scud missiles at Israel, hoping that an Israeli response would lead the Arab states to quit the US-led coalition. However, under American pressure, Israel refrained from retaliating against Iraq. Israel had hoped that the American administration would remember its contribution to preserving the coalition, but it soon became apparent that the United States sought first of all to compensate the Arab regimes for their participation in the coalition, and the latter asked the Americans to promote the idea of an international conference.

Consequently, the Americans stepped up their pressure on the Shamir government to accept the call to convene an international conference designed to resolve the Palestinian issue and facilitate peacemaking between Israel and its neighbors. In discussions with Israeli representatives, the Americans emphasized that this time the conference could bring enormous political benefit to Israel: after the Shiite revolution in Iran, and against the background of Saddam Hussein's aggression, the leaders of the Gulf states saw potential in an alliance with Israel against the Iraqi and Shiite threat. In fact, the peace treaty that Israel signed with Egypt no longer generated denunciations; instead, it served as a model.[38]

As in the case of the London Agreement, Shamir was opposed in principle to the format of an international conference. He feared that Israel would find itself under a coordinated assault by the world powers and Arab states, and thus preferred direct and separate talks with each of the states involved. After US officials promised that they would not support a Palestinian state or PLO representation in the negotiations, and that following the conference's opening ceremony Israel would negotiate separately and directly with each of the sides, Shamir accepted the invitation to the conference, scheduled to begin on October 30, 1991, in Madrid. Here was another irony, reflecting the influence of Israel's domestic situation on its foreign policy: under a hawkish government, Shamir agreed to a format he had emphatically rejected when heading a national unity government that included the Labor Party. Nonetheless, he did not retreat from his rigid views on an accord with the Palestinians or soften his opposition to any territorial concessions.[39] The Madrid Conference began with tough speeches delivered by representatives of all the sides—speeches that reflected basic national narratives. However, for the first time since the armistice agreements in 1949, there were bilateral and multilateral channels of conversations between Israel and Arab states aimed at achieving a comprehensive peace. The talks between Israel and the Jordanian-Palestinian delegation were designed to find a solution for the territories in the framework of a confederation or an independent Palestinian entity. Another objective was to reach agreement on peace accords between Israel and Jordan, Syria and Lebanon, and later with Arab states that do not share a border with Israel. While the bilateral talks aimed to promote peace agreements between Israel and its neighbors, the multilateral sessions—that included representatives of thirteen Arab states, Israel, the United States, Russia, Japan, and the European Union—were designed to discuss Middle Eastern cooperation in the areas of economics, environment, water, refugees, arms control, and more.

The conference did not produce any real breakthrough. But it had enormous historic importance for the peace process in the Middle East because (as the Middle East expert Itamar Rabinovich emphasized) it was the first time that all of the stakeholders in the Arab–Israeli conflict participated together in a diplomatic process, and the first time in history that Israel conducted negotiations with a Palestinian delegation (as part of a combined Jordanian-Palestinian team) acceptable to both sides. Thus, the Madrid Conference's importance as a historic milestone, from the perspective of the twenty-first century, even surpasses that of the peace treaty with Egypt and the Oslo Accords, which largely reflected the same formula as the one proposed in Madrid: direct channels of dialogue aimed at realizing the vision of comprehensive peace in the region.[40] However, in practical terms, the talks conducted in 1991 and 1992 with the Jordanian-Palestinian delegation (initially led by the Palestinian physician Haydar Abd al-Shafi) were fruitless.

Beilin also considered the Madrid Conference an important first step in laying a foundation for the technical format of negotiation—direct bilateral and multilateral talks. However, under the Shamir government, the sides remained far apart; it was difficult to find common ground for progress.

The conference also had an impact on the dialectics within the Israeli political system. As Shamir's position softened, at least concerning Israel's participation in the conference and negotiations, members of the Labor Party dared to express increasingly dovish views. Thus, contrary to Labor's traditional stance, the party's central committee approved a decision in August 1991 to allow some Palestinian East Jerusalemites (only those with another residence outside of Jerusalem) to participate in elections in the territories. The central committee also approved an official statement of support for a Jordanian-Palestinian confederation. Although it stopped short of recognizing the option of an independent Palestinian state, it cleared initial ground for this path. In parallel, Beilin accelerated his contacts with senior Palestinian figures—including members of the joint Jordanian-Palestinian delegation, as well as others who were not permitted to participate in the delegation because of their PLO affiliation. His partners in this dialogue were primarily intellectuals such as Hanan Ashrawi, Ziad Abu Zayyad, Radwan Abu Ayyash, and Sari Nusseibeh. In these conversations, Beilin tried to promote an idea he had already publicly expressed in January 1991: an Israeli withdrawal from the Gaza Strip as a first stage in the establishment of an Israeli-Jordanian-Palestinian confederation.[41] In this sense, the return to the opposition enabled Beilin and Peres to float proposals and ideas in freer discourse with the Palestinians, because their proposals were not binding in any case. For example, Beilin's archives reveal that on April 6, 1991, during a meeting with Faisal al-Husseini, Peres advised al-Husseini to stick with the formula of a confederation with Jordan and to put aside the demand for an independent state due to public opinion in Israel.

Peres: "Don't present your goals now. Choose a confederation with Jordan over any other idea. [Also] don't raise the issue of the right of return, because that will frighten the Israelis."

Al-Husseini rejected Peres's advice: "We're interested in independence to ensure the realization of the right of return, not to destroy Israel. We're willing to cooperate with Jordan, but not necessarily according to the agreement here"[42]—that is, a confederation that does not include an independent Palestinian state, but only autonomy.

The subject of confederation and its implications also arose during a visit by Peres and Beilin in Egypt on July 14, 1991, when the two met with President Mubarak and his adviser Osama al-Baz. Al-Baz, then in charge of the Palestinian portfolio, noted King Hussein's fear that in the absence of an accord between Israel and the Palestinians, and against the background of the anticipated mass immigration of Soviet Jews to Israel, a demographic change would induce many residents of the territories to migrate to Jordan, thus changing the identity of the Hashemite Kingdom and undermining its stability.

Al-Baz: "I've seen King Hussein every month during the past three years. He's fearful of the immigration from the Soviet Union and that it will cause an exodus of Palestinians to Jordan."

Mubarak asked to tone down the frequent declarations by Israeli politicians about the need to "warm up" the peace with Egypt and expand it to include cultural and economic relations. "I [also] want to create an impression of warm peace with Israel. The Arabs have come to terms with the peace between Israel and Egypt, but we must not create the wrong impression that strengthening the peace means accepting Israeli policy."[43] The anticipated immigration from the Soviet Union was perceived at that stage in the Arab world as a factor that could generate an enormous change in Israel's standing, and it was also mentioned in other discussions. A summary written by an Israeli participant after a different meeting in Cairo—attended by young Labor members including Burg and Beilin, upon the invitation of Boutros-Ghali—indicates that the Egyptians believed that the immigration of Soviet Jewry could also contribute to a positive development in the peace process.

"The Russians are secular," noted al-Baz during that meeting. "It will be difficult for you to change them and their worldview. They're educated, and all they want is quality of life. It was a mistake by the Arabs to oppose the immigration from the Soviet Union. Because they can change the Israeli outlook. You just need to make sure they don't go to the territories. You need to connect their interests to yours. The peace lobby in Israel should work to win the support of the Russians." On the other hand, he called the Arabs of Israel "divided and discordant assholes." Amr Moussa, the Egyptian foreign minister, added, in a sort of warning: "We've always complained that the Palestinians haven't changed, but they've changed."[44]

Al-Baz's disparagement of the Arabs of Israel can be understood in light of Egypt's disappointment over their failure to coalesce as a political force to strengthen the left in Israel, while his positive attitude toward the impending Russian immigration can be seen as evidence of the fact that the Western secularization thesis was also a dominant part of the worldview of secular leaders in Arab states. That is, the liberal Western perception that divided religious and secular people in a binary way, and identified the religious element as the obstacle to peace, led the Egyptians to assume that the secularity of the immigrants would make them a decisive electoral force on behalf of the Israeli left. As we know, this did not happen. On the contrary, in the absence of a religious connection, the immigrants from Russia based their connection to Jewishness and Israel on reinforcing the national dimension in their secular worldview. Thus, most of them became strong supporters of the right, regardless of their relation to Jewish religious tradition.[45]

# Part B

# 6

# The Big-Small Upheaval: From Opposition to Oslo

## 1

The years 1990–92, the Labor Party's second period in the opposition, marked the peak of the party's reformation.

The process was both personal and substantive. Although Rabin and Peres continued to compete for the party's leadership, there was a change of generations in the middle echelons. The older generation, which was still active in the party and was represented by people like Emanuel Zisman, Shlomo Hillel, Yisrael Kessar, and Ora Namir (the latter two even challenged Rabin and Peres for the party's leadership), lost its power and influence, and the Mashov alumni from the 1980s became the dominant politicians in the party. The rising stars in the party were in their early forties—a young age in Israeli politics in the late twentieth century. Most of them were Israeli-born or had immigrated to Israel at a young age, and embodied a more diverse and up-to-date mosaic of Israeli society: Avrum Burg represented the liberal religious camp, while Nissim Zvilli and Amir Peretz represented the second generation of Mizrahi Jews; Yael Dayan stood out for her feminist views; Haim Ramon was seen as a quintessential and energetic sabra; Nawaf Masalha represented the Israeli Arab who was at home in both cultures; and Hagai Merom represented the kibbutz movement. Beilin completed the mosaic as a representative of the educated and enlightened Tel Avivian, whose feet were in the Middle East, but whose eyes looked toward the Western world.

Together, they were able to win the central committee's approval for a number of landmark decisions in the history of the Labor Party. One decision, led by Burg, called for severing the state-religion connection that Ben-Gurion had instituted. (After Burg's proposal was approved, Peres convinced him to promote a softer version.) Another decision called for a settlement freeze in the West Bank and Gaza Strip, and expressed readiness for an accord with Syria based on territorial compromise in the Golan Heights. The party's central committee also recommended revoking the law prohibiting meetings with the PLO. And though most party members had yet to accept the idea of a Palestinian state, the ideological change was clear: the party had become less like its security-minded predecessor, Mapai, and more like a European-style social-democratic party.[1] By contrast, the Likud under Shamir's leadership appeared gray and less relevant.

An important decision by Beilin at this stage was to establish the Economic Cooperation Foundation (ECF) in conjunction with Yair Hirschfeld, Boaz Karni, and others. The ECF is a nonprofit organization that works to promote Israeli-Palestinian cooperation through economic projects, research, and position papers. For Beilin, it offered what vote contractors provided to other politicians: a significant entity that supported his initiatives. Its small staff paved the way to the Oslo Accords.

Another important decision by the Labor Party was to adopt, for the first time in Israel, a framework of primaries for the party's leadership and list of Knesset candidates. Like many developments in the party (including the Oslo process), the decision to hold primaries was driven more by the ongoing struggle between Rabin and Peres than by principled support for open primaries as an expression of democracy.

After "the stinking maneuver," Rabin resolved to again compete for the party's leadership. He was supported by many party members who had concluded that Labor's chances of returning to power were slim under Peres. Rabin sought to hold the elections for party leader on August 1, 1990; Peres preferred to postpone the vote for another year. The central committee convened on July 22, 1990, to vote on Rabin's proposal. Peres delivered an impassioned speech in which he accused Rabin of subversion ("I wrote a book?" he asked, referring to Rabin's memoirs, which included a description of Peres as an "indefatigable schemer.") Rabin spoke dispassionately about his achievements in the unity government. His tone of speech also expressed his distaste for the party's institutions, where Peres's supporters were the majority. Indeed, Peres won 54 percent of the votes, and the elections for party leader were postponed. This time, however, the central committee's power could not withstand public opinion (which favored Rabin, according to the surveys) and pressure from senior party members, who feared that Labor would remain in opposition without a more electable leader. As the elections approached, more and more Labor MKs declared their support for Rabin. When Navon, Peres's friend, also switched his support to Rabin, this trend appeared to be unstoppable. In a difficult conversation with Peres, who was ready to propose the candidacy of Amos Oz in a desperate attempt to prevent Rabin from becoming the party leader, Navon reminded Peres how he himself had abandoned his patron, Ben-Gurion, in 1968 after deciding, together with a majority of Rafi members, to merge with Mapai and form the Labor Party. Navon reminded Peres of how difficult this decision was, but that it was justified after realistically assessing the situation.[2]

Rabin, suspicious as usual, was wary of relying on politicians who switched to his camp, and demanded that the upcoming elections for the party's leadership be held in the format of primaries, allowing tens of thousands of party members to participate. After his proposal was approved, the two camps prepared for elections, scheduled for February 19, 1992. The Rabin camp chose as its slogan: "With Rabin, We'll Win." Peres's advisers suggested the slogan: "With the Best, We Win." The circle of Peres supporters continued to dwindle as the elections drew near. Hagai Merom advised Peres to drop out of the race and aim for an agreement with Rabin that would secure Peres's standing. Beilin found it difficult to advise Peres on a course of action. His loyalty was assured, but he was aware of the slim chances of winning. In his eyes, both slogans were valid—Peres was the best, but Rabin could win.

Yisrael Kessar and Ora Namir also were competing for the party's leadership. Peres tried to convince Kessar to drop out: most of Kessar's supporters were Histadrut activists and Arabs, and the assumption was that most of them would vote for Peres if Kessar were not on the ballot. But Peres's clout diminished together with his chances of winning. Kessar remained in the race and Rabin was victorious with just over 40 percent of the votes. Peres had to settle for the No. 2 slot on the Knesset list, after Rabin. Beilin's standing also declined. His efforts to sever the connection between membership in the party and the Histadrut angered the trade federation's loyalists and, despite his high media profile, Beilin was relegated to the twenty-fourth spot on the Labor Party's list of candidates. Again, this showed that Beilin did not draw his political power from the public, but from his roles in the top echelon in the political system.

While the political fortunes of Peres and Beilin declined within the party, surveys indicated growing public support for Labor as the elections approached. The elections were moved up from November to June after Shamir's right-wing partners quit the coalition, leaving him without a Knesset majority. Shamir's willingness to participate in the Madrid Conference, and his decision not to retaliate against Iraq for firing Scud missiles against Israel during the Gulf War (a wise decision, based on the IDF's assessment that it would be impossible to eliminate the missile threat completely, and in response to the American administration's demand) stirred fierce criticism in the right-wing parties Hatehiya, Tsomet, and Moledet. The government fell in early 1992 when the three parties left the coalition in protest. This suggests that Shamir acted shrewdly as a politician when he preferred unity governments that enabled him to cast the "blame" on the left. Without the Labor Party in his government, the accusations about his excessive "moderation" fell entirely on him.

The criticism against Shamir and his government also intensified in the wake of a series of knifing attacks against Israelis by lone assailants from the territories, which shook Israelis' sense of personal security. In a deeper sense, this criticism reflected the connection between the neoliberal trend that engendered greater individualization in Israeli society, and the fact that Israeli society regarded a threat to personal security as more egregious than a threat to national security. That is, Israelis were prepared to absorb broad security incidents—for example, the intifada and the missile barrage from Iraq—but found it hard to accept the privatization of the risk at the level of attacks against citizens in the streets, though the strategic weight of such attacks was negligible. In addition, the fact that these knifings began at the very time that the uprising in the territories had waned a bit, brought more Israelis to realize that the conflict could only be resolved through diplomacy. In this context, it is noteworthy that some members of the young generation in the Likud also disagreed with Shamir's refusal to recognize the Palestinians' right to self-determination. (He viewed them as an indistinct part of the Arab nation.) For example, Roni Milo advised Shamir to adopt Beilin's proposal to start with a withdrawal from Gaza, arguing that this would lighten the demographic burden and portray Israel as an initiator on the diplomatic front. But Shamir rejected any notion of withdrawal. Both before and after the elections, he repeated on several occasions the statement that capsulizes his view of the Arabs and of the multitude of peace initiatives: "The sea is the same sea, and the Arabs are the same Arabs." That is, the Middle Eastern conflict is still over the right of the Jews to a state, and the Arabs—whether Palestinians, Jordanians, or others—still reject this right.

The Shamir government also faced economic crisis in light of the budget demands created by the massive wave of immigrants from the former Soviet Union. The economy was in recession and unemployment soared to 12 percent. Shamir refused to freeze construction in the settlements in exchange for loan guarantees Israel requested from the United States for immigrant absorption, and this portrayed him in public as a leader who was ready to sacrifice everyday needs for the sake of an outdated ideology. (The American condition for the loan guarantees was based on concerns that Israel would channel most of the immigrants to the territories, and thus establish irrevocable facts on the ground.)

The elections were also held in the shadow of numerous corruption affairs that naturally aroused the public's disgust with the government, similar to the feelings the prevailed on the eve of the upheaval in 1977. There was also widespread resentment about the surge of religious legislation—a function of the coalition's dependence on the ultra-Orthodox parties—including restrictions on "immodest" advertisements and public transportation on the Sabbath.

2

The Shamir government made an important and lasting impact on the state's future by enacting two basic laws—Basic Law: Freedom of Occupation and Basic Law: Human Dignity and Liberty. This effort was led by Amnon Rubinstein (Shinui) and Dan Meridor (Likud); Beilin was among its supporters. This legislation reshaped the relations between the legislative, judicial, and executive branches, and established a liberal-secular framework for court rulings.[3] These two basic laws empowered the Supreme Court to overturn legislation that violates human rights.[4]

It is worth pausing to consider the question of how such liberal legislation was enacted under a right-wing/ultra-Orthodox government, because this question is related to changes that occurred in the methods of struggle between the liberal camp and the "Jewish"/conservative camp in Israel, and reflects the nature of the confrontation between the camps in the twenty-first century.

Meridor, who served as justice minister in the Shamir government, says the successful passage of these laws can be attributed to a prosaic reason. Shamir, who considered himself a supporter of individual rights, simply took little interest in legislative processes and their significance, and gave Meridor a free hand to operate in this area as long as it did not rattle the coalition.[5] At the same time, it seems that the religious parties' MKs did not realize the full implications of these laws,[6] in part because the legislation did not address important rights such as freedom of religion, equality, and freedom of speech, and because Basic Law: Human Dignity and Liberty was worded somewhat vaguely. On the one hand, the law stated that it could not be used to override previous legislation; thus, it was not revolutionary and Israelis would remain subject to rabbinical courts. On the other hand, the law can be interpreted as authorizing the overturn of a rabbinical court ruling if the complainant makes a convincing case that the ruling violates his dignity and freedom.[7] In this way, the legislation strengthened human rights in Israel.

Only in retrospect, it became clear that these basic laws facilitated a deviation from the "politics of accommodation" that had characterized Israeli governments since the days of Ben-Gurion. The "accommodation" approach was designed to resolve conflicts through compromise in a society that was divided on ideological or religious issues, while avoiding definitive decisions.[8] Indeed, since the 1990s, these basic laws led to High Court decisions that changed the traditional Jewish character of Israel (for example, legalizing the import of non-kosher meat)[9] and engendered an ongoing conflict between adherents of former Supreme Court president Aharon Barak's doctrine, which asserts that "everything is justiciable," and critics who accuse the Supreme Court of overstepping its bounds.

For our purposes, the identity of this legislation's proponents is important: Rubinstein and Meridor, who led the legislative effort, and Beilin, who supported it (though he was not one of its leaders), came from different parties, from different sides of the political spectrum in Israel. However, in many ways they embodied the same image of the liberal Israeli: enlightened, secular, nationalist, and Ashkenazi. Almost *ahusalim* [as noted earlier, a Hebrew acronym for Ashkenazi, secular, Israeli-born, socialist, nationalist Israelis]. Just the socialist component was missing. Professor Ran Hirschl identifies a constitutional revolution in the basic laws the Knesset enacted in 1992 and argues that their enactment at this stage was not coincidental. The new laws, he explains, were the Israeli chapter in a global transition to juristocracy in the late twentieth century—that is, the transfer of power and authorities from representatives and lawmakers to judges. In Israel, this action was prompted by an awareness that the secular-bourgeois hegemony was imperiled due to demographic and sociological changes. Therefore, the transfer of power to the Supreme Court was designed to leave control and power in the hands of the threatened class. Indeed, diverse groups had entered the Knesset, with values and inclinations different from those of the old elite, and it was clear that this trend would only strengthen in the future. Consequently, the representatives of the old hegemony—Meridor, Rubinstein, and the thirty-two MKs (including Beilin) who voted in favor of the basic laws and shared a neoliberal secular agenda—decided to fortify the Supreme Court while they still had the power to do so.[10] This assertion points to this episode under the Shamir government as the opening round of the raucous cultural battle raging in the second decade of the twentieth century. It also helps to explain the sense of urgency that characterized the Rabin government after the Labor Party's victory on June 23: it recognized that due to the demographic and social changes occurring in Israeli society, the liberal camp's window of opportunity was closing. In his conversations with Peres and Rabin at the time, Beilin expressed this urgency as a principle that should guide the government's policy.

Indeed, Labor's victory represented an opportunity, almost at the last moment, while it was still possible for the liberal camp to form a coalition under its leadership. The media called this turn of events "the small upheaval." In retrospect, however, its repercussions for Israeli society were of no lesser magnitude than the upheaval of 1977.

The left's victory, etched in the public memory as Rabin's achievement, did not, in fact, reflect the wishes of the voters. The Labor Party did, indeed, win forty-four seats and Meretz another 12 (about 20% more than the combined seats of Ratz, Mapam, and Shinui in the outgoing Knesset), and the Likud slipped to only thirty-two seats, but the number of votes for the left-wing bloc was several thousands less than the number of votes for the right-wing bloc and religious parties. If the threshold percentage had not been raised, the Hatehiya party would have entered the Knesset and Shamir could have formed a government.[11] Thus, in light of the demographic changes, which were also related to the high birthrates in the ultra-Orthodox sector and the growing strength of the traditional dimension in Israel, it seemed like almost the last chance of the liberal camp in Israel to govern.

Rabbi Ovadia Yosef's bold decision to instruct Shas to join the leftist government this time provided the underpinnings for the only political alliance capable of promoting peace accords—an alliance of the liberal camp with ultra-Orthodox and Mizrahi Jews. But this alliance was based on agreements between the leaders of the respective publics—without a sincere effort to foster agreement between the citizens themselves. This type of alliance only arose one other time in subsequent years, when Ehud Barak formed the last leftist government in 1999, and that alliance, too, collapsed before the end of its term. Perhaps an attempt to promote dialogue between the different publics during the days of the Rabin government would have also helped to fortify this alliance in the future. But this did not happen.

In any case, in July 1992, fifteen years after the upheaval, the Labor Party returned to power under the leadership of Yitzhak Rabin. The new government relied on the sixty-two MKs of Labor, Meretz, and Shas, with a "security net" provided by five MKs from Hadash and the Arab Democratic Party. It was one of the most active and important governments in the history of the State of Israel.

## 3

Prior to the Labor Party's internal elections to choose its Knesset slate, Rabin, who had already defeated Peres in the vote for party chairman, called upon all Labor voters to choose Peres for the top spot in the list. This projected a sense of responsibility and reduced tensions within the party. As noted, Peres was, indeed, elected to the first slot. However, Rabin's approach was purely instrumental and did not indicate a sincere intention to reconcile with his rival. This was saliently underlined on the evening of the victory.

When the election results were announced, Peres hurried to the Dan Hotel, where the party's leaders and activists were gathering. Some of the activists received him with cries of joy and jubilation. Rabin's associates, who were still getting organized at his home, reported to him that Peres was receiving a hero's welcome at the hotel, as if it were his personal victory. This was the background to Rabin's dour appearance on the stage and his joyless speech featuring his famous declaration: "I will navigate." Peres, standing at the far edge of the stage, needed no further explanation. He felt unduly insulted again. The depth of Rabin's antipathy for Peres was in full display to Israeli citizens watching the television broadcast. Even at the moment of his greatest victory, Rabin primarily emphasized the hierarchy of relations he intended to establish with Peres.

Relations between the two continued to be strained during the formation of the government. It was rumored that Rabin intended to assign a minor role to Peres, perhaps even relegating him to the role of minister without portfolio. When Rabin presented the new government on July 13, it turned out that Peres received the portfolio he desired, the Foreign Ministry. However, Rabin significantly narrowed the foreign minister's purview. He denied Peres the right to intervene in the direct contacts with Arab states and the Palestinians, which were underway in Washington in the wake of the Madrid Conference. Rabin also stipulated that he would personally handle all of the critical issues pertaining to relations with the United States. Peres was left with the multilateral talks conducted on the sub-ministerial level, which addressed secondary issues that would become relevant only after achieving peace.

Peres had no alternative but to agree and hope that he would eventually be able to expand his range of activity. He again appointed Beilin to serve as his deputy. At first, Peres and Beilin tried to persuade Arab states to upgrade the multilateral talks to the ministerial level. Peres believed, much like Herzl, that regional economic prosperity would lower national and political tensions. Thus, he tried to explain to his Arab interlocutors the importance of raising the level of the talks, even if the topics were ostensibly secondary in importance and would only become applicable after concluding peace treaties. But this effort failed, primarily due to Saudi opposition. The Israeli press ridiculed Peres as "the foreign minister for cocktail affairs." Beilin understood that Peres's diminished status offered some potential advantage. That is, the exclusion of Peres from the central arena of diplomacy gave him the freedom to explore activity and formulas for negotiation that were considered unacceptable, and this is the key for understanding the developments in Oslo.

After assuming his post, Beilin asked to review all of the reports on the diplomatic talks conducted since the beginning of the Madrid Conference. He was particularly interested in the meetings held between Israel and the Jordanian-Palestinian delegation, and quickly identified the impasse. The fact that Rabin kept Elyakim Rubinstein in the role of cabinet secretary and as the head of the Israeli delegation in the talks with the Jordanian-Palestinian delegation did not boost the Palestinians' optimism about negotiations under Rabin's government; it conveyed the message that there was no real difference between the new government and its predecessor vis-à-vis the territories. It is doubtful that the Yiddish jokes Rubinstein told during the meetings did much to brighten the mood.

The attempt to dictate to the Palestinians who their representatives could be— that is, the prohibition of PLO members from participating in the negotiations—was absurd in terms of its utility. The members of the Palestinian delegation not only received instructions from the PLO, but also presented positions that were more rigid than those of the PLO—after all, they could not be seen as less loyal to the national cause. Faisal al-Husseini was allowed to join the Palestinian delegation only in the ninth round of talks. Al-Husseini was one of the leaders of the first intifada, the son of Abd al-Qadir al-Husseini (the commander of Palestinian fighters in the Jerusalem area during the War of Independence) and a relative of Mufti Haj Amin al-Husseini (the most prominent Palestinian leader in the pre-state period). His inclusion in the delegation was a gesture by the Rabin government. Under Shamir, Israel had refused to allow residents of East Jerusalem to participate as Palestinian representatives because they resided within the boundaries of Israel. (Israel officially annexed East Jerusalem in 1980.) Rabin agreed to allow al-Husseini to join the delegation based on the latter's additional residence in the territories outside of Jerusalem. But in conversations with Beilin, al-Husseini expressed his bitter disappointment with the negotiations.[12] He complained about the absurdity of forcing the Palestinians to negotiate in a joint Jordanian-Palestinian framework, when everyone knew that the Palestinians received their directives from the PLO (Dr. Saeb Erekat, a member of the delegation, later admitted that he had acted as Arafat's direct surrogate) and after King Hussein had publicly washed his hands of the territories. Al-Husseini was particularly peeved by Rubinstein, who proposed discussing municipal elections instead of general elections in the territories, arguing that for the Palestinians' sake, it would be best to avoid elections that could reflect the power of Hamas.[13] From Israel's perspective, al-Husseini concluded, the Palestinians would be free, at best, as mayors. The historian Avi Shlaim, who studied the peace process, wrote:

> At least one thing was clear at the end of the twenty months and ten rounds of Arab–Israeli peace talks: the Madrid formula was not capable of ushering in a new era of peace in the Middle East, and a new formula had to be found.
>
> Although the Madrid formula involved Israel in indirect negotiations with the PLO, Rabin resisted for a whole year the calls for formal recognition of the PLO. He saw Yasser Arafat as the main obstacle to a deal on Palestinian autonomy, and did his best to marginalize him, pinning his hopes on the local leaders from the occupied territories, whom he considered more moderate and more pragmatic. Experience taught him, however, that the local leaders could not act independently of the PLO chairman in Tunis, and that, consequently, if he wanted a deal, he would have to cut it with his arch-enemy.[14]

With encouragement from Peres, Beilin began to explore other options—alternative paths.

**4**

One of these paths began when Beilin was still an opposition MK, busily preparing for the Knesset elections. On April 29, 1992, he went to a meeting at the Tandoori restaurant in Tel Aviv. Though he was not a fan of Indian cuisine, he could not refuse an invitation to meet there from Terje Rød-Larsen, a Norwegian sociologist from the Fafo Research Foundation. Rød-Larsen had conducted research on the living conditions of the Palestinians in the territories and was captivated by the idea of promoting peace. Joining the two at the meeting was Dov Randel from the Histadrut's International Relations Department.

Beilin was not in high spirits, largely due to Peres's precarious standing in the party. The battles between the Peres and Rabin camps had also prevented Beilin from playing a significant role in the election campaign; all that remained for him was to volunteer for meetings in the Arab sector, aimed at strengthening Arab support for the party on election day. In any case, Rød-Larsen surprised Beilin during the meal by telling him about a meeting he had had with Fathi Arafat, the brother of the PLO chairman, and with Abu Ala (Ahmed Qurei), who headed the PLO's economic branch. His impression from that meeting, Rød-Larsen said, was that the PLO was ready to compromise in order to reach an accord if the Labor Party, indeed, rose to power. Rød-Larsen proposed convening a meeting between Faisal al-Husseini and Israelis in the Norwegian capital, Oslo, to discreetly discuss possibilities for advancing the process, separately from the futile talks in Washington. Beilin thanked him for the information, and emphasized that as long as the Likud remained in power he saw no chance of reaching an agreement, even in theory. On the other hand, if Rabin became prime minister, he would be open to ideas, because one of his main campaign promises was to conclude an agreement on Palestinian autonomy within nine months.

Beilin chose the Middle East expert Dr. Yair Hirschfeld, who had already served as his contact person with the Palestinians, as the Israeli representative for the proposed talks in Oslo. On June 19, less than a week before the elections, al-Husseini, Rød-Larsen, Hirschfeld, and Beilin met at the American Colony Hotel in East Jerusalem and agreed to set up a secret channel of informal talks that would present any conclusions it reached to the government—if the Labor Party was victorious in the elections.

On September 9, less than two months after the formation of the Rabin government, Jan Egeland, Norway's deputy foreign minister, arrived for a visit in Israel. His bureau chief was Mona Juul, Rød-Larsen's wife. In a conversation that Egeland and Juul conducted with Beilin, Hirschfeld, and Beilin's adviser Shlomo Gur, the deputy foreign minister suggested implementing the proposal outlined at the Tandoori restaurant. The plan was not only to hold discussions with al-Husseini, but also with a direct representative of the PLO.

When Beilin came to update Peres on the Norwegian proposal, he found the foreign minister in a downcast mood. Angry and insulted, Peres told his deputy that Rabin had refused to allow him to meet with al-Husseini. Beilin was in a bind. He chose not to tell Peres about the Norwegian proposal to host meetings with al-Husseini in Oslo, but also decided not to personally participate in the talks. He refrained from telling the Norwegians why he was not participating; he did not want to reveal Peres's diminished standing in the government. After conducting consultations, Beilin decided that Dr. Ron Pundak, a former defense official who specialized in Jordan, would also represent him in the Oslo talks. At this stage, the law prohibiting direct meetings with PLO officials was still in effect. Beilin had already submitted a bill to revoke this law in the previous Knesset, but it was rejected—in part, because of opposition from hawkish Labor MKs. On December 2, 1992, with pressure from Meretz, a bill to overturn the prohibition came before the Knesset again, this time as government-backed legislation, and it passed its first reading by a one-vote margin. Though Rabin himself refrained from voting, it signaled the winds of change.

5

The meetings in Norway were preceded by two meetings in London, on December 4 and 6, 1992. Participants in the London meetings included Hirschfeld, Pundak, Abu Ala, and the PLO's representative in London, Afif Safiya. Beilin was also in London, preparing for the multilateral talks planned at the Madrid Conference. Hirschfeld updated Beilin only after the fact, to avoid implicating him in the deliberate violation of the law. Hirschfeld reported: "The meetings were held upon the initiative of Ashrawi and al-Husseini in order to create a secret channel and check the readiness of PLO-Tunis to move forward and reach an Israeli-Palestinian agreement."[15] Beilin was the only Israeli politician informed about the content of the conversations, and he made it clear to Hirschfeld and Pundak that they were operating alone, without the approval of the foreign minister and prime minister.[16] Though the decision to keep Peres in the dark was not an easy one, and could have harmed their relationship, Beilin preferred this path. Otherwise, he might have forced Peres to choose between two complicated options: to inform Rabin about the secret contacts, knowing that he was likely to forbid them, or circumvent the prime minister, and thus jeopardize his position in the government.

To quiet his conscience, Beilin decided to update Peres if the conversations reached a deeper level. The Palestinians, on the other hand, assumed that if Beilin knew, then Peres knew, and that Rabin, of course, was overseeing everything. Although the Palestinians were well versed in the intricacies of Israeli politics, they failed to appreciate the full significance of the hostility between Rabin and Peres. However, Beilin vaguely reported about the possibility of moving toward direct talks with PLO to the US assistant secretary of state, Edward Djerejian, and his deputy, Dan Kurtzer, who were in London for the multilateral talks. This happened on December 4, after Hirschfeld and Abu Ala met for the first time in London. Beilin asked Djerejian and Kurtzer whether they would be willing to provide an American umbrella for secret talks between Israel and the PLO after the Knesset approved the final reading of the law revoking the prohibition on meeting with PLO representatives. At this stage, Beilin thought it would be best to conduct the talks in the United States. But the two American diplomats explained that this was impossible because a majority in Congress still opposed recognizing the PLO. This seminal moment led Beilin to understand that the only practical option was a secret channel in Norway, which only he and his advisers would know about at first. His main concern was that the Mossad would detect the meetings and update the prime minister, so he decided not to inform any Foreign Ministry personnel except his secretary Orit Shani and his adviser Gur. On the Palestinian side, Abu Ala reported that both Arafat and Abu Mazen (Mahmoud Abbas), who was considered responsible for the Israeli portfolio in the PLO, were aware of the talks and their significance. The two sides agreed on the basic objective: an interim accord on autonomy, followed by negotiations on a final status agreement that would include discussion of the confederation option.

On December 6, 1992, Pundak, Hirschfeld's partner in the talks, sent the following encrypted message to Beilin:

> Here's a report on two meetings that Hirschfeld held with Hanan Ashrawi's "friends." The Palestinians seek to reach an initial agreement quickly. In their view, if they don't advance peace, they'll lose control to Hamas and the extremist organizations. They suggest that the Americans offer the "conventional gestures" via Faisal al-Husseini and Hanan Ashrawi, a proposal for an agreement on principles. [But] they don't believe the new administration will renew the dialogue with the PLO and ask us to launch a public campaign to renew the discourse. They are already now ready to discuss Rabin's proposed federation idea in a positive way.[17]

This report revealed part of the complexity of the relations between Israel and the Palestinians. The main reason for the PLO's readiness for flexibility and negotiation was its fear of Hamas gaining strength, while the PLO's weakness was the very reason that impelled Israel to pursue an agreement with the PLO. At the same time, the Palestinians' desire to promote their cause in the American administration via Israel reflects the extent to which Zionism, from its earliest days, was boosted by the perception of Jewish influence. Herzl believed that this perception would help him promote the Zionist cause in his initial meetings with Russian and Turkish officials, who thought that American Jewry could convince the US administration and financial investors to assist their countries.

In any case, December was not the ideal month to start negotiations. On December 13, Hamas militants abducted a Border Police officer, Haim Toledano, and demanded the release of Ahmed Yassin, the Hamas founder who was sentenced to life for inciting to abduct and kill Israeli soldiers. The government prepared to conduct negotiations and demanded to first receive a sign of life. Two days later, Toledano's corpse was found. In response, the government instructed the IDF to launch an operation against Hamas in the territories. More than 1,000 members of Hamas and Islamic Jihad were rounded up in the operation. On December 17, the government decided, in an unprecedented move, to expel 415 of these detainees to Lebanon. It seemed that the leftist government was more aggressive than its predecessor, and the possibility of a diplomatic accord appeared faint.

Meanwhile, Beilin prepared for the talks scheduled to take place at a pastoral guest house about 100 kilometers south of Oslo, as planned in the meetings held in early December in London. The first round of meetings in what became known as the "Oslo track" began on January 20, 1993, a day after the Knesset revoked the prohibition on meeting with PLO officials, and continued through January 22nd. Abu Mazen, who led the talks on the Palestinian side, decided that Abu Ala would be joined by Hassan Asfour, a close associate of Arafat, and Maher al-Kurd, Arafat's economic adviser. Abu Ala asked Beilin to personally participate in the talks, but the deputy foreign minister chose to continue to orchestrate the negotiations remotely, from the Foreign Ministry's offices in Jerusalem and Tel Aviv, receiving updates by telephone and encrypted telegrams.[18] The second round was slated for February 11 and 12. The absurdity in the fact that the Israelis and Palestinians did not speak each other's language was conspicuous in the talks. Abu Ala, who was meeting for the first time with Israelis, insisted on speaking Arabic in order to ensure the precision of his words, and al-Kurd translated his words into English. This was time-consuming, though the participants felt from the outset that something of real significance was afoot.

The central idea of the negotiations was to infuse the Camp David Accords with content on the Palestinian issue. That is, the aim was to implement Begin's plan of administrative autonomy: to grant the Palestinians broad autonomy for an interim period, during which the Palestinians would choose their leaders in free elections, who would then negotiate with Israel on a final status accord. At an early stage in the Oslo talks, the "Gaza first" idea was raised—an Israeli withdrawal from Gaza even before the elections for the Palestinian leadership. The idea was to give the Palestinians a clear benefit that would demonstrate Israel's seriousness, while relieving the demographic and security burden entailed in controlling the Gaza Strip. The proposal to "get rid of" Gaza, even before conducting Palestinian elections, was also part of the motif of urgency that guided Beilin. However, the sides did not engage in in-depth discussion of this idea. On the question of East Jerusalemite Palestinians participating in the Palestinian elections, the Israelis proposed (as already approved by the Labor Party's central committee) that they could vote, but as foreign residents. To compete in the elections, a Palestinian resident of East Jerusalem would be required to have an additional address outside of the city. It was decided that the critical issues of the right of return, borders, and the status of the Jewish settlements would only be decided in a final agreement.

The secrecy of the Oslo channel, which also left Peres out of the loop, is evident in the fact that the foreign minister (accompanied by Pundak, Hirschfeld, and Avi Gil, and after receiving Rabin's okay) met on January 9, 1993, in Jerusalem with Faisal al-Husseini and explained why Israel would not conduct direct negotiations with the PLO. Peres's remarks are interesting, because he outlines his far-reaching vision, including the removal of nonconventional weapons from the Middle East after reaching a full regional accord. Peres said:

> We know that you speak with the PLO in Tunis, and we don't prevent you from doing so. But we have two problems with direct talks with the PLO. One is that the PLO also speaks on behalf of the Palestinian diaspora, and just as we don't speak in the name of the Jewish people in the exile—it also cannot. The second is that the PLO is still linked to acts of terror and this is a cause of rancor—even if sometimes exaggerated—for us. The situation could change if the PLO abandons terror for the period of negotiation, and is very clear in calling for a two-state solution. We suggest you choose representatives and begin negotiating an interim accord to avoid complicating the situation concerning the map and relations between the peoples. . . . . I know that you're concerned that the temporary will

become permanent, but I can promise you that even if we don't agree on the map, we'll agree on a timetable. And secondly, we accept 242 and 338. Wherever there is Palestinian life—will be under your control. Wherever there are Israelis—under our control. And other areas—under shared control. You'll be able to enact laws in your area, and we'll have our laws [in the areas] under our control . . . we'll leave Jerusalem for the end. You'll be able to vote, but any concession now in Jerusalem would lead to the loss of a majority under any government. Concerning confederation—the economic world is becoming global. . . . It's early to talk about this, but we'll be open to an economic partnership. . . . Concerning security, you need to consider our needs in regard to missiles with nonconventional weapons, and we'll be willing to have full inspection. We can cooperate. We'll build a canal from the Red Sea to the Dead Sea.[19]

Al-Husseini was more succinct in his responses. He was primarily wary of a gap between promises in private conversation and their lack of implementation. "We need steps from your side," he said. "Under Shamir and under Rabin nothing has changed, and I'm losing my credit among the people. Every step from your side is an investment in the moderates."[20]

# 6

On February 11 and 12, Beilin's representatives met again with Abu Ala. This time, Abu Ala said that before making concessions and agreements, the PLO needed to understand whether the channel was authorized and backed by Rabin. With disappointment, he cited reports in the Israeli press that Rabin had said that another five to ten years would be needed before reaching agreement in negotiations. Of course, the Israeli representatives dodged this question. After all, at this stage Rabin knew nothing about the Oslo talks.

The two sides had already reached agreement on the basic outlines of an accord: Israel would transfer authorities for self-rule of Palestinian life in a range of fields, and elections for a temporary Palestinian council would be held within a few months, which would choose representative for signing an autonomy accord with Israel. Two years after signing the agreement, Israel would fully withdraw from the Gaza Strip, which would be governed under an Egyptian or international trusteeship. At this stage, negotiations on a final status accord would commence. The sides did not agree on the Palestinian council's legislative authorities. The Palestinians sought to achieve the nearest thing to a sovereign state, while the Israelis wanted to allow only legislative authorities at the municipal level. One of the central problems was the mutual suspicion of the two sides (which persisted throughout the process); each side feared that the other would fail to carry out the agreements. The Israelis rejected Abu Ala's proposal to form an international council to arbitrate disputes over implementation of agreements.

It was easier to agree on the way in which the accord—if achieved—would be brought before the two sides. Similar to Peres's plan at the time of the London

Agreement, here, too, the intention was to present the conclusions of the Oslo talks to the Americans and ask them to submit them to the Israeli prime minister and to al-Husseini as the representative of the Palestinians, as if the ideas were the American administration's own initiative. The assessment was that presenting the agreements as an American initiative would make it easier for both the Israeli side and the Palestinian side to withstand domestic opposition. At this stage, it was decided to present the accord during a shuttle diplomacy mission of Secretary of State Warren Christopher. And if Rabin and al-Husseini agreed, there would be a public signing ceremony.

7

Only in early February 1993, when the talks produced basic agreements, Beilin decided to share the secret with Peres. His main fear was that Peres would complain about being kept in the dark for so long, and not about the initiative itself. Knowing the stuff that politicians are made of, Beilin also was concerned that Peres might be inclined to belittle the agreements emerging in Oslo because he had no hand in them.

The tactic Beilin chose later served Peres when he came to inform Rabin: he presented the developments without any drama, almost nonchalantly, as if this were just one of many options, but one that deserved attention. Beilin's concerns quickly faded. Peres responded to the update in a matter-of-fact way, and since he had never previously heard of Abu Ala, he asked for more information on the Palestinian representatives and their political importance. He did not address the fact that Beilin had concealed these developments from him, as if this were standard procedure, and promised to get back to Beilin with an answer after reviewing the matter. Beilin appreciated the way Peres responded. In Beilin's eyes, one of Peres's strengths as a leader was that he allowed freedom of action to those around him—especially to Beilin, who had been at his side for about fifteen years. Peres made sure to garner credit for diplomatic gains, but was ready to allow his associates to act independently during the process itself—a quality atypical of most politicians. In this, too, Peres was undoubtedly influenced by his mentor, Ben-Gurion, who surrounded himself with young people who were allowed independence in implementing the general policy of the "old man."

Beilin could now only wait in suspense for Peres's answer; it was clear that the Oslo process would be a nonstarter without the foreign minister's support. Several days passed before Peres responded. It was clear that he had studied the documents carefully. Peres had reservations about granting election rights to Palestinian residents of East Jerusalem and the proposed international trusteeship for the Gaza Strip. However, in general, he saw the Oslo talks in a positive light. Now Peres had the task of informing Rabin and convincing him to agree to continue the talks in Oslo.

Since the establishment of the government, Peres had regularly updated Rabin on every diplomatic option that crossed his path. He realized that to win Rabin's trust he had to tread carefully in even the smallest matters and consistently brief Rabin on his activities. They established a routine of meeting privately every week, without recording notes of the meeting. They allowed themselves to speak freely in these meetings and their working relations began to improve. Nonetheless, the cloud of suspicion never completely lifted. Peres would tell Beilin that during these tête-à-têtes, Rabin sounded well-intentioned, but that he feared Rabin would renege on some of their agreements. This would be easy to do, since the content of the meetings was never documented. Therefore, after each meeting, Peres would quickly write a summary for himself to keep a record of the key points. Rabin also did not change his basic view of Peres; when he met privately with Beilin, he would complain about Peres, without taking into account Beilin's close relationship with the foreign minister.

Still, now in the eighth decade of their lives, Rabin and Peres also recognized the fact that it might be their last opportunity to advance their objectives. They were now the last two "tribal elders" in the Labor Party, and were fully aware that their combined experience was invaluable. In intimate forums, Rabin was a different person than he was in meetings with many participants. Sometimes he surprised Beilin with his cordiality and openness to different proposals. Beilin hoped he would react this way to Peres's update, and he waited in the foreign minister's office after Peres left for his one-on-one meeting with Rabin. Indeed, the prime minister surprised Peres by responding calmly. He was neither thrilled nor horrified by the talks and agreements with PLO representatives. Rabin asked Peres to oversee the talks and continue with the Oslo track as long as it was not detrimental to the official channel of negotiations in Washington. Peres and Beilin felt a sense of relief and tried to find an explanation for Rabin's calm response. Perhaps he simply did not believe the Oslo effort was particularly important, and may have preferred to keep Peres busy with this. Another conjecture attributed his response to the importance Rabin placed in his campaign promise to achieve an agreement with the Palestinians within nine months. Therefore, he was not in a hurry to reject any option, especially when the Washington talks were going nowhere fast.

Thus began the involvement of Peres and Rabin in the Oslo process and the Oslo Accords: with lukewarm consent. Some like to claim that Peres deviously dragged Rabin into the Oslo process, but Beilin's archives indicate otherwise. Rabin was updated on developments almost immediately after Peres learned of them, and the two jointly assumed responsibility for the process, starting in February. It is true, as described below, that Rabin was, as usual, a bit more skeptical. It is also true that from this stage, Peres was more excited and confident than Rabin was about the Oslo path.

The myth of the complete exclusion of the Americans from the talks is also inaccurate. The American administration was not updated in the initial stages about the seriousness and importance of the contacts in Oslo, because the Israeli side was also unsure about this at the outset. However, as Hirschfeld noted in a report he prepared on the Norwegian track: "The American administration was in the picture from the beginning of the contacts. The Americans adopted the position that each of the channels should be allowed to operate separately."[21] It seems amazing that while Israel's prime minister and foreign minister knew nothing about the Oslo talks, the American administration was being briefed on the developments. However, while it is chronologically correct to say that the American administration "was in the picture from the beginning of the contacts," this is a bit of an overstatement. Beilin reported to State Department officials Djerejian and Kurtzer on the talks weeks before informing

Peres and Rabin, but he did not go into the details. The Americans themselves did not appreciate the importance of the talks, and as long as Rabin and Peres were not involved, the information did not receive significant attention in the White House. The initial contacts were seen as another nonbinding and unpromising effort.

Hirschfeld wrote in his report:

> After making the connection, the Norwegian government took responsibility for the logistics and various coordination. From January until mid-May 1993, five meetings were held between PLO representatives—Abu Ala, head of the Economic Department, who was also in charge of the multilateral negotiations, Maher al-Kurd, Arafat's economic advisor, and Hassan Asfour, Abu Mazen's political advisor—and Pundak and Hirschfeld. The talks were held with the knowledge of a very small circle in the top PLO echelon, headed by Arafat.

During the first talks, possibilities were examined for reaching an accord based on three main principles:

1. the gradual transfer of authorities;
2. the Palestinians' suggestion to implement autonomy first in Gaza; they emphasized that it was clear to them that Peres supported the idea and there were supporters in the opposition, too. Jericho was an addition raised later;
3. promoting cooperation in all fields of life, particularly in economic development.

> Another goal was to examine the management of security issues during the interim period, responsibility for the Jewish settlements, topics for negotiation on the final status accord, and the legal standing of the autonomy. . . .The PLO personnel expressed views that were more moderate in a number of central areas, and Israel's positions were accepted vis-à-vis interim agreements in these key areas: removing Jerusalem from the autonomous region, while preserving the [Palestinians'] rights to participate in elections; Israel's responsibility for overall security; the autonomy's authority would not apply to the settlements and Israelis.[22]

Peres was mainly worried about the participation of East Jerusalem Arabs in the Palestinian elections, because he feared that the political system and Israeli public opinion would find this hard to digest. Nonetheless, he was surprised to learn that the Palestinians were not insisting on another idea that was raised, of an Israeli withdrawal from Jericho together with Gaza.

Rabin himself regarded the Oslo track as an auxiliary channel. Prior to the meetings scheduled for March 20, he asked to instruct the teams to demand that the PLO tell the members of the Palestinian delegation to renew the talks in Washington. (The Palestinians had quit the talks, alleging that the Israeli side was not serious about negotiating.) In return, Israel would agree to continue the talks in Oslo. At this stage, the paradox of the Middle East was evident in its full glory: Israel wanted to exploit the secret channel of direct talks with the PLO in order to make progress in the Washington channel, which was ostensibly conducted without the PLO's involvement, though it was clear to all that the PLO stood behind the Palestinian delegation. The PLO found itself in a trap: it wanted to conduct the talks with Israel on its own and directly. However, in an effort to convince Israel of the sincerity of its intentions and its goodwill, the PLO accepted Rabin's demand and instructed the members of the delegation to renew the negotiations in Washington. The absurdity of these moves cried out to high heaven: Why not conduct direct negotiations between Israel and the PLO? After all, it was in Israel's own interest to talk with the key Palestinian player, and it was clearly in the PLO's interest to strengthen its status as the entity that openly manages the Palestinians' fate. But from Rabin's perspective, it was impossible at this stage to cancel the talks in Washington and openly focus on the direct conversations with the PLO in Oslo, because this would signify official Israeli recognition of the PLO. And Rabin believed this recognition was excessive compensation for agreements that had yet to be signed.

Still, the fact that it was only thanks to the secret talks in Oslo that the PLO agreed to instruct its delegation to renew the talks in Washington in April, illustrated to Rabin the benefits of direct negotiations with the PLO. Rabin's decision to adopt Oslo as the preferred channel was also spurred by messages he received from the Democratic president, Bill Clinton (who entered office in January and immediately showed his commitment to achieve peace in the Middle East), and from the new secretary of state, Warren Christopher, expressing their disappointment over the lack of progress in the Washington track. But at this stage, he still preferred to pursue the Oslo talks without making them public.

The Palestinians had concerns of their own. Abu Ala feared that Israel was exploiting the talks in Oslo only to pressure the PLO to instruct the Palestinian delegation to renew the official talks in Washington, and would not honor the promises the Israeli representatives made in Oslo. Abu Ala wanted to know which channel Rabin was committed to, and noted that Arafat saw the Oslo talks as the primary channel. To illustrate their seriousness, the Palestinians updated the Egyptians, who also gave their blessing to the Oslo process. The members of the Palestinian delegation in Washington, on the other hand, were unaware of the developments in Oslo. At this stage, the compartmentalization was very high in Tunis, and besides Arafat and Abu Mazen and the negotiators themselves, no one in the organization knew about Oslo.

However, as the talks in Norway became more serious and in-depth, disputes arose on issues that the two sides had already agreed upon during the initial meetings. In March, the Palestinians demanded an earlier withdrawal from Gaza, and wanted the elections to be held under international supervision. The Israeli representatives did not oppose an early timetable for the withdrawal, but rejected international supervision, fearing a precedent that would impose foreign intervention in the territories. At the same time, new agreements were reached. It was agreed that the Palestinians in East Jerusalem would vote at polling stations adjacent to the holy sites, which were already viewed as international. It was also agreed that Israel and the Palestinians alone would define the legislative powers of the Palestinian council to be elected. In addition, the Israelis agreed to establish an arbitration institution that would address cases of disagreement in implementing the accord. The arbitration, however, would be limited to specific topics, and would be initiated only after attempts at direct dialogue failed. The Norwegians suggested bringing representatives of the American administration into the picture to help overcome the obstacles in negotiations, and the Palestinians proposed increasing the Egyptians' involvement.

The media in Israel and the world continued to focus on the Washington channel. In March, Rabin visited the White House and agreed to include a Palestinian resident of East Jerusalem in the Washington talks in exchange for the Palestinians agreeing to drop their constant demand to involve the PLO directly. It was agreed that the talks in Washington would resume in April, but the absurdity was that the representatives in those talks were unaware of the agreements that had already been reached in Oslo, and the negotiations in Washington became pointless.

In May 1993, Peres decided the time had come to deepen the contacts in Oslo and proposed conducting the negotiations himself. Rabin refused, arguing that the foreign minister's direct involvement would commit the government and narrow Israel's range of maneuver. Peres accepted the decision with disappointment, but insisted on raising the echelon of negotiators. Rabin agreed, provided that it did not involve a civil servant or politician. Peres chose for this task Uri Savir, the Foreign Ministry's director-general, who until then knew nothing about the Oslo talks.[23] Rabin was wary of negotiations conducted exclusively by Peres's aides, and soon afterward requested that Joel Singer join the Israeli negotiating team in Oslo. Singer, the foreign minister's legal adviser, enjoyed the confidence of both Peres and Rabin. The participation of Savir and Singer was initially presented as merely intended to assess the progress of the talks; the idea was to avoid giving the Palestinians the impression that the arrival of "official" negotiators signaled a change on the Israeli side. However, their positions in the Foreign Ministry and Singer's expertise in contract law clearly indicated that the talks had reached a new stage in which the Israeli leadership was preparing for the possibility of signing an official accord. As the talks continued, Savir and Singer assumed a central role in the negotiations.

Rabin, who had yet to inform anyone in the Prime Minister's Bureau about the talks in Norway and the agreements reached there, formed a team of four to oversee the negotiations and regularly discuss their progress: Peres, Beilin, Singer, and himself. The team met once a week, primarily on weekends. The meetings were usually held at Rabin's office in the Defense Ministry, or at the Accadia Hotel, where he was staying on weekends while his apartment in Tel Aviv was undergoing renovation. There were also meetings at his official residence in Jerusalem, and a few at the Prime Minister's Bureau. These low-profile meetings were necessary to prevent gossip about what was happening.

Since Peres flew overseas frequently in his role as foreign minister and Singer was still working at a law firm in Washington, some of the meetings were held just between Beilin and Rabin. The two did not become friends, but a direct and open relationship developed, and the talks were more candid than ever.

In one such meeting, Beilin suggested dropping the insistence on autonomy for an interim period—an idea proposed at Camp David and at the Madrid Conference, and which served as a basis for the Oslo talks—and skipping directly to negotiations on a final status accord. In Beilin's view, a rare situation had emerged within Israel and internationally and it should be exploited: a Palestinian partner who was ready to step back from many of its past demands, an Israeli prime minister who was prepared to negotiate with the PLO, and a young American president who was seeking his first international achievement and would be willing to work hard to reach an accord. There was an opportunity for a far-reaching move, Beilin argued. Rabin rejected the idea. He explained that if the talks on an interim accord failed, it would be possible to return to them in the future. But if the talks on a final status accord failed, it would be almost impossible to return to discussing interim arrangements. There was logic in Rabin's assessment, but that conversation led Beilin to think about another diplomatic initiative, which he would also need to initiate without the backing of Rabin and Peres: opening another secret channel for talks on a final status accord, in parallel to the Oslo talks. But this awaited further progress in the Oslo negotiations.

In early June, the Palestinians presented positions that were more hardline. Pundak and Hirschfeld attributed this to the fact that "the circle of those who knew the secret in the PLO had widened and Arafat had intensified his direct involvement."[24] Thus, even those who supported direct contacts with the PLO regarded Arafat as a more radical element in the organization.

Disagreements also arose among the Israelis. Singer, Savir, and Beilin believed that the time had come to propose official Israeli recognition of the PLO, and thus put an end to the hypocrisy and absurdity of conducting negotiations with an organization that official Israel was unwilling to negotiate with. This would also enable Israel to demand a PLO commitment to completely stop all violent activity. Pundak and Hirschfeld also agreed with them. Peres, on the other hand, argued that it was premature to recognize the PLO and that Israel should save this important bargaining chip for later in the negotiations. Nonetheless, he did not oppose the idea of allowing top PLO leaders to settle in Gaza immediately upon its transfer to Palestinian control.[25]

## 8

On June 6th, Peres and Rabin met for one of their regular update sessions. Peres returned from the meeting pale and angry. Those who claim that Rabin never wholeheartedly supported the Oslo process can point to this meeting as evidence.

Rabin surprised Peres with a demand to stop the process, arguing that the agreements were vague and their implementation could endanger the security of Israel's citizens. He had concluded that PLO-Tunis was seeking to undermine the new leadership emerging in the territories, and that Israel should focus on negotiating with that local leadership in the Washington channel.[26] Peres, stunned, consulted with Beilin and the two found it hard to explain Rabin's change of mind. Only a few weeks earlier, Rabin had approved sending Singer and Savir to Oslo, a decision that indicated his interest in advancing toward an accord there. The day after his meeting with Peres, Rabin sent him a letter in which he described Oslo as a "danger":

> Pursuant to our conversation on this matter on Sunday, June 6, 1993, I'd like to reiterate the main points I mentioned. In the current situation, the so-called "Oslo contacts" constitute a danger for continued negotiations on peace. . . . First, they give an opportunity for [PLO] Tunis officials to bypass the Washington talks and weaken the positive element in them—the residents of the territories who are included in the Palestinian delegation. The Tunis officials are the radical factor among the Palestinians who support the peace process, and are those who are preventing the more moderate ones from advancing in the negotiations with us. This was clearly expressed in the ninth (the latest) round of negotiations. Moreover, they are preventing members of the Palestinian delegation from engaging in dialogue with State Department representatives in Washington. It is quite possible that Tunis officials aim to torpedo any chance of reaching serious negotiations in Washington and force us to negotiate only with them. . . . I wish to stop the contacts pending further investigation.[27]

Upon Peres's instructions, Beilin asked Hirschfeld and Pundak to compose a letter addressing Rabin's reservations. The letter they prepared noted that, in any case, the Washington talks were slated to reconvene on June 15, and if Rabin believed in this channel, there was no reason not to continue in it. However, the two emphasized, it was clear that without Oslo, no progress could be made in Washington. They also noted that the agreements in Oslo offered the Palestinians self-rule only in exchange for a complete halt to terrorism, and that Israel would retain security powers during the interim period, including responsibility for the security of the settlements. The transfer of Gaza to the Palestinians, they added, would only relieve Israel of a demographic and security burden. The letter also stated that an agreement in Oslo would boost economic prosperity in Israel because of the cooperation it could potentially facilitate with Arab states. Hirschfeld and Pundak promised Rabin that his reservations would be discussed throughout the process. Peres gave the letter to Rabin, reminding him that it had been agreed to postpone discussion of the critical issues (borders, settlements, and Jerusalem) until the sides began negotiating a final status accord.

In Peres's office, they waited for a response.

On June 11, Rabin summoned Peres, Beilin, and Singer to his office. They were surprised to find him in a relaxed mood. He sounded satisfied by the fact that authorities would be transferred to the Palestinians gradually, and that the Civil Administration and military government would not be dismantled immediately. Rabin emphasized that Israel's Oslo negotiators must stand firmly behind his demand that security and foreign affairs remain in Israel's hands during the entire interim period. Singer tried to take advantage of the congenial atmosphere to discuss the possibility of mutual recognition between Israel and the PLO. But Peres quickly intervened, saying there was no justification for this now and that Israel should continue to demand the PLO's blessing for electing a new Palestinian representative body in the territories. Rabin said he "agrees with Shimon." Singer was insistent. He politely asked permission to raise this possibility with the Palestinians as his personal proposal. Rabin's response was surprising: "In your own name, offer whatever you wish."[28] This was the first time that Rabin approved considering the idea of recognizing the PLO, and this occurred only a few days after he had rejected the Oslo process in its entirety.

The question of what caused Rabin's sudden and strong opposition to the Oslo process—and what led him to quickly return to it—remains a mystery.[29] Uri Saguy, the head of military intelligence from 1991–95, suggests an interesting possibility, also expressed in Arab sources: Rabin suspected Peres and Beilin of sending messages to Arafat that included requests to stall the talks in Washington, while Rabin was still hoping to leverage the Oslo process to advance the negotiations in Washington. Though Rabin understood it was impossible to negotiate without a connection to the PLO, he continued to distinguish between the PLO-affiliated representatives in the territories and the Tunis-based PLO leadership. "I'm not placing myself as a judge," Saguy later wrote, "but I have a firm belief that the negotiations with the Palestinians in Washington were delayed and even undermined to a significant extent by other people on the Palestinian side and by some in the Israeli Foreign Ministry, who believed that the negotiations should be conducted in a different format and by other people."[30] Martin Indyk, who served as a special assistant to Clinton during this period, admitted that despite his intimate familiarity with the Oslo process and its various aspects, he found it hard to explain Rabin's position on Oslo.[31] Rabin's letter to Peres was later leaked to the press and right-wing circles cited it to claim that Rabin was dragged into an agreement against his will. But his rapid return to the Oslo path and his involvement in the details of the discussions throughout the process indicate otherwise.

Another hypothesis is that Rabin may have given a green light for the first stages of the Oslo talks with the goal of using it to achieve compromises in the Washington track. According to this premise, once the talks resumed in the United States, Rabin decided that the Oslo path had run its course and that the agreements reached in Norway should be brought into the official track.

Ephraim Sneh, who was close to Rabin, offered a different explanation. In this account, since the prime minister continued to have doubts about Oslo and lacked confidence in Peres's representatives, and because he also understood that the Washington track was going nowhere, he wanted to secretly pursue a third track, bypassing both Washington and Oslo, and asked Sneh to lead this mission. Indeed, Rabin sent Sneh to meet with Nabil Shaath, who was very close to Arafat and served as the PLO's head of foreign affairs. The meeting took place in London on June 7, a day after Rabin had met with Peres and instructed him to suspend the Oslo process. However, after Rabin understood from Sneh that he could not open a third channel with Shaath because Arafat saw Oslo as the best path for extracting concessions from Israel, Rabin discarded the idea of creating a third track.[32] Perhaps Sneh's account most accurately explains Rabin's conduct, because his suspicion of Oslo was also reflected in another channel he tried to pursue at this stage (unbeknownst to Beilin and Peres), which began with serious conversations between Haim Ramon and Ahmed Tibi, as

Arafat's representative. Rabin renewed his support for the Oslo process only after realizing there was no alternative.

Another possible explanation is that between June 6 and 11, Rabin conducted a lesson in leadership, making it clear to Israel's negotiators in Oslo (Peres's men) who the real boss was. He wanted to emphasize their duty to precisely convey his demands, without glossing over anything. Perhaps he was concerned that the negotiators were overly inclined to compromise. The lesson in leadership may also have been designed to put pressure on the PLO's negotiators. Simple psychology may have also played a part: Rabin suddenly felt apprehensive, but was reassured by the letter of clarification from the Israeli negotiators in Oslo.

In this context, it is worth examining the relationships in the Israeli team that was privy to the Oslo talks. Rabin was the ultimate decision-maker, but operated completely on his own and kept his closest advisers in the dark about the Oslo process. Michael Bar-Zohar, Peres's biographer, correctly noted that "in addition to being an extraordinarily suspicious person, Rabin had to rely on information channeled to him from Peres, whom he totally distrusted, and from Peres's young gang, including Yossi Beilin, who were completely devoted to him."[33] Beilin sensed the weight of this solitary burden on Rabin's shoulders. While Peres could call upon the assistance of his aides, Rabin read every document alone. He was usually focused and remembered in detail the questions raised in previous meetings. However, he was occasionally overwhelmed. One time, Beilin asked Rabin if he had noticed a relatively minor clause that had changed from one draft to the next. Rabin read it again, admitted that he had not noticed, and said he did not agree with the change. On the way out of the meeting, Peres asked Beilin why he had drawn Rabin's attention to the change: the main thing is to get him to sign.

In any case, after June 11, the Israeli negotiators were again authorized to work toward an accord, but were also required to clarify several critical subjects: security arrangements, the status of Jordan and Egypt in the accord, the question of who would sign the accord on each side, and the type of regime to be formed in Gaza.

On June 28, an important meeting took place between al-Kurd, Abu Ala, Singer, Hirschfeld, and Pundak.

The Palestinians were apparently aware of the efforts to create additional channels of negotiation and Singer needed to reassure them. "I saw Rabin's response before I came here [to Oslo] and after . . . he told me there's only one back channel, Oslo. There are all sorts of people getting involved, and Rabin can't prevent this. There's no need to harm the channel in Washington, but whatever is agreed here—will be implemented there. Rabin went over the drafts sentence by sentence, and he wants to know that there isn't any trick or conspiracy here."[34] Abu Ala noted that the Palestinians also have reasons to suspect the Israelis, and added: "It's not easy for us either."

After his preliminary remarks, Singer asked to address the security arrangements, which were discussed only in general since no military experts were present: "Rabin wants that anywhere the IDF withdraws—army and Israeli vehicles will [still] be able to travel in the streets."

Abu Ala replied with a series of questions that actually pertained to the final status accord: "What do you think about Jerusalem? What about the Kalandia airport? Why do you object to having the [Palestinian] Authority's headquarters in Jerusalem? What about the institutions that are already located there? What will you announce about [continuing] the settlements? Will they be completely halted? The number of settlers will remain [unchanged]? Responsibility for the settlements is yours, [but] what about outside of them? What's the difference between a political settlement and a security settlement?" He also proposed leaving "part of the agreement secret. That would help."

In concluding his remarks, Abu Ala added a concrete demand concerning the security arrangements: "We want our security forces, supported by an Egyptian force and international forces—Scandinavian, American, or others—to manage the security." He noted: "If the IDF wishes—it can return within an hour. But an IDF presence in the territory will not be accepted. We need 10,000 fighters."

"In what structure?" the Israelis asked.

Abu Ala: "I don't know. But besides the settlers and IDF soldiers—all the rest [must be] under Palestinian control."

Singer: "Not necessarily. Local electricity, roads to the settlements and to a Palestinian village [that is, approval to use electric and construction infrastructure]—those will not be under your jurisdiction. . . . Some areas will be under your responsibility, some not."

Abu Ala: "That's not a problem."[35]

## 9

In his memoirs, Efraim Halevy—the deputy director of the Mossad from 1990–95 and Mossad chief from 1998–2002—laments the absence of defense experts in the early discussions in Oslo. Though Halevy supports a two-state solution and appreciates the historic importance of the Oslo Accords, he claims that clearer and more effective security arrangements could have been formulated if security professionals had been involved in the negotiations from the outset. These improved arrangements, he argues, would have prevented some of the lacunae in the accords and thus strengthened the foundations of peace.[36]

A similar concern was expressed in real time by Johan Jørgen Holst, one of the prominent supporters of the Oslo track, who replaced Thorvald Stoltenberg as Norway's foreign minister in April 1993. He warned against "constructive ambiguity" on security matters and other issues, aimed at facilitating an agreement while sidestepping contentious details.

On July 27, Holst wrote to his Israeli counterpart that "the situation in the 11th round of talks is not clear and it seems that each side is interpreting things in its own way." He identified the lingering suspicion between the two sides as the main problem. Holst added that he had learned from a conversation with Abu Ala that the Palestinians feared that "Israel wanted to retain full security control," which would undermine any chance of a state in the future, and that Israel's aim was to separate the PLO from the Palestinian people.[37] Peres was concerned about the pessimistic tone of a key person involved in the talks. He tried to reassure Holst and convince him that there were grounds for postponing issues until the final status negotiations. Peres wrote in response: "We don't want to control the future and the lives of Palestinians. . . . We understand from your letter that the PLO also understands that the time is right, but I fear that they are inclined toward a solution that is too perfect. . . . The problem is that the Palestinians want to decide on the parameters for the final accord now, but we know that it's impossible to guarantee the future, and creating a new reality is the only alternative."[38]

In any case, it was evident in meetings held on July 25 and 26 that the two sides had moved further apart, including backtracking on some agreements they had already reached. On July 29, Singer sent a worried telegram to Rabin, Peres, and Beilin classified as "top secret."

> On July 25-26, I participated in a meeting with PLO representatives in a small town near Oslo, based on the optimistic messages I had received from the Norwegian foreign minister Holst, who met with Arafat last week. . . . Therefore, we expected that the discussion would focus on the five points that remained open in the last joint draft, from July 6th, and on the three points we sought to revise according to the prime minister's instructions (on security, legislation and Jericho as the site of the autonomy's council). . . . It turned out that while they accommodated us on one important point (the participation of Jerusalem residents in elections), on many other points they reopened subjects that had already been closed. . . . We reacted very strongly. . . . We emphasized that their conduct stirred doubts about the seriousness of their intentions. . . . Nonetheless, we decided to try one last time. . . . They took our words very hard and, consequently, a gloomy atmosphere prevailed between the two camps.[39]

Later in the telegram, Singer described the issues in dispute:

> Concerning Resolution 242 [and 338], they wanted to stipulate that the negotiations on the final status would lead to the implementation of those decisions, while we're prepared to affirm that the permanent accord will constitute implementation of those decisions. . . . Concerning the reference to "the legitimate rights and just demands of the Palestinian people," we asked to add that their fulfillment would be expressed in a final status agreement. . . . Concerning the topics for negotiation on the final accord, they asked we already agree now to discuss Jerusalem, refugees, settlement, security arrangements, borders, relations, and cooperation with neighboring states. On the other hand, we preferred wording in which each side lists the topics it will raise in negotiations. . . . On the subject of the involvement of Jerusalem residents in elections, the PLO made a big step to accommodate us and agreed to drop their demand that the final accord stipulate the right of Jerusalem residents to vote and be elected. . . . They added that they want to put off the early transfer of authorities until the IDF withdraws from Gaza and Jericho, and explained to us that they want the authorities to be transferred to the PLO Tunis

leadership, which will come to Gaza, and not to Palestinians inside [the territories]. They demanded that the PLO bring its security police, while we're willing for them to only recruit police personnel who have Jordanian citizenship. They asked for control of the Jordan bridges and crossings between Gaza and Egypt—we made it unequivocally clear that we did not agree.[40]

Singer also added his assessment of the Israeli media's impact on the Palestinians' attitude toward Israel's positions. In the recommendations section, he suggested that "the prime minister and foreign minister announce that Israel has reached the limit of concessions, because the PLO reads the Israeli press with a magnifying glass," and he complained about the damaging way in which Israeli politicians were trying to promote additional mediation channels on their own initiative. "[Yossi] Sarid promised [the Palestinians] a connection between the autonomy's council and Palestinian institutions in Jerusalem," while "[Haim] Ramon [operated] via Ahmed Tibi." These efforts, Singer wrote, entice the Palestinians to wait for additional changes in the Israeli stance, and weaken the bargaining power of Israel's representatives in Oslo. Singer was unaware that Rabin had sent Sarid and Ramon to these meetings in order to check alternatives to Oslo because he was still skeptical about what was happening there.[41]

# 10

The basic idea behind the Oslo Accords was that the peace process with the Palestinians should be divided into two stages: in the first stage, an interim agreement would be signed that would establish autonomy, help build relations of trust between the two sides, and allow for an assessment of the agreement's implementation; in the second stage, a final status accord would be negotiated and signed at the end of five years. The deep question that remained hovering in the air pertained to the final accord, but during the days of negotiation, Rabin and Peres refused to clarify among themselves their broad strategic objective. The Palestinians thought that the permanent accord would upgrade the autonomy to statehood. Rabin and Peres were far from this. It was clear to Beilin that the final status agreement would lead to a Palestinian state.

The Israeli side did agree that it was possible and worthwhile withdrawing the IDF from Gaza and Jericho in the initial stage; this would both test the Palestinians and give them a tangible achievement. Israel was slated to withdraw from most of the territories later in the interim period, but would refrain from dismantling settlements and retain security responsibility for the settlements and borders.

The hope was that a positive reality created during the interim period would make it easier for the two sides to compromise on the core issues in the final status accord, including the status of the refugees, Jerusalem, and the borders.

The Palestinians agreed in principle to accept this framework. The main obstacles that remained concerned the legislative authorities of the elected council, the formal status of Gaza and Jericho, the geographic demarcation of Jericho, the corridor between Gaza and Jericho, and whether Arafat would be called "president" (a title that would accord the autonomy a near-state status) or only "chairman." In parallel, they tried, unsuccessfully, to already raise issues that were slated for the final status negotiations.

Even though the negotiations were conducted with PLO representatives, the possibility of Israel officially recognizing the organization did not come up for discussion until late July; the Americans also opposed Israeli recognition of the PLO at this stage.[42] While Rabin authorized Singer to raise the idea as a personal initiative, the Israeli plan was to gain the PLO's consent to hold elections in the territories and then continue the official negotiations with Palestinian representatives chosen in those elections. However, the fact that Israel was negotiating with an organization it had yet to officially recognize (the PLO) raised questions: Who would sign an agreement reached in Oslo? And who would present it to the leadership on both sides? One idea was to give the draft agreement to the Americans, and the Americans would then present it to Rabin and al-Husseini, the head of the Palestinian delegation in the Washington talks, for its official signing. Another suggestion was to have Peres and al-Husseini sign the agreement.

In late July, the Norwegian foreign minister proposed to Peres that he meet in secret with Arafat. Peres feared that news of the meeting would get out and adversely affect Israeli public opinion, even before reaching an agreement. However, for the first time, he did not rule out meeting with Arafat after the signing of an accord. Beilin, on the other hand, wanted to leap forward. He believed it would be best to recognize the PLO as part of the agreement, and thus prepare public opinion on both sides to appreciate its historic significance and the mutual acceptance it expressed. According to the report from Holst, who met with Arafat on July 20, the latter also recognized the historic importance of the Oslo track and saw the agreement as a dramatic step toward full reconciliation between the Zionist movement and the Palestinian national movement. However, in his conversation with Holst, Arafat also frankly expressed his worries about the repercussions of the agreement, because the Palestinians would be giving more than they receive. Israel, Arafat said, would present the military withdrawal from Gaza as a valuable diplomatic quid pro quo, while, in fact, it relieved Israel of a security headache and demographic burden. But he could not say this publicly without dishonoring Gaza and its residents. Arafat was also concerned about access to Gaza and Jericho and passage between them; he feared that Israel had a grand, secret plan to create a sort of cantonization of the territories, which would sever the various regions and make it impossible to achieve a real state in the future. Therefore, he announced he would not sign an agreement unless it includes a mechanism for free passage, controlled by the Palestinians, between the different parts of the territories. In addition, as an Arab and Muslim leader, he was obliged to demand recognition of the Palestinians' natural, historical, and religious connection to Jerusalem. Arafat summed up his concerns in a more embittered strategic assessment: an agreement in Oslo might only lead to limited autonomy for the Palestinians, while Israel would immediately receive a bridge to the Arab world, including the Gulf states, which would then abandon the ongoing struggle for a Palestinian state.[43]

Arafat's pessimistic (and perceptive) assessment on the eve of signing the agreement not only indicates a keen understanding of Israeli interests and of his own standing in the Arab world, but also helps to explain the difficulties that arose in implementing the

Oslo Accords. Arafat feared from the outset that an agreement in Oslo would be seen as an Israeli concession, rather than what it actually was—a successful strategic maneuver by Israel; this would put the Palestinians in an inferior position. Thus, it is easy to understand why he did not intend to completely abandon the option of terrorism as an alternative to continuing the process.

The scholar Yoram Peri, who served as Rabin's adviser, offers an interesting analysis of Israel's deep interests in Oslo that validate Arafat's concerns to some extent: Israel did not seek to deceive Arafat, but the primary flaw of the Oslo process was that the political echelon (and later, the military establishment) adopted the process because of strategic and security considerations, and not as a result of profound thinking about the moral essence of resolving the conflict.[44] At the center of these considerations was the assessment that the principal threat to Israel in the twenty-first century would be states in the second circle, headed by Iran. Thus, it was best to exploit the current situation, including the collapse of the Soviet Union, to compromise on the territories, whose importance diminished in the era of ballistic missiles. Israel could then rid itself of the conflict with the Palestinians and achieve peace accords with the neighboring states, thus freeing it to concentrate on meeting the threats from the second circle. Beilin himself noted in a speech at the Meretz convention in 2005 that the primary strategic reason that impelled Rabin to support Oslo was that he saw a future threat from Iran. Thus, he wanted to resolve the Israeli-Palestinian conflict as soon as possible in order to focus on the Iranian threat.[45]

"Of course, the accord with the Palestinians was designed to ease the demographic distress and security burden entailed in control over them, and from Rabin's desire to exploit the diplomatic window of opportunity in the early 1990s after the dissolution of the Soviet Union," Beilin frankly notes today. He goes on to explain:

> But, to a very great extent, Rabin pursued peace out of fear of the nuclear [threat]. He said he wanted to reach peace before Iran attained a nuclear weapon that could change the balance of power in the Middle East. In fact, in the early days of the government, the Mossad began to work intensively on this issue. Ephraim Sneh, who was close to Rabin, also worked a lot on this. In a way, this suggests that Rabin thought that Israel could not prevent Iran from going nuclear, and thus had to pursue peace accords before strategic changes occurred in the region.[46]

The fear of Muslim nuclearization that occupied the Israeli leadership already at the time when the Dimona reactor was built in the 1950s,[47] intensified since the 1970s and developed under Avraham (Avrasha) Tamir into what the historian Shlomo Aronson calls "the Tamir school": the need to reach an accord on the territories before a Muslim state develops a nuclear capability.[48] A significant part of the motivation for a peace treaty with Egypt should also be understood in this nuclear context. In the 1980s, Israel was mainly troubled by the nuclear option in Iraq and Pakistan. In 1980, as opposition leader, Peres proposed a "policy of opposition to supplying nuclear weaponry to any state [in the Middle East] that is in a state of war [with Israel],"[49] and he justified the need for territorial compromise as part of preparation for the more severe threat.

In Yoram Peri's view, since the readiness for compromise with the Palestinians drew from security considerations, it lacked a moral impetus and attentiveness to the Palestinians' plight. Without these components, it is difficult to inject real content in peace accords, Peri argues. This also explains why the leaders of the defense establishment supported the Oslo Accords when informed about them early in the process, and then adopted a different stance during the second intifada, when Arafat was perceived as instigating terrorism: the Israeli perspective on the Palestinians was and remains purely military, and this prevents an understanding of the complexity of Palestinian positions and motives.[50]

# 11

In August 1993, in the context of US-mediated talks between Israel and Syria, Rabin publicly repeated an earlier declaration about the formula for peace with the Syrians: "The depth of the withdrawal will reflect the depth of the peace." In reiterating this, Rabin was signaling progress and Israel's readiness to compromise on the Syrian track. Since he had already emphasized that Israelis would not be able to contend with withdrawals on two fronts, this declaration posed a threat to the Oslo process. The background to Rabin's remarks included a secret promise he made (in the presence of Israel's ambassador in Washington, Itamar Rabinovich) to Secretary of State Warren Christopher on August 3 that in exchange for full peace with Syria, he would be willing, contrary to his campaign promises, to withdraw to the lines of June 4, 1967.

Although Peres and Beilin were unaware of this promise at the time (Rabinovich updated Peres only after Rabin's assassination), Rabin's declaration on the formula for peace with Syria worried them—not because they opposed a deep withdrawal from the Golan Heights, but because of Rabin's conviction that it would be impossible to conclude agreements in parallel with both the Palestinians and the Syrians. Beilin, feeling a sense of urgency, tried to convince Rabin that there was no contradiction between the two tracks, and that Israel should promptly pursue accords on all fronts. But Rabin remained unconvinced. Thus, his declaration in August about "the depth of the withdrawal will reflect the depth of the peace" can be seen as another expression of Rabin's skepticism about the Oslo process. Indeed, in Rabinovich's view, Rabin remained skeptical about Oslo until almost the last moment. (In any case, when the secretary of state returned to Israel on August 5 after presenting the prime minister's position in Damascus, Rabin was disappointed. Assad set conditions of his own, rejected the idea of a gradual Israeli withdrawal over five years, and refused to normalize relations with Israel at the beginning of the withdrawal process. Rabin decided to step away from the Syrian track for the time being.)[51] It is possible, however, that Rabin's public statement about Syria was a tactical move. That is, it was intended to push the Palestinians toward an agreement and warn that Israel would otherwise turn to a different track.[52]

Indeed, the Palestinians were more forthcoming in a meeting on August 14 and agreed to postpone decisions on the border crossings (between Gaza and Egypt and between Jericho and Jordan) until the stage of detailed negotiation, after signing the initial agreement. It was also agreed that Arafat would suffice with the title of "chairman."

In exchange, Israel promised to transfer Gaza and Jericho to the Palestinians before signing a detailed agreement on self-government in the territories, several months after the signing of the initial agreement. This paved the way for signing the Oslo I Accord. Internal political developments in Israel also strengthened the desire to sign an agreement as soon as possible: in the wake of a Supreme Court ruling that Interior Minister Aryeh Deri would need to step down from his position after his indictment on charges of financial corruption, it was clear to Rabin and Peres that Shas would likely quit the coalition before long, undermining the stability of the government.

Peres had a diplomatic visit scheduled in Stockholm in August, and he decided to wait there and monitor the latest developments in Oslo. He hoped to come to Oslo and be present at the ceremonial signing of the first, basic agreement. August 19 was expected to be the day of decision. Uri Savir and Abu Ala worked out the final details. The Palestinians consulted with PLO officials in Tunis. The Israelis spoke with Peres, who supervised matters from Stockholm, and with Beilin, who remained in Jerusalem and updated Rabin over the telephone.

At the very last moment, a substantial problem arose: the Palestinians insisted on managing the autonomy from a Palestinian institution to be established in Jerusalem. The Israelis refused. In the end, the Palestinians relented in exchange for a letter promising that the status of their existing institutions in East Jerusalem would not be harmed. (For this reason, the institutions of the Palestinian Authority were established in Ramallah, which became a sort of Palestinian capital, even though it lacked historical importance, other than its proximity to Jerusalem.) Savir and Abu Ala signed the agreement that night (August 19) and Peres arrived in time for the signing. He stood close by and watched with excitement.

The basic agreement, which was simply called the Declaration of Principles, was general. It recognized UN Security Council Resolution 242 as the foundation for continued negotiation—that is, land for peace—and included Israel's withdrawal from Gaza and Jericho as a precedent-setting step toward withdrawing from the rest of the West Bank. The precise map of Israel's withdrawal would be decided in ongoing negotiations. The Palestinian autonomy arrangement was slated to last five years in the initial stage, with the sides hashing out the details of the final status accord during that period. There was no mention of a Palestinian state, but the autonomous authority was promised independent mechanisms—for example, a police force. In fact, the wording of the agreement left many details for the future. However, the bottom line was historic: Israel and the PLO agreed on the basic outlines of a solution of peace. Peres updated Rabin over the telephone and told him that Abu Ala and Savir would sign the agreement that night—Rabin approved and did not elaborate in his response.[53] The signing ceremony took place in secret, filmed with a personal video camera. The question of whether to conduct another ceremony, public and festive, in full view of all, remained open.

An attack in Lebanon that took the lives of seven IDF soldiers that same day was a reminder of the complexity of the conflict. Peres considered postponing the signing of the agreement, but Rabin joylessly gave the green light to sign the accord. In any case, Peres instructed the Israeli team not to toast the agreement with champagne, as planned, because of the circumstances. Festive or not, Peres defined the event as the Palestinians' Balfour Declaration.[54] Thus, in less than eighty years, the Zionist movement evolved from the needy party to the one that granted rights to the national movement that competed with it over the same piece of land.

## 12

Rabin now decided to brief the head of military intelligence, Uri Saguy, on the Oslo talks. A memo Beilin wrote to himself a few days after the signing indicates that Saguy reinforced Rabin's concerns about the security aspects of the agreement, which committed the Palestinians to conclude the conflict peacefully, without a direct reference to unconditionally stopping terrorism. Beilin describes a phone call from Rabin in this memo:

> The prime minister called and said that the head of military intelligence had seen intelligence material about Oslo, including a call to the Americans . . . he [Rabin] asked if the agreement talks about a cessation of terrorism. I told him it didn't. And that it's mentioned in the seven points. They pertain to the intifada. He said the intifada is not so important to him if they stop terrorism. He [Rabin] asks us that they talk with the Norwegian [Holst], because if he wants to implement the agreement—they cannot continue with terrorism.[55]

A seven-point agreement appended to the Declaration of Principles included an explicit commitment by the Palestinians to renounce terrorism, but did not obligate the PLO to quash terrorism conducted by other Palestinian organizations. Rabin, as reflected in his conversation with Beilin, was troubled at the last moment by the possibility that even if the intifada (which had died down in any case) ended under the PLO's control, terrorists would emerge from other organizations in the territories and overshadow the benefits of the accord.

Immediately after the agreement was signed, Peres flew to the United States, upon Rabin's directive, to update the American administration on the developments. Due to the importance of the events, Peres suggested that Rabin himself fly to meet with Clinton, but the prime minister decided against this. The briefing was held in California, in the presence of Secretary of State Christopher, special Middle East coordinator Dennis Ross, and another White House staffer from the Middle East desk. Peres and Ambassador Rabinovich represented Israel, and the Norwegian foreign minister, Holst, was also present. The minutes of the meeting indicate the mix of the ideological with the personal, and both high and low politics.

> Peres emphasized: "What we bring [the signed agreement] is not a government decision. For now, only the prime minister and foreign minister are updated, and we need government approval. We caught the PLO at a low point, but we must be careful about pressure that would lead to the collapse of the partner."
> Christopher: "You're right. You need to preserve a reliable interlocutor."

Ross wanted to hear the Israelis' assessment of the possibility that Arafat would not keep his word and would not implement the agreement.

Israel's foreign minister stated confidently: "Our assessment is positive. He has no alternative due to his strategic situation."[56]

Peres asked the Americans to prod the Arab states to recognize Israel as a sort of reward for the agreement with the PLO. He singled out Tunisia, Oman, and Morocco as potentially ready to extend such recognition, and did not rule out the possibility of Saudi recognition of Israel. Peres also emphasized the need to provide an economic umbrella for the Palestinians, and asked the Americans to grant financial assistance to the Palestinian National Council that was slated to be elected.

The conversation in California also included discussion of holding a public signing ceremony. Peres suggested a festive ceremony that would underline the importance of the event and stir excitement in public opinion. In retrospect, Beilin contended that this was a mistake: the celebratory announcement of the agreement, which was actually a statement of principles that postponed the critical issues for future negotiation, was detrimental to both sides. "The ceremony at the White House created the erroneous and problematic impression of a diplomatic earthquake and of an Israeli-Palestinian peace that wasn't there," Beilin later said. "Oslo became much more dramatic than it actually was. It was not an Israeli-Palestinian peace accord, unfortunately."[57]

The Americans rejected the proposal to present the agreement as the fruit of their own initiative. However, they promised Peres, who was haunted by the precedent of the London Agreement, that they would back the accord.

When Peres returned to Israel, preparations began for presenting the agreement to the government and then to the public. Already in the days after the signing, news items began to appear about contacts with the PLO, but the general picture was not yet clear to journalists and the public. Unlike its usual practice when reporting historic events, *Yedioth Ahronoth*, the first newspaper to expose the contacts, chose a dry, factual headline: "Peres meets secretly in Sweden with senior PLO official."[58] This time, it seems, the factual description in the headline was shocking enough in itself. It took the media and the public a few days to understand that Israel had reached an agreement with the PLO and, as is customary in Israel, the national feeling very quickly swung from surprise to fear to euphoria, reflected in headlines such as "Enough tears and blood."[59]

On August 30, the government discussed the principles of the agreement. Clouding the festive moment was a long list of people who felt insulted at being left in the dark about the Oslo process. The cabinet secretary, Elyakim Rubinstein, who led the Israeli delegation in the Washington talks, came to the meeting with a frown. He told Beilin that he also could have reached an agreement, even earlier, if Rabin had given him the flexibility accorded to the Oslo negotiators. Eitan Haber, Rabin's bureau chief, was also disappointed and considered resigning over the fact that he was kept unaware of these developments. Rabin explained to Haber that he himself was doubtful about the possibility of reaching peace. The IDF chief of staff, Ehud Barak, was worried about security breaches. He expressed his concern about friction between the IDF and the Palestinian police force, and about protecting roads between the settlements following the IDF withdrawal. Nonetheless, Barak told Beilin that if he were a government minister, he would vote in favor of the agreement, even with a heavy heart. Motta Gur, the deputy defense minister, expressed indignation at not being informed of the contacts (though he felt better after learning that Rabin had also refrained from briefing his closest associates, including Haber and the director of the Prime Minister's Office, Shimon Sheves). Deri, surprisingly, praised the agreement, but announced that since he planned to resign from the government because of his indictment, Shas would not assume responsibility and would abstain in the vote. In the end, all of the ministers, except for two abstentions (Shimon Sheetrit and Deri), voted in favor of the agreement.

Beilin felt that this was a sort of anti-climax.

Immediately after signing the agreement, the sides continued to negotiate on mutual recognition between Israel and the PLO. (In the document signed in Oslo, there was no Israeli commitment to recognize the PLO, though the act of signing alongside Abu Ala constituted de facto recognition.) The agreements reached on this issue were expressed in an exchange of letters between Rabin and Arafat. Israel committed to recognize the PLO, and the PLO committed to recognize Israel's right to exist in security. In the negotiations that preceded the exchange of letters, Arafat demanded mutual recognition in exchange for a commitment by both sides to refrain from using violence and military force. For Arafat, the IDF's operations as the occupier in the territories were parallel to acts of terror. Rabin rejected this wording. Arafat ultimately agreed in his letter to renounce terrorism and prevent his men from conducting acts of terror. However, he emphasized the distinction between stopping the intifada and abandoning the path of terrorism—because the intifada was a popular uprising and not a PLO initiative, and it would end when the vision of peace is realized.[60]

This disagreement contains one of the seeds of calamity that weighed upon the Oslo process and hindered implementation of the agreements it produced: a lack of trust in the purity of the other side's intentions, a key condition for establishing true peace. Both the Israeli side and the PLO marched forward into a fog of suspiciousness. While the Oslo agreements blazed the trail to an accord, they were insufficient to free the sides from the constraining paradigm of the basic narrative of the conflict, in which two national movements, Jewish and Palestinian, fought for control of the same piece of land. In a letter Hirschfeld and Pundak sent to Beilin just six months after the signing of the agreement, they identified this impediment. In their view:

> From a technical perspective, the breakthrough entailed an agreement to separate the interim and final accords—and required the Palestinians' willingness to implement the interim accord prior to elections in the territories. Previously, the Palestinians would only agree to an interim accord if the final accord was concluded in advance. This was their concession. . . . In principle, the Oslo agreement was a successful idea that failed in implementation because both sides refused to relinquish their basic narrative, according to which the other national movement is competing against it.[61]

Under Israel's pressure, Arafat agreed to include in his letter a promise to change the Palestinian National Charter and revoke the articles calling for the destruction of Israel—without stipulating a deadline for making this revision. (The charter is the PLO's formative document, originally adopted in 1964 and revised in 1968. It rejected the right of the Zionist movement to a Jewish state in Palestine, claiming that the Jews are a religious community only.) Israel accepted Arafat's commitment to stop PLO terrorism and renounce terrorism in principle, without vowing to act against other terrorist organizations. The Israelis understood that a commitment in writing to act against Palestinian organizations would create difficulties for Arafat vis-à-vis Palestinian opponents of the agreement and portray him as Israel's subcontractor. Thus, from the first moment, the Oslo agreement and the letters attached to it included tacit understandings and attempts to circumvent or take into account the views of extremists on both sides, instead of blazing a new path toward peace by insisting on a new paradigm, free of the suspicions of the past, in order to make it possible to remove them in practice.

In this context, the Israeli demand to amend the Palestinian Charter is an example of a paradox that characterized Oslo: on the one hand, it offered the hope of historic reconciliation; on the other hand, it was an arrangement based on the perception of the other as an enemy. After all, the amendment of the charter was meaningless if it did not derive from the free will of the Palestinians. (In any case, it had only declarative value. Therefore, some on the Palestinian side compared the Israeli stance on this issue to a demand to amend the biblical text concerning the Jewish connection to the Land of Israel.)

During the conversations on this issue, Arafat explained that the Oslo agreement in itself revokes the charter's articles pertaining to Zionism. In any case, he emphasized, amending the charter would require a two-thirds majority of the members of the Palestinian National Council (the PLO's supreme legislative authority) and that this level of support could not necessarily be mobilized. Still, as noted, he committed to trying to fulfill this demand. Israel responded in a short letter signed by Rabin, which included recognition of the PLO as a representative—not the exclusive one—of the Palestinians. Rabin signed the letter with a simple Pilot pen on live television on September 9. He appeared to be moved by emotion, though it was not joy. His facial expression when he signed the letter, like the look on his face when he shook Arafat's hand at the public ceremony held four days later, showed how difficult it was for him to officially recognize the PLO and its leaders as representatives of the Palestinians for negotiation.

## 13

The public signing of what was officially called the "Declaration of Principles on Interim Self-Government Arrangements" took place on September 13, 1993. As suggested by Peres, it was decided that the ceremony would be held in a festive atmosphere on the White House lawn. The events during the forty-eight hours that preceded the signing again demonstrate that grand diplomatic history is made by people, with their weaknesses and tendencies to be petty, even in moments of grace.

Rabin preferred not to participate in the ceremony. He favored a more modest and businesslike proceeding, and might have sufficed with the signing that had already occurred in Oslo and the letters attached to the agreement. But he was compelled to agree, because that is not the way history is made in the modern era. All of the sides prepared for the festive ceremony in Washington, but the level of representation remained an open question. The White House debated this question and initially decided to leave the signing at the level of foreign ministers. But as the date of the ceremony approached, and the world media devoted great attention to the upcoming event, President Clinton decided to participate himself. Rabin's advisers, and Shimon Sheves in particular, believed that the prime minister's absence would give a huge political advantage to Peres. They persuaded Rabin, as Clinton had proposed, to fly to Washington. Arafat also wanted to participate in the ceremony and gain international legitimacy. Thus, at nearly the last moment, the ceremony was upgraded to include the participation of Clinton, Rabin, and Arafat. Rabin called Peres and invited him to fly with him.

Peres was angry and disappointed. After all, he was the one who had persuaded the Americans to host a festive ceremony, while Rabin had opposed the notion. And Peres had felt all along that Rabin was half-hearted about the Oslo process. He summoned Beilin, Savir, and Avi Gil for urgent consultations on Saturday morning. Peres complained that due to considerations of political prestige, Rabin was granting Arafat a large and premature quid pro quo in his readiness to appear with him. Beilin told Peres that the participation of Rabin and Arafat would strengthen their commitment to the process and have a positive impact on public opinion in Israel and beyond. But Peres remained unconvinced. He felt that Rabin's motivation was different: he was trying to steal the glory from him. Peres reminded Beilin that the Oslo agreement would never have occurred if they had not been forced to search for an alternative channel to the Washington talks favored by Rabin. After venting his bitterness, Peres announced that in the current situation, it would be best for Rabin to fly alone. The foreign minister's advisers tried to convince him that this would be a mistake. They reminded him that David Levy, the former foreign minister, had acted this way when choosing to skip the Madrid Conference after Shamir decided to lead the Israeli delegation. History does not remember those who were absent, only those who attended, his advisers argued. In the end, Peres relented. However, when compiling the list of invitees to the White House ceremony, perhaps distracted by anger, he left out the names of two key people: Hirschfeld and Pundak, who had conducted the Oslo negotiations from the outset. They ultimately found their way to the ceremony as invitees of the Norwegian delegation.

On the White House lawn, Peres signed the Declaration of Principles on Interim Self-Government Arrangements (usually referred to as the Declaration of Principles Agreement or the Oslo I Accord) on behalf of Israel and Abu Mazen signed on behalf of the PLO. Secretary of State Warren Christopher and Russian Foreign Minister Andrei Kozyrev also signed the agreement as witnesses. The agreement stipulated, in general terms, that Israel would withdraw from Gaza and the Jericho area, and later from additional territory in the West Bank. It also provided for the formation of a

Palestinian police force that would be authorized to carry weapons. However, Israel retained responsibility for defending against external threats on the borders and for protecting Jewish settlers.

Based on this agreement, detailed accords were later hammered out—including the Cairo Agreement in May 1994 and the Oslo II Accord in October 1995. The latter provided the specifics of what was outlined in the Declaration of Principles: how the autonomous Palestinian Authority would be established, election procedures for the PA's council, the transfer of authorities pertaining to education, culture, health, welfare, taxation, and tourism from Israel to the PA, and the powers of the Palestinian police and the restrictions under which it operates.

The autonomy was designed to last for five years, during which time a final status accord would be negotiated, based on UN Security Council resolutions 242 and 338. All of the critical issues—whether autonomy would turn into statehood, the status of Jerusalem, the right of return for refugees, security arrangements, borders, and the fate of the settlements—were postponed, as noted, to the final status negotiations.

Nonetheless, it is difficult to exaggerate the excitement stirred by the ceremony on September 13, 1993. After Peres and Abu Mazen signed the agreement, millions of people around the world watched as the prime minister of Israel and the leader of the Palestinian national movement, two men who represented one of the most complex and bloody conflicts in the twentieth century, shook hands. Rabin mumbled something to Peres when he shook Arafat's hand. At first, it was difficult to decipher his words. However, his reluctance was conspicuous, and this made the moment even more authentic and moving. It later became apparent that Rabin had told Peres: "Now it's your turn"—as if asking Peres to join him in dirtying his hands.

# 14

Today, more than two decades after the signing of the Oslo I Accord, it is easy to point out its flaws. Still, the agreement was a historic breakthrough, primarily in the mutual recognition of the legitimate rights of both peoples and the readiness of the accepted leadership of both peoples to engage in dialogue. It broke the taboo that had impeded any potential coexistence agreement.

From Rabin's perspective, Israel's recognition of the PLO was a function of exploiting an opportunity, the right timing, and the desire to fulfill his campaign promise of reaching an agreement with the Palestinians within nine months. He did not yet think in terms of two states, but sought a more relevant and effective sequel to the 1978 Camp David Accords.

Beilin felt great satisfaction about the role he had played in the process. He had already concluded in the late 1970s that the key to ensuring stable Jewish existence in the Middle East was to partition the land and engage in dialogue with the PLO. Though Rabin and Peres were ultimately responsible for the agreement as the state's leaders, Beilin was, in fact, the architect of the process that began in Oslo. Nonetheless, he recognized that the Oslo I Accord between Israel and the PLO was only the first step. It was a bold and pioneering step, but still only the beginning. And knowing that time was not on the side of the peacemakers (due to political, demographic, strategic, and psychological reasons) and that the process had many opponents, Beilin began to formulate the next plan: to accelerate the timetable for achieving a final status accord.

Indeed, more and more opponents rose up against the agreement on both sides. Some opposed the agreement and partitioning on theological grounds (religious Jews and Hamas supporters). Immediately upon the signing of the agreement, they were joined by naysayers and critics from two main directions: in the radical left in the West, and among a few PLO factions, some argued that Israel did not intend to withdraw from the territories. According to this view, Israel was merely exploiting the weakness of the PLO—which had no alternative but to accept Oslo if it wanted to preserve its standing—to cleverly perpetuate its control of the territories. The PLO was relegated to a solely municipal role, in which it would serve as Israel's subcontractor on the ground: a classic case of post-colonialism.

The Israeli right, on the other hand, claimed that the agreement awarded a terrorist organization the right to enter and control the territories and its Palestinian residents, just when its importance was waning and the intifada was dying out. About two years after the agreement, in one of his last television interviews, Yitzhak Shamir argued that Israel's fundamental error stemmed from its haste in pursuing an accord. Thus, Israel rushed to conclude an agreement in Oslo, even though the PLO had been "close to extinction" at the time. According to Shamir, to achieve true peace, Israel should have waited patiently and calmly for the PLO to disappear, and for a new generation to emerge in the territories, free of past grudges, and capable of discussing a peace accord.[62] Thus, as a representative of the right, the fundamental principle in Shamir's outlook, was a different perception of time that required restraint and waiting, and was anchored in Jabotinsky's notion of the "iron wall."

Beilin, who was interviewed alongside Shamir, agreed that time was of predominant importance. In Beilin's view, however, the agreement with the PLO actually saved Israel at nearly the last moment, because if the PLO had, indeed, become "extinct" (that is, lost its influence among the Palestinians), Israel would have been compelled to engage in a much more difficult and complex dialogue with Hamas as the PLO's successor.

This analysis underscores the secular versus religious dichotomy that characterizes Beilin's liberal perspective. In this view, the secular person is expected to be more flexible and moderate than the religious person. Without this distinction, it would be hard to understand why Beilin assumed it would be impossible to reach an accord with Hamas. After all, the PLO had also refused for years to recognize Israel, and perhaps the religious dimension might have actually facilitated an agreement with Hamas.

In any case, it seems we can explain the weaknesses and flaws of the Oslo agreement by blending the arguments of the right and the radical left: the fact is that Israel did not go all the way in either direction. It did not wait for the natural development of a local Palestinian leadership, but also continued to treat the PLO with obstructive suspicion after deciding to recognize it. Rabin declared in his speech on the White House lawn: "Enough. Let us pray that a day will come when we all will say: Farewell to the arms." Meanwhile, however, the Israeli sword continued to hang over the Palestinians' neck as a potential threat. Similarly, the military suit Arafat wore at the peace ceremony also indicated that he continued to wield the potential threat of returning to the path of terrorism.

In any case, the opponents of the agreement were still a minority in September 1993. Surveys found that over 60 percent of Israelis were optimistic and supported the Oslo process, and there was even stronger support in the Palestinian public. Some viewed the agreement as the greatest achievement of the Zionist movement: integration in the Middle East with the consent of the Palestinians and Arab states. The mainstream media expressed euphoria over the dawning of a new era. It suddenly seemed that Shamir's defeat in the last elections had historic significance, beyond politics, by blocking the road to the Greater Land of Israel. It was symbolic and significant that Roni Milo, a member of the "princes" generation in the Revisionist Party, and a loyalist and favorite of Shamir, publicly announced his decision to give the agreement a chance. In the Knesset vote on the Oslo agreement, on September 23, Milo abstained, together with two other Likud MKs—Meir Sheetrit and Assad Assad. Shas MKs also abstained. With the support of Hadash and the Arab Democratic Party, the agreement won Knesset approval by a vote of sixty-one to fifty.

The Knesset debate, however, was stormy. Opponents of the agreement, such as Yehoshua Mazza, argued—as Begin had claimed during the vote on German reparation payments in 1952 —that only Jewish MKs should be allowed to participate in the voting. This argument reflected the crisis the opponents of the agreement were experiencing and the deep significance they attributed to it—primarily the fear of losing the Jewish identity of the state, an identity that was linked to the Land of Israel since 1967. This connection is largely attributable to the fact that in the Jewish state, unlike Jewish communities abroad, there is very little discussion of Jewish values (religious, cultural, social, and philosophical). In this situation, the only way to sustain Jewish identity is to cling to the soil, metaphorically and ideologically. Still, as noted, the mainstream media focused on the positive future that awaited. Tawfik Ziad, a Hadash MK, succinctly described the collective feeling: "The rejectionists here cannot stop the imperative development. They cannot stop peace. That large stone, the stone of peace, has started to roll from the top of the hill and no power can stop it."[63] Few understood the threatening and tragic meaning the opponents of the agreement found in his remarks.

# Peace Contends with Reality

## 1

Beilin met Arafat and the PLO's leadership for the first time only after the ceremony on the White House lawn. In October 1993, he flew to Tunisia, where Arafat received him in his office. As usual, Arafat was effusive in warmly welcoming his guest. He got up from behind his desk and sat beside Beilin to avoid a sense of hierarchy, and offered to pour Beilin's cup of tea himself—with honey instead of sugar, while noting its health benefits. Beilin was not overwhelmed by the gesture—which Arafat made toward most of the people whose favor he sought—and was eager to discuss the matters at hand.

Arafat told Beilin that four key issues had to be addressed in order to advance the process: 1) the release of Palestinians imprisoned for acts of terror; 2) the repatriation of Hamas and Islamic Jihad members expelled to Lebanon; 3) the complete halt of closures that Israel occasionally imposed on East Jerusalem; and 4) the release of Ahmed Yassin, the leader of Hamas in the territories. In regard to the fourth request, Arafat wanted Israel to emphasize that were it not for his efforts, Yassin would still be languishing in an Israeli prison.[1] It was clear that at this stage, before his arrival in the territories, Arafat's main objective was to secure his standing among the Palestinians. He was concerned about Hamas, Islamic Jihad, and the Popular Front, and about his opponents in the PLO. Arafat explained that he supports, in his long-term vision, the formation of a confederation living in peace with the other states in the region. Beilin promised to convey the Palestinian leader's messages to Rabin, and asserted that it was essential for Arafat to help ease the Israeli public's fears about him and his intentions. He asked for a symbolic gesture and suggested that Arafat replace his military uniform with a civilian suit. Arafat responded to Beilin's suggestion in a way that is unconventional in dialogue between Western leaders: prolonged silence. Ashrawi, who was present at the meeting, took the initiative after a long pause in the conversation and said that the chairman dresses in the way his people understand him, and that without his uniform, he would become a different person in their eyes.[2]

In accordance with the Declaration of Principles signed in Washington, the next stage was to negotiate the details of the withdrawal from Gaza and Jericho, and the establishment of the Palestinian Authority. However, Beilin's primary focus was already on reaching a final status accord between Israel and the Palestinians. During his meeting with Arafat, he suggested—without the knowledge of Rabin and Peres—reconstructing the Oslo model: establishing a secret channel to discuss final status issues, in parallel to the official negotiations on the interim accord. Arafat agreed. Thus, an additional track was initiated between Beilin and Abu Mazen, who did not plan to return to the territories at this stage.

At the same time, Beilin sought to convene a forum of experts in Israel—including academics and former officials from the defense establishment and Foreign Ministry—to brainstorm about Israel's needs in the final status accord. The forum met for the first time in April 1994. Economic Cooperation Foundation personnel, including Boaz Karni and Oslo negotiators Yair Hirschfeld and Ron Pundak, were among the participants. There was a consensus among most of the forum members: time was of the essence.

Contrary to the view of Rabin and most of the state's leaders, who saw the five-year interim period as essential for examining Arafat's intentions and the Palestinians' capacity for self-rule and for preventing terrorism, Beilin and the experts he convened believed it would be best to shorten the interim period and strive to reach a final status accord. In their view, Israel should exploit public support and the diplomatic opportunity—the PLO's weakness, the collapse of the Soviet Union, and a supportive administration in the United States —to resolve issues that might prove unresolvable if postponed to the future. In other words, they believed Israel should strike while the iron was still hot. The forum's discussions continued until May 1995, and the notes from these meetings reveal disagreements among proponents of an accord. For example, the economists in the forum advocated stronger restrictions on allowing Palestinians to work in Israel in order to strengthen the workforce in the territories, while the security-oriented members advised against separating the Israeli and Palestinian economies, fearing that unemployment in the territories would lead to violence. In the latter's view, economic dependence would help prevent the option of terrorism if the negotiations stalled. While most of the discussants assumed that Jewish settlements would be dismantled in the natural course of progress in negotiations, Beilin thought that Israel should seek an agreement that would leave most of the settlements in place, under Palestinian sovereignty, in areas not included in the settlement blocs Israel planned to annex.[3]

The idea of leaving the settlements intact in the final agreement did not only arise because of fears about the difficulty in evacuating them.[4] It stemmed mainly from a more profound conception of the meaning of peace. For Beilin, peace should include living under foreign sovereignty because, in any case, Israel and Palestine would establish some form of confederation. In this context, we should note an interesting document that Hirschfeld presented to Beilin regarding the final agreement slated to be signed in 1999. In fact, the document offered a detailed Israeli vision for the next fifty years. The first decade of peace was expected to shape democratization processes among the Palestinians and neighboring states, and to boost the growth of the middle class in the region, strengthen authentic leaders who draw their power directly from their people, and reduce defense spending in favor of investment in narrowing social disparities. On this subject, Hirschfeld's paper also noted the social dangers a peace agreement would pose: the anticipated growth in the Israeli and Palestinian economics was likely to widen disparities, which would undermine stability in these societies. This, in turn, would weaken support for continuing to advance and deepen the peace process. Therefore, Hirschfeld suggested placing emphasis on developing regional infrastructure systems during the first decade. The second decade would focus on economic cooperation between Israel, Jordan, Palestine, Egypt, Syria, and Lebanon. During the third decade, the aim would be to rid the region of weapons of mass destruction and strengthen the ties between the Middle Eastern community and the Gulf states. The fourth decade would witness the realization of a joint Middle East union, similar to the European Union, through an economic, cultural and security alliance, in which the Jewish state would be one of the member states of the regional federation.[5]

"The 50-Year Vision," which reads today like a pipe dream, reflected the optimism that prevailed at the time of its writing, soon after the signing of Oslo I.

On May 4, 1994, Rabin and Arafat met in Cairo to sign an agreement in the presence of representatives from Egypt, the United States, and Russia. The Cairo Agreement specified the details of the Israeli withdrawal from Gaza and Jericho, and the powers of the PA, and established the basis for subsequent IDF withdrawals from Palestinian urban centers. The agreement stipulated that the PA would receive executive, judicial, and police authorities to govern the areas from which the IDF withdraws, replacing Israel's Civil Administration. Both sides committed to take action to prevent terrorism and to form a joint committee with Egypt and Jordan to discuss permitting the return of Palestinians who left the territories in the wake of the Six-Day War.

However, the viewers of this event, broadcast live on television, saw the leaders continuing to wrangle while already on the stage. Although Israel released about 1,400 Palestinian prisoners earlier that day as a gesture to Arafat prior to his planned arrival in Gaza on July 1, the latter claimed that the Israeli map attached to the Cairo Agreement unduly narrowed the boundaries of Jericho. He also complained about the security arrangements at the border crossings. Arafat consented to sign the agreement only after Rabin promised him a letter stating that the maps attached to the agreement would be subject to further discussion. The cameras caught Mubarak chastising Arafat: "Sign, you dog!" The open dispute on the stage reflected the high level of suspicion between the sides, though they continued to move forward together.

Soon afterward, the Oslo track produced nearly miraculous scenes: in late May 1994, in accordance with the Cairo Agreement, PLO forces began to arrive in the territories. Israeli soldiers and Palestinian police officers patrolled together, and Palestinians handed flowers to the soldiers. On July 1, Arafat returned to Gaza in a festive convoy that crossed the border from Egypt to Gaza. The return of Arafat, whose convoy was protected in part by IDF helicopters hovering above, stirred excitement in the territories and throughout the world—including many Israelis who could not help but identify with the Palestinians' feeling of liberation. There were numerous reports in the press about the IDF's plans to shorten compulsory service in light of the diplomatic developments. No settlements were evacuated, and it appeared that Israel had benefited without paying a steep price.

But there was a darker side, too: fierce opponents of the agreement arose in Palestinian society, particularly among Hamas and Islamic Jihad members. From the signing of Oslo I until the murder of Rabin in November 1995, Israel was rocked by a wave of attacks, unparalleled since the pre-state period of civil strife: 164 Israelis were killed and hundreds were injured. Most of the attacks were carried out by Hamas suicide bombers, and some by Islamic Jihad. However, a critical fact should be noted in this context: until the massacre committed by Baruch Goldstein in the Cave of the Patriarchs in February 1994, the Hamas attacks were sporadic and conducted within the territories, usually against military targets.

On the eve of Holocaust Remembrance Day, which also marked the fortieth day since Goldstein's shooting spree in Hebron, Hamas carried out a suicide attack in Afula. The driver of a car packed with explosives pulled up alongside an Israeli bus and detonated himself. Consequently, the IDF stepped up its activity against Hamas personnel in the territories, and the organization responded by intensifying its attacks. Horrific scenes of dead and injured people in the streets of Israel—scenes graphically covered by the media, which did not refrain from close-up photographs of the victims—became a painful routine. On the other hand, the IDF conducted operations against Hamas personnel and demonstrated, despite the withdrawals, that it could do as it pleased in the territory earmarked for autonomy; many Palestinians were injured or killed in these operations.

Government officials tried to explain to the Israeli public that a distinction should be made between the PLO and Hamas, and that the attacks were aimed in part at undermining the PA. However, many in Israel concluded that the PA was responsibility for preventing terrorism.

But the situation was more complex: while the PA worked to thwart attacks by Hamas terrorists against Israel, it had to be careful not to lose its standing in the territories and appear as collaborating with Israel. The PA was already suspicious of Israel, partly because the agreements between Israel and the PLO were sometimes vague. For example, there was no explicit Israeli commitment to stop construction in the settlements, though the Declaration of Principles stated, in the style of constructive ambiguity: "The two parties agree that the outcome of the permanent status negotiations should not be prejudiced or preempted by agreements reached for the interim period." The Palestinians interpreted this as an Israeli promise to refrain from construction in the settlements during the period of negotiations. The Rabin government was, indeed, inclined to curb settlement activity and limited building permits to cases involving natural growth in the settlements. However, as the IDF withdrew from Palestinian cities, the government began to pave roads to ensure the safety of Jewish settlers, largely due to the problem of terrorist attacks. These access roads, which bypassed Palestinian cities and villages, gave the Palestinians the feeling that the Oslo agreement was designed to imprison them in enclaves. And when this trend expanded, it was seen as characteristic of an apartheid regime.

Infighting within the PLO also hampered the implementation of the Oslo Accords and sometimes made it difficult for the organization to maintain a stance in favor of continued negotiations according to the original plan. This was viewed in Israel as a struggle between hawkish opponents of the agreement and dovish supporters, but talks Beilin conducted with al-Kurd, Arafat's economic adviser, indicate a more complex picture. Beilin summarized his impression:

> Al-Kurd describes the fierce struggle within the PLO between Arafat's camp, which includes Farouk Kaddoumi [head of the PLO's political department who opposed the Oslo Accords and only later returned from Tunis to Gaza] and Yasser Abed Rabbo [a PA minister], versus the camp of Abu Mazen and Abu Ala, as a battle for political power, and not as a struggle between moderates and extremists. Al-Kurd, unquestionably a moderate, represents Arafat and is loyal to him, and it was precisely this loyalty that led to his exclusion from the June 1993 talks. . . . The rivalry between the camps induces Arafat to try to maintain an appearance of independence, even at the price of opposing agreements concluded by Abu Mazen and Abu Ala, who treat the process as their baby, and try to thereby strengthen their standing. . . . In al-Kurd's view, Arafat is basically a pragmatist, without a clear ideology. If not for the struggle between the camps, he would proceed to immediately implement the Declaration of Principles . . . [but] Abu Ala does not always update Arafat . . . and when Arafat discovers he wasn't updated, he automatically becomes an oppositionist.[6]

Beilin's assessment indicates that like the Israeli political arena, where the array of forces is generated by a combination of ideology, strategy, internal politics, and personal interests, the Palestinian positions on Israel and the peace process did not only reflect their approach to the peace process, but also stemmed from partisan and personal struggles within the PA and Palestinian society.

In any case, less than a year after the signing of Oslo I, it was already clear that the historic mutual recognition between Israel and the PLO was not enough to resolve the tangle of difficulties en route to peace.


# 2

In parallel to the talks on interim accords after the Cairo Agreement, the secret track between Beilin and Abu Mazen and their advisers deepened. The goal was to try to draft a final status agreement to present to the leaders. The sides tried to address the core issues, including the volatile question of refugees.

The refugee issue has two intertwined dimensions, practical and theoretical, because the theoretical dimension could have practical implications for Israel. Since the days of the first Ben-Gurion government, which decided to prevent the return of refugees who were expelled from their homes or who abandoned them during the War of Independence, there was no change in the Israeli position: absolute opposition to granting the right of return because it could undermine the Jewish majority in Israel.

From a moral perspective, Israel justified its stance by claiming that the refugees were not expelled but fled of their own volition after trying to prevent the creation of the Israel during the War of Independence. (At the end of the war, there were an estimated 700,000 refugees. If refugee rights are extended to the third generation, they number over five million today.) Israel's official position remained unchanged even after many cases of expulsion were uncovered by the "New Historians." From a legal perspective, Israel also bases its opposition to allowing the return of refugees on the UN partition resolution of November 1947, which established the right to a Jewish and democratic state. Therefore, the return of refugees would prevent Israel from being a Jewish state in terms of the demographic majority (or would prevent Israel from being democratic, if it chose to remain Jewish without a majority).

Ben-Gurion called the demand to allow the return of refugees a "bluff" and "one of the rationales for destroying Israel." According to Ben-Gurion, that is precisely why Arab states refrained from granting citizenship to refugees in their states, preferring in many cases to settle them in refugee camps: to use them as a threat.[7] It is true that Israel has absorbed a limited number of refugees as part of a humanitarian policy of family reunification,[8] but it has rejected every proposal for mass repatriation. At the end of the War of Independence, during the armistice talks with Syria, the Syrians proposed a joint resolution of the problem: they would grant citizenship to 250,000 refugees in exchange for a full Israeli withdrawal from the Sea of Galilee, and Israel would absorb the rest of the refugees. Israel rejected this proposal. The refugee issue became taboo. Ben-Gurion also rejected a proposal from President John Kennedy, who suggested that Israel absorb 10 percent of the refugees and promised that the rest would be absorbed in Arab states within a decade. The Israeli prime minister explained that as long as there is no Arab readiness for real peace and recognition of Israel's right to exist as a Jewish state, Israel's consent to absorb refugees would mean that Israel would find itself "at the same point in negotiations, but after already absorbing 100,000."[9] The historical irony is that despite its official stance, Israel allowed about 62,000 Palestinians refugees to return under family reunification provisions in the years preceding the Oslo agreement, and another 30,000 returned during the following decade. That is, nearly 100,000 refugees returned to Israel, and tens of thousands more returned illegally.[10] Thus, what was perceived as taboo, actually occurred to some extent, and this did not undermine the demographic balance in Israel.

In this context, the importance of the theoretical dimension of the issue becomes salient. Israel not only refuses to physically absorb the refugees, but also declines to take declarative responsibility for their plight. One of the reasons for this is the fear that acknowledgment of responsibility for the plight of the refugees would be tantamount to adopting the Palestinian narrative on acts of expulsion, spontaneous and planned, which created the *Nakba*, the Palestinian catastrophe in 1948. Israel's concern is that this would cast a historical shadow over one of the pillars of the Zionist narrative: the portrayal of the War of Independence as a justified and moral fight for Jewish independence. In the twentieth century, however, it is doubtful whether this would undermine the justification of Israel's existence. Indeed, the Palestinian narrative has permeated Israeli academia, becoming almost mainstream in humanities departments, and is prominent in the media and public discourse.[11] In this sense, the political system lags behind academia and the public system, and it is certainly possible that in a context of peace, most Israelis would not be shocked by accepting responsibility for the events of 1948 in all of their complexity.

On the other hand, the stance of the Palestinian leadership is not conducive to compromise on this issue. It does not suffice with the right to return of those who were expelled, but also demands granting this right to the descendants of those who were forced to flee in the heat of war. As noted, an estimated five million Palestinians meet this definition of entitlement to the right of return. Besides their moral argument, the Palestinians base their legal case on UN Resolution 194, passed in December 1948, which "resolves that the refugees wishing to return to their homes and live at peace with their neighbors should be permitted to do so at the earliest practicable date, and that compensation should be paid for the property of those choosing not to return."

The historical irony (one of many in the Arab–Israeli conflict) is that when the UN Resolution was adopted, the leaders of Arab states and Haj Amin al-Husseini, the preeminent figure in the Palestinian national movement, were among its prominent opponents—because of the resolution's implicit recognition of the legitimacy of the Jewish state ("live at peace with their neighbors").[12] However, after the PLO recognized Israel's right to exist, Resolution 194 took on added validity from the Palestinian perspective.

Beilin did not have a magic formula that would satisfy the Palestinians while still addressing Israel's interests. He believed that the return of even several hundred thousand refugees to their homes in Israel would undermine Israel's existence as a Jewish and democratic state. Nonetheless, he thought there was a realistic chance of resolving the dispute, because it was clear to both sides that there was no prospect of Palestinians returning en masse to Israel, even if permitted to do so.

Against this background, Beilin sought to resolve the issue through formal Israeli acknowledgment of responsibility for the plight of the Palestinian refugees, and absorption of a limited number of refugees. This approach of apologizing or acknowledging responsibility for suffering has been used as an effective tool in various settings in the international system since the Second World War. The effectiveness of this approach can be explained in light of the postmodern emphasis on understanding "the other" and on psycho-historical analysis, which draws a parallel between collective national feelings and personal feelings. In this context, the clash of conflicting narratives is seen as a battleground in itself, which must be neutralized.

According to Mark Amstutz, a political science professor who studied conflicts in Argentina, Chile, Northern Ireland, and South Africa, the ethics of asking for political forgiveness is anchored in the idea of "restorative justice." Unlike "compensatory justice," which requires a tangible exchange or concession on a concrete matter in dispute, restorative justice also entails taking moral responsibility for past injuries and a readiness to recognize the narrative of "the other." In this way, it helps to begin a new historical page.[13] According to Amstutz's research, in order to achieve the restorative effect of taking responsibility, all of the sides involved in the conflict should participate in the process. The injuring side should sincerely acknowledge the injustice it caused and show readiness for historical revision; this includes expressing remorse and offering compensation. The injured side is required to drop its demand for full retroactive compensation for what it perceives as injustice, and should appreciate the signification of the request for forgiveness.

In the Israeli-Palestinian case, too, it was important to find a formula that would ensure Palestinian acceptance of Israel's acknowledgment of its responsibility. Otherwise, the acknowledgment of responsibility might only intensify the conflict and create an opening for additional demands—legal and national, personal and collective, even among subsequent generations—based on the Israeli confession. The wording Beilin proposed to Abu Mazen stopped short of apologizing or accepting explicit and comprehensive responsibility for the refugees' plight. Instead, his wording was more subtle and ambiguous in recognizing "the material and emotional suffering" inflicted upon the refugees. This was accompanied by an expression of Israel's readiness to participate in providing monetary compensation in the framework of an international fund to be created for rehabilitating the refugees.

## 3

While Beilin and his colleagues explored formulas for the final status agreement, the interim agreements continued to encounter difficulty due to the terror attacks and internal opposition to the Oslo process on both sides.

During the course of 1994, Arafat tried unsuccessfully to reach an accord with Hamas leaders. The friction within his team continued and, of course, this did not help to advance the peace process with Israel: Abu Mazen remained in Tunis and moved to the territories only in 1995. He now publicly headed the final status talks from the Palestinian side, but held no position in the executive or legislative branches.

Another problem pertained to the impact of the interim agreements on the Palestinian economy. Without an improvement in the life of the average Palestinian, there was no point in the rapprochement with Israel or possibility of mobilizing popular support. In a meeting with Terje Rød-Larsen in August 1994, Beilin raised the possibility of forming an investment house in Cyprus to channel funds for establishing enterprises in the territories; the idea was that Israel would oversee and be a partner in the investment activity. Rød-Larsen did not reject the idea, but expressed a concern that was often voiced by the Palestinians about "Israeli neocolonialism"— that is, the continuation of the occupation through other means. The creation of a joint investment house might be seen as an example of the relations described by dependency theory in postcolonial discourse. According to this theory, the relations between "developing" and "developed" states, in the context of globalization processes, are wrapped in financial instruments that provide benefit to the developing states, but also perpetuate their dependence on developed states and favor the center over the periphery.[14] This was not Beilin's intention. However, he told Rød-Larsen: "If the choice is between hunger [in Gaza] and neo-colonialism—I prefer neo-colonialism. Because at the moment, there is no better solution."[15]

In any case, it was announced in October 1994 that Peres, Rabin, and Arafat would receive the Nobel Peace Prize. The news made waves in the world, and indicated the importance of their achievement as an international symbol of conflict resolution. The decision was also designed to express support for the Israeli-Palestinian peace process. However, against the background of terror attacks and concern for the future of the process, many in Israel and abroad were incensed by the decision. One of the members of the Nobel Committee, Professor Kåre Kristiansen, resigned in protest, claiming that Arafat had yet to prove he had abandoned the path of terrorism. In an interview with the Israeli press, Kristiansen stated: "It's a mistake to award the Nobel Peace Prize for a process when we don't know whether it will succeed or fail."[16] At one stage—in part, to emphasize that the Israeli-Palestinian peace process was still in its infancy—some members of the committee considered awarding the prize to Beilin and Abu Ala as architects of the agreement. It turned out, however, that the deadline for submitting nominations had already passed. Michael Melchior, the chief rabbi of Norway (and later a minister in the Barak government) called Beilin and told him about the proposed nomination. Knowing the leaders involved, Beilin said it was better off this way, adding that those who bear responsibility for implementing the agreement should receive the prize, not those who initiated the process.

The hope was that the decision to award the Nobel Peace Prize to Rabin, Peres, and Arafat would mark one of the celebratory moments of the Oslo process and boost support for it. But Israel's political reality came and dashed this hope. For many of the opponents of the agreement, acceptance of the prize indicated the Israeli leadership's detachment from the reality on the ground. A motion for the agenda submitted by Likud MK Uzi Landau, who did not shrink from comparing Oslo to the Munich Agreement, reflected the prevailing mood:

> Imagine that on December 10, 1938, they had awarded the Nobel Peace Prize in Oslo, in an impressive ceremony, to Adolf Hitler, the German fuehrer, Neville Chamberlain, the prime minister of England, and Daladier, the prime minister of France, for their contribution to world peace following the signing of the Munich Agreement. . . . 56 years later, on the 10th of December, 1994, the curtain rises on a shameful scene, and other names for those characters appear on the stage in Oslo. . . . Here is the price of that peace process, for which you received a prize, in people killed during the past years. Just two weeks ago, the IDF Spokesperson's Office published the data and said there were 114 killed in the intifada. In six years, there were 114 killed, compared to 102 killed since the agreement you signed—a similar number.[17]

At this stage, the leftist camp responded by mainly ignoring the explicit comparisons to the era of the Third Reich and the tally of dead bodies. Peres, who was present in the Knesset debate, dryly muttered: "How is that relevant?" Beilin did not even bother to participate in the discussion. The feeling was of feverish activity accompanied by harmful verbiage from the political right. The significance and impact of such comparisons—or, more precisely, the inroads they made in public opinion in Israel—were not accorded sufficient attention.

But it was impossible to completely ignore the growing disappointment in the public, and even supporters of the process began to sound more and more apologetic. The term often used by Oslo supporters to refer to those killed in terror attacks, "victims of peace" (ironically, a term first used in public by Likud MK Meir Sheetrit in a Knesset debate on September 21, 1993), was perhaps true from a historical perspective, but did little to persuade or console. After all, what was the point in territorial concessions if they did not prevent victims? The word "victims" (*korbanot*) in Hebrew also refers to the sacrificial offerings described in the Bible. Indeed, the victims were almost seen as sacrificial offerings on the altar of peace,[18] rather than victims who paid the price on the road to peace. Furthermore, by using the term *korbanot*, with its theological connotation in Hebrew, the peace process was depicted in religious terms, which infused it with a messianic dimension. That is, the current situation could be seen as an apocalyptic war that would usher in a messianic era.

Representatives of the government, including Beilin, tried to press Arafat to take stronger action against Hamas and Islamic Jihad. Paradoxically, however, the more receptive Arafat was to Israeli pressure, the weaker he became among his people because of his apparent collaboration. This trap made it difficult for Arafat's personnel to combat terrorism, especially in light of the fact that he was still inclined to regard terrorism as another instrument in his political-diplomatic toolkit. The Israelis complained that Arafat often responded to their remarks by espousing hallucinatory conspiracy theories about the perpetrators of the terror attacks. One of the emissaries who met with Arafat reported to Beilin: "The meeting with Arafat left a harsh impression. Either he's an outstanding actor or he's out of his mind. Arafat claimed that the Shin Bet and Hamas were conspiring against him. According to Arafat, the Shin Bet is arming Hamas in order to push him into a corner."[19] Arafat's conspiracy theories led many in Israel to treat him as an irrational actor. But this was a superficial understanding of Arafat. His talk of conspiracies reflected the secularization of the world, including the Arab world, because conspiracy theories are used in the modern era to explain what would be attributed to divine intervention in the ancient world.[20] In particular, it seems that Arafat used conspiracy theories to convey a more complex message: I cannot and do not want to cooperate with you to that extent.

At one point, even Beilin publicly declared: "If the situation does not calm down and terrorism is not significantly curbed, it will be possible to say: the rotten fruit of peace. Then we will no longer be able to continue the negotiations and we will not sign a permanent accord."[21] But he was convinced that the complexity of the situation required resilience, because he did not see the terror attacks as a side effect of the peace process. On the contrary, Beilin believed that the attacks could be attributed to the fact that the diplomatic process was still incomplete.

But the attacks were not the only consequence of the peace process. The Oslo process provided great diplomatic benefits to Israel vis-à-vis its neighbors in the Middle East, boosted its standing in the world, and opened new markets for the Israeli economy. On October 26, 1994, Israel signed a peace treaty with Jordan. The peace with Jordan made public the relations that had been conducted quietly for decades, since the Yishuv period, between the Zionist movement and the Hashemite Kingdom. Only after the accord with the Palestinians could King Hussein sign a peace treaty without forfeiting his legitimacy. There was a strong consensus in Israel in favor of the peace with Jordan, which did not require significant concessions from Israel. Certainly, this support also was attributable to the fact that Israelis viewed King Hussein as "Western."

Nonetheless, the perception that peace with Jordan was one of the salient fruits of the Oslo agreement failed to completely take root among the Israeli public. A suicide bus bombing in Tel Aviv on October 19, a week before the treaty was signed, and the death of Nachshon Waxman (an Israeli soldier abducted by Hamas, who died during a failed IDF rescue attempt) several days earlier, dampened the excitement about peace with Jordan. This diminished the government's ability to leverage the peace with Jordan to boost the public support required for advancing in the diplomatic channel with the Palestinians.

4

The early 1990s were seen as a "window of opportunity" for advancing the peace process in the Middle East. The disappearance of the Soviet Union as a backer of the Arab states, Clinton's Democratic administration in the United States, the Labor Party's return to power in Israel, the PLO's weakness in the wake of the First Gulf War, globalization processes described by political scientists as signaling the decline of the national era—all seemed conducive to facilitating peace between Israel and the Arab states. The portrayal of Shi'ite Iran as a threat to the Sunni states in the Gulf and Middle East, and the weakened footing of postwar Iraq also boosted the chances of reconciliation and even alliances between Israel and the Sunni states.

In particular, Israel sought to reach an agreement with Syria, whose leaders were hostile toward the Oslo Accords and were seen as capable of impeding Israel's rapprochement with its neighbors. Soon after the signing of Oslo I, in a meeting Beilin held with members of the Foreign Ministry's Planning Division, it was agreed that in order to achieve the broader objective of the Oslo process—peace treaties with Arab states—Israel would have to compromise vis-à-vis Syria. "It is doubtful that progress in negotiations with Jordan will lead to the normalization of Israel's situation in the Middle Eastern arena," read a document summarizing the meeting. "Syria will continue to be the key to this."[22] Beilin came away with the same conclusion after meeting with Abd al-Rahman bin Khalifa, Bahrain's ambassador in Washington, to discuss forging closer relations between Israel and Bahrain: Israel would need to overcome the Syrian obstacle. The ambassador acknowledged the "negative attitude toward Israel" in his country, but told Beilin: "If there is peace in the Middle East, Israel's relations with Bahrain will perhaps be better than with Israel's neighbors. . . . Syria is the key to this. If there is peace with Syria—the Middle East problem will be resolved."[23]

In accordance with the resolutions of the Madrid Conference, talks between Israeli and Syrian delegations were also being conducted in Washington. There was no progress in these talks, but Rabin's election victory in 1992 raised renewed hopes for Israel's northern front. Assad allowed the hundreds of Syrian Jews remaining in the country to emigrate in 1992 as a goodwill gesture, at the request of the Americans. Israel was also asked to make a gesture of its own. Peres and Beilin were less involved in the Syrian track, which was Rabin's domain. He was assisted primarily by Itamar Rabinovich—the head of the Israeli delegation in the talks with Syria, and later Israel's ambassador in the United States —and by top IDF officers. But the composition of the negotiating team was not the reason for failing to reach an agreement with Syria. The Syrians were more rigid and fully aware of their importance and the enormous leverage they held over Israel's ability to break through the circle of hostility in the Middle East. The price they demanded in exchange for peace was high. They were unwilling to suffice with an Israeli withdrawal from the Golan to the border demarcated in 1923 by France and Britain, the powers that ruled the region at the time. During Israel's War of Independence, the Syrians breached this border and now demanded that Israel retreat to the armistice lines of 1949 (the border in effect on June 4, 1967, on the eve of the Six-Day War). This would allow them a foothold on part of the Sea of Galilee.

When Rabin promised Secretary of State Christopher a withdrawal from the Golan Heights, he did not draw a specific map, assuming that it would be possible to compromise on the question of borders. But the Syrians would not budge. They also never "bought" the Oslo Accords as an expression of Israel's readiness to make concessions. In October 1993, about a month after the signing of the Declaration of Principles, during a private conversation between the Syrian foreign minister, Farouk al-Shara, and Lee Hamilton, the Democratic chairman of the House Foreign Affairs Committee, al-Shara claimed that it was clear to the Syrians that "Israel was not giving up anything." Hamilton was not sure what he meant, and emphasized that Israel would be withdrawing its army from the West Bank and Gaza Strip. The Syrian foreign minister asserted in reply that Israel had not relinquished East Jerusalem or agreed to grant the Palestinians a state, but received recognition of its right to exist and a PLO commitment to abandon terrorism. Hamilton tried to clarify which steps Israel could take to prove its sincerity to the Syrians. "Any type of complete withdrawal,"[24] al-Shara replied. The conversation, which was intended to reach Israeli ears, conveyed a clear message: the Syrians would insist on returning to the borderline they held on the eve of the Six-Day War, even though this line included territory they had captured, while demanding that Israel relinquish territory it had captured.

Since Rabin believed that the Israeli public would be unable to cope with two concurrent withdrawals, some Foreign Ministry officials believed that Israel should slow its efforts on the Syrian track. Beilin, on the other hand, continued to believe in the urgent need to exploit the window of opportunity. According to reports the ministry received from people who met with Assad, the Syrians believed that Rabin, unlike other Israeli leaders, was both serious in his intentions and politically strong, and thus the chances of an agreement increased. In September 1994, Beilin received a report stating that "Assad's position in the past was that there was no difference between a government headed by the Alignment or the Likud. . . . His view has apparently changed, and he understands that the leader he can reach an accord with is Rabin." The report emphasized the need to understand the cultural differences and the disparity between the fundamental perceptions of the East versus the West—assuming that Israel represents the West. "When you tell the Syrians they have to take into account public opinion in Israel as a factor . . . they get angry and respond that the perception in Israel that Assad does not have the same problem of internal public opinion is insulting," the report stated. "Assad is moving forward in slow steps toward an agreement with Israel. It's his way—to act slowly. That's how it was, for example, on the matter of permitting Syrian Jews to leave for the United States. It took 16 years for this to be realized."[25]

The talks conducted between the military chiefs of staff of Syria and Israel stirred hope that soon gave way to disappointment. Dennis Ross attributed the blame to Syrian dissatisfaction with Israel's approach. Beilin summarized Ross's remarks after a meeting with him:

> The Syrians are the ones who proposed the meeting of the military chiefs of staff and, in their view, they complied with Israel's request to move to a higher echelon. Thus, they were disappointed that instead of Israel responding in kind, they heard [from IDF Chief of Staff Ehud Barak] that it's only the beginning of the process. According to Ross, Barak presented the key points of the security outlook in an excellent way, but Assad was expecting to hear something different. The conversations are serious, but the negotiation is psychological in this reality. Assad decided that if there was a breakthrough on the issue of security, it would be the key. Rabin also holds a similar view—that security arrangements should be discussed first.[26]

Beilin assumed that Rabin had instructed Barak to take a tough stance in the talks because "Rabin does not believe that peace with Syria would give him a victory in the elections. Peace with Syria means a withdrawal, and this step is not popular today. Personal security is a much more important element."[27] The failure of the talks between the chiefs of staff prompted Beilin to consult with Prof. Muhammad Muslih—a historian of Palestinian origin, who was close to the regime in Damascus—in order to understand the Syrians. Muslih said that Israel's search for Syrian strategy from an intelligence and political perspective would not produce results:

> The number of top Syrian officials who know Assad's strategy toward the peace process is very limited. Perhaps none of them know the full strategy. . . . The Syrians are aware of the fact that time is not on their side and that the chances of achieving the objective—Syrian dominance in the area that was once the Levant— have diminished. . . . Nonetheless, Assad is not prepared to concede his positions, even if this means he will not achieve an Israeli withdrawal from the Golan, and the status quo will continue for years. From his perspective, this means that at least he did not give in to Israel and that Syrian history will record this. . . . Assad is in the process of abandoning his basic view that the United States will "sell" him Israel, but apparently, this hope has yet to fade completely. Improving relations with the United States is very important to Assad. He realizes that countries that clash with the United States do not fare well. This is so important to him that he refrains from publically criticizing Hussein and Arafat, too, who paved the way to separate peace agreements with Israelis (though he totally opposes their moves, which weaken him, as noted).[28]

Mark Rosenberg, a businessman who met with President Assad and top Syrian leaders, and later visited Israel, also emphasized the need to understand that the Syrians operate with a different mindset: "Rosenberg noted the Syrian regime's lack of understanding of the domestic constraints, both in Israel and in the United States. They [the Syrians] are convinced that Rabin and Clinton can make any decision and are not limited."[29]

Besides the question of the borderline (that is, the depth of Israel's withdrawal from the Golan Heights), the disagreements with Syria centered on security arrangements after the Israeli withdrawal, including the size of the area to be demilitarized and the nature of the warning stations Israel sought to deploy on Mount Hermon. However, while there were serious disagreements on these matters, Rabinovich explains the difficulty in achieving an Israeli-Syrian accord by noting Assad's primary motive for negotiating with Israel: his desire to establish closer relations with the United States. While Israel, Syria, and the United States shared responsibility for the failure of the talks at this stage (they were renewed after Barak became prime minister), the principal stumbling block was the fact that Syria under Hafez al-Assad was negotiating with the United States and not with Israel. From Syria's perspective, the talks were aimed to pave the way to good relations between Washington and Damascus. Assad was, indeed, willing to sign an agreement with Israel—but only if all his conditions were met in full.[30] By its very readiness to engage in talks with Israel, Damascus hoped to achieve its primary objective of warming US-Syrian relations. Achieving an accord with Israel was of lesser importance from Syria's perspective.

The French foreign minister, Alain Juppé, offered a different explanation for the failure of the talks with Syria: the Israeli interest was to use an accord with Syria to achieve a breakthrough to Arab states and thus strengthen its standing in the region— what Beilin and Peres called a "comprehensive peace." Syria, which considered itself a regional power, was wary of bolstering Israel's clout in the region and thus preferred to maintain the status quo.[31]

Therefore, it seems that Peres's aspiration for a "new Middle East"—an expression he coined in his effort to persuade the Israeli public of the potential advantages of an accord with the Palestinians—was strategically counterproductive. First, the goal of fashioning a "new Middle East" in a cultural region that relied on ancient traditions was seen as a threat by Arab leaders, not as a promising development. Second, what Israel defined as an era of prosperity was interpreted as an Israeli ambition to establish cultural and economic dominance in the region. The difficulty of Arab leaders in contending with the "new Middle East" was evident in reactions to the first MENA (Middle East and North Africa) economic conference, held in Casablanca about a year after the signing of the Oslo I Accord.

The MENA conference was seen in Israel as evidence of the enormous economic potential offered by the new agreements in the Middle East. In great excitement, Israel sent a large delegation to the conference, including business people, cultural figures, and entrepreneurs from various fields. The number of Israelis at the conference certainly did not reflect Israel's relative size in the region. Furthermore, Israeli business people were conspicuous in approaching their Arab counterparts, brimming with confidence and brandishing a host of proposals for joint ventures. Dan Propper, the head of the Manufacturers' Association of Israel at the time, remembers: "There was great euphoria . . . the Casablanca Conference was aimed at triggering economic peace in the region and creating connections between business people in Israel and the states of the region. For the first time, officially and in front of the cameras, we met in Morocco with business people from states that then, and today too, we could only imagine meeting. Manufacturers and business people from Arab states embraced us."[32]

However, the Arabs apparently viewed these developments differently. In April 1995, Beilin (who did not attend the MENA conference in Casablanca) met with senior American officials to prepare for the next economic conference, slated to convene in Amman in November. He was asked to convey a request to the Israeli delegation: keep a lower profile this time. David Aaron Miller, a top State Department adviser on the Middle East, stated at the meeting that the Casablanca conference had "stirred anger against Israel." According to Miller, "The Egyptian complaints pertained to the excessive number of Israelis there, and the exaggerated emphasis [of the Israeli proposals] on building financial frameworks and institutions. Their concerns are directed at the effort [to create] a new Middle East. The bilateral relations are not yet ripe for making this leap." Beilin said in response that he did not think Israel should comply with the Egyptian demands, "but should be aware of them." Ambassador Indyk noted that even though the next conference would be in Jordan, which was considered more comfortable for Israel, there was no reason to expect a different approach "because the Jordanians will also have an interest in pleasing the Egyptians."[33] The remarks in this meeting reflect a basic flaw in the Israeli vision of peace: the closer Israel came to realizing its aspiration of integrating into the region, the more it was held back by Arabs fears of Israeli economic and cultural dominance. In this context, we can only return to the Herzlian error, already expressed in *Altneuland*—the belief that the Jewish state could integrate in the region by virtue of the economic and technological prosperity it would bring, without stopping to ask: why would the Arabs want the change offered by the Jews? What are the implications of this change in terms of the threat to existing arrays of power and culture in the Middle East? And why should the Arabs adopt the Jewish state as the vanguard instead of aspiring to be its own vanguard?

This leads us to the "Mizrahi" dimension lacking in the Israeli leadership's approach to the Middle East. That is, perhaps there is a problem in the fact that the State of Israel's leadership (including Beilin) has always been predominantly Ashkenazi. Perhaps the peace camp in Israel should adopt a slower clock that recognizes the needs and concerns of the Arabs through a basic affinity with the characteristics of their culture. A little-known fact is that until the beginning of the British Mandate, about 40 percent of the Jews in Palestine were of Mizrahi descent (Sephardim and Jews from Islamic lands). Recent studies describe the extensive collaboration between Mizrahi Jews and Arabs, based on their cultural, linguistic, and geographic affinity.[34] Thus, perhaps the absence of Mizrahi leadership in the Zionist movement, indeed, exacerbated the conflict. I am not referring here to the radical calls in recent years for solidarity between leftist-Mizrahi Jews and the Palestinians because, paradoxically, proponents of identity politics, who emphasize the Mizrahi identity as supreme, ignore the fact that most Mizrahi Jews give precedence to their Jewish identity. What is possible and desirable is an attempt to position Mizrahi Jews as a bridge between Zionism and the Palestinians (as the Arabs of Israel could be on the Palestinian side). On the other hand, even when recognizing Zionism's flawed understanding of the Arabs' complex disposition, the question remains of what Israel should do now: can it adopt the viewpoint of the peoples of the Middle East, to the point of trampling Israel's own aspirations and objectives?

# 5

Israel's unique position as a state straddling the East-West axis—that is, a state that represents the West and is supported by it, while being situated in the East and seeking to integrate into it—led the Jordanian royal house to try to mobilize Israel for establishing a new Middle East alliance.

This occurred in the 1990s, prior to the second Gulf War (in which the United States under President George W. Bush toppled Saddam Hussein's regime). During the course of many conversations between the Jordanians and the Americans, the Jordanians argued that contrary to the Americans' view, Iraq was the key to stability in the Middle East. The Jordanians tried to persuade their interlocutors to draw Iraq into an alliance of moderate states and to focus on the effort to marginalize Iran.[35]

When the Jordanians realized they could not convince the Clinton administration to seek rapprochement with Iraq and isolate Iran, they turned to Israel, hoping to mobilize its assistance in lobbying the US government on this issue. In March 1995, Beilin had a fascinating conversation with the Jordanian prime minister, Abd al-Karim Kabariti, who asserted that peace could be achieved between Israel and Iraq by creating an Israeli-Sunni bloc. Kabariti argued that the time was ripe for exploiting Saddam Hussein's weakness—just as the PLO's weakness was later exploited to reach an Israeli-Palestinian accord—in order to promote an initiative that would reshuffle the cards in the Middle East. In this context, the Jordanian prime minister contended that the United States did not sufficiently understand the common interest of Israel and the Sunni states. According to Kabariti:

> The Israeli mistake is in unquestioningly accepting the American stance of "dual containment." This is an empty slogan, which no one has operationalized. It is essential to decide who the enemy is. Our enemy and yours is Iran, and the Americans are making a mistake when they think that Iraq is the enemy. The president of Iraq is at one of the weakest points in his history, and is ready today for things that he wasn't ready for in the past, and perhaps won't be ready for in the future. Israel should not regard Jordan as a buffer between it and Iraq, but rather a bridge to it. Saddam Hussein is not your problem. You should make contact with him and exploit the situation. This could change the map of the Middle East.

Kabariti added that relations with Iraq could also help to solve the Palestinian refugee problem because the development of Iraq would require Saddam Hussein to obtain "working hands." For this purpose, he would grant citizenship to skilled Palestinians.[36]

The wisdom of the Jordanian viewpoint became apparent only years later, when the US Army became entangled in an endless civil war in Iraq after toppling Saddam Hussein's regime. This civil war also contributed to the formation of the Islamic State jihadist organization. Contrary to earlier Western assessments, recent studies indicate that the organization was not created by Al-Qaeda. The civil war that erupted following the collapse of the Saddam Hussein regime engendered an alliance between extreme jihadists and secular supporters of the Ba'ath Party. This led to the surprising formation of a radical Salafist party that evolved into the Islamic State organization.[37]

Beilin did not reject the Jordanian viewpoint, but replied that in this case—as in 1993, when North Korea sought closer relations with Israel, which rejected these feelers out of loyalty to American policy—"though Iraq is a complex subject, we are operating in full coordination with the United States and no change in policy is expected."[38]

Another interesting point raised in the conversation between Kabariti and Beilin related to the dissonance between public declarations and policy behind the scenes. Beilin noted that though he was aware that the denunciations of Israel by official Jordanian representatives were directed at domestic public opinion, "extreme statements are liable to become policy, even when there is no intention behind them."[39]

This remark on the gap between declarations and policy stemmed from the bitter experience Beilin had accrued in conversations with Arab leaders. When he started out as Peres's adviser and was first exposed to contacts with Arab leaders, he was often excited to hear optimistic statements, behind closed doors, about Israel and about ending the conflict. He was inclined to believe that such statements symbolized possibilities that would develop in time. However, as time passed, he realized that despite his curiosity and excitement when hearing the "truth" behind the scenes, the public statements dictated the reality, binding the leaders to their words and shaping public opinion. This perception also influenced the way he reads history books that draw from archives and expose surprising statements spoken in private. Beilin attributes only marginal value to such statements. Therefore, he was disappointed when Kabariti asked him to disregard the denunciations of Israel he would continue to make because of domestic needs.[40]

In any case, the Jordanians continued to press Israel to create channels of communication with Iraq and to persuade the Americans on this issue. Beilin summarized another meeting with Kabariti a year later, in March 1996:

> Kabariti said that King Hussein encouraged him to work on the subject of Israel's relations with Iraq, and added that Hussein would be willing to help in any way in this matter. According to Kabariti, this move would lead the entire Arab world to open up toward Israel. He said that he had also spoken about this with Dennis Ross [and other American officials], who strongly opposed any connection with Iraq. In this context, he quoted the king, who said there were two alternatives: The sanctions would continue as long as the current regime exists, or contact would be made with the regime.

Beilin said that Israel would not act on this subject without consulting with the United States, and promised to pass the message on to his higher-ups.[41]

As history shows, it was to no avail.

# 6

Naturally, public and media attention focused on the diplomatic accords the Rabin government pursued. However, the Rabin government was very active in other areas, including an effort to change Israel's economic structure.

Haim Ramon, the health minister, orchestrated the passage of the National Health Law on June 15, 1994. The legislation severed the connection between membership in the Histadrut and membership in the Clalit HMO, thus ending the Histadrut's control of one of the central health services in Israel. Ramon contended that the law actually helped the Histadrut by relieving it of the HMO's heavy debt and placing it in the hands of the government. In the long term, however, due to its loss of control of the Clalit HMO and the citizenry's newfound freedom in choosing a health fund, Histadrut's standing weakened and its revenues declined as the number of members dwindled.

Ramon, with Beilin's enthusiastic support, made the reform of the Histadrut his flagship project. In pursuit of this goal, he resigned from the government in February 1994 and formed the "Haim Hadashim" (New Life) faction in the Histadrut. The new faction competed in the elections for the Histadrut's Executive Committee in May 1994 and defeated the Labor Party slate led by Haim Haberfeld. Ramon became the chairman of the Histadrut, ending over seventy years of control by Mapai and its successor, the Labor Party. In an absurd twist, Rabin and Peres (less conspicuously) were pleased by Ramon's victory over their own party.

The Histadrut under Ramon instituted far-reaching reforms, entailing deep cuts in its bureaucracy and the sale of most of its enterprises and assets. It later also separated from its pension funds. As noted, these moves were supported by the leaders of the Labor Party, who were attentive to the public's hostility toward the labor federation at this stage. Consequently, the Histadrut lost its decades-long standing as a central social and economic institution in Israel. It is still powerful in its shrunken role as a workers' organization, thanks primarily to the strong unions at the Israel Electric Corporation and the large ports.

Beilin is still proud of Ramon's policies, which were based on ideas they discussed when they were members of Labor's Young Guard. Beilin explains today:

Since I was the *Davar* newspaper's Histadrut reporter and knew every corner there, I became closely familiar with the crooked relations between the trade unions and the Histadrut and the cases of personal corruption. Though I believe in the right to unionize, the Histadrut became a monstrous bureaucracy over the years, which needed to be addressed. The Histadrut was an organization that handed out jobs without any reason or justification. It drove me crazy. For example, when Motta Gur completed his term as IDF chief of staff, he was appointed director-general of Koor Mechanics though he was unqualified for the position. He had military qualifications, but found himself director-general only because the Histadrut had become a place that arranged jobs for former officials. And that's just one example.

Moreover, since the party was required to back the Histadrut, which demanded support for its companies, the party backed Solel Boneh, which was the leading building contractor in the territories in the 1970s and 1980s. This absurd situation had a practical impact on the positions of party members, because if they wanted to support Solel Boneh, they couldn't oppose continued construction in the settlements. Another example was the opposition of union leaders in the military industries to measures I tried to promote in the 1980s against relations with South

Africa. A blow to relations would also mean a blow to deals with the military industries, and since the military industries were owned by the Histadrut, the party was obligated to it. This created an absurd situation in which, under the cloak of socialism, members of the Labor Party became proponents of right-wing or immoral views.

Beilin could not accept "the situation in which you had to be a Histadrut member to become a member of the Labor Party." He explains:

> Besides the inherent absurdity of this, the connection between the party and the Histadrut, in the era of primaries, gave enormous and corruptive political power to vote contractors in the large unions. And the fact that someone who wanted to be a member of a different HMO could not continue to enjoy the conditions to which Histadrut members were entitled, made a mockery of the original idea of providing services to the citizen.

Beilin also argues today that there was a need for a reform in the Histadrut in order to make it, and the entire Israeli economy, more efficient. Though he is largely correct, we cannot ignore the fact that the reform also had a negative impact on worker-employee relations in Israel. The Histadrut's weakness engendered a process of privatizing labor relations in Israel. Despite the growth in population, the number of unionized workers has dropped from about two million in the early 1990s to about 600,000 today. This phenomenon came in the wake of dismantling the welfare state, executed in no small part by leaders of the Labor Party. This not only affected economic growth and widened disparities, but also had repercussions on the Labor Party and the Israeli left, which originally drew from socialist ideas. It is no coincidence that the Labor Party fell from forty-four seats in the 1992 Knesset elections to fifteen in the 2013 elections. Since 1999, Labor has struggled to garner more than twenty seats. (In 2015, under the name Zionist Union, the party won twenty-four seats, including six allotted to the Hatnuah faction led by Tzipi Livni.) In retrospect, Nissim Zvilli, who participated in the programs to reform the Histadrut, concluded: "It was a far-reaching mistake to completely destroy our organizational infrastructure. In this way, we lost four to five seats in the peripheral cities and neighborhoods, places where the Labor Party never had anything to sell except for the Histadrut."[42] But Beilin believes it was impossible to act otherwise, and that the good of the state, even if at the expense of the party, required the cleaning of the Histadrut's stables.

Still, from a contemporary perspective, and in light of the widening gaps in Israel, Beilin thinks that the reforms instituted in Israel, which propelled it toward a neoliberal economy (primarily at the fault of Likud governments, in his view), should be reexamined. "The leaders have a duty to reexamine their views as time goes by, in accordance with the weaknesses created in the system from time to time," he says today. Beilin elaborates:

> In the 1990s, it was correct to open the Israeli economy to the world, and to correct the flaws of the Histadrut. I believed, and still believe, that the state does

not need to be the owner of any company, including hospitals. Privatization is fundamentally the right move. But now it is necessary to examine how social responsibility is maintained through regulation. How to safeguard the workers' conditions while also maintaining competition. I'm in favor of organized labor and against companies that prevent this. And I think that since 1977, there has been a process of disarray in market conditions, but the current reform cannot be executed with the tools Mapai used. The world is flat today, and it's impossible to entrench ourselves with a nationalized economy cut off from the world. But it does frighten me to see the dependence on plutocrats and how the free market is becoming a monster. Therefore, regulation that sets wage ceilings, for example, is essential and fitting. The Israeli economy needed to change, and rightly so, because it always frightens me to remain in the same place. Today we need a new social-democratic initiative to inject remedies for the damage that came with neoliberalism.

## 7

Though Beilin is primarily identified with the peace process, his original dream was to be appointed to a job that did not exist in Israel's governments—minister for affairs of the Jewish people. (Interestingly, Ariel Sharon also wanted to establish this position in the 1970s.) He did not intend to only engage in Diaspora affairs. The ministry he envisioned would, in the spirit of Ahad Ha'am, address the cultural and moral significance of the Jewish people in the modern era, in Israel and abroad.

Beilin is an outlier in this regard among Israeli politicians, who generally focus their attention exclusively on Israel. The story of Israel, in Beilin's eyes, is a chapter in the Jewish question and its meaning. For him, the fulfillment of the Zionist project entails more than securing sovereign existence in the Land of Israel. Beilin did not realize his hope of establishing a ministry for the Jewish people's affairs, but at many junctures of his career, he worked on issues pertaining to these affairs, especially Jewish immigration and absorption. As deputy finance minister, he initiated the formation of an absorption cabinet in 1989 to prepare for the anticipated wave of immigrants from the Soviet Union. Beilin was one of the proponents of granting a general "absorption basket" the immigrants could use as they wished, allowing them to choose their place of residence and occupation without government intervention. Beilin is proud of his approach, which reflected the lessons he drew from Israel's absorption of large waves of immigration in the 1950s. He is probably unaware of the historical irony in the fact that the correction inspired by the flawed absorption of Mizrahi Jews was implemented to absorb Ashkenazi Jews in the 1990s.

In any case, along with the desire to encourage Jewish immigration, Beilin is also concerned about assimilation in the Diaspora. In this context, he initiated the Birthright project.

Assimilation is a topic that is not easy for a liberal person to oppose. During the Emancipation period, as assimilation among European Jews was rising, the struggle against this trend was one of the motives for Zionism among liberal Jews who were quintessentially secular, including Jabotinsky and Herzl. But in the twenty-first century, deep in the era of globalization, when identities are already fluid, and when people from different places in the world connect due to cultural, technological, athletic, and other preferences, it is difficult for an enlightened and fair person to publicly demand from young people to forego a loving relationship with another person only because that person does not belong to the same religious or ethnic category.

However, Beilin knows that assimilation is the big question that is almost never raised in Israel as a threat to the existence of the people, even though less critical security threats are defined as "existential" on the public agenda. While it is hyperbole (and distasteful) to call assimilation, as some do, the "quiet Holocaust" or "the sweet Holocaust," any attempt to discuss the future of the Jewish people cannot disregard this phenomenon. According to a survey conducted by the Pew Research Center in 2014, about 58 percent of Jewish adults in the United States are assimilating—that is, are married to non-Jews. (This is admittedly a simplistic definition of assimilation, as we note below.) And the rate soars to 71 percent among non-Orthodox Jews. This is not limited to the demographic loss. American Jewry constitutes an elite group in culture, science, and business, and support for Israel would suffer without it.

The question of what caused such a steep increase in assimilation (only 17 percent of US Jews assimilated in 1970) raises more conjecture than answers. In some ways, assimilation can be seen as proof of the historical necessity of the State of Israel for the Jewish people. Only in Israel—by virtue of being the majority—Jews continue to marry other Jews and are not assimilating. But this perspective is far from sufficient. Indeed, Israel's founding fathers believed that the creation of the state would also strengthen Jewish identity in the Diaspora, yet the result is the opposite. Is it possible that Israel's existence has actually reduced Diaspora Jews' fears about the future of the Jewish people and, consequently, they feel less of a commitment to preserve their Jewish identity? Many secular Jews regard the ultra-Orthodox as responsible for keeping the embers of Judaism alive; perhaps US Jews look at Israelis in the same way? Or perhaps rising assimilation stems from the fact that the Jewish state has turned out to be just another state entity, lacking any unique values?

But who is defined as assimilating, and what, in fact, is assimilation? Should a Jew who marries a non-Jew and educates his children as Jews—with his non-Jewish (and non-converting) wife's consent—be considered someone who is assimilating? Should a person be defined as a "Jew" only according to Orthodox criteria? Shouldn't Orthodoxy be required to adapt Jewish law to the existence of mixed couples? And perhaps the religious Jews are right—without a commitment to the Jewish religion, the Jewish people will shed its values and lose its cohesion? But is the religious commitment toward the idea or toward the ethnic affinity?

Assimilation is also a chapter in a broader story of a secularized world in which national and cultural boundaries are blurring. When a Christian American does not regard his religion as a barrier between him and others, why should a secular classmate do so? And in general, in deeper philosophical terms, without reference to the Jewish question, assimilation is ostensibly a positive sign of an enlightened era, in which people mix with others without differentiating by religion or race.

The question of assimilation is complex, with no clear-cut answers. And since assimilation is occurring overseas, the issue generally receives scant mention in the Israeli media. This is a ridiculous situation: we accept as natural the warnings by Israeli leaders about threats to the Jewish people's existence, while part of the people is already disappearing.

Against this background, it was important for Beilin to place the question of assimilation at the center of the Israeli agenda.

Since Beilin is not a religious person, he could not suggest the traditional Jewish identity as a formative and uniting framework. On the other hand, he sees no secular cultural alternative to the Orthodox Jewish identity other than living in Israel. Only in Israel can "a Jewish normative culture and system" exist that is able to preserve Jewishness for the coming generations—without coercion. Therefore, he believes that the only optional remedy for assimilation (besides the Orthodox formula) requires, at the very least, visits to Israel, which can strengthen the connection to it—and, indirectly, the connection to Jewishness—among the young secular generation of Diaspora Jewry.[43]

Despite the fact that the Jewish people today is divided almost equally between those living in Israel and those living in the Diaspora (primarily in the United States), Beilin does not support Ahad Ha'am's formula of two centers—one in Israel and one in the Diaspora. He believes that "only Jerusalem can ensure ongoing Jewish life, even if it does not surpass America intellectually." Since Ahad Ha'am's vision of a Jewish moral-cultural center has not been realized in Israel, in part due to the preoccupation with security and economic challenges, Israel's attraction for those who attribute importance to the survival of Judaism as a culture stems from the simple fact that only in Israel is it possible to live in a Jewish majority, in a Jewish-Israeli culture tied to the religious Jewish tradition but without requiring observance of its commandments. Only in Israel do the laws and norms draw from the historical Jewish culture.[44]

Secular Judaism, Beilin believes, has yet to find an alternative to religious symbols as a unifying cultural factor. At the same time, he recognizes the process that Diaspora Jewry is undergoing, which his former student, Professor Yossi Shain, defined as "the Israelization of Judaism." That is, the focus of identity of the Jewish world, at least since 1967, is Israel—regardless of whether this is expressed in criticism of Israel or in unqualified identification with it.[45]

Beilin wants to deepen this "Israelization" and use it as a common denominator to prevent the loss of interest in the continued existence of the Jewish people, because in many ways he is concerned about the future. The generation that experienced the Holocaust was tragically and indelibly imprinted with a consciousness of the uniqueness of Jewish existence. But as that generation dies out, there is less commitment to Jewish identity, especially among the successful communities in the Western world, where religious identity is losing its importance. Paradoxically, the longed-for peace is also liable to accelerate the process of alienation from Jewishness, because as the situation and standing of the Jewish community in Israel improves, and the more its future is ensured, there will be less concern and interest in it. Accordingly, the connection with Israel will weaken. Only an intimate familiarity with life in Israel can preserve the connection between Diaspora Jewry and Israel, and perhaps even pave the way toward a shared culture.

This is the background for the "Shovrim" (Vouchers) program that Beilin began to promote in 1994, a program known today as Birthright (or "Taglit" in Hebrew). The goal was to encourage Jewish youth to become acquainted with Israel, and the idea was to entice them to visit by subsidizing their trip. Today, this seems simple and trivial, but until the project got underway, the Jewish Agency and Jewish organizations leaned toward a different approach: to encourage young people to immigrate to Israel after acquiring a profession and completing their studies. Beilin thought this approach was wrong because it was doubtful whether the organizations could, indeed, generate mass immigration, and because once young people acquire a profession, they usually seek relevant work in their country of residence. He thought it would be better to suffice with a more modest objective—a visit to Israel, which would generate a natural attraction for living in Israel, or at least strengthen the connection to it. And, in this context, it would be best to focus on young people who have yet to complete their studies because that is when a person's identity is formed and people are more open to change. In addition, Beilin felt that the Zionist establishment should move away from the outdated approach that identified Israel primarily as a historical phenomenon and, instead, present Israel as an attractive tourist destination.

Brian Lurie, a liberal rabbi active in San Francisco, proposed institutionalizing the initiative and establishing a fund of $30 million—to be jointly financed by the Jewish Agency, Diaspora Jewry, and the Israeli government—that would subsidize trips to Israel for 50,000 young Jews. Beilin, on the other hand, proposed fully funding such trips (and prepared plans that described the economic implications of the project). Since most of the Diaspora youth in the Western world travel abroad in any case, they must be offered a decisive advantage to choose Israel as their destination—and this advantage would be a cost-free trip. Opponents of his proposal argued that the trip participants would be more committed to the program if required to pay at least some of its cost.

In the framework of Birthright, Beilin sought to achieve another significant change in Israel-Diaspora relations: to reduce Diaspora Jewry's philanthropy to Israel as much as possible, and to channel donations to projects focused on strengthening the ties between Jews in the Diaspora and Jews in Israel. In his view, collecting donations for Israel perpetuated an exilic mentality, which also has an impact in deeper contexts, and harms Israel's image as an advanced Western nation that can mobilize funding in other ways. The image of Israel as a needy country is also indirectly detrimental to encouraging immigration from the United States. (Similarly, Beilin opposed the Project Renewal urban revitalization program conducted under the Begin government, which was funded by donations from world Jewry. While Begin viewed the donations as a symbol of Jewish solidarity, Beilin believed they create an equation in which the Jew living in the West is the wealthy one who financially supports the poor Israeli living in Israel, thus perpetuating relations based on a consciousness of deprivation.)

The counterarguments were many. Donors insisted that transferring money to the state and its institutions enabled them to concretely express their identification with

Israel. Government officials argued that the state still needs the money of world Jewry and that Israeli budget allocations should give priority to the development towns, in keeping with the traditional Jewish teaching that "your city's poor come first" when it comes to giving charity.

There were also intense discussions on the question of whether to fully fund the trip to Israel. Charles Bronfman, who was captivated by the idea and later became one of the key funders of the project, argued at first that no one appreciates a free gift. But the main person responsible for stalling the project was Rabin, who had difficulty understanding its importance and believed that the state budget, in any case, should be used to meet the needs of the state and its citizens, and not to finance visits by Jews to Israel.[46] The first prime minister to embrace the idea was Netanyahu. In 1998, after being promised the participation of funders like Bronfman, Lynn Schusterman, and Michael Steinhardt, he agreed to allocate state funding for the project. Birthright was launched in 2000 and subsequent prime ministers continued to support it.

To date, over 650,000 young Jews have toured Israel in Birthright programs. About 80 percent of the program participants are from the United States, with the rest from various countries in the Jewish Diaspora. The tours include holy places (such as the Western Wall) and sites connected to the history of Zionism and central events in Israeli history. Since 2007, Sheldon Adelson, known for his hard-line right-wing views, has contributed enormously to the project, which has led critics to decry Birthright as a project that tends to promote an ultra-nationalist perspective. Critics also charge that Birthright tours are militaristic, as expressed in activities with IDF soldiers, and note that the tours do not visit the territories, which could expose the visitors to the dark side of the occupation.

In any case, Birthright is today considered one of the most important projects addressing the continuity of Jewish life, and in an era in which the political divisions over Israel's path are a cause of internal dissension in Israel and in the Diaspora, this project is perhaps one of the last successful Zionist initiatives on which there is a consensus of support.

# 8

After Peres and Rabin took over the reins of the Oslo channel, Beilin spent many hours in meetings with Rabin—some of them with Peres and Savir, and some one-on-one.

The relationship that developed between the two was complex. Beilin's close relations with Peres colored Rabin's attitude toward Beilin from the outset. At the same time, Beilin found it difficult to accept the blend of Rabin's extreme shyness and his ability to bluntly hurl insults at his interlocutors. This character flaw was also detrimental to creating a consensus around the peace process, because there were instances when, as prime minister, he could have absorbed the criticism directed at him and played the role of the conciliatory father of the nation, displaying empathy toward all parts of the society, but. Instead, he almost automatically responded with the frankness and directness that characterized him. For example, he said in reference to Golan Heights residents who opposed an Israeli withdrawal: "They can spin around like propellers."

And in response to criticism from Jewish settlers, Rabin publicly declared: "I don't give a damn about them."

In later stages, when the diplomatic process advanced and the political critique escalated to accusations of treason and death threats against Rabin, Beilin identified with Rabin's anger. Rabin could not understand how anyone could accuse him of treason. But in early stages of the process, at least in response to fierce criticism that did not exceed the bounds of political discourse, Rabin's rhetoric contributed to polarization and sometimes put the government in an adversarial position vis-à-vis significant segments of the public. Of course, Rabin's responses also expressed his integrity and leadership (and, to some extent, contributed to his popularity and the admiration felt toward him). Beilin appreciated how Rabin withstood pressure and the fact that he took responsibility for failures, but was often disappointed to discover a tendency toward close-mindedness and lack of imagination. In any case, a friendship did not blossom from the many hours the two spent together. (Beilin also did not regard himself as a friend of Peres, despite their closeness and the affection he felt toward him.) But a relationship of mutual regard and openness developed between Rabin and Beilin, which also stemmed from the businesslike approach of both men.

Nonetheless, and despite an agreement between Peres and Rabin that Beilin would be appointed minister after the resignation of Haim Ramon in February 1994, Rabin delayed the appointment. Only in July 1995, in parallel to the appointment of Ehud Barak as interior minister, Rabin agreed to fulfill his agreement with Peres. In front of the cameras, Rabin, with his bashful grin, declared: "Yossi has come of age." There was an element of affection in this expression, but also a bit of disparagement, perhaps reflecting the fact that Rabin still regarded him as one of Peres' boys. Beilin was happy about the promotion, though he realized it was mainly attributable to the thaw in relations between Peres and Rabin, and less because the prime minister really wanted to promote him.[47] Since his primary focus was the peace process, Beilin did not want to be appointed minister of economy and planning. He ultimately agreed to take on this portfolio, but set an extraordinary condition: that he be allowed to dismantle the Ministry of Economy and Planning. When he said this to Rabin, the prime minister chuckled and predicted that Beilin would come to him in another six months demanding a budget increase for the ministry. Beilin vowed that his unique contribution as minister of economics and planning would be to save the economy the money required to run the ministry, which was tailored for Yaakov Meridor in the Begin government and whose authorities previously belonged to various divisions in the Finance Ministry and Prime Minister's Office. Rabin did not live to see the fulfillment of Beilin's promise. The ministry was dismantled after Rabin's assassination, under a new government formed by Peres.

# 9

On September 28, 1995, Rabin and Arafat returned to Washington to sign the Interim Agreement on the West Bank and the Gaza Strip, better known as Oslo II.[48]

The agreement was designed to expand Palestinian control in the territories and regulate the relations between the sides until the conclusion of a final status accord in 1999. It called for the IDF to withdraw from most of the large Palestinian cities, established a Palestinian police force of thousands of armed personnel, and divided the West Bank and Gaza Strip into three categories: Area A—under full Palestinian civil and security control; Area B—under Palestinian civil control and Israeli security control; and Area C—under Israeli control.

In a preliminary discussion of the agreement in the Knesset, Beilin went up to the podium to represent the government. In his speech, he acknowledged the difficulties the agreement posed, but argued that it expressed a necessary risk for those who no longer wish to rule over another people. Beilin presented the agreement as the fulfillment of the autonomy plan the Begin government signed as part of the peace treaty with Egypt. In light of the importance of the speech, which sheds light on Beilin's perception of the process and his responses to arguments from the right, it is presented here at length:

> In 1978, a certain agreement was signed that has since become known as the Camp David Accord, and it spoke about autonomy for the Palestinians in Judea and Samaria and the Gaza Strip, and a strong local police. This document remained a document for many years, and it's difficult to know exactly how the people who wrote the document envisioned this autonomy operating on the ground. Only in the Oslo agreement did this document become a basis for an agreement that had to implemented. . . .

> Undoubtedly, when this becomes a reality, it raises quite a few problems. . . . After turning this document into reality, a group emerged from those who supported the Camp David Accords who said: This is not what we had in mind, and maybe it was actually a mistake from the start. Another group of Knesset members opposed the Camp David agreement in principle then, or entered the Knesset afterwards and said that it was a bad deal, and here's the proof—when it comes to implementing the agreement, it leads to an undesirable outcome in their eyes. But I want to turn to MK [Avigdor] Kahalani, who basically approves the move—so I understand and know—but his remarks, when it comes to implementing this move, raise question marks that make it really impossible. It's impossible to want to stop ruling over another people, but also to stay there; it's impossible to leave, but also say that places like Ramallah or Bethlehem are on the way to Jerusalem; that there's a big problem with leaving cities like Qalqiliya lest it become a source of terrorism; that there's a big problem with leaving Jenin and Tulkarem because of their proximity to the Israeli border, and the same applies to Qalqiliya.

> After all, we need to make a decision here—and we'll make it, I hope, soon—and it is a historical decision to a large extent: Are we ready, because we don't want to rule over another people, to leave a significant part of the West Bank and find security arrangements that can ensure reasonable security for us? And for us—that's for Israelis, regardless of whether they live on this or that side of the Green Line. We either say: This involves so many risks—and all of the question marks you

raised are question marks, I can't refute them and say they're nonsense, especially what you asked at the end—is it possible to guarantee that no Jew will be killed. Who can guarantee? Just as you can't guarantee that no Israeli will be killed in the current situation, I can't guarantee that no Israeli will be killed in the new situation. We don't live in an insurance firm, where each of us is a better agent than the other. Therefore, in my opinion, whoever makes the fundamental decision that in order to stop ruling over another people we should leave the densely populated areas in the West Bank and Gaza, also needs to accept the conclusion that there is no alternative but to take that risk involved in leaving, if you can make reasonable security arrangements. . . .

Concerning the security of the residents in Judea and Samaria—this is undoubtedly the primary effort. It's a lot of money, it's a lot of effort, and there's nothing more important in this agreement from our perspective than to achieve security both for them and for the residents living in sovereign Israel. . . . We insisted in Oslo on something that not many believed was possible to achieve—that during the entire interim period, all of the communities would remain intact. So there's an argument whether this is sufficient and, on the other hand, there's an argument whether it wouldn't have been best to reach an agreement on moving some of them . . . in any case, we insisted on all of them remaining in place. . . .

In my humble opinion, after a few difficult months of adjustment, of an attempt to reach some sort of modus vivendi, this experiment of "Gaza and Jericho first" has been one of the most successful experiences in the history of our relations with the Arabs. I recently asked for statistics on attacks in Gaza. In 1992, seven Israeli citizens were murdered. In 1993, eleven Israelis were murdered. Since May 1994, the beginning of the autonomy, two Israeli citizens have been murdered in Gaza. . . . It seems to me that the story of Gaza and Jericho is an extraordinary successful story. . . . If we can implement this type of accord, with roads that will cost a lot of money, with an army that will continue to protect the settlements and the settlers, we'll reach a situation in which security will increase rather than decrease, on both the sovereign side of the Green Line and the other side of it.[49]

The most noteworthy element in Beilin's speech is his emphasis on the decision to build a network of bypass roads in the territories—later seen as an expression of an apartheid regime, fueling the conflict—and to bolster the IDF's protection of the settlements, instead of beginning to plan their evacuation.

It seems that this emphasis, and Beilin's rhetoric in the speech in general, was a response to the turbulent mood in Israel and the desperate attempt to contend with growing opposition to the agreement. The moral and uplifting arguments expressed when the Declaration of Principles was signed were now absent from Beilin's remarks, replaced by a slightly apologetic presentation, which rationally analyzed the advantages of the agreement, including a reference to the decline in the number of Israelis killed. This was his way of trying to lower the flames of opposition in the Knesset and in the public. In retrospect, however, it seems that shifting the public debate from the advantages of peace from the moral and strategic perspective to a limited security discussion, which included a tally of dead, served the interests of the opponents of the agreement. After all, it is more difficult to explain ongoing acts of terror under a diplomatic accord than in the absence of an accord. The balance sheet of bereavement dampened the excitement and drained the human energy that sustain trailblazing peace agreements, leaving center stage for the energy of the opponents.

Indeed, when the agreement was presented to the Knesset for ratification on October 5, the atmosphere was tumultuous. A rally organized by the right-wing opposition was held in Zion Square in central Jerusalem, with Netanyahu, Sharon, and Moshe Katsav among the speakers. Many demonstrators joined in malicious chants against Rabin and Peres, including "Rabin's a traitor" and "Death to Rabin." Some of them continued their unruly protests at the entrance to the Knesset. In the Knesset plenum, Rabin delivered the main speech. In his programmatic address, he outlined his vision and reasons for opting to negotiate with the PLO. Two important statements stood out:

The first statement referred to the source of the conflict and addressed one of the basic flaws of Zionist thinkers—ignoring the existence of the Arabs of Palestine. It is no secret that the establishment of the modern Jewish national movement was accompanied by polemics and proposals on a range of social, economic, and theological issues. But one central question—regarding the Arab population that has lived here for centuries—was relegated to the margins of the debate (though there was some discussion of the need to reach an accord and compromise with the Arabs).[50] Therefore, many attributed profound significance to Rabin's declaration in his speech that "we didn't come here to an empty land." This was interpreted as an expression of historical remorse, a sort of belated apology for the early Zionist blindness. Thus, it seemed that his remarks marked a substantive and genuine change in Jewish-Arab relations in the disputed land.

However, Rabin also made another important statement. He declared that the primary motive for the Oslo agreements did not derive from a historical-moral outlook, but rather from his desire to separate from the Palestinians as quickly as possible in order to prevent the development of a binational state. Accordingly, he stated his readiness to establish an independent Palestinian entity that would be "less than a state"—terminology the Palestinians would be loath to accept. Rabin went on to sketch his red lines: rejection of a full withdrawal to the lines of June 4, 1967, a united Jerusalem under Israeli sovereignty, annexation of settlement blocs, and demarcation of Israel's eastern border in the Jordan Valley, where Israeli settlements would remain. Although these red lines essentially blocked any possibility of winning Palestinian consent (and, in fact, seem to correspond to those of Benjamin Netanyahu in the twenty-first century), the Knesset vote on the interim accord (Oslo II) was seen as a battle between two opposing worldviews that would decide the future of Israel. The fact that the agreement was approved by a slim margin of two votes (61 to 59) reflected the huge divide in Israeli society and clouded what should have ostensibly been celebrated as one of the Zionist movement's greatest achievements.

Beyond the ideological conflict, many accused the Rabin government of "buying votes," because Oslo II would not have been approved without the support of MKs

Alex Goldfarb and Gonen Segev (who later served a prison sentence for smuggling drugs and was arrested in May 2018 on suspicion of spying for Iran). The two men were elected to the Knesset as members of the right-wing Tsomet party, which opposed the agreement, and then formed a separate faction and joined the coalition in exchange for generous political benefits and promises. But historical accuracy requires noting that the opponents of Oslo also received support from MKs who crossed party lines: Emanuel Zisman and Avigdor Kahalani, who were elected on the Labor Party slate, voted against the agreement after quitting Labor and forming the Third Way party.

## 10

Beilin today says that he had already concluded at this stage that there was a fundamental flaw in the Oslo Accords:

> We opened too large an expanse of time and let the extremists on both sides undermine the agreement. The second mistake is that we were certain the terrorism would come from the Palestinian side. We weren't prepared for the massacre by Baruch Goldstein in the Cave of the Patriarchs in February 1994, which ignited the fire. With the initial signing of the agreement, we saw that a large majority of the public supported the peace accord, and we thought that was enough. We didn't understand that an extreme minority could be much more effective than the moderate majority.

Therefore—and in light of Rabin's remarks about "an entity that is less than a state," and considering the difficulties that Arafat faced from opponents of the accords in Palestinian society—Beilin sought to accelerate the secret talks he conducted with Abu Mazen on a draft of the final status agreement, with the aim of surprising the two leaderships with a memorandum of understandings. The talks were held under the auspices of the Swedish government. The Israeli negotiators included Yair Hirschfeld, Ron Pundak, and, sometimes, Nimrod Novik. On the Palestinian side, the participants included Hussein Agha and Ahmad Khalidi, intellectuals living in London, and Hassan Asfour, a confidante of Arafat. On October 31, 1995, the two sides reached understandings that were summarized in a draft agreement, and Abu Mazen came to ECF's modest Tel Aviv office to celebrate the occasion. The agreement was not formally signed, but it offered a detailed framework for a final status accord.

A Palestinian state would be created, encompassing 95.5 percent of the territories. Israel would annex the large settlement blocs, where about 70 percent of the settlers lived at that time. There would also be land swaps: in exchange for 250 square kilometers that Israel would annex in the West Bank, the Palestinians would receive 200 square kilometers in the northern Negev. The Jordan Valley and areas at the northern end of the Dead Sea that were not under Israeli sovereignty would be gradually transferred to the Palestinians. After the establishment of Palestine, Jerusalem would be divided administratively. Formally, it would remain united under Israeli control, but the Palestinian flag would fly over the Temple Mount, and the Palestinians would manage the Islamic holy sites and establish their capital in the Abu Dis neighborhood in Jerusalem.

It was also agreed that Israel would consent to the limited entry of refugees to the Palestinian state and recognize their plight in an official declaration. Israel would also participate in an international conference on compensation for refugees, and continue to allow family reunification and the return of refugees under humanitarian criteria. On the subject of settlements in the territory of Palestine, it was agreed that they could remain under an innovative condition: they would not be defined as settlements for Jews only. Palestine would be demilitarized, and Israel would be allowed to maintain a "low-signature" military presence (that is, warning systems, without the conspicuous presence of soldiers) for twelve years.[51] The draft agreement did not include a commitment by the Palestinians to formally declare an end to the conflict—a demand raised by Ehud Barak in later negotiations.

Though the agreement was unsigned and not all of the details were fleshed out—for example, the precise formula of the accord in Jerusalem—its primary importance was in laying the groundwork that was acceptable to the PLO's second-in-command and to the person who led the Oslo process from the Israeli side. The main progress from Israel's perspective included the land swaps, the proposal to leave settlements intact in Palestinian territory, and the Palestinian agreement to essentially concede the right of return to Israel. From the Palestinian perspective, the Israeli side agreed to a Palestinian state for the first time, expressed readiness to declaratively recognize the refugees' plight, accepted a Palestinian capital in Jerusalem and Palestinian control of the Islamic holy places, and civil control in the Jordan Valley. Encouraged by the achievement, Beilin decided to update Rabin and Peres as soon as possible.

Recognizing the importance of the document, Beilin thought it would be best for Rabin and Peres to present it to the public during the next election campaign, assuming that it would boost support for the Labor Party and help it win another four years for implementing the agreement. In October 1995, during the Labor Party convention, he also proposed moving up the elections (without revealing the secret agreement with Abu Mazen). While Beilin sought early elections because he was concerned about the erosion of public support for Rabin, the latter opposed Beilin's proposal and called it a somewhat impudent attempt to impose his view on the party's leaders. "Yossi, with all due respect for your part in the Oslo agreement," Rabin declared at the convention, "you could have roamed around there for another three years without any result if only the election results were different, while the leaders of the current government, not a single one, including Shimon, would have borne responsibility."[52] The proposal was rejected and removed from the convention's agenda. Rabin believed he could win the next elections and there was no need to rush ahead.

In late October, Rabin was also worried about the rally planned for November 4 in Kings of Israel Square in Tel Aviv, aimed at re-energizing supporters of the peace process. Despite his initial reservations about the idea, in part due to concerns about a sparse turnout, Rabin was persuaded (largely under pressure from the former mayor of Tel Aviv, Shlomo Lahat) to appear and deliver a speech in a joint display of strength with Peres. Beilin, who was busy polishing up the draft of the final status agreement, did not place much importance in the rally. He thought it was a good time to fulfill a commitment to deliver a series of lectures in the United States before focusing on promoting the final status accord. He scheduled a meeting with Rabin for early November—planning to tell the prime minister about the understandings with Abu Mazen at that meeting—and flew to New York.

# After Rabin's Murder

## 1

While in New York, Beilin met at his hotel with Amos Oz and told him about the agreements with Abu Mazen. In the midst of their conversation, Beilin's bureau chief called and frantically reported that Rabin had been attacked at the conclusion of the peace rally. Beilin found it difficult to understand, and thought she was referring to another one of the many verbal assaults against the prime minister. "They shot him," she explained. Beilin and Oz hurried to Beilin's room to watch the news broadcasts on CNN.

As noted, Beilin did not feel great affection for Rabin, and Rabin was not enamored with the man he called a poodle. Beilin was angered by the failure of both Rabin and Peres to overcome their mutual animosity, though he believed there were, indeed, moments when their gestures—including their famous embrace at the peace rally, moments before Rabin's assassination—expressed authentic appreciation of their partnership in the process. Beilin had reasons not to like Rabin as a person—and yet he wept. Oz was also caught up in emotion.

Oz and Beilin quickly contacted Ehud Barak, then serving as interior minister, who was staying at the same hotel. Arrangements were made for the three to board a mournful flight to Israel that night. While on the plane, Beilin thought appreciatively of the heavy historical burden Rabin had borne and his ability to persevere in leading the country along the path he had chosen, despite the personal attacks against him. To some extent, Beilin felt personally responsible for the murder, as the person who had paved the route that ultimately led to the assassination. He also thought about the vagaries of history, which would remember Rabin as someone who was murdered because of his pursuit of peace, though he actually had a hard-line security-oriented worldview. Beilin was also worried about the future of the Jewish state; according to Israel's ethos, this type of political murder could never have occurred. In parallel, he began to wonder what he should do in the wake of the assassination. He had planned to present the agreements with Abu Mazen to Rabin and hear the prime minister's views on the final status accord. In Beilin's conversations with Barak during the flight, the two recalled memories of Rabin, both recent and distant, and discussed what was likely to happen in the wake of his assassination. Neither could imagine how things would unfold.

After the initial shock from the murder, and from the fact that Yigal Amir, a law student at Bar-Ilan University, who had studied at the ultra-Orthodox Amiel Yeshiva, but wore a knitted yarmulke (associated with national-religious Jews), had managed to penetrate Rabin's thin security detail and fire three shots, Israeli society turned to what was called a "national self-reckoning."

Some preferred to narrowly focus on the security blunder of the Shin Bet, which had assumed that a Jew would not harm the prime minister. (This assumption is actually anchored in theology, drawn from expressions such as "a Jew who sinned is still a Jew" and "all Jews are responsible for each other," though Jewish history, and certainly Zionist history, primarily during the Yishuv period, is full of Jews who harmed and even murdered other Jews for political reasons.)

Some described Amir as a "wild weed," a twenty-five-year-old youth with an unstable personality, who did not represent a larger phenomenon. Others pointed to the incitement by right-wing politicians who had accused Rabin—directly and indirectly—of treason. The public spotlight largely turned toward the radical rabbis in the national-religious camp, who had attached contemporary political commentary to terms from Jewish law, such as *din moser* (a Jew who informs on a fellow Jew to a non-Jew) and *din rodef* (a Jew who endangers a fellow Jew, knowingly or unknowingly). Whether directly or indirectly, the rabbis thus provided a license to murder the prime minister in order to prevent him from endangering Jews or the Land of Israel.

On the other hand, some right-wingers complained that the muzzling of Oslo opponents by the media and the government had led to an outburst, expressed in the terrible murder. For example, Benny Begin explained, less than two months after the murder: "Every organized, systematic, calculated attempt has been made to strangle democracy in Israel by silencing the parliamentary opposition, and a cynical attempt has been made to create an atmosphere in which opposition to the Oslo Accords is identified in people's minds with the abominable murder."[1]

Each of these arguments contains some truth, but the perspective of over twenty years helps to understand Rabin's murder in a slightly different way.

Israeli society was built upon a socialist ethos, which began to fade after the Ben-Gurion era, and especially after 1977. The alternative ethos that emerged after Begin's rise to power strengthened the Jewish identity of the state, and prominently emphasized the connection to the territories as an expression of a tradition-friendly stance. When the government decided to relinquish the territories, no unifying ethos remained. Amir's bullets were fired through this void.

Rabin's assassination was also the product of a change in Israel's cultural profile in the 1990s: Along with the privatization of the economy, structural changes occurred during Rabin's term that led to the opening of new world markets to Israel. With growing international trade, products became available in Israel that previously could only be purchased overseas. This affected consumption habits, which became more diverse and accentuated the disparities between the different classes in the society. The Oslo Accords, and the dissolution of the Soviet Union that preceded it, engendered new and renewed diplomatic relations with many states, including China and India, and countries in Eastern Europe and Africa. The world opened for Israelis, primarily middle-class Israelis, in an unprecedented way. At the same time, a massive wave of immigration arrived from the Soviet Union, which was different from previous waves of immigrants in that the immigrants were not required, and did not want, to assimilate in the melting pot and relinquish their unique cultural traditions from their country of origin in order to become Israelis. This fact also expressed the erosion of the value of collectivism that had characterized the society in its formative years—and which continued to significantly characterize Israeliness until the 1980s—and its replacement by a more individualistic approach. Part of the old Israeliness and its cohesive glue was lost.

In this context, it should be noted that the "tribal campfire" of Channel 1 was replaced by the blossoming of cable channels, which began to air in 1989. In particular, the introduction of commercial television broadcasts fostered a new form of statism (*mamlachtiyut*). In his book *Channel 2: The New Statism*, Noam Yuran argues that Channel 2 only gave a new form to the old statist content, and that besides mocking the aesthetics of the original tribal campfire, Channel 2 did not challenge the old narrative. Instead, it presented the same statism in more emotional and commercial colors.[2] But as Roland Barthes noted, form is also a type of content. The salient characteristics of commercial television—the commitment to the viewer's desires and the needs of the advertisers, who themselves act in accordance with the viewers' wishes—made the public discourse more superficial. This cultural climate discouraged attempts to conduct in-depth discussions of the significance of the Oslo agreement, preferring to portray it as a chapter in a TV series that opens with an idyll and moves on to tragedy in a wave of terror attacks. The complexity required for digesting a process like Oslo did not find a place in the discourse of the 1990s.

Commercial television also contributed to accelerating the processes of individualization and Americanization in Israeli society by exposing the society to American products and programs, without offering the values of civic nationalism on which the American nation was built. Thus, Israeli society discarded its original values without finding an alternative. Against the background of this analysis, the assassination of Rabin not only reflects a climactic point in the national dispute, but also expresses the evisceration of values from this dispute, in parallel to the declining power of Israel's formative ethos. In many ways, it can be said in retrospect that Rabin was murdered because it was already possible to murder the leader of a state whose values and solidarity were no longer strong.

In this context, the sociologist Michael Feige argues that contrary to the customary identification of Amir with the national-religious camp, the assassination can actually be explained by Amir's alienation within that camp. Since 1967, members of the religious-Zionist camp had, indeed, tended to oppose and cry bitterly against withdrawals and concessions—for example, the withdrawal from Sinai and the disengagement from the Gaza Strip—but at the same time, they refrained from actually rebelling against the state's institutions and maintained the tense balance between the sanctity of the state and the sanctity of the religion. If there is something in Amir's biography that helps to explain why he fired the shots and not someone else, it is the fact that he was always rejected by the national-religious camp and was unfamiliar with the implicit codes of the Zionist-religious language, which knows how to oppose without crossing the boundaries. "Amir's act," Feige correctly notes, "is connected to complex Israeli interaction between religion and ideology, ethnicity and class, centrality and peripherality."[3] That is, the murder should be understood beyond the general and explicit story line of a religious right-wing Jew who murdered the prime minister: We should note that Amir was a Mizrahi Jew in an Ashkenazi society, a national-religious Jew in an ultra-Orthodox yeshiva, and a university graduate who was largely rejected by his classmates and by the girls he courted because of his different ethnic origin and socioeconomic status. Rabin, in this context, represented for Amir not only the leader who was ready to give up parts of the Land of Israel, but also the ultimate symbol of the classic sabra. Rabin was also the successful and popular Israeli that Amir was unable to be.

Indeed, during the days of Rabin's government—which invested enormous sums in the education system and in the periphery that boosted economic growth and the standard of living—little media attention was devoted to the complex and stratified fragments that characterized the society and separated the center from the periphery, the religious from the secular, and various ethnic groups from one another. Although the murder was associated at the time with the religious-secular and right-left debate, it is hard to dismiss the thought that in Israel today, which is immersed in a "culture war" and ethnic self-reckoning, many more would be inclined to describe the story of Rabin's murder as shots fired by a rejected Yemenite against an Ashkenazi Jew regarded as the "salt of the earth." That is, the battle over the territories did not derive only from the old internal Zionist debate between maximalists and proponents of compromise. At a deeper level, this battle reflected a broader array of rifts that were further exacerbated by neoliberalism and intersected with issues of ethnicity, class, and identity. These rifts shattered the Israeli center that had prevailed until the 1980s. The shots fired at Rabin were therefore the most terrible expression of this dispute, and the inability to overcome it.

## 2

Rabin's assassination reinforced Beilin's belief that time was not on the side of the liberal camp in Israel. He hoped that Peres, who replaced Rabin as prime minister, would push toward a final status accord before it was too late. Ostensibly, it should have been easier to convince Peres of this than Rabin, yet this was not the case. Beilin felt that the circumstances in which Peres became prime minister weighed upon him. The enormous energy he typically displayed was gone, giving way to a cautious and hesitant stance. During the first conversation between Peres and Beilin after the murder, it seemed that the spark in Peres's eyes had dimmed.

Beilin presented the draft of the final status accord to Peres and emphasized its advantages: Though the Jordan Valley would come under Palestinian sovereignty, the Jordan River would remain Israel's security border and no foreign army would enter this area. Tens of thousands of settlers would come under Israeli sovereignty by annexing the large settlement blocs, and the settlements beyond the border would not be dismantled; an agreed solution would be found to provide security for them. Residents of Jewish settlements in Palestine could choose compensation or remain under Palestinian sovereignty, while retaining their Israeli citizenship (as long as the settlements are not defined as exclusively for Jews).[4] The Palestinian flag would fly on the Temple Mount, but the Holy Basin would remain an ex-territorial area that would essentially keep the city undivided. The Palestinians would call their capital Al-Quds, but it would be in Abu Dis; they would control the eastern neighborhoods of Jerusalem, which anyway were populated by Palestinians. There was also a proposal to form a joint city council, with representatives from the Israeli and Palestinian quarters; the council would choose the mayor.[5] Beilin emphasized that the partition of Jerusalem would strengthen the Jewish majority in Israel. The Palestinian state would be demilitarized. In exchange for relinquishing the settlement blocs, the Palestinians would be compensated with the desolate Haluza Sands area adjacent to Gaza. And if the Jordanians and Palestinians agreed the confederation option would also remain open. Israel would officially recognize the plight of the Palestinian refugees, but they would not be allowed to return to Israel except in special humanitarian cases. An international committee would be formed, chaired by Sweden, to help rehabilitate the refugees. Israel would share in paying the expenses, but after these arrangements were made, the Palestinians would present no further demands to Israel on this subject. Beilin suggested that Peres ask the United States to upgrade Israel's status by making it a member of NATO and to ensure Israel's qualitative advantage. He hoped that Peres would adopt this format.

Peres was not convinced. He sounded skeptical and pensive. He was ready for the first time to publicly express support for establishing a Palestinian state in Gaza, but preferred to leave the future of the West Bank open, and to involve Egypt, Jordan, and the Palestinian state in Gaza in determining its future status. In other words, Peres wanted to extend the interim agreements. The lesson he drew from Rabin's assassination was completely different from that of Beilin. Instead of urgently pursuing a final status accord, Peres preferred to wait patiently with interim agreements until the two peoples were ripe for peace and the mutual concessions it required. While Beilin believed the best course would be to formulate an agreement and submit it to a referendum, or present it as the basis for elections, Peres preferred to continue with the same coalition and focus on strengthening the interim agreements and trying to make progress in negotiations with Syria. In Peres's view, there was no chance of formally signing an agreement with Arafat based on the Beilin-Abu Mazen understandings in the current situation. Furthermore, the Israeli public had suffered a shock and would oppose conceding the Jordan Valley, he contended.[6]

Beilin was disappointed. Nonetheless, he agreed with Peres that it was essential to mend the rifts in Israel and chose to pursue this aim in the political arena. He believed that in light of the soul-searching in the national-religious camp, it would be possible and worthy to bring the NRP into the government, and to win the support of the ultra-Orthodox parties from outside the coalition. Zevulun Hammer, the moderate leader of the NRP, also thought the circumstances mandated its participation in the left-wing government. The two agreed that in exchange for the NRP's support for the government, which would continue to negotiate withdrawals, the final status agreement would be put to a referendum or new elections would be called. Beilin considered this a comfortable solution for closing the ranks for the time being. However, Yossi Sarid, who was then competing against Shulamit Aloni to lead the Meretz party after Aloni was forced to resign from the Education Ministry (Sarid replaced her in early 1996), believed that the national-religious camp's self-reckoning required it to sit in the opposition. During the initial weeks following the assassination, Peres enjoyed high approval ratings and Sarid thought this should be leveraged to promote an unequivocal left-wing agenda.[7] And since without Meretz's support it would be impossible to expand the government, the coalition format remained unchanged: the Labor Party, Meretz, and Yiud (the faction of Gonen Segev and Alex Goldfarb), supported from the outside by Hadash and the Arab parties.

At the same time, there were several personnel changes in the government. Barak proposed that Peres appoint him defense minister and Beilin foreign minister. Beilin supported the proposal, but Peres preferred to give Barak the Foreign Ministry portfolio and have Beilin serve as a minister in the Prime Minister's Office. In this role, Beilin would deal with the sensitive issues of negotiation. Peres kept the defense portfolio for himself, following in Rabin's path and the original example of Ben-Gurion, who also served as defense minister during much of his tenure as prime minister.

It was important for Peres to demonstrate military might. During his days as prime minister, the IDF conducted many preemptive actions in the territories—activities that were seen by the Palestinians as a sign of continued control over their lives. On January 5, 1996, in a sophisticated operation entailing explosives planted in a cell phone, the Shin Bet orchestrated the killing of Yahya Ayyash (known as "the engineer"), who had masterminded major suicide bombings in Israeli cities in 1994 and in early 1995. After emerging from the melancholy that struck him in the weeks following Rabin's assassination, and after realizing that he would not succeed in promoting negotiations with Syria, Peres became convinced that it would be best to move up the elections. In the wake of the targeted killing of Ayyash, Peres believed that his political standing was strong enough to carry him through early elections that would bolster the leftist bloc and his legitimacy as someone directly elected by the public. The elections were set for May 1996.

Besides its effect on the prime minister's standing, the liquidation of Ayyash was intended to weaken Hamas and boost morale in the Israeli public. But hopes of subduing the Islamic organization were dashed as Hamas responded quickly and brutally to Israel's killing of "the engineer." It soon became apparent that Ayyash had managed to train a cadre of terrorists: Between February 25 and March 4, Hamas militants carried out four suicide attacks, claiming the lives of fifty-nine civilians and soldiers. The March 4 attack, which Hamas perpetrated in conjunction with Islamic Jihad, occurred near Dizengoff Center, one of the salient symbols of the Tel Aviv lifestyle. In light of the ghastly images of dismembered limbs, charred bodies and buses, there was a growing feeling in the public that the Oslo agreement had proved that in exchange for withdrawing from Palestinian cities and villages, Israel would receive blood and the loss of security.

The Israeli leadership continued to press PLO leaders to combat terrorism. Abu Mazen sent a message via the Jordanians that he would be willing to assume a more dominant role in the negotiations, even if this meant a dispute with Arafat, if Israel evacuated settlers from Hebron and the Gaza Strip. "Otherwise," he said, "it will be impossible to successfully implement the Oslo agreement, an agreement for which there is no alternative."[8] But if there had been a chance to evacuate the settlers from Hebron following the shocking massacre in the Cave of the Patriarchs in February 1994, now, when many Israelis were blaming the terror attacks on the Palestinian Authority, which controlled the area, this possibility was gone.

Israel tried unsuccessfully to defeat Hamas with force, though there were also indirect contacts between Hamas and Israel in an effort to achieve a ceasefire after the killing of Ayyash. Beilin's archive contains a document describing a meeting in Jordan between Steve Cohen, a Jewish-American professor, and Mohammad Nazzal, a senior Hamas official who introduced himself as representing the Hamas political bureau and Khaled Meshal. According to the document, Nazzal told Cohen:

> The political bureau of Hamas has decided to propose a written or oral agreement entailing a commitment not to attack Israeli civilians, in exchange for halting the attacks against Hamas leaders. The proposal is acceptable to their military wing. They do not want to conduct negotiations now with Israelis, but with someone authorized by Israel, who needs to be an external witness.

The document explains that Hamas offered to distinguish between attacks aimed at harming soldiers on both sides of the Green Line, which would continue, and attacks aimed against civilians.

> In their eyes, the attack at Beit Lid is an attack against soldiers, while the attacks against the buses in Tel Aviv and Jerusalem constitute an attack against civilians. Therefore, they won't attack civilians, and in exchange, if we catch Hamas leaders, we'll be able to arrest them, but not kill.

The document concludes with several questions:

Should we ask Steve to speak with someone in the Shin Bet?
Should we demand a general ceasefire that would not distinguish between soldiers and civilians?
Should we forget the whole thing?
Should we ask Steve to return to Jordan and speak with Nazzal?
> p.s. Nazzal offered the body of Ilan Sa'adon in exchange for not extraditing Abu Marzouk. After hearing in response that Israel would prefer [to receive] information on Ron Arad, Nazzal said: "We have connections."[9]

This attempt to reach a ceasefire with Hamas did not succeed—like a number of other attempts occasionally mentioned in the newspapers of the period. The fighting continued to rage, extinguishing public faith in the Oslo process.

3

In April 1996, an Israeli "interests office" opened in Tunis and relations with Arab states continued to deepen, behind the scenes, during the course of the year. But here, too, the progress fell far short of what the Peres government had hoped, and Tunis also encouraged Jerusalem to lower its expectations. The message conveyed from Tunis after opening the interests office was that this should be seen as the climax of the process at this stage, and not as a starting point. A document in Beilin's archives notes: "Due to internal and external constraints—the Egyptians opposed opening a parallel office in Tel Aviv . . . [Tunis] prefers a cautious and gradual development of relations. Full relations will be established, in their view, only in circumstances of comprehensive peace."[10]

Peres had hoped to reach election day with a comprehensive vision of peace coupled with a tough security stance. The sorrow and self-reckoning in the wake of Rabin's murder was supposed to help him. However, he arrived at the finish line accompanied by public anger over the suicide attacks and without the support of the Arab public, which held Peres accountable for the Kafr Qana incidents during Operations Grapes of Wrath in Lebanon. In early 1996, Hezbollah intensified its activity against the IDF in the security zone, and after dozens of Kiryat Shmona residents were injured in a Katyusha barrage against that town, the IDF launched an operation against the organization, with heavy bombing and shelling of Hezbollah bases and Shi'ite villages in southern Lebanon. During this operation, the IDF mistakenly shelled a UN post in Kafr Qana, where a group of Lebanese refugees had taken cover. According to initial reports, which were later refuted, over a hundred people were killed in the shelling, including many children. Peres expressed sorrow, but did not apologize. The pictures of the refugees' corpses led many Arab citizens of Israel to feel that the Palestinians were again paying the price, even in Israel's battle against Hezbollah. The operation did, indeed, stop Hezbollah's Katyusha attacks against Israel, yet the mood in the Jewish public was far from celebratory. The understandings reached with Hezbollah after the operation—which essentially involved Israel and Hezbollah agreeing to limit their fighting to the security zone—recognized Hezbollah as the sovereign in southern Lebanon and thus strengthened its standing.

Nonetheless, few could believe that on May 29, 1996, in the first direct elections for prime minister in Israel, the Likud candidate would win, even if by less than half a percent. In retrospect, the surprising victory can be explained in two ways, which are almost contradictory. The first is that the elections expressed a rational vote by most Israelis, who concluded, despite the shock of Rabin's assassination, that the Oslo Accords should be halted or significantly slowed in the wake of the string of attacks. The second explanation identifies the Likud's victory as part of an ongoing process of replacing the original Israeli elites, a process that was unnaturally suspended in the 1992 elections only because of a split among the right-wing parties.

In this context, the Likud was boosted by the underdog mentality of its voters: They saw themselves as fighting for their objective outside of the establishment—against it, in fact. Thus, with most of the media and Israeli establishment favoring Peres (directly or indirectly), it was easier for Netanyahu to mobilize voters. Indeed, Israelis who identify as anti-establishment and feel a sense of deprivation have continued to favor Netanyahu in the twenty-first century, despite the fact that the right has been in power almost continuously since the upheaval of 1977.

The anti-establishment sensibility of Likud members and supporters is deeply rooted. The Revisionist movement was established by Jabotinsky in 1925, and it stood in opposition to the Yishuv's leadership and the Israeli establishment until 1977. Moreover, in Israel's formative years, during the Ben-Gurion era (1948–63), the Revisionists, represented primarily by Herut (formed by Begin and other Irgun members when the state was declared), was discriminated against by the establishment—in employment, budget allocations, and political legitimacy.[11] It is customary to describe the exclusion of the Revisionists from government coalitions and institutions by citing Ben-Gurion's famous rule: "without Herut and Maki"—that is, without the Revisionists and the communists. In terms of political legitimacy, this approach applied more to Herut. For example, Meir Vilner, one of the leaders of the communist party, was invited to sign the Declaration of Independence, while Menachem Begin, the Irgun leader who fought (albeit separately) for independence and the expulsion of the British, was excluded from the broad circle of signatories.

By 1996, Israeli society had undergone many changes—and the process of change continues today, more than two decades later. The historical-ideological background to the hostility between the workers' camp and the Revisionist camp has dimmed. However, over the years another process occurred that helped to preserve the sense of deprivation and underdog mentality: the sense of discrimination felt by Mizrahi Jews, who began to support Begin in the mid-1950s. In many ways, their sense of discrimination blended with the sense of discrimination felt by the original Revisionists. Thus, a sense of deprivation continues to characterize those who vote for the right. Consequently, the Likud is perceived as representing the "common folk" and those who are anti-establishment, while the Labor Party is seen as representing the elites that control the institutions of government, although their power has waned since 1977. Whether these sensitivities reflect a particular mindset or deep-rooted identities, they still play a role in Israel and have an impact on election results.

This helps to explain why the bandwagon theory failed to predict the outcome of the 1996 elections. According to this theory, undecided voters tend to "jump on the bandwagon" and vote for candidates who are leading in the polls. In this case, Peres initially had a commanding lead in the polls. Many right-wing voters, influenced by Rabin's assassination, were thinking about abandoning the Likud this time. However, as the polls continued to point toward a Peres victory, more and more of these wavering voters decided to return to the fold and vote Likud. As far as they were concerned, the repercussions of Oslo not only pertained to territorial compromise (which was and still is acceptable to most of the public), but also involved the battle over the state's identity and culture. Oslo was perceived as part of a process designed to make Israel more cosmopolitan and less Jewish, and thus posed a threat to the identity and cultural-historical heritage of traditional and Mizrahi voters.

This raises the question of how the Likud—whose political origins were in the Revisionist Party established by secular Ashkenazi Jews from the petty bourgeoisie— became a source of identification for Mizrahi and religious Jews.

Menachem Begin was largely responsible for this. He strayed from the ideology of Ze'ev Jabotinsky in his approach to religious matters, and adopted the Jewish tradition as a unifying and inclusive factor in his national outlook.

Begin's approach was also contrary to that of Ben-Gurion and the labor movement. The latter aimed to transform the Jewish society of immigrants into a Hebrew-Israeli nation, based on the values of socialism (rather than the values of religion). This led to the conceptual, and sometimes practical, exclusion of Mizrahi and religious Jews. On the other hand, Begin recognized and honored the traditional heritage of Mizrahi Jews, thus placing them on an equal footing with Ashkenazi Jews.

The Mizrahi and religious connection with the Likud, therefore, was not the result of false consciousness or of emotional manipulation by its leaders.[12] It is a chapter in the process Begin launched to expand the boundaries of participation and belonging in Israeli society.[13] This also created an ideological alternative to the common denominator offered by the left. And in the right's hold on power in recent decades in Israel, we can conclude that the "Jewish" common denominator defeated the "Israeli" one.

In this context, it is interesting to note a meeting Beilin had with Rabbi Menachem Froman a few months after the Oslo agreement. Froman, the rabbi of the Tekoa settlement, was a maverick. In his worldview, the Palestinian-Israeli conflict is one central chapter in the overall Arab–Israeli conflict, which could be resolved by creating a bridge between Judaism and Islam. He believed it was possible to resolve a territorial and diplomatic dispute by recognizing and agreeing on religious values common to Jews and Muslims.

Froman found it absurd that the Rabin government and the PLO were trying to build a secular bridge to peace and reach an accord based on their fear of the religious extremists on both sides, while there was already a common denominator among religious leaders—their belief in God. In his view, the transcendental outlook shared by Judaism and Islam could remove political obstacles, which are material in essence, through a unifying faith in something greater and more significant than concepts such as sovereignty and borders. If we agree that the land belongs to God, we can agree to live together with a flexible division of sovereignty, without a defined separation. Froman did not merely preach, but conducted dialogue with Palestinians, including Hamas members. This dialogue was seen as a bizarre sideshow in the atmosphere that sanctified the liberal and secular element common to the Israeli and Palestinian leadership. The appeal of this idea may, indeed, be confined to the theoretical aspect, but it is worthy of discussion.

During his meeting with Beilin, Froman said:

> There's a need to formulate a policy vis-à-vis the Muslim world. In light of the peace process with the PLO, there is also a need to talk with Palestinian extremists. . . . Today, Israel has no policy on this matter. For example, the subject of Jerusalem. We're discussing the subject with the Palestinians and are not taking

into account the significance vis-à-vis Jordan and Saudi Arabia. Or Turkey. [We] don't have the tools to address the subject. We need to develop these tools because there is an institutional Islam and a fundamentalist Islam. And with Hamas we'll need to talk, sooner or later. If we get to know them, access to them will be easier.[14]

One of Froman's associates, whose name is not mentioned in the notes of the meeting, told Beilin to remember that despite the PLO's image as a secular Palestinian movement, religious contexts also underlie its policy:

We don't attribute enough importance to this. There is a deep context to Arafat's statements in South Africa [a reference to a speech in Johannesburg in which Arafat compared the Oslo process to a treaty the Prophet Muhammad signed with a Jewish tribe during a period of weakness, with the intention of violating it once he gained strength]: Arafat spoke as a Muslim. Therefore, we should accentuate the shared history and commonalities between the religions (for example, against idol worship, on subjects of prayer, the negative attitude toward usury, opposition to abortion, and so on.) There are many organizations that can help to mediate. Hassan, the king of Morocco. Prince Hassan from Jordan. How, for example, do we relate to the subject of mosques?[15]

Beilin was not dismissive of this message and proposed forming a committee to discuss the interfaith connection. However, he did not delve deeply into this subject or promote it. Froman's view remained esoteric in the Israeli public and in the political system. (Froman died in 2013 and his daughter-in-law was injured in a terror attack in Tekoa in 2016.)

4

After the Likud's victory, Beilin held conversations with a number of right-wing Israelis in an attempt to decipher the riddle of Netanyahu and understand his intentions. In a meeting with Natan Sharansky, who then headed the Yisrael B'Aliyah party, the latter predicted that Netanyahu would support the Oslo process. Sharansky added that unlike himself, who "had strong reservations about Oslo, Netanyahu was closer to Beilin than to him on the political-diplomatic issue."[16] But it soon became apparent that this assessment was mistaken. Netanyahu's victory did not kill the peace process. He simply killed it slowly. Upon assuming office, Netanyahu announced that he would honor the Oslo Accords, while making sure to implement them on a basis of mutuality: "If they give, they'll receive; if they don't give, they won't receive," he often declared in a patronizing tone, which also expressed his skepticism and suspiciousness. Before long, it was clear that mutuality could also be a formula for stalemate and foiling the process.

Netanyahu met with Arafat and shook his hand, but did this to avoid violating agreements signed under an international umbrella. Though his attitude toward Oslo was fundamentally negative, he did not want to get on a collision course with the

United States. During Netanyahu's term, the peace process lost whatever remained of its initial utopian significance, and was reduced to pedantic negotiation between two sides that lacked faith in each other's intentions. The draft of a final status accord reached by Beilin and Abu Mazen was tossed into the dustbin of history. In any case, Netanyahu preferred continuing the interim agreements in a limited format.

At the end of Yom Kippur in September 1996, Netanyahu authorized the opening of one of the Western Wall tunnels to tourists. The exit from the tunnel was located in the Muslim Quarter of the Old City. Netanyahu's action came despite warnings from security officials that the tunnel opening was likely to spark riots. Indeed, Arafat encouraged a violent response, fueled by baseless rumors about an Israeli attempt to take control of the Temple Mount. During the disturbances, IDF soldiers and Palestinian police officers fought each other for the first time. In the clashes, 17 soldiers and about 100 Palestinians were killed. (The IDF casualties were caused, in part, by a lack of preparedness.) Israel described the Palestinian police officers, who had previously conducted joint patrols with IDF soldiers, as traitors. Bumper stickers with the slogan "Don't give them rifles" were distributed throughout Israel. (Ironically, this is the title of a pacifist song that Natan Alterman wrote seventeen years after the First World War, in protest over the use of chlorine gas during that war.)[17] The slogan blamed the Oslo planners for arming Palestinian Authority personnel.

In the wake of the violent events, and under American pressure, the Netanyahu government approved the Hebron Agreement in January 1997, which apportioned control in the city. However, the peace process itself sputtered in the climate of mutual distrust and in light of the noncompliance of both sides with agreements reached earlier. Israel complained that Arafat was not making a sufficient effort to prevent terrorism and stop incitement in Palestinian educational institutions. Arafat, on the other hand, wrote to Secretary of State Madeline Albright on November 18, 1997, that Israel was supposed to have withdrawn from 90 percent of the territory by 1997 (according to his interpretation of the accords), but failed to fulfill its commitments on this matter. Though the number of terror attacks decreased during Netanyahu's term—largely because Hamas had less incentive to undermine the process, which was moribund in any case—the relative calm was not exploited to advance the process.

In late September 1997, another entanglement occurred. In a daring assassination attempt in Amman, Mossad operatives were able to spray poison on Khaled Meshal, the head of Hamas's political bureau. The poison was designed to kill Meshal without leaving a trace. But the operation went awry and two Mossad agents were arrested. King Hussein was incensed by the violation of Jordan's sovereignty, which also violated an Israeli commitment to refrain from acting within the bounds of the kingdom. In order to prevent a crisis or even the severing of relations, and to facilitate the release of the two agents, Netanyahu acceded to the king's request to release from prison Sheikh Ahmed Yassin, the leader of Hamas in the territories. Yassin's release not only strengthened Hamas, but it also underlined Arafat's weakness: Ever since the signing of Oslo I in Washington, Israel had ignored his request to release Yassin as a gesture toward him. This gesture would have portrayed Arafat to the Palestinians as powerful vis-à-vis Israel, while Yassin would seem weak in comparison.

These events were not accidental. Netanyahu used them to undermine the fundamental idea of the Oslo Accords—whose aims included boosting the status of the PLO as the central Palestinian organization.

According to the original plans, the signing of a final status accord was slated for May 4, 1999. However, under Netanyahu, the sides found it difficult to even agree on implementation of the interim agreements. Netanyahu agreed in principle only to withdraw from 8.5 percent of the territories.[18] The Palestinians accused Israel of violating the Oslo Accords, while the Netanyahu government claimed that the Palestinians were the ones violating the principles of the agreements by refraining from revoking clauses in the Palestinian Charter that called for Israel's elimination, by enabling the continuation of incitement against Israel in the Palestinian media and educational institutions, and by failing to thwart terrorism emanating from the territories.

The impasse in negotiations created tension between Israel and the American administration, and Netanyahu sought to enlist the assistance of the Jewish lobby in the United States. On May 15, 1998, prior to the opening of the AIPAC conference, Beilin decided to make an exception to his practice of not interfering in relations between Israel, the US administration and American Jewry while a member of the opposition, and published a call to AIPAC members in the *Washington Post*. (The American businessman Steve Berman funded the publication of Beilin's manifesto.) Beilin wrote that AIPAC's adoption of Netanyahu's stance, which was contrary to the administration's position, would be a departure from the organization's basic principles of "deepening and strengthening Israel's relations with the United States."[19] What Beilin did not dare to publicly declare was his assessment that the Jewish lobby thrives on confrontations between Israel and the administration, because it is the best time for raising money and enlisting new volunteers for the organization. In this context, paradoxically, the good relations that prevailed between the administration and Israel during the days of Rabin and Peres diminished AIPAC's importance, while fulfilling the organization's objectives.[20] Netanyahu, who tried to maneuver between pressure from the administration and Palestinian demands, on the one hand, and pressure from the parties in his right-wing coalition, on the other hand, was compelled to sign the Wye River Memorandum on October 23, 1998, which was intended to translate some of the withdrawals planned in the Oslo II agreement into practical steps. Netanyahu could not admit this, but because of his troubled relations with the PA, the Wye agreement was largely formulated, with support from the State Department, in secret conversations held at the residence of Mohammed Bassiouni, Egypt's ambassador in Israel. The participants in these talks included Beilin, Ramon, and Novik on the Israeli side and Palestinian representatives Abu Mazen, Saeb Erekat, and Mohammed Dahlan, who was then the head of Palestinian Preventive Security in the Gaza Strip.

The agreement stipulated that Israel would transfer another 13 percent of the West Bank to the PA and continue its withdrawal from Hebron; in exchange, the PA would endeavor to collect illegal weapons in the territories, stop incitement against Israel, and ratify the revocation of clauses in the Palestinian Charter that call for the destruction of Israel.[21] The signing of the Wye Memorandum weakened the coalition, as several

MKs quit the government in protest. Consequently, the government fell after failing to pass a state budget for 1999, and the political system prepared for elections. The Labor Party believed it could regain power in light of the consensus in the public and in the political arena that Netanyahu had failed as prime minister. The hope was to return to the Oslo path and advance toward a final status agreement that would turn the three years of Netanyahu's rule into a temporary detour.

Though Netanyahu was, indeed, defeated, history compels us to regard his first term as dominant in shaping Israel's path. He returned to power in 2009 and, as of the writing of these lines, his tenure as prime minister is second only to that of Ben-Gurion. It is worth taking a moment to reflect on Netanyahu before returning to the story of the 1999 election campaign.

Many people, in both the left and the right, define Netanyahu as a hesitant leader who recoils from difficult decisions, and as a conservative who seeks to perpetuate the status quo. However, in attempting to understand the secret of his leadership, we find that hesitancy and caution do not necessarily characterize him. A cautious leader would not have ordered the opening of the Western Wall tunnels or the assassination of Khaled Meshal, and certainly would not have dared to confront the US administration on the question of the peace process (during his first term) or on the question of how to prevent Iran from acquiring nuclear weapons (in his subsequent terms, vis-à-vis the Obama administration). A cautious leader would not have been able to institute significant economic reforms, contrary to the wishes and interests of many of his voters, as Netanyahu did as finance minister from 2003–05. It is also unnecessary to identify Netanyahu, contrary to another popular thesis, with the neoconservative stance of the American right. His policies are devoid of optimistic aspirations, unlike those of the neoconservatives who seek to spread the values of democracy. He has no ambition of influencing the Middle East region or inducing a change in it.

What characterizes Netanyahu is profound pessimism, and the motif of mutuality—his mantra when trying to conduct the Oslo process during his first term—is tailored to his worldview. To understand Netanyahu in this context, it is essential to read one of the formative articles written by Ze'ev Jabotinsky: "Man is Wolf to Man." In the article, which draws from Thomas Hobbes's notion of "war of all against all" in humankind's natural state, Jabotinsky writes: "A fool is someone who believes his neighbor, even a most good-hearted and pleasant neighbor." The solution proposed by the founder of the Revisionist movement includes "separatism, distrust, standing on guard at all times, with a sailor's cane in hand at all times," in order to "hold some ground in the battle of wolves."[22] Without venturing into the realm of psychology, it seems that Netanyahu's family biography[23]—a strong father who felt that the academic world and the political system failed to appreciate the value of his research, and a brother who was destined for greatness, but was killed during the Entebbe operation—also contributed to the pessimism in his worldview.

Paradoxically, Netanyahu's pessimistic dimension is also evident in the fact that despite his reservations about the PLO, he did not believe that a complete rejection of the agreements with the PLO would produce a better option. He clearly did not regard Arafat as a partner and was not hopeful about surprising diplomatic gambits (including, for example, the feelers he put out to Syria early in his first term). However, he was also not inclined toward grandiose military solutions, because he believed that Israelis would not tolerate a large number of casualties. For Netanyahu, life and Jewish history mainly pose a range of threatening possibilities, and therefore his policy is characterized by measured maneuvers, without any inspiring vision.

Netanyahu's victory in 1996 can be defined as a victory of his natural pessimistic outlook, which later dovetailed with the pessimism in Israel vis-à-vis the peace process after the outbreak of the second intifada in September 2000. However, in 1999, there was still a sense of hope in Israel. The promises of Ehud Barak, the new Labor Party leader (who ran under a new political mantle called One Israel), to renew the peace process, and his military background as IDF chief of staff, brought the reins of power back into the hands of the leftist camp.

# The End of the Conflict and Its Continuation

1

After Netanyahu's victory in the 1996 elections, a turnover of leadership began in the Labor Party. Peres was forced to recognize the fact that his tenure as party chairman was over, and the party prepared to elect a new leader. Still, Peres wished to continue to enjoy a senior (and ostensibly symbolic) position as party president. Ehud Barak, who was planning to run for party chairman, was wary of Peres and sought to reduce his power as much as possible. Thus, Barak tried to block Peres from even the symbolic role.

The relations between Barak and Beilin were good—relative to what was happening in the political arena in general, and in the Labor Party in particular. They first met when Beilin was cabinet secretary and Barak was chief of IDF military intelligence, and despite their fundamental disagreements concerning Oslo, there was mutual respect between them. Nonetheless, and although Beilin had never seen himself as a candidate to lead the party or the state, he decided to compete against Barak for leadership of the Labor Party. One reason for this was the decision by Haim Ramon, Beilin's preferred candidate to succeed Peres, not to run after the party's central committee rejected his demand for completely open primaries—that is, primaries in which every citizen could vote and not just party members. In Ramon's assessment, he would be unable to defeat Barak in primaries open only to party members, mainly due to the opposition he had stirred when instituting reforms at the Histadrut. As a lesson from the Rabin–Peres rivalry, Ramon preferred to build a sound relationship with Barak, and to prepare to compete against him in the future.

There was another reason behind Beilin's beilin to run: now, when Peres was no longer the power broker in the Labor Party, he sought to build an independent power base in the party. To some extent, Beilin's disappointment over Barak's hostility toward Peres also contributed to his decision. And while it was reasonable for Beilin to assume that he would lose to Barak, who was portrayed as Rabin's successor, he felt it was important to present an alternative to the policy of Barak, who at that stage expressed opposition not only to a Palestinian state, but also to another subject Beilin advocated—withdrawing the IDF from the security zone in southern Lebanon. (Barak contended that a full withdrawal would be tantamount to "abandoning" northern Israel.)

In February 1997, shortly before the tragic accident in which seventy-three IDF soldiers were killed when two Yasour transport helicopters collided en route to the security zone, Beilin initiated a meeting at the home of Likud MK Gideon Ezra to promote, together with other MKs, the idea of withdrawing from Lebanon. On February 10, the Labor Party's Knesset faction met for its weekly meeting. In a gloomy atmosphere in the wake of the helicopter disaster, a consensus emerged against Beilin's position. Binyamin (Fuad) Ben-Eliezer nearly accused Beilin of high treason: he claimed that Beilin's declarations on this issue were encouraging Hezbollah to continue its attacks. Ephraim Sneh was more moderate, but also thought that Beilin was weakening Israel's position. Even Peres joined the critics, though implicitly, contending that the situation in Lebanon had to be resolved as part of an agreement with Syria.

Barak attacked Beilin personally, claiming that he lacked responsibility and an understanding of defense matters, and that Beilin's remarks were driven by his affection for newspaper headlines.[1] Barak's verbal assault was also aimed at June, when the party's primaries would be held. Besides Barak and Beilin, two other candidates were vying for the top party post: Shlomo Ben-Ami, who grew up in Kiryat Shmona and offered voters a candidate of Sephardi origin, and Sneh, who was considered a long shot.

As expected, Barak won in the first round, garnering 50.3 percent of the votes. Ben-Ami received 14 percent and Sneh about half as many as Ben-Ami. The surprise was Beilin, who won the support of 28.5 percent of the party members who cast their ballots; some of these voters were Peres loyalists and others were members of the young generation in the party. Beilin's strong showing demonstrated that his political standing was no longer solely dependent on his patron.

Prior to the Knesset elections, primaries were also held for the party's list. Beilin and Ben-Ami adopted the unconventional strategy of presenting themselves as partners running together. The result proved the wisdom of this move: Ben-Ami came in first, and Beilin landed in second place. (In the list of Knesset candidates, they received the fourth and fifth slots, because the first three places were reserved for Barak, Peres, and David Levy, respectively.)

The Labor Party appeared to offer a fresh and cohesive team, and Barak was bursting with ideas. To extract the party from the ethnic trap, he apologized on behalf of the party for the way the Mapai establishment absorbed the immigrants from Islamic lands. Barak also facilitated Labor's merger with two other parties: the Gesher faction of David Levy, who had left the Likud, and Meimad, whose leaders were religious Jews with moderate views on religion and the peace process. Barak chose the name "One Israel" for the combined list, aiming to appeal to new religious and Mizrahi constituencies that identified less with the Labor Party.

In the elections for the 15th Knesset, which again included direct elections for prime minister and a separate vote for a Knesset list, Barak defeated Netanyahu, winning 56 percent of the votes cast for prime minister. This was a major achievement.

However, the election results for Knesset representation indicated that the right-wing and religious dimension in the Israeli public was continuing to strengthen. Shas won seventeen seats. In his victory speech on election night, May 17, 1999, Barak promised the crowd gathered in Rabin Square the "dawning of a new day." But the jubilant crowd called for excluding Shas from the new coalition ("Just not Shas!") and thus reflected the left's alienation from trends that were impossible to stop.

Barak, whose party received only twenty-nine seats (the Likud fell to nineteen seats) ultimately formed a coalition with Shas as a central partner and crammed into his coalition parties whose ideologies were incompatible: Meretz, United Torah Judaism, the NRP, Yisrael B'Aliyah, and the Center Party.

In addition, the way that Barak distributed ministerial portfolios—appointing party leaders to head ministries for which they were unsuited—shook the Labor Party's internal equilibrium. In fact, this method of assigning ministerial roles was largely aimed to clip the wings of the party's top leaders. Barak assigned Ben-Ami to the Ministry of Public Security, Beilin to the Justice Ministry, and Ramon was relegated to minister without portfolio. Beilin was angry and suggested to his colleagues that they jointly decline Barak's ministerial appointments. However, they rejected his proposal and he was reluctant to be the sole rebel.

On the diplomatic front, Barak promised rapid decisions and asked the public to judge him based on "the test of results." This reflected a Machiavellian view, as opposed to a Kantian focus on intentions. Barak began his term as prime minister with a sense of urgency.

Barak declared that he would seek to conclude a final status accord with the Palestinians—precisely what Beilin wished. However, it later became apparent that his aspiration to end the conflict was rooted in suspicion and pessimism concerning Arafat and the Palestinian national movement, not unlike Netanyahu's outlook. Still, there was a decisive difference between the two: unlike Netanyahu, Barak was ready to embark on a diplomatic initiative in order to test his pessimism.

About a year and a half after his election, Barak presented the most daring formal proposal that any Zionist leader had offered a Palestinian leader. However, during an in-depth conversation with Beilin several months after entering the prime minister's office, in which he asked for a detailed explanation of the Beilin-Abu Mazen understandings, Barak revealed how limited his vision was from the outset.

## 2

The conversation between the prime minister and the justice minister took place in early October 1999 at Barak's home in Kochav Yair.

Barak laid out his plans in the meeting, though he mainly sought to draw from Beilin's insights and knowledge about the peace process. But Barak did not intend to assign Beilin a role in conducting negotiations. He believed it would be best to assign this mission to people perceived by the public as more hard-line; Barak was concerned that Beilin's conciliatory image would reduce public support for peace talks. In this context, as noted in the meeting summary written by Beilin, "Barak spoke about the political space he has," and was interested in the models of negotiation—that is, whether it would be better "to conduct secret or open talks."[2] Barak wondered what the Palestinians were aiming to achieve. Beilin said that one of the problems in conducting talks with the Palestinians stems from the fact that they do not conduct strategic discussions among themselves from which it is possible to deduce their objectives. Therefore, it is only possible to understand them during the course of the negotiation itself, in which their positions can change. "The Palestinians did not conduct serious discussions among themselves, and thus we can learn about their flexibility only from the negotiation itself, which was with Abu Mazen's team."

Nonetheless, from his experience in contacts with Abu Mazen, Beilin said that in his assessment, "on the subject of borders, there will be flexibility on their part if we revise the 1967 border lines [that is, land swaps, and the transfer of Haluza Sands in exchange for the settlement blocs]."

On the issue of refugees, Beilin believed the Palestinians would be ready to accept "returning to a state of Palestine, a significant monetary arrangement, and a statement about family reunification." In his view, it would also be possible to agree with the Palestinians on leaving some of the settlements under Palestinian sovereignty, and he also believed that they would be willing to build their capital in Abu Dis. Beilin added that the Palestinians understood Israel's security constraints and concerns, and would therefore agree to a demilitarized state that would include an Israeli presence within its borders, as long as Israel places a time limit on these necessary security arrangements and they do not become permanent.[3]

Barak said he wanted "in a short time" to reach a final status accord that would include a Palestinian state. But he surprised Beilin when he said—in response to the Beilin-Abu Mazen understandings, which proposed a state on 95 percent of the territories—that when he "looks at the map, he sees that 50 percent of the West Bank also constitutes a state." Barak explained that he sought "Israeli control of the border with Jordan until negotiations are concluded," and hoped to achieve "economic separation." He told Beilin that Clinton had said to him "that he'd like to [finish] by mid-2000."

Barak thought a lot about how to conduct the negotiations and explained that he "is reluctant to suggest ideas for a final status accord himself, and would like [academic and public] institutes to initiate" them. Nonetheless, he expressed his confidence in his interpersonal ability and powers of persuasion. Therefore, Barak said "he would like very much to conduct intimate dialogue with Arafat, despite all the problematic aspects," and guaranteed that he could "explain to him that it's a critical moment—like Ben-Gurion in his hour." In addition, the prime minister shared his assessment that "on the issue of Syria, there are contacts that might make it unnecessary to return to the border of June 4th."[4]

A salient element missing from Barak's remarks was an attempt to understand the complexity of the Palestinian stance beyond Israel's tactical needs in negotiation. His assertion that the Palestinians could actually maintain a state on 50 percent of the territory indicated his obliviousness to the Palestinian ethos and narrative. (For the Palestinians, even a complete withdrawal to the 1967 lines was a painful and historic compromise on greater Palestine.) Moreover, the summary of his conversation suggests a disparity between Barak's rhetoric on the need for peace and the mechanism he envisioned for securing the accord: massive separation, which is contrary to the concept of peace between nations.

Barak spoke in detail about his plan to build a modern border to separate Israel and Palestine. In Barak's mind, the 400-kilometer border would incorporate ten sophisticated, fingerprint-activated border crossings. The separation would also be expressed in economic detachment and in the dismantling of all Jewish settlements that are not annexed to Israel.

Based on security considerations and Barak's assessment of Israeli public opinion, the only arrangement he could envision was a consensual divorce. Barak insisted that he could persuade the Palestinians to make do with a state that would encompass just 50 percent of the territories and consist of several blocs connected by bridges and tunnels. He emphasized that Palestine's military capability would be limited and that Israel would maintain a presence in the Jordan Valley. He knew, of course, that his plan did not meet the Palestinians' aspirations, but believed that his proposal was the only realistic formula, at least "until peace is embedded in the hearts."[5]

Barak sought to navigate the process almost on his own. He told Beilin that it was best to remove the United States from the equation as an aggressive mediator (like the role it had played during Netanyahu's term) in order to avoid harming relations if disagreements arose between the sides.[6]

Beilin left the meeting disturbed by the disparity between Barak's positions and those of the Palestinians. He believed that the Palestinians would accept, at most, Israel's annexation of 3-5 percent of the territories—the main settlement blocs, which would bring 70 percent of the settlers within Israel's borders. Beilin also thought the Palestinians would insist on controlling the Jordan Valley and, in particular, would reject any Israeli sovereignty over the Holy Basin in Jerusalem.[7] Nonetheless, he appreciated the prime minister's genuine desire to achieve a permanent accord. Beilin understood that Barak wanted to avoid additional withdrawals under the interim accord until concluding final status talks, and told him he would do whatever he could to help Barak advance the negotiations.

Arafat, in clear contrast to Barak's desire to quickly reach a final status accord, was willing to accept a gradual process, as long as it progressed as he wished. He was disappointed by Israel's intention of postponing the withdrawals stipulated in the Wye Memorandum. However, the Palestinians expressed optimism about Barak after the Netanyahu years and the frustration they had experienced under Israel's right-wing government.

## 3

Another issue on the Barak government's agenda was the IDF's presence in southern Lebanon. In May 2000, the government ordered the IDF to unilaterally withdraw to the international border with Lebanon. Barak made this decision in light of the failed talks he conducted in Shepherdstown with Syria's foreign minister, Farouk al-Shara, and President Clinton. After a meeting in Geneva between Clinton and Assad also failed to produce a breakthrough, Barak had to forego his preferred option of withdrawing from Lebanon in the framework of a comprehensive agreement with Syria, and decided to take action unilaterally.

Barak demonstrated his leadership capacity in deciding to retreat to the international border, but the story of the withdrawal from Lebanon would not be complete without noting Beilin's persistent activity on this issue. As mentioned, Beilin had long advocated pulling the IDF out of the security zone in southern Lebanon, and two years prior to the withdrawal he published a book on the subject: *A Guide to Leaving Lebanon*.[8]

Since the limited withdrawal to the security zone in 1985 and until 2000, despite the array of changes in the Lebanese reality, Israeli policy had remained largely unchanged. IDF activity in Lebanon continued to be based on a vague decision to redeploy in the security zone.[9]

Most of the public also regarded the security zone as a necessity. A significant change in the public's stance began only in the wake of the helicopter disaster in February 1997. The search for the soldiers' bodies continued for a long time and the pictures broadcast on television were heartrending. In April 1997, a group of four mothers of soldiers serving in Lebanon set out to mobilize public pressure for an IDF withdrawal. The media called the group the "Four Mothers" and the members of the group adopted this name. Beilin met with them behind the scenes and encouraged them to expand their activity. In September 1997, after concluding that the group was not attracting enough media attention, he decided to form the Movement for a Withdrawal in Peace from Lebanon. The movement was led by retired IDF officers Col. Yonatan Lerner and Col. Asher Sadan, together with academics and politicians. The goal was to prepare a plan for a unilateral exit from Lebanon in the absence of a diplomatic agreement, and to present it to the public as an alternative to the security zone—at least until reaching an accord with Syria that established relations between Israel, Lebanon, and Syria.

Like other initiatives by Beilin, this protest movement was not anti-establishment in character. It operated as a nongovernmental organization and mobilized about 3,000 volunteers at its peak.[10] Beilin published articles in favor of the withdrawal, and was the movement's representative in interviews; in 1998, he began presenting the withdrawal plan in his media appearances.[11] According to the plan, the IDF would unilaterally pull back to the international border, and a third party would assume responsibility for the resultant vacuum in order to ensure the security of Israel's northern communities.

The plan was rejected by the leaders of both the Labor Party and the Likud, who argued that it would abandon the security of the communities in northern Israel and boost Hezbollah. However, the repeated attacks by Hezbollah, as well as political considerations and the broader diplomatic context (the fading hope of an accord with Syria), prompted both candidates for prime minister in 1999, Barak and Netanyahu, to promise they would endeavor to withdraw from Lebanon after the elections. And, indeed, on May 24, 2000, after it was clear that negotiations with Syria had collapsed, the IDF pulled out of Lebanon.

The withdrawal itself, partly because the element of surprise was crucial, was executed hastily. The pictures of Hezbollah fighters celebrating, showing off the plentiful equipment left behind by the retreating IDF soldiers, were disconcerting for Israelis. Contrary to Beilin's original plan, the security zone was not handed over to a third party (the Lebanese army or an international force). The South Lebanon Army (SLA) was quickly dismantled and hundreds of its fighters fled in panic to Israel. Many accused the state of abandoning the SLA fighters and of harming the IDF's image as an army that does not recoil from its enemies.

However, the ensuing years demonstrated that in terms of ensuring quiet on Israel's northern border and preventing bloodshed, the unilateral withdrawal was justified and effective. The number of IDF casualties was drastically reduced, and Israel's northern communities have usually enjoyed quiet. Although the Second Lebanon War (which erupted in July 2006 after the abduction of two IDF soldiers on the border) claimed the lives of more than 160 Israeli soldiers and civilians, this can be attributed to the rash Israeli decision to strike against Hezbollah when the IDF was not suitably prepared for this.

Still, Israel failed to realize its hope of transferring the security zone to the Lebanese army and UN forces, or leaving it in the hands of the SLA, due to the prevailing diplomatic and military conditions in the Middle East. Instead, Hezbollah forces took control of southern Lebanon. Armed by the Iranians and the Syrians, Hezbollah became a significant and incessant threat to Israel, even when the border was quiet. The question of whether Hezbollah would have strengthened and armed within Lebanon even without an Israeli withdrawal remains an open question, which, as noted, is a function of the overall strategic situation in the Middle East.

# 4

After the withdrawal from southern Lebanon, Barak focused most of his efforts on the Palestinian front. He adopted a grandiose notion of ending the conflict between the Zionist and Palestinian movements with the thrust of a single conference. He wanted to convene the conference by September 2000, the target date he had set for reaching a final status agreement. The Palestinians were wary of a conference because they doubted it would lead to an agreement. Under American pressure, however, they agreed to participate in it.

The conference was scheduled to begin on July 11, 2000, at Camp David. Shlomo Ben-Ami and Abu Ala conducted secret talks in Stockholm in preparation for the conference, but failed to formulate clear agreements that could be implemented. On the eve of the conference, when Abu Ala sought to renew these preliminary talks, this time in Cairo, Barak refused to authorize Ben-Ami to continue the discussions with Abu Ala. Barak feared that the Palestinians would raise additional demands for Israeli concessions before the conference opened.[12] The prime minister believed in his ability to sew up all the details and achieve a historic breakthrough at the moment of truth, in the discussions at Camp David.

Barak did not reserve a place for Beilin in the Israeli delegation, but sent him on a round of secret conversations with leaders of the settlers. Beilin recorded his impressions in a personal letter to the prime minister.

To: The prime minister
From: Yossi Beilin

From May 28-31, I held a round of meetings with some of the contacts in Judea and Samaria —Yisrael Harel, Rabbi Yoel Ben-Nun, and Zvi Moses—as you requested. Here are my impressions:
The real source of power remains in the hands of the founding core of Gush Emunim members and not the officials in Judea and Samaria. When it comes to fateful decisions, only they can give the ideological approval. Benny Katzover,

Menachem Felix, Hanan Porat, Daniella Weiss, the rabbis, and also Uri Ariel and Zambish [Ze'ev Haver] . . . the idea that emerged is to create a forum of intensive dialogue. The aim is to explain to their leadership the difference between holy and Holy of Holies. . . . From our perspective, we should emphasize the historic achievement of the settlers, that 80% [of the settlers] would remain within Israel and that annexation would receive international legitimacy.[13]

The description of the authoritative leadership among the settlers reflects the rapid and radical developments they underwent. At the time of Beilin's talks, the founding generation of Gush Emunim still held the reins. Subsequently, ideological groups emerged, including the "hilltop youth" and other extremist and independent groups, which do not recognize the authority of the old leadership, and this could make it harder to reach an accord with the settlers during a future evacuation.[14] On the other hand, the fact that Israel's annexation of the settlement blocs, where about 80 percent of the settlers live, is not regarded as an insurmountable obstacle by the Palestinians, indicates that in many ways the settlement enterprise won.

This helps in understanding what is usually portrayed as an ongoing Israeli strategic blindness vis-à-vis the settlements—that is, the continuation of construction in the territories despite the fact that all of the governments since 1967, without exception, have understood that at some stage Israel will need to reach some sort of accord. Soon after the Six-Day War, the Eshkol government stated that Israel would aspire to reach an agreement in exchange for a withdrawal, whose details were left unclear. In Golda Meir's government, Dayan championed the policy of open bridges, aimed at strengthening local leadership as a foundation for negotiation in the future, and the Begin government proposed autonomy. Even Shamir said that his plan was to wait for leaders to arise in the territories after the PLO is eliminated in order to try to reach an agreement with Palestinian moderates. This does not mean he would have agreed to a Palestinian state, but he, too, recognized the need for some sort of diplomatic accord. Since Oslo, every Israeli government has accepted the principle of withdrawal, at least on the declarative level. Nonetheless, in parallel, another historical truth stands out: all of the governments, leftist and rightist, have supported the settlements, whether directly or indirectly.

The Palestinians' reported acceptance of the idea that a large majority of the settlers would be annexed to Israel explains this ostensible contradiction and suggests there was an ongoing Zionist strategy behind the settlement project—a strategy that applied the same motif that guided Ben-Gurionist policy: grab as much as possible. The governments of Israel recognized the need to compromise, but sought to stall and establish facts on the ground until reaching a situation in which Israel could leave the maximum possible in its hands.

Indeed, if Israel manages to sign an agreement that offers a Palestinian state while also approving the annexation of most of the settlers, it would be possible to say in historical perspective that the settlement project triumphed. For some reason, this viewpoint is missing from the public debate, which still examines the settlements issue as a zero-sum game in peacetime. This is one of the basic mistakes of the Zionist left, which refrains from emphasizing the fact that the division of the land will be accompanied by annexation of 80 percent of the setters, perhaps because this would justify the entire settlement enterprise. And perhaps this was Beilin's intention in suggesting that a distinction be made between the "holy" and the "Holy of Holies" vis-à-vis the settlements in the final status accord.

## 5

Beilin is primarily described in this book in the context of diplomacy, which was the focus of his activity. But he was a secondary player most of the time in the Barak government, and concentrated mainly on his role as justice minister. In principle, and contrary to subsequent justice ministers, his aim was to preserve the power and public standing of the Supreme Court, and he supported the view advocated by Aharon Barak (president of the Supreme Court from 1996–2005) that "everything is justiciable."

In Beilin's eyes, Aharon Barak's view was a worthy model for judiciously balancing the tension between Israeli's Jewish and democratic dimensions. Beilin was fundamentally opposed to the type of initiatives proposed by Daniel Friedman, the justice minister in the Olmert government, to reduce the power of the Supreme Court, including limiting the term length of Supreme Court presidents. Beilin also opposes changing the composition of the committee that selects judges and restricting the Supreme Court's purview.

The fact that few laws have been overturned by the High Court during more than two decades of judicial review of Knesset legislation, and the fact that judicial review has been conducted in a cautious and moderate way, support Beilin's contention that Israel has maintained an appropriate balance between the branches of government. He trusts the judgment of the Supreme Court, even today, when its composition has become more conservative and less committed to Aharon Barak's classic liberal position. The Knesset is the sovereign, but democracy requires protecting the rights of the minority no less than implementing the wishes of the majority. For this reason, it is important to protect the power of the Supreme Court. In order to implement the "general will" that embodies the collective will of the individuals who constitute the society, it is essential to maintain a balance between the legislative and judicial branches. ("General will" is a concept popularized by Jean Jacques Rousseau, who contrasted it to the "will of all," which reflects a mix of irreconcilable private interests.) Therefore, it is important to maintain the requirement of a special majority of eighty (of a total of one hundred and twenty) MKs, which expresses the interests of the coalition and some members of the opposition, to overturn a Supreme Court ruling in the case of disputes between the Knesset and the court.

Nonetheless, Beilin is critical of some aspects of Barak's court. He notes, for example, that under Aharon Barak's inspiration, and in light of his eminent standing, the High Court sometimes permits the state to act beyond the Green Line in a way that is contrary to international law and whitewashes its actions. "Barak accepted the judicial bubble created in the territories, and though he wanted to burst it, he didn't think he could do so."[15]

Beilin is a long-time proponent of the idea of a constitution for Israel. He does not accept David Ben-Gurion's argument that the absence of a constitution allows the authorities the flexibility required to address the various streams that comprise Israeli society. Beilin believes that a constitution could regulate and establish the character of Israel. It is possible to understand Ben-Gurion's opposition to a constitution during the state's formative years in order to prevent a rift with religious Jews and to allow Israeli society to define its values over time. Today, however, especially in light of the many legislative initiatives by the Netanyahu governments to limit minority rights, the time is ripe for a constitution that would explicitly express the values of the society and state.

In any case, Beilin's primary achievement as justice minister was his work to promote the "Shin Bet Law" (though the legislation was officially enacted in 2002, when Beilin was no longer justice minister.) For the first time, the law defined the organization's roles, structure, and authorities, including oversight methods. Until then, the Shin Bet had operated in accordance with government decisions, and not in a statutory framework.

While working to formulate the law, Beilin encountered opposition from security officials and MKs (including Reuven Rivlin, the future president), who demanded that the law permit the use of moderate physical pressure during interrogation. In one of Beilin's conversations with Ami Ayalon, the Shin Bet director at the time, the latter tried to convince Beilin why it was essential for the law to allow moderate means of torture. He showed him a presentation and tied his hands, attempting to demonstrate that such methods did not constitute unbearable torture, and that without them it would be difficult to deal with "ticking bombs." Beilin remained unconvinced and his successor, Meir Sheetrit, followed Beilin's lead on this issue. The legislation was ultimately enacted without the clause permitting physical pressure. A clause was added to the Prevention of Terror Ordinance that promises legal protection for Shin Bet interrogators if accused of employing physical pressure when necessary. However, under the Shin Bet Law, it is forbidden in principle to use violence when conducting interrogations.

While at the helm of the Justice Ministry, Beilin prepared the foundations for a High Commission for Human Rights, designed to coordinate legal appeals from citizens and organizations, and sought to promote legislation that would ensure representation for Arab Israelis in government corporations and agencies. In addition, a number of judges had to step down after coming under criticism from Beilin, who monitored their performance while attending court in disguise—a practice that riled the association representing judges in Israel.

In 2000, Beilin was one of the only ministers to support joining the signatories to the Rome Statute, which established an international criminal court to prosecute people accused of genocide, war crimes, and crimes against humanity. In discussions on this issue, Beilin argued that there was a moral flaw in Israel's opposition to signing the Rome Statute, considering the fact that Israel was founded in the wake of the Holocaust. However, as in the case of Israel's relations with South Africa in the 1980s, his position encountered opposition by the government, the defense establishment, and the attorney general. A main reason for this opposition was an article in the Rome Statute introduced by Arab states, which defines as a war crime the transfer of a population from an occupying state to an occupied territory. In light of its settlement enterprise, Israel was concerned that charges of war crimes might be filed against politicians and army officers under this article. Since the Rome Statute stipulated that non-signatory states cannot be brought to trial, the Israeli establishment preferred to ignore it. There was a consensus on this matter between Israel, the Pentagon, and most members of the US Senate, who feared that American army personnel would be brought to trial. Only in 2000, after a battle by President Clinton himself, who argued that joining the Rome Statute would continue the American legal tradition of fighting war crimes that started with the Nuremburg trials, a compromise was found that enabled the United States, and Israel in its wake, to sign the statute. The signing came on the last day on which it was still possible to become a signatory without the statute applying retroactively to crimes from the past, which eased the concerns about the prosecution of Americans and Israelis.[16]

Beilin also fought to protect the independence of the National Labor Court, which tended to support workers in conflicts between workers and employers, based on the assumption that the employer generally has the upper hand. (Yosef "Tommy" Lapid from the Shinui party, who replaced Meir Sheetrit as justice minister in 2003, made the National Labor Court subordinate to the Supreme Court as part of the extensive neoliberal policy of the Sharon government, which was inclined to weaken the status of workers.)

Toward the end of his term, Beilin sponsored two ostensibly procedural amendments that bolstered the status of opposition leader and the stability of governance. In 2000, he introduced Amendment 8 of the Basic Law: The Knesset, which established a statutory basis for the position of opposition leader and requires the prime minister to brief the opposition leader on sensitive matters. A year later, the Basic Law: the government was amended to discontinue direct elections for prime minister—a method that was originally designed to strengthen governance, but turned out to encourage voting for small parties, thus deepening the polarization in the Knesset.

As the Barak government began to come apart in 2000, Beilin found himself with the additional role of minister of religious affairs. (He also sought to shut down this ministry. Tommy Lapid later did this, based on Beilin's plan.) It is interesting that in this role, he tried to amend the Law of Return to make it more restrictive. From Beilin's perspective, Israel is a land of refuge for members of the Jewish people and not for the distressed people of the world in general. Even previously, he had stated: "In the current situation, the law and its later amendments are being exploited by hundreds of thousands who are ready to wrap themselves in a tallit and phylacteries, recruit two witnesses to say they had a Jewish grandfather, or who are simply imposters seeking to flee the hunger in the world, and are supported by a few missionary rabbis ready to collaborate with them."[17] Beilin proposed that a non-Jew with a Jewish grandfather could immigrate to Israel under the Law of Return only if the grandfather resides in Israel, or immigrates together with the grandson. His objective was not to reinforce the strict Orthodox stance on the definition of a Jew, but to strengthen the Zionist component in defining a person as a Jew—that is, both the grandfather and the grandson would have to take the trouble of living in Israel. In any case, his proposal was not accepted.

Another initiative, which Beilin jointly promoted with Professor Shahar Lifshitz, aimed to introduce a "partnership covenant" as a path for de facto civil marriage, without requiring legislation challenging the rabbinate's control of family law. This initiative also was rejected.

6

On May 19, 2000, President Clinton's national security adviser, Sandy Berger, landed in Israel to conduct meetings in preparation for the Camp David summit. One of these meetings was with Abu Mazen and Beilin. Berger wanted to understand the nature of the agreements the two had reached in 1995, and asked them both if they still stand behind them. Abu Mazen smiled and asked Beilin to respond first. After Beilin responded affirmatively, Abu Mazen also confirmed his commitment to the understandings achieved five years earlier, but emphasized that he was speaking for himself only.

Beilin understood from Berger that President Clinton regarded the Abu Mazen-Beilin agreements as a basis for an accord and Beilin conveyed this message to the prime minister. About a month later, upon Barak's request, he presented the agreements in a cabinet meeting. Beilin reiterated the familiar points: Palestine would be a demilitarized state encompassing about 95 percent of the territories. About 130 settlements would be annexed to Israel as part of the blocs, and about fifty would remain in Palestine. The Jordan Valley would also be transferred to Palestine, but the IDF would remain there for an extended period. Western Jerusalem would be recognized as the capital of Israel, while Israel would recognize the area defined as Al-Quds in the period prior to the Six-Day War as the Palestinian capital, which would also include partial sovereignty on the Temple Mount. Jerusalem would be divided, municipally, between the Jewish and Arab neighborhoods, and the sovereign status of particular neighborhoods that remained in dispute would be determined by a joint committee that would discuss this question under no specific deadline.

Barak was not particularly impressed by the Beilin-Abu Mazen understandings. He intended to present a tougher version of them at Camp David.[18] For example, he told the ministers that he would demand an end-of-conflict declaration. No such declaration was included in the Beilin-Abu Mazen understandings, based on a recognition that life is stronger than words, and that the agreement should be allowed to bring an end to the conflict in a natural way.

Beilin understood from Barak that he rejected any concession on the Temple Mount and sought to limit the Palestinian capital to the confines of Abu Dis. He had already sensed that Barak had strong reservations about the Beilin-Abu Mazen understandings from his facial expression when the prime minister returned the document of understandings to him after having asked to examine it. Barak did not appear enthusiastic.

These were ominous signs regarding the summit's prospects. But since President Clinton also wanted to convene the summit, and since Barak promised behind closed doors and publicly to make every effort for peace, or that he would at least reveal the Palestinians' real positions, Beilin was inclined to believe that it was right to participate in it. Nonetheless, he had the feeling that both objectives—reaching peace or revealing the Palestinians' stance—were equal in importance to Barak.[19]

Arafat also felt hesitant about the summit. On July 21, Barak sent Beilin to ask Mubarak to speak with Arafat and convince him to participate in the summit. During a two-hour conversation with the Egyptian president, Beilin promised in Barak's name that Israel intended to go far. At the end of their conversation, Mubarak called Arafat, who was meeting at the time in his Bethlehem office with Ben-Ami. Arafat spoke with Ben-Ami about the Pact of Umar—the capitulation of Byzantine Jerusalem to the Muslim conquerors led by Caliph Umar Ibn al-Khattab. According to Arab tradition, the pact, signed in 638, prohibited Jews from living in Jerusalem.[20] In retrospect, Arafat's words echoed in Ben-Ami's ears as a warning about his unwillingness to accept anything less than full Palestinian sovereignty over the Temple Mount. By citing this historical event, Arafat sought to illustrate how faithful his negotiating stance would be to the Muslim narrative. However, in the moment of truth, Arafat agreed in the telephone conversation with Mubarak to participate in the summit. In retrospect, Beilin calls this one of the most superfluous diplomatic achievements in his life.

Much has been written about the failure of the Camp David summit—a failure that engendered the second intifada. The bloody events that began at the end of September 2000 had severe repercussions on the peace process. The intifada was interpreted in Israel (in large part due to the decision by Clinton and Barak to blame the Palestinian side for the failure of the summit) as ingratitude of Palestinians: they not only rejected Israel's generous proposals, but also responded with violence and suicide bombings. As this narrative took root, many Israelis from the Zionist center and left, who had supported the Oslo process, lost their faith in the good intentions of the Palestinians. Consequently, the Zionist left lost its pool of supporters in the center of the political map. We will discuss this at length below, but first will address the question of why the summit failed, and whether it was wise to convene it in the first place.

Scholars and participants in the process have offered a variety of answers to this question. Edward Said, who opposed the Oslo Accords, believed that the summit failed because the peace process, as charted in Oslo, was ultimately nothing more than an Israeli ploy designed to relegate Arafat to the role of mayor of Gaza and Ramallah, and to enable Israel, under the guise of achieving the longed-for peace, to establish relations with the Arab states, which in any case did not regard the Palestinians' plight as a problem that directly affected their interests. The Israeli journalist Amira Hass, who chose to live in Gaza and Ramallah in order to cover the process from the other side's perspective, believes that the Camp David summit collapsed because the Palestinians rejected the logic of Oslo: to perpetuate the occupation without paying for it.

On the other hand, Joel Singer, who conducted the decisive stages in the Oslo talks, offers a more complex view. In his assessment, the model proposed at Camp David is still the only realistic solution, and it will be adopted in the end. But the Palestinian narrative requires a bloody war of independence before the Palestinians will agree to compromise, and that is the historic role of the second intifada. The philosopher Slavoj Žižek argued that the West must accept the need of the oppressed side, especially in advance of an accord, to express its liberation in a revolution that requires blood and tears.

Another explanation points to the different perceptions of time in the East and the West. While Barak looked at a digital clock that told him to seek an end to the conflict during his first government and before Clinton completed his term, Arafat's analog clock ticked at a much slower pace, allowing for the time required to digest the change in the situation. Therefore, it was a mistake to demand that Arafat end the conflict at that time.

Yasser Abed Rabbo, who was then the Palestinian culture minister, offered a more concrete explanation. He argued that it was a mistake to discuss the Temple Mount, because there is no solution for this issue. In retrospect, Mubarak also concluded that it was wrong to impose a summit that aspired to end the conflict before resolving the basic disagreements.

Beilin believes that the failure stemmed from the disparity between Barak's authentic desire to make fateful decisions and the limited compromises he was willing to offer.

In this context, it is important to note that by the time Barak departed for the summit in July 2000, his coalition had already collapsed. Thus, his hope of arriving at the summit reinforced by a partnership with the right had faded. Meretz quit the coalition in June over a dispute between Education Minister Sarid and his deputy minister from Shas, Meshulam Nahari, and Barak's decision to support the latter. The NRP, Shas, and Yisrael Beiteinu also left the coalition in opposition to the compromises expected at Camp David. At the last moment, Foreign Minister Levy also chose to resign in protest over the anticipated concessions. In a no-confidence vote on the eve of the trip, the government was outvoted 54 to 52, but survived because a Knesset majority of 61 votes was required to unseat Barak. His shaky standing naturally affected his ability to maneuver at the summit.

There are numerous versions of what occurred at the summit—almost as many as the number of participants. There is no disputing the fact that Israel's representatives floated far-reaching proposals to the Palestinians and that the latter rejected them. In this sense, we can understand Barak's disappointment over Arafat's refusal to take a "Ben-Gurionist action" and follow the example of the State of Israel's founding father, who agreed to the UN partition plan in 1947 despite the fact that the Jewish state was apportioned only 55 percent of the western Land of Israel.[21] However, the comparison to Ben-Gurion and the days of the Yishuv is flawed because the pre-state Jewish community developed amid a sense of the wonderful achievement of returning to the homeland after 2,000 years; accordingly, there was a readiness to compromise with the Arab residents of the land. By contrast, the Palestinian national movement emerged amid a sense of the homeland being robbed by the Zionists and, consequently, the Palestinians took a hard line against a compromise that does not even grant them all of the territory between the Green Line and Jordan. In any case, when Ben-Gurion adopted the partition decision, he also took into account the impending War of Independence, which offered prospects of expanding the borders.

The Camp David summit opened with a fundamental disagreement. Both sides publicly recognized UN Resolution 242 as an agreed basis for negotiations, but the Palestinians demanded that their interpretation of 242 (that is, requiring Israel to withdraw to the lines of June 4, 1967) serve as the starting point of discussions on a compromise, while Barak had the opposite in mind: the discussions at the summit would lead to agreements on land (not all of it) in exchange for peace; these agreements would supersede 242 from a legal perspective.[22]

In Beilin's view, the Palestinians saw Barak's stance, as presented prior to the summit, as preliminary proof of his limited intentions.[23] However, Barak softened his positions during the summit. He agreed to compromise on annexing only 9 percent of the territories to Israel and to relinquish sovereignty over some of the Arab neighborhoods in Jerusalem. This was not enough for the Palestinians. The Americans proposed transferring the Arab neighborhoods adjacent to the Old City to Palestinian administration while leaving them under temporary Israeli sovereignty, with the hope that both sides would become more flexible in time and reach a final decision on sovereignty. They later suggested that the Muslim Quarter and Christian Quarter come under Palestinian sovereignty, while the Jewish and Armenian quarters remain in Israel's hands. In regard to the Temple Mount, the Americans proposed dividing sovereignty vertically: Palestine would have sovereignty over the upper party, where the Dome of the Rock and Al-Aqsa mosques are located, while the lower part, sacred to Jews (the Western Wall), would be under Israeli sovereignty. The Palestinians rejected this idea also. The demilitarization of the Palestinian state, on which there was agreement in principle, also remained unresolved when the sides came to work out the details. The Palestinians agreed to a "non-militarized" state, while the Israelis insisted on a completely "demilitarized" state. The Palestinians conditioned their acceptance of IDF warning stations in the territories on the presence of Palestinian officers at the stations; the Israelis rejected this condition. The Palestinians refused to allow Israel to use Palestine's airspace for training flights, despite the protection the Israeli Air Force could provide for an unarmed Palestinian state. (Israel provided such protection for Jordan during the Black September events in 1970, when it deployed forces to deter the Syrians from intervening in the battle of Palestinian organizations against King Hussein.)

# 7

## The Camp David Summit, Haniyah's Journal

The Middle East is complicated, and the relations between its players are sometimes driven by conflicting interests. The seemingly irrational element of the conflict is, in fact, part of the rationale, and the memoirs and testimonies published about the Camp David summit indicate that the failure to understand the irrational element played a central role in the failure of the summit and the peace process. Of the many sources available, I have chosen to present the diary of Akram Haniyah—editor-in-chief of the Palestinian newspaper *al-Ayyam*, a senior member of Fatah and an adviser to Arafat.

As a member of the Palestinian delegation at the Camp David summit, he wrote a daily summary of the events and meetings in real time. The diary provides an authentic and instructive account of the failed summit from a Palestinian perspective. Haniyah wrote the diary in Arabic, with the conciseness the genre demands. It is presented here in its entirety in English translation. (The diary was transferred to Beilin's archive for analysis and historical documentation.)

## July 11

First meeting in the evening: Clinton, Barak, Arafat, and Erekat. The topic: Jerusalem.

Clinton: "I don't know how to solve the problem."

Arafat: "It's easy. The east is our capital. The west—their capital. The city is open with cooperation in all fields, including infrastructure and security."

Clinton: "Israel won't give up sovereignty in Jerusalem."

Erekat: "Israel argues that it won't accept the return of refugees because of the demographic problem. How can it reconcile this with its willingness to annex 250,000 Palestinians in East Jerusalem? The U.S. position is corpus separatum. No country recognizes Israel's annexation of Jerusalem, including the United States. Therefore, it needs to be affirmed from the outset that Jerusalem is the key to an accord. Not to consider partial or full deferment of the subject, or to think that peace is possible when Israel is holding sovereignty there."

Arafat tells how every time he mentions holy Jerusalem in his speeches, he is interrupted by thunderous applause. . . .

Clinton: "I suggest forming committees that will meet tomorrow: Jerusalem, borders, settlements, security, refugees."

Arafat: "Agree and appoint as follows: Refugees—Abu Mazen and Nabil Shaath. Borders—Abu Ala, Dahlan, and Asfour. Jerusalem—Abed Rabbo and Saeb Erekat."

## July 12, morning

The Palestinian borders committee met this morning with the Americans, headed by [Madeleine] Albright.

Albright: "I'd like to present a paper tomorrow, so I'm asking for ideas, from the Israelis, too."

Abu Ala: "Before we propose ideas, it's important to understand your position on land swaps. We're willing, provided it's based on identical value and size. First, we need to decide on borders, and then on swaps."

Albright: "Israel is requesting a security presence in the Jordan Valley under Palestinian sovereignty for a limited period of time."

Erekat: "The border between Jordan and Israel in the south is 625 kilometers. Along our territory, the border stretches over 1,000 kilometers. In the south, there's not a single soldier. Why is it essential in our territory?"

Albright: "I suggest a three-sided meeting. Agreed?"

Two hours later, Ben-Ami, Amnon Lipkin-Shahak, Yisrael Hasson, and Gilad Sher join the meeting.

Ben-Ami: "Why can't we discuss swaps? 80% of the settlers will be annexed in the blocs. An Israeli presence in the [Jordan] Valley will be removed gradually, and will be under Palestinian sovereignty. Israeli sovereignty on the Jordan River and the Dead Sea."

The Palestinians together: "That's not a basis for negotiation or for peace. You came to Camp David to sabotage it and blame us. The '67 lines and evacuation of the settlements is required for reaching peace."

Dahlan: "It's only possible to communicate with you via Hezbollah's method."

Albright: "I'm adjourning the meeting."

## July 12, evening

Erekat with Clinton.

Erekat: "Did you invite us in order to reach an agreement, or to assign us the responsibility for failure? Barak is a right-winger. He rejected Oslo, and before Camp David he was ready to unite with the Likud."

Clinton asks that Arafat send a team to him and says he will also invite Israelis tomorrow.

Agreed.

## July 13

Three-way meeting with Clinton, Sher, Abu Ala, and Erekat.

Clinton: "I ask for your patience. I'm interested in an agreement. I want to formulate a basis for an agreement and present it to Barak and Arafat tonight."

Erekat: "The gap is wide. Presenting a paper will entangle the sides. This type of paper needs to be well-prepared."

Sher: "I'm ready to formulate a paper that will include the sides' agreement based on a partition into Israel and Palestine. From this, there would be no losers or winners."

Erekat: "What about Jerusalem?"

Sher: "A special regime in a format of functional autonomy."

Erekat: "If that's your stance, it will perpetuate the conflict for a millennium. Don't dream that the Jews will control the historical and religious rights of three billion Muslims and Christians. The Palestinians were authorized by the Muslim and Christian Arabs to liberate Jerusalem."

Sher: "Is that a threat?"

Erekat: "You're ruling by means of occupation. We can contend with occupation. But you want to move from occupation to an accord—without changing the situation. This would be giving Palestinian consent for continuing the occupation in other ways."

Abu Ala: "In Stockholm, and even earlier, the Israeli side offered us more. This is a serious step backward."

## July 13, evening

Clinton meets Arafat and tells him that Barak is interested in new ideas.

Arafat: "What about Jerusalem?"

Clinton: "The paper I have includes the position of the Palestinians, who demand a capital in East Jerusalem, and the position of Israel, which wants a united Jerusalem under Israeli sovereignty."

Arafat: "I won't accept any paper stating that Jerusalem will be Israel's capital. The Haram [Temple Mount] will be under Israeli sovereignty? That contradicts the basis for negotiations and is contrary to international legitimacy."

## July 14

The three committees met during the day but made no progress. In the evening, Clinton hosted a dinner, including *kiddush* [blessing over wine on the eve of the Jewish Sabbath].

## July 15

At a meeting of the borders committee, Clinton could be heard screaming at Abu Ala: "You're not being serious. I'm the president of the United States. I don't have time to waste with you! If that's your approach—I'll pack and leave. Give me an idea. Show ideas on the map. Illustrate ideas, needs, what you're ready to do. You're just raising difficulties."

Abu Ala did not respond.

Afterwards, Clinton asked to meet one-on-one with Arafat. In the conversation, he said that he wanted Arafat to send him two representatives that night, with latitude to negotiate and with new ideas. At midnight, Erekat, Dahlan, Sher, and Ben-Ami went to him. Clinton locked them in until dawn.

**July 16**

During the meeting, Ben-Ami presented new ideas.

Jerusalem: The external [Palestinian] areas will be outside the boundaries of the city, under Palestinian sovereignty. The internal areas will receive broad functional autonomy and services will be connected to the Jerusalem Municipality. The Old City will be under Israel's sovereignty, with a special regime, to be formulated in dialogue, that will apply to the Muslim, Christian, and Armenian quarters. The Haram will be a Palestinian custodianship, which will be transferred to them via the UN and Morocco. Consequently, the Palestinian state will have responsibility and full authority on the Haram al-Sharif, including security. The sovereignty that will remain in Israel's hand will be soft.

Borders: Israel will annex 10% along the Green Line, and in exchange, the Palestinians will receive a safe passage that will operate without an Israeli presence. In addition, Palestine will receive areas at Israel's ports and one at Ben-Gurion Airport. On the eastern border, Israel will have security control over 10% [of the territory] under full Palestinian sovereignty, and the evacuation will be gradual, starting one year after the agreement and culminating at the end of ten years. So, at the beginning, the size of the state will be 90%.

Erekat: "On the subject of Jerusalem—for us, it includes the Old City, Saladin, Bab al-Amud, Sheikh Jarrah, Wadi Joz, Silwan Valley, Jabal al-Mindal, a-Tur, and Ras al-Amud—all these are Palestinian areas that will be transferred to our sovereignty with arrangements that will ensure an open city and cooperation. We understand the Jewish need regarding the Jewish Quarter and the Western Wall. About borders—the basis is the line of June 4th. If there are minor revisions, they will be discussed based on land swaps equal in value and size. We won't agree to have settlers in our territory. Special arrangements can be made for the movement of people, goods, and vehicles between the states. In regard to refugees—the right of return must first be recognized; and those who don't choose to return will be compensated. Security: All of Israel's needs will be honored as long as it is not at the expense of Palestinian sovereignty and land. And also, based on mutuality and not a one-sided need. We're ready for any model of security: Egyptian, Jordanian, or as proposed to Syria and Lebanon."

After the meeting, Arafat sent a letter to Clinton:

Borders—a withdrawal to 1967 in accordance with resolutions 242 and 338. We're ready for adjustments based on mutuality in quality and quantity. Refugees according to [Resolution] 194. Holy Jerusalem—Palestinian sovereignty, an open city, consideration of Israel's needs in the [Jewish] Quarter and the Western Wall. End of conflict at end of implementation.

Clinton proposes to Arafat:

Borders: In the east, Israel will annex 20% of the valley along the Jordan [River]. Will deploy forces in 10% of the West Bank for twelve years. In the west, Israel will annex 9% of the West Bank in exchange for 1% adjacent to Gaza, Haluza. Refugees—he didn't elaborate, but consensually. Security: international forces in the Jordan Valley. Jerusalem—In the Old City, the Muslim and Christian quarters under full Palestinian sovereignty. The Jewish and Armenian quarters under Israel. The Haram: residual sovereignty to Israel and sovereign custodianship [that is, partial sovereignty for Israel, while the Palestinians would have sovereignty under a sort of trusteeship regime]. The internal areas—Ras al-Amud, Silwan, Sheikh Jarrah, and Wadi Joz—broad functional autonomy for the Palestinians under Israeli sovereignty. End of the conflict—this package ends the conflict.

## July 19

Arafat responded in writing: "Mr. President, in light of the importance of the matters under discussion, especially Jerusalem, and in light of your proposal, we find it important to coordinate and discuss with the Palestinian leadership, considering the Palestinian situation, of which you're aware. We are willing to continue the negotiations at a place you find appropriate via a negotiation team, [but] we [must] note to you that your proposal cannot be a basis for a just and lasting permanent accord, and this is in light of international law that constitutes the basis for Madrid and all of the agreements signed since then. We would like to emphasize that we are sincere in our desire to reach an accord that will resolve all of the disputes pertaining to the permanent agreement."

Abu Mazen left for his son's wedding. Now Erekat and Asfour are responsible for Jerusalem. Security: Abu Ala and Dahlan. Refugees: Abed Rabbo and Shaath. During the course of the day, there were six meetings between Clinton and Arafat. Without progress. Clinton announced that he was leaving for Japan. Everyone packed.

Clinton went back to Arafat and asked for tentative approval, in principle, of his ideas, and wanted Arafat to explain his reservations. "Don't lose my friendship and the friendship of the United States," he said. "Don't lose the friendship of the Congress."

Arafat: "I appreciate your efforts and your friendship, but I cannot betray my people, the Arabs, the Muslims, the Christians. We are now too weak to liberate Jerusalem, but someone will come and do this in another year, two years, a decade or a century, and will fly the flag of our state there. I led the Palestinian people from the diaspora and reached a peace process of the brave, based on international legitimacy. I won't be the Palestinian leader who gives legitimacy to Israeli sovereignty on the Haram. I thank you for your efforts, and may God help us."

Clinton: "[When you agree to compromise] you are not betraying the Muslims and the Arabs. I'm ready to speak now with Mubarak, with Abdullah, and with the Saudis to have them help to defer the subject of Jerusalem, or resolve part and defer part."

Erekat: "We must not declare the process a failure, because that would mean that the region and its inhabitants would be hurled into a maelstrom of blood. Don't hurt Egypt, or other Arabs, by involving them now. We'll need Egypt to support the agreement when it is reached. If Egypt is inside, and accepts the compromise, it will come under attack by extremists and won't be able to contribute. Mr. President, it seems that you've internalized Barak's position, and you're starting from the point of what he can do. How can you speak about the Muslim and Christian quarters and forget the Armenian [Quarter], Wadi Joz, Sheikh Jarrah, etc. and leave them for Israeli sovereignty? It's illogical. And what you said about the Haram, it means we'll start to count how many Palestinians blow themselves up in Jerusalem and in Tel Aviv, because you're giving legitimacy to extremists to wave the banner of liberating the Haram."

Clinton spoke with Arafat on the telephone afterwards, and wished him a good trip. A quarter of an hour later, Clinton got back to Arafat and the Palestinians and said that Albright would continue in his absence, until his return on Sunday. He asked that the three committees meet continuously until July 23rd. Arafat agreed and canceled his return.

*   *   *

The discussions on July 19, as described in Haniyah's diary, highlight one of the most difficult obstacles in the path to ending the conflict: the failure of the United States and Israel to understand the Arab perspective of the conflict.

While Clinton was pressing the Palestinians to adopt his proposals, which he regarded as a deal offering enormous benefits to the Palestinians relative to their current situation, Arafat, the leader of a secular Palestinian organization, explained that he did not approach the conflict only with a view to the present, but also with an eye to the past and the future. For Arafat, the conflict was not only territorial or national, but also religious. Therefore, he considered three dimensions of time—past, present, and future.

More precisely, the national conflict is anchored in theology. Thus, what is seen in Western eyes—according to a cold, rational calculation—as a Palestinian achievement, is a defeat in the perspective of Muslim history and Islamic values. For this reason, Arafat explained that while it was possible to compromise on the other material issues of the conflict, the Palestinians could not compromise vis-à-vis the Temple Mount: if he consented to such a compromise, history would record him as the one who granted legitimacy to Jewish control of the site. Arafat emphasized that no Palestinian, even the most moderate and secular, would be willing to be remembered in history as the one who gave the Jews an official hold on the Temple Mount. This highlights a paradox: it was more comfortable for Arafat to accept the status quo, with Israel as the occupier of the Temple Mount, than to accord Israel limited rights to the site.

This means that Barak introduced a superfluous obstacle into the negotiations by demanding that any agreement declare that it signifies the end of the conflict. The Palestinians could only agree to this demand if Israel surrendered the Temple Mount. But someone who asks the Palestinians to compromise on their rights vis-à-vis the

Temple Mount, cannot demand that they declare an "end of conflict," because this would compel them to publicly renounce their aspiration to restore Islamic control of the holy site. It would have been wiser to seek an end to the conflict in practice, rather than through declarations—via a diplomatic accord that facilitates coexistence, which in turn would eliminate the desire to renew fighting. However, Barak was blind to this Palestinian catch-22.

Similarly, Clinton was blind in his efforts to pressure Arafat via Arab states. As Erekat perceptively explained, the power and importance of any leader in the Arab world would be diminished the moment he provided support for a compromise on the Temple Mount, thus reducing the value of this support. This would also place the leader's regime in jeopardy, subjecting it to the anger of the masses. Furthermore, a concession on Palestinian sovereignty on the Temple Mount would only strengthen the status and significance of the Haram among Muslims, and thus stir a mass movement demanding its complete liberation.

This line of reasoning leads to the conclusion that the only path to ending the conflict requires Israel to relinquish sovereignty over the Temple Mount, which, in fact, did not assume an important place in Zionist ideology until 1967. However, in the wake of the Six-Day War, the religious and the national elements blended so much that even a decidedly secular person like Barak referred to relinquishing the Temple Mount as a blow to the "Holy of Holies." Therefore, if there is a possibility of resolving the Temple Mount conflict between the two national movements, it lies in the dimension that was missing from the summit: a connection to religion —in the spirit of Rabbi Menachem Froman—that would enable and ennoble the Israeli secular leadership to yield sovereignty over the Temple Mount.

The Temple Mount question brings us to the conventional belief that a national conflict, in light of its rational dimension, is more easily resolved than a religious conflict. However, in the Israeli-Palestinian context, the attempt to neutralize or extract the religious dimension from the resolution of the conflict might actually make it more difficult to defuse.

There were those in the Zionist movement who realized this early on. For example, the Brit Shalom movement, already in the 1920s, advocated a Zionism that would pursue modern and collaborative development of the values of religious tradition and culture on both sides in order to prevent a clash between Jewish and Arab nationalism in Palestine. The religious dimension can also bridge disagreements because it alleviates the need to fight over the "here and now" in this world, deferring disputes to Providence in the future, while allowing for coexistence in practice. Religion, therefore, is not only a threat. For example, the Western world was horrified when Khomeini's fundamentalist Shiite regime in Iran replaced the shah's secular regime, which sought to skip over the Muslim era and connect modern Iran to the Persia of Cyrus and Darius. However, contrary to his predecessor, Khomeini opposed nuclear development because it threatened the natural order of the world as God created it. He declared that the atomic infrastructure the shah had built in Iran was designed to serve as the "toys of the [Western] satans"[24] (though he later changed his stance).

In Israel, the liberal camp is generally wary of addressing the religious dimension of the Israeli-Palestinian conflict because of a radical secular view of religion and its perception of extremist believers as threats to the enlightened way of life. But religion—in its moral sense, as a cultural identity, representing values that can bridge between believers of different faiths—is a spiritual inspiration that could also support a new secular Jewish identity which is also less nationalist. "The spirit of man, precisely when it is profound, cannot be soothed without religion," claimed A. D. Gordon, one of the leaders of socialist Zionism. Perhaps the tempestuous and innovative spirit of Zionism suffers from the lack of a religious anchor. And perhaps this type of anchor could have dispelled the insistence on controlling the Temple Mount—control that is military in essence—and convert it to a purely spiritual attachment to it. Otherwise, a superfluous paradox arises: secular Jews seek a national-material foothold at a place that is wholly spiritual-religious.

The history of Islamic lands also teaches that when the focus of identity of Jews and Muslims was religious, they generally managed to coexist, despite some occasional tensions and outbursts of violence. Zionism, which gave precedence to the national dimension instead of religious identity, did not eliminate the religious component in favor of complete secularity, but used religion in an instrumental and convoluted way. Consequently, the religious component plays a visible-invisible role in the conflict, which dangerously erupts like a sort of demon in a troubled soul. Instead of repressing this religious component until it bursts out in the hands of ultra-nationalist extremists, it would be better to mobilize it to help mitigate the conflict.

Let's return to the diary of the summit.

## July 20

> The Palestinians sought to coordinate a timetable for meetings. Shlomo [Ben-Ami] and Gilad [Sher] said they hadn't received instructions from the prime minister for this. Erekat tells that Barak is in depression. Except for Sher, he hasn't met with anyone for four days, between the 20th and the 23rd, and has secluded himself in his room.

> Erekat reported to Albright that the Israelis refuse to meet. Albright spoke with Barak, who told her, "Arafat has to accept Clinton's proposal before we can renew meetings." According to Barak, "Arafat cannot receive concessions, put them in his pocket, and ask for more."

> Albright invited the two delegations. Barak was the only one who didn't come. She announced that the president's proposal is off the table.

## July 21

> Shlomo announced that he's no longer authorized to discuss the subject of Jerusalem. Erekat went to Albright and told her what Shlomo said. Albright asked him not to update Arafat about this, and that he [Erekat] and Ben-Ami should discuss the major principles in the meantime.

> Erekat to Albright: "I can't mislead Arafat."

Albright: "Don't tell him. It will blow up everything."

At night, Albright telephoned Arafat and told him that Barak agreed to a meeting on the subject of Jerusalem between Erekat and Shlomo.

## July 22

The Palestinians report backtracking in Israel's positions on all subjects.

## July 23

Clinton returned from Japan. Erekat delivered a message to him from Arafat on what had occurred in his absence. Clinton asked to meet Arafat and asked that two from each side continue to discuss the subject of borders, Jerusalem, and the refugees. Arafat agreed. Clinton sat with the four at night. The Israelis demanded annexing 9% of the blocs along the Green Line. They will give 1% adjacent to Haluza, and want three warning stations—north, center, south—and a security presence in specific areas in the Jordan Valley, under Palestinian sovereignty and for a limited time. The Palestinians refused.

## July 24

Clinton met members of the refugees committee in the morning. The Palestinians demanded the right of return. To start with the refugees in Lebanon and to establish an international fund for compensation. (Clinton, as promised, did not ask to convene the team on the subject of Jerusalem.)

At 7 PM, Clinton summoned Arafat, who came to him with Abu Ala and Saeb Erekat. Alongside Clinton were Albright, George Tenet, and Sandy Berger.

Clinton: "Why didn't you accept my proposals?"

Arafat: "I won't betray my people. Do you want to come to my funeral? I'd rather die than agree to Israeli sovereignty over the Haram. I also won't sell out the Armenians; they're part of the Palestinian people. I won't be recorded in Arab and Muslim history as a traitor. As I promised my people, we will liberate Jerusalem! If not now, maybe in a thousand years."

Clinton (furious): "Barak offered compromises and concessions, and you're refusing to present anything. The discussion is about statecraft, not about religion. You could never have dreamed of sovereignty in the Muslim and Christian quarters and full authority over the Haram, and all in the framework of a sovereign state. You could never have dreamed of this! You missed an opportunity in 1947 when you opposed the partition; you lost again in 1978 [the autonomy plan incorporated in the Egyptian-Israeli peace treaty] and now again!? You won't have a state. Our relations are finished. Congress will vote to stop assistance and we'll treat you as a terrorist organization. You won't find anyone in the Middle East who will give you the time of day. You can receive support from the churches—you brought all of them to Bethlehem 2000—and you can return to Gaza as a hero. But the morning after, you'll be alone and deprive your people of everything it is being offered. Then your people will judge you. The Muslims will also say that Clinton offered you a state and control over the Haram. . . . You'll be the reason the Haram remains under Israeli sovereignty. Barak made many concessions—you haven't budged. You only want to keep in your pocket what Barak already gave you."

Arafat: "I'm the leader of the Palestinian people, and I represent the Arabs, Muslims, and Christians in all matters related to the Haram and the Church of the Holy Sepulcher. I won't betray their trust in me. Even if you offer me a state, and Haifa and Jaffa—without sovereignty over the Haram, it won't happen! Time will tell."

Clinton: "You're free to do as you please."

Tenet: "You're putting an end to the relations between us. You're throwing everything away. You're sentencing your people to a continuation of the state-less situation."

Berger to Clinton, in front of everyone: "You're losing a lot on the domestic front in the United States, and there are many issues in Congress and you have a broader responsibility. I'm begging you to close this summit. Arafat is not willing to move forward."

Albright: "Barak offered more than what we expected from him, and you haven't presented a thing."

Erekat turned to Albright: "It's true that there's no price to pay for attacking us, blaming us, and threatening us. We don't have a lobby that will change your thinking. I'm aware of the depth of the alliance between you and Israel, and your political blindness toward Israel. But now you're threatening the region and its peoples, and pushing them to drown in a cycle of violence and blood. Your position serves Bin Laden and all of the extremists in the Arab and Muslim world."

Erekat to Clinton: "Mr. President, I expected you to be the leader of the world with your wisdom and your vision, and that you'd keep away from threats and deliberate with us with a bit of fairness. We're a people that agreed to a state on 22% of original Palestine. And the Israelis discuss one time on a basis of historical considerations, one time on religious [considerations], and a third time according to the needs of public opinion in Israel, a fourth time on the basis of what they call security needs, and a fifth time according to psychological reasons of the people in Israel. The Palestinian people stood against this superpower with a stone in hand. If there isn't peace for us—there will not be peace for anyone.

I'm speaking to you from a broken heart, and wish to apologize to every Palestinian I personally convinced to support peace during the past twenty years. You'll bear responsibility for every Palestinian or Israeli who is killed if you continue in this method. This summit produced great progress. We never dreamed of talking about

Jerusalem, borders, and refugees—and here, it's happening. Please, Mr. President, don't throw away this process, because its failure means turning off the lights in the Arab and Muslim world, and I don't know when we'll be able to turn them back on again."

Clinton to Arafat: "I have a proposal: Within an hour, you send me Erekat, and I'll ask Barak to send Ben-Ami. I'll sit with you for as long as needed to discuss two questions: How we get out of the impasse and ideas for Jerusalem."

Arafat agrees.

Albright to Arafat: "Your stance is honorable and you're a man of faith. I expected the ceiling of your expectations to be lower than what you presented. But now I must admit that I respect your demands."

About an hour later, Erekat returns to Clinton and finds Ben-Ami there.

Clinton to Erekat: "You said that we need to continue the process, and that we've made a lot of progress at the summit and attained many achievements. What do you propose now?"

Erekat: "I suggest preparing a joint, three-sided announcement recapping the summit, describing the progress, and stating that despite the progress there are still wide gaps, but that the sides have agreed to continue in the process with the aim of implementing 242 and 338. The United States will continue to be a full partner, and the sides will continue in their efforts to reach an agreement by September 13th."

Ben-Ami: "If the summit ends without any agreement, it will mean that the process collapses and the peace camp in Israel collapses, Israel's government falls, and perhaps a unity government with Sharon will be formed."

Erekat: "That's not logical. Barak has no political chance without an agreement."

Clinton: "This isn't the place for a political argument over the internal situation in Israel. I suggest a three-sided announcement promising the continuation of the process or an announcement that the process collapsed. A third alternative is to postpone the topic of Jerusalem and resolve all the rest, or to defer part of the discussion on Jerusalem for two years and resolve the rest."

Erekat: "The last two proposals are totally unacceptable, and the announcement about the collapse of the process would bring destruction to the region."

Clinton: "I'll decide later. Meanwhile, I'd like new ideas for Jerusalem."

Ben-Ami: "This is our official proposal: the external areas—under Palestinian sovereignty. The internal—autonomy with broad authorities, but under our sovereignty. We can grant sovereignty over a neighborhood or two. In the Old City—a special status for the Muslim, Christian, and Armenian quarters with security cooperation. The government of Palestine will be able to establish its center near the Haram and under its sovereignty. The sovereignty on the Mount will be divided: The Palestinians will be the sovereign on the Haram in the framework of a trusteeship regime (sovereign custodianship), including responsibility for security, while Israel will have partial sovereignty (residual custodianship), with Jewish prayer permitted at an agreed-upon space on the Haram."

Erekat: "You're retreating from previous promises. This is the tradition of Israeli negotiation."

Clinton: "There are two proposals [regarding Jerusalem], one of which has yet to be discussed with Barak. One, the formula that Shlomo Ben-Ami presented. The second, the external areas under Palestinian sovereignty, with the internal under Israeli sovereignty but under broad Palestinian autonomy. The Muslim and Christian quarters will be Palestinian. The Armenian and Jewish will remain under Israel's sovereignty. In regard to the Haram—it will be transferred to Palestine by the Security Council. Prayer will be permitted for Jews on the Haram."

Clinton asks to present this to Arafat.

Erekat: "There's no need. He cannot accept it."

Clinton: "Go, deliver it, and come back and report."

Erekat goes and returns with a short letter from Arafat to the president: "We appreciate your proposals, but they cannot serve as a basis for peace negotiations, and contradict the possible solution and international legitimacy."

Clinton: "I expected this. We'll think tonight about announcing the conclusion of the summit."

The three parted ways before dawn.

**July 25**

Clinton and Berger invite Barak, Danny Yatom (the head of the security-diplomatic staff and former Mossad chief), Arafat, and Erekat.

Clinton: "I'm sad that we were unable to reach an agreement, but there was considerable development in the positions of the sides. I ask the two sides to do their utmost to reach an agreement by September."

Arafat: "We'll make every effort."

Barak: "We must not allow the process to collapse. We hoped for an agreement, and we need to continue in this effort."[25]

8

Perhaps if Barak and Clinton had kept their promises to the Palestinians at the end of the summit—not to declare it a failure and not to cast the blame on Palestinian rejectionism—it might have been possible to prevent the outbreak of violence that began in October and quickly escalated into what is known as the second intifada or Al-Aqsa Intifada. On the other hand, perhaps nothing could have prevented the wave of violence after the failure of the talks and the subsequent stalemate.

One way or the other, after the Camp David summit failed, Barak (as usual) pursued two contradictory paths: on the one hand, he continued to examine the possibility of convening another summit in which the disputed issues would finally be resolved, especially the issues of the Temple Mount and the refugees.[26] On the other hand, he worked to strengthen his political standing at home, and Israel's international standing, by promoting the claim that the concessions he offered had "revealed Arafat's true face."

In this sense, Beilin was justified in feeling concerned and uncertain about whether reaching an accord was more important to Barak than revealing Arafat's "true face." At the same time, from Barak's perspective, he was not wrong in his analysis. After all, he, indeed, offered the Palestinians a state—something Israel had never offered before. During the talks at Camp David, the map of the Palestinian state the Israelis proposed grew from 77 percent of the territories to nearly 90 percent.[27] The Palestinians proposed a map that left 1.6 percent of the territories in Israel's hands (including Ariel, Alfei Menashe, and Karnei Shomron) and demanded an Israeli withdrawal from Gush Etzion and the Jewish neighborhoods in East Jerusalem, except for Har Homa. In addition, they insisted on land swaps in exchange for the 1.6 percent they were willing to cede to Israel. That is, they demanded territory from Israel equal in scope to the land Israel would annex in the West Bank. They examined the border between Israel and the proposed Palestinian state with a fine-tooth comb. A disagreement arose over an issue that is less familiar to the Israeli public—46 square kilometers (0.8% of the West Bank) in the Latrun area. This area, referred to as no man's land, remained in Israel's hands when the armistice agreement was signed with Jordan at the end of the War of Independence, though Israeli law was not applied to it. Israel claims it as part of Israel de facto, while the Palestinians regard it as occupied territory that should be returned.

In cold terms of profit and loss, Arafat should have accepted the offer that gave him a Palestinian state for the first time in Arab history (and definitely more than he had prior to the summit). But as we have seen, he was influenced by forces that lie beyond these cold calculations. In any case, the fact that Arafat lost does not mean that Israel won. The Israeli-Palestinian conflict is not a zero-sum game, and the success of the peace process is a shared interest. The culpability of Arafat is still a failure for Israel. The Palestinians' point of departure draws from a historical narrative that associates the Zionist idea with the theft (intentional or not) of their lands. From their perspective, even if they received full sovereignty over all of the territory beyond the Green Line, they still would only have 22 percent of Mandatory Palestine. In this context, Arafat had little room to compromise—and certainly had few options as the representative of the Muslim interest vis-à-vis the Temple Mount. After reading Haniyah's summit diary, it is no surprise that Arafat and the members of the Palestinian delegation portrayed themselves as heroes when returning home from the summit. That is, they heroically withstood the pressure of the two superpowers—the world's greatest superpower (the United States) and the strongest power in the Middle East (Israel) —and did not surrender. The Americans, indeed, exerted enormous pressure on the Palestinians.

After the summit, Barak refused to meet with Arafat. His intention was to weaken the Palestinian leader's standing as a statesman, and he believed this would help to soften Arafat's positions. In September, when the two met by chance at an elevator in the UN building, Arafat tried some subtle humor, asking Barak's wife Nava: "Who is this man next to you?" Barak responded with a cold smile.

Barak finally agreed to meet with Arafat in late September. Arafat suggested Abu Mazen's home as the venue, but Barak insisted that the meeting take place at his home. He finally, and uncharacteristically, was persuaded to act in accordance with the local custom (at least outwardly) and asked the mediator, the Jewish-American businessman Daniel Abraham, to embrace Arafat and say: "This is a hug from Barak. We live in the Middle East and are committed to its customs. In the last three meetings, I was in the Palestinian Authority, and therefore I ask that you honor me and come to my home."[28] Arafat consented and Barak had a chance to learn a thing or two about the importance of respecting others.

The meeting was held on September 25th in a positive atmosphere. (Barak called it "strengthening the connection.") But it was too little, too late. Three days later, the opposition leader, Ariel Sharon, chose to conduct a well-publicized visit to the Temple Mount, which the Camp David summit had shown to be the heart of the conflict. (It is very possible that Sharon was aware of this fact and that it influenced his decision.) Riots erupted in East Jerusalem in the wake of the visit, and later spread through the West Bank and into the State of Israel, eventually escalating into what is known as the second intifada (in Israel) or the Al-Aqsa Intifada (the accepted Palestinian name). Thus began a bloody period that the Middle East expert Uriya Shavit rightfully calls "the Palestinian war of attrition."[29]

The question of whether Arafat orchestrated the riots or was swept up in them is difficult to answer. In many ways, the frustration in the Palestinian street was authentic, and the riots were led by local leaders. However, Arafat clearly sought to exploit the anger and frustration as leverage against Israel, and played a real part in the intifada.

At the same time, the misguided stance of Barak, who believed that portraying the Palestinians as recalcitrant would bring international pressure upon Arafat to shed this image, was undoubtedly a factor in the events. Since Arafat believed the Palestinians could compromise no further, the only alternative he saw was to plunge the parties into another round of violence that would also exact a price from Israel and force it to reexamine its positions.

Beilin participated in efforts to prevent the escalation and understand the Palestinian stance. In a meeting after the summit with Faisal al-Husseini, Beilin sought to decipher the Palestinians' attachment to the Temple Mount, explain its significance to the Jews, and find a bridge between the two leaderships. Beilin said during the meeting that a confrontation over the Temple Mount would spiral out of all proportion, and emphasized that Israel had no desire or plan to harm Islamic holy sites.

Al-Husseini responded with a series of questions: "Let's assume there's an earthquake while you still have sovereignty—will you then, when setting out to rebuild the Mount, construct the Temple there?"

Beilin replied in the negative. Secular Israelis, he explained, have no such aspiration, while religious Israelis are waiting for the days of the Messiah.

Al-Husseini nodded in acknowledgment and posed another question, which he quickly answered himself: "Okay, but after the earthquake, will the Jewish public allow you to rebuild our mosques there? The majority will say that its work was done by the hands of nature and now the place should be left in ruins."[30]

The mix that al-Husseini expressed—of the natural and the cultural, of the mythical and the rational, and of the political and the theological—was an indication of how difficult it will be to unravel the complications of this conflict.

In another meeting, this time with Dahlan and Muhammad Rashid, Arafat's confidante and economic adviser, Rashid noted the need to reinforce the Israeli peace camp with religious moderates and mentioned Aryeh Deri, who was then serving a prison sentence, as an option. Without him, Rashid believed, it would be difficult to mobilize the Shas party's support. He said to Beilin that if the peace process was important to him, he should lobby to pardon Deri. Beilin was horrified by the suggestion, which for him expressed disregard for the rules of sound governance and law in Israel.[31] He also reported this to Barak.

Undoubtedly, Rashid's suggestion was morally flawed. But it indicates how the achievement of peace, in the sense of ending the conflict, requires tackling many sensitive and complex issues, some of which might also require some unsavory work.

## 9

On October 12, 2000, two IDF reservists took a wrong turn and ended up driving into Ramallah. The two—Vadim Norzhich and Yossi Avrahami—found themselves alone in the heart of the city. They were relieved to see Palestinian police officers and quickly explained that they had lost their way and asked for directions back to their base. The policemen took another course of action: they arrested the two, took their rifles and led them under threat to the local police station. En route to the station, the soldiers were beaten by passersby.

The rumor of the soldiers' presence at the police station made waves. Hundreds gathered at the entrance of the station, demanding to hand over the soldiers. The police officers acceded to the demand and opened the door to the room where the beaten soldiers were being held. The soldiers were murdered in a lynching documented in part by Italian television cameras. Their dead bodies were tossed out of the windows of the station.

The horrific scene, broadcast on Israeli television in a censored version that was still threatening and revolting, was an additional breaking point in the Israeli public's attitude toward the Palestinian Authority. The pictures from Ramallah reinforced collective feelings of anger and fear in a range of contexts. For example, the fact that one of the soldiers was an immigrant from Russia stirred memories of pogroms against Jews. And the helplessness of the IDF soldiers, who served in the strongest army in the Middle East, tragically encapsulated Israel's psycho-historical status as "Samson der nebechdikker [nerd]" as Levi Eshkol once said in his picturesque Yiddish: the poor little hero. The fragility of Israeli power was exposed and touched raw nerves. There was also humiliation and anger, primarily directed at the Palestinian police officers, who seemed to substantiate claims about the security errors of the Oslo Accords through their active assistance in the lynching. Orientalist images of bloodthirsty Arab mobs also entered into the mix.

Beilin too was horrified by the lynching. It was the lowest point he experienced in the history of the conflict. "The night of the lynching in Ramallah was the most terrible moment," he recalled:

> Because there is something cold in the incidents of the suicide bombers. A person comes coolly and with a sort of insane faith and kills himself and those around him with calculated cruelty. But the hateful eyes you saw in the lynching, you don't see in the suicide bomber. Or those hands at the window, of the one who takes pride in having human blood on his hands. Therefore, the sight of the hands and of the surrounding crowd was from my perspective the deepest nadir.
>
> In my eyes, the biggest question for our generation is the Holocaust. Why it happened. And how innocent and orderly people drew the most terrible things from within them. And my answer is that apparently each one of us has dark recesses we are not even aware of. That in each of us there is the very best and the very worst. And what happened in the lynching in Ramallah is that suddenly you saw the very worst. The most terrible evil. Which isn't Arab or Palestinian evil, but human evil. And it's evil that also exists among us. Evil that also exists among our good children who were the best pupils and the most devoted in the classroom, and suddenly found themselves doing awful things in the intifada.
>
> To see that person, who might be a gardener somewhere, and perhaps even a glazier or carpenter who also worked in Jerusalem, and might very well be quite a good person—that really shocked me. I thought about the fact that it's very likely that he returned home that evening and caressed his child's head, and ate dinner with his wife and watched a little Al-Jazeera and even told her there had been a little turmoil in the city that day. From my perspective, the fact that such primal forces could spring from a regular person, perhaps even a good man, to the point that he was willing to murder people who did nothing to him, and to become excited and enthused by it, and to stand that way at the window—that's the most horrific thing. For me, that was the most frightening moment. After all, everything we did was aimed at repressing those forces. Everything I've done all these years is an attempt to stop the madness. Not to let the evil and the deranged and the primeval get the better of us here.[32]

The lynching was one of a number of severe incidents in October. Arabs in Israel launched violent demonstrations to express solidarity with their brethren in the territories, and there were Jews in Israel who feared this could lead to civil war. The heavy-handed response by the police cost the lives of thirteen Arabs (twelve citizens of Israel and one resident of Gaza), adding to Arab Israelis' disappointment in the State of Israel and their sense of alienation from it.

The events threatened to destroy the trust not only between the peoples, but also between the leaders and politicians who had become accustomed to ongoing dialogue, even during stormy times. It seemed that the curtain had fallen on the option of coexistence, and the fact that Hezbollah launched its first attack against IDF soldiers since Israel's withdrawal to the international border—three IDF soldiers were abducted on October 7, and Israel did not know for years whether they were alive or dead—reinforced the sense of isolation and the danger lurking at Israel's doorstep. The New Middle East that Peres promised seemed very far away, indeed.

Nonetheless, at lower echelons, Israelis and Palestinians made efforts to renew reconciliation. On October 18, about a week after the lynching in Ramallah, Pundak sent to Beilin and Barak a concise summary of talks he conducted over a period of about three weeks with Marwan Barghouti, the commander of Fatah's Tanzim forces, who was seen as one of the future leaders of the Palestinian Authority. Barghouti, who played a key role in the first intifada and was expelled to Jordan for this activity, supported the Oslo Accords and the peace process. However, when the second intifada erupted, he became one of its leaders.

Pundak reported that Barghouti was asking that the Israelis understand the complexity of the situation from the Palestinian viewpoint. Barghouti argued that the military and diplomatic pressure Israel was exerting left no recourse for the Palestinians other than violence—violence that could only be quelled when the Palestinians feel Israel's good intentions expressed on the ground. "During the past three weeks, I conducted talks with Barghouti every day and night," Pundak wrote:

> He vowed that the lynching shocked him and that he would have prevented it bodily. He asked that the IDF stop using live fire. Claims that it fans the flames. He also suggests stopping the humiliating public pressure of Israel against the PA as in—"Only if they do such and such, we'll lift the closure." He asked for conciliatory statements. For example, for the prime minister to say that he understands the importance of East Jerusalem for the Palestinians and the Haram for the Muslim world, and that these things will be taken into account in the permanent agreement. He gave the impression that they would continue the unarmed popular demonstrations in a relatively reduced way until the Arab summit convenes.[33]

An interesting addition was the Tanzim commander's request from Israeli leaders to refrain "from demonizing Barghouti, because even if he is tough, he believes in an accord."[34]

These words are instructive not only because they show how dialogue can continue even under fire, but primarily because of their content: Barghouti, who represented the young generation of Palestinians born and molded in the territories under Israeli occupation, frankly explained that supporters of the peace process in Israel must accept the need of the oppressed for violence. But the question is whether the Israelis could, indeed, have viewed themselves as Goliath, accepting the anger of David, when the historical contexts and diplomatic circumstances in the Middle East led them to feel like David, surrounded by giants who threatened to annihilate them.

## 10

After the outbreak of the intifada, Beilin made various efforts to calm the situation. In December, Barak and Beilin met with King Abdullah in Jordan. One of the main topics in the conversation was a question that troubled Israel and stirred disputes within its defense establishment: Is Arafat leading the intifada or at the very least "controlling the height of the flames" (as described in the jargon of security officials)? If so, Arafat was the key to ending it. Or was he compelled to adapt himself to the prevailing disappointment and frustration in the Palestinian street, which sparked the uprising?

King Abdullah too had no definitive answer. "Jordan," the king said, "is interested in stopping the violence. I contacted Arafat a number of times and said to him: 'You've mobilized the entire Arab street on your side. Al-Jazeera has mobilized to broadcast harsh pictures. What is your objective? Where are you leading?' He was evasive. Jordan and Egypt tried to influence him, but Egypt's agenda is not always clear."[35]

In their conversation, Abdullah promised that "any agreement of the Palestinians with Israel will be acceptable to the Arab world." But Barak cynically added: "except for a concession on sovereignty over the Haram." The king suggested using the assistance of international observers in any accord. And in regard to the Temple Mount, he warned that turning it into a religious issue would incite the masses. Interestingly, Abdullah suggested emphasizing that the Temple Mount would be under Arab—not Muslim—sovereignty, thus neutralizing the Iranians' connection to the Mount. "Why do you need the Iranians there?" He promised that the accord would guarantee the rights of Jews on the Mount.

To ease the minds of Israelis vis-à-vis the right of return, the king spoke about a survey that found that most Palestinians are willing to receive compensation instead of actually exercising the right of return. "The problem is that Arab public opinion thinks that Israel also rejects the return to [the state of] Palestine," he added. That is, one of the problems related to this issue was the way in which it was marketed to the Arab public. At the end of the meeting, the king committed to a future of peace with Israel, and promised that no political pressure would ever lead him to "pardon the murderer of the schoolgirls" (a reference to the Jordanian soldier Ahmed Daqamseh, who fired at a group of Israeli schoolgirls visiting Naharayim on March 13, 1997, killing seven of them). "Over my dead body," he said. The king added "that his vision of the era of peace includes Jordan, Israel, and Lebanon as a flourishing economic bloc."[36] (Daqamseh, indeed, released only after serving a full sentence, in March 2017.)

Despite Israeli hopes to the contrary, the Jordanians had no leverage they could use to stop the Al-Aqsa Intifada, or at least deescalate it. In an earlier conversation, Nabil Shaath, the PA's minister of planning who was also in charge of international cooperation, had advised Beilin that Israel should not aspire to extinguish the intifada though its overt and covert relations with Middle Eastern leaders because the intifada was an expression of popular frustration over the failure to win independence. "You can't expect to stop the intifada by pressing a button," he said. Shaath explained that since it was a popular protest, he couldn't say whether Arafat was controlling it or using his skill in gauging public opinion. "It's somewhere in the middle."[37]

The Al-Aqsa Intifada was a fatal blow to the Barak government. Efforts intensified in the political arena to replace the government or dissolve the Knesset. In secret talks with Sharon's associates,[38] Barak tried, unsuccessfully, to assemble a unity government. In early December, in an effort to position himself as proactively choosing to seek a renewed vote of confidence from the public, Barak announced his resignation as prime minister and called early elections.

Since the Knesset itself did not disband, the elections were held this time only for prime minister. The ideal candidate of the right, and the most popular one according to the polls, was Benjamin Netanyahu, who planned to return to politics from the hiatus he had taken after losing to Barak in 1999. However, only members of Knesset were eligible to compete for prime minister, and Netanyahu was not an MK at the time. There was support in the Knesset to amend this restriction and allow Netanyahu to run against Barak, but Netanyahu refused to enter the race unless the Knesset was also dissolved. His bitter memories from the shaky coalition he led in his first term—and the fact that the Likud had only nineteen MKs in the Knesset at the time, and perhaps had fears about leading Israel at one of its most difficult moments—contributed to his decision not to compete. This paved the way for Sharon to run as the candidate of the right, after he defeated Ehud Olmert in the Likud's internal elections.

During the election campaign, and toward the end of Clinton's term in the White House, Barak accepted an American proposal to renew negotiations. The talks were slated to be held at Taba, in the Sinai, against the background of the Clinton parameters unofficially presented to the two sides in late 2000. The key points included establishing a Palestinian state on 94–96 percent of the West Bank, compensation for the Palestinians of 1–3 percent of the territory they relinquished, a safe passage between Gaza and the West Bank, leaving 80 percent of the settlers within the boundaries of the State of Israel, territorial contiguity for the two states, and reducing the number of Palestinians harmed by the border arrangements. Other options were also raised, such as leasing territory.[39]

The Israeli side decided to accept President Clinton's proposal to continue negotiations, despite the fact that many questioned the moral and legal right of a transition government to commit to concessions and agreements that would bind the government that replaces it. Beilin supported renewing the negotiations. He believed that precisely because Barak had lost power, he would be less constrained by political interests, and the Israeli negotiating team could be more candid and bold in the talks. In addition, as in previous cases, Beilin acted in accordance with his belief that as long as there was no legal prohibition, politicians should take advantage of almost every opportunity they have to make an impact on the future—even if contrary to public opinion, which at this stage opposed the talks.

The Taba conference opened on January 21, 2001, and lasted one week. During this time, IDF soldiers and Palestinians continued to clash. Somewhat absurdly, and perhaps typical for the Middle East, progress was achieved—even though the two peoples had seemingly lost all trust in each other by this stage. To this day, the nearly official (but unsigned) Taba understandings are the closest thing to a peace accord between Israel and the Palestinians

This can be attributed in part to the composition of the Israeli delegation, which was more dovish. To a large extent, the composition of the delegation was forced upon Barak, who had lost his political power. Barak may also have agreed to a more "leftist" team because he realized that he would likely lose the elections and had nothing to lose in public opinion. Unlike Camp David, Beilin was directly involved, assigned to discuss the subjects of refugees and the right of return. Sarid also participated. Ben-Ami, Sher, and Shahak led the delegation. (Along with Dahlan, the Palestinian delegation was led by Erekat, Shaath, and Abed Rabbo, who was suspicious of Israel's intentions since the beginning of the Oslo process. Representatives of the American administration and the European Union also participated in the conference, acting as mediators.) Though aware of the critique of the conference's legitimacy, Beilin hoped that the talks would yield progress. In this context, Dahlan promised surprising flexibility. "I know that in the past Arafat said that he intended and he didn't intend—now he does."[40] Brig. Gen. Shaul Arieli, who represented Israel in the delegation on questions pertaining to borders, claims that Barak was serious and authorized him to present a map to the Palestinian side.[41] Barak himself explained that he was skeptical about the conference and its results, but feared that nonparticipation in the conference would play into the hands of the Palestinians, who would be portrayed as the side that was more committed to peace.

# 11

Against the background of the Taba talks and the upcoming elections for prime minister, the first significant conflict arose between Peres and Beilin, a confrontation that also clouded their relations in subsequent years.

Beilin believed that achieving a draft agreement, backed by a halt to the intifada, would change the nature of the battle between Barak and Sharon; the polls were predicting a victory for the latter. Beilin thought that an agreement would enable Barak to compete not only as someone who failed in his peace efforts, but also as someone who had a substantive plan for change. His hope was that the public could be convinced that the bloody events of the second intifada were the death throes of the historical conflict between the two national movements. Despite Sharon's projected victory, Beilin believed that the public still harbored reservations about Sharon after the commission of inquiry into the Sabra and Shatila events recommended dismissing him as defense minister in 1983. Incidentally, Netanyahu held the same view when he decided to take a timeout from politics in 1999, and this was the main reason he supported Sharon's appointment as his replacement during his temporary leave. That is, he thought he was leaving the leadership of the Likud in the hands of someone who could not pose a threat to him.

However, as the intifada became more violent, the possibility of Sharon becoming prime minister, which seemed like a radical idea in 1999, became more realistic, certainly in light of the disappointment about Barak. Against this background, Peres believed that the only way to defeat Sharon was to place himself as the leader of the

Labor Party instead of Barak. Peres showed Beilin surveys indicating that he could defeat Sharon and that he had a better chance of doing so than Barak. He asked for Beilin's support, but Beilin disappointed him by opposing this idea. Most of the other Labor MKs also did not support Peres's bid to return as party leader in the ninth decade of his life. Peres did not give up. According to the new law on direct elections for prime minister, an independent candidate could also participate in the race after collecting the signatures of ten MKs. Peres hoped that the Meretz MKs, who were disappointed with Barak and had quit his government, would provide the required signatures.

He returned to Beilin with the new idea, but his former protégé argued that Peres's candidacy, in addition to Barak, would guarantee Sharon's victory. Peres remained unconvinced and raised a counterargument: in a three-way competition, none of the candidates would win the required majority in the first round, and it would be easier for him in a second round. Beilin contended that Peres's candidacy would cause irreparable damage to the Labor Party, and Peres replied that it was Barak's candidacy that would destroy the party's future. The argument ended in disagreement. Peres, who did not compete in the end (after failing to convince Meretz MKs to back his candidacy), was angry at Beilin, while Beilin was disappointed in his mentor. This episode in their relationship remained a secret, and only years later Beilin admitted that it was "the heaviest cloud that weighed upon our close relations of a quarter of a century. And even if we overcame it, it was there, without a doubt, somewhere in the sky."[42]

# 12

At Taba too, the negotiators drifted into arguments on historical questions. In one such argument, pertaining to the right of return, Beilin pulled out a manifesto published by the workers' council in Haifa on April 28, 1948, urging the city's Arabs not to leave and promising them equal rights in a Jewish state. Shaath claimed that this was at best an example of a tiny island of humanity in a general Zionist episode that was catastrophic for the Palestinians.

Nonetheless, historical questions did not prevent constructive discussions and surprising agreements. For example, the Israelis presented the following draft that won the support of the Palestinians in principle, and marked a significant narrowing of the gaps between the positions of the two sides.

> Israel will keep in its possession 4% of the blocs beyond the Green Line and another 1% for security needs and for the populated areas around Jerusalem. The settlers will be evacuated without other options, except for the areas of the blocs. Land swaps will be made in exchange for the territory around Gaza, including for the safe passage between Gaza and the West Bank in the area south of Hebron. The land swaps will be on a scale that represents a withdrawal from all of the 1967 territories for the Palestinians. . . . An international plan will be formulated to help absorb 25% of the settlers in Israel. There will be Israeli soldiers along the

Jordan [River] border under UN supervision, not [operating] independently. The agreement will include recognition of the end of the demands and of the conflict, and will constitute the implementation of 242. Israel will call upon the world to recognize Palestine, and Palestine will call upon the Muslim world to recognize Israel. . . . Solution for the refugees—they will be entitled to return to [the state of] Palestine. A Palestinian outside of Palestine will be entitled to a Palestinian passport, subject to law. The Palestinians will also have a right to return [in limited numbers] to Canada, Australia, certain European countries, and Israel. Jerusalem will be divided: the Jewish neighborhoods under Jewish sovereignty; the Palestinian ones under Palestine's sovereignty. But Jerusalem will remain a single unit in terms of the possibility of entering its parts. East Jerusalem, including the Arab neighborhoods, will be annexed to Palestine, including neighborhoods where property was purchased by Jews. Ma'alei Adumim will remain under Jewish sovereignty, but will not be expanded eastward. The same applies to Pisgat Ze'ev. The Muslim and Christian quarters—under Palestinian sovereignty.[43]

As noted, this draft was not signed as a document of shared understandings. However, it signaled a shared direction. At one stage, Israel presented a map that offered 93 percent of the territory to the Palestinians, and Israel's representatives agreed to add land from inside Israel in the framework of land swaps, which were not marked on the map. But it is doubtful whether it was an "official map"—that is, approved by Barak as an agreed Israeli version.[44] There was also agreement on restricting the armament of the Palestinian state, on three Israeli warning stations in Palestinian territory, and on the deployment of international forces in Palestine for an undefined period of time. The sides did not agree on the characteristics of the warning stations and the Palestinians rejected Israel's request to conduct training maneuvers and military activity in the territories. They also insisted on complete control of their airspace, contrary to Israel's position.[45]

Another interesting element in the Taba talks pertained to the nature of Israel's declaration on the refugees. It was understood that few would actually be absorbed in Israel (Beilin and Shaath unofficially agreed on the gradual absorption of 40,000 refugees.)[46] The idea of acknowledging some responsibility for the refugees' plight had been raised earlier and was discussed here. The innovation in the proposed draft, which was prepared in advance of the Taba talks, was the linking of Jewish distress throughout history with the contemporary Palestinian misery. This raised an original idea of a narrative of common distress. Here is the draft declaration:

The State of Israel is certainly aware of the suffering of the Palestinian refugees and their longing to return to their country. From a historical experience of pain and the desire to return to the homeland, the Jewish people identifies with the refugees' demand. The Zionist vision never included the desire to uproot people from their land. . . . And thus, after losing a third of its people in the Holocaust, the people in Israel accept Resolution 181 of 1947 regarding the principle of two states—Jewish and Arab—in western Palestine. The Arab state was slated to include a Jewish minority, and the Jewish state was slated to include an Arab minority. The war in

1948 created a tragedy in which hundreds of thousands of Palestinians became refugees. Some of them left in fear, some left despite Israeli pressure to stay, and some were forced to leave under Israeli pressure and joined the Arab forces hostile to Israel. Regardless of the reason, the outcome is tragic and demands a fair solution. The solution must also take into account the actual situation in the existing reality and the establishment of the Palestinian state in the homeland of the Palestinian people, including full self-determination. Israel is committed to making an important contribution to resolving the problem, without harming and undermining its character as the homeland of the Jewish people now, and for the coming generations.[47]

In July 2001, about six months after the Taba conference, Shaath told Beilin at a meeting in Holland that the right of return issue could be resolved in practice via an Israeli statement recognizing the refugees' suffering, because, in any case, the great majority would not seek to exercise this right in Israel. Arafat himself confirmed that the Palestinians realize that the right would not be fully exercised in practice. "We understand the demographic fears of Israel . . . when we implement Resolution 194, these fears should be taken into consideration."[48] In the same conversation in Holland, Beilin suggested a mechanism to resolve the refugee problem within five years: the Palestinian refugees in Lebanon would receive first priority. A minority of them would be absorbed in Israel; the rest would be compensated or absorbed in other countries. The aim would be to dismantle UNRWA (the United Nations Relief and Works Agency for Palestine Refugees in the Near East) within five years, marking the end of the problem. Shaath agreed in principle, but noted the urgent need to achieve a consensus on this issue in the wake of globalization and neoliberalism: independent subgroups were gaining power at the expense of states and national movements, and Shaath warned that many Palestinians might begin to demand the right of return and compensation on a personal basis, via new organizations that are not subordinate to the PLO and their state, even after the issue is officially resolved by the leaderships. "Everyone understands that the right of return will not be realized in practice and will not harm Resolution 181 [which stipulates] that Israel is Jewish," Shaath said. "The problem is how the Arab world will look at someone who accepts compensation and does not return to his homeland. . . . And there's also a problem of the privatization of the right of return—each person is liable to join a private organization of his choice."[49]

Therefore, while the Taba talks ended without an official signing of an agreed-upon and joint text, they produced progress. It is true that the media and public opinion did not attribute importance to these negotiations because they were conducted under a government whose days were numbered. However, more than a year later, when the journalist Akiva Eldar published the agreements (as documented by the European Union's representative Miguel Moratinos) in *Haaretz*, it became clear that the talks had great potential for real rapprochement between the two sides.

At Taba, it was decided that the land would be divided in principle according to the lines of June 4, and that land swaps would be on a 1:1 basis. That is, the Palestinians would receive land in the exact amount of the territory ceded to Israel in the settlement blocs. Still, disagreements remained on the question of the territory to be annexed by

Israel. Israel demanded 6 percent of the territories that contained the main settlements, and the Palestinians agreed to Israel's annexation of 3 percent. Israel's representatives gave up the Jordan Valley settlements in the talks and promised to dismantle them. The Palestinians demanded and won an Israeli concession on sovereignty in part of the Old City, and agreed in exchange to discuss Israeli annexation of the neighborhoods built around Jerusalem after 1967. Nonetheless, they refused to recognize the annexation of Har Homa, Givat Ze'ev, and Ma'alei Adumim. It was agreed that Israel would have sovereignty over the Jewish Quarter and part of the Armenian Quarter, and that the holy places would be administered by a joint body. The Temple Mount issue was not resolved, but the sides did not rule out a proposal to grant international sovereignty over the Mount to the members of the Security Council and Morocco (or another Muslim state) for three years. The Palestinians would be the temporary "guardians/custodians" until an agreement was reached, by the end of the three-year period. In regard to the refugees, besides a declaration in which Israel recognizes their plight, it was agreed that Israel would gradually absorb 25,000–40,000 refugees, and that the others would receive monetary compensation. No agreement was reached on the question of the Israel Air Force's right to train in the skies of Palestine, but it was agreed that the accord would signify the end of the conflict.[50]

Beilin believes that not only was progress made in the talks, but the fact that it was achieved after the crisis at Camp David and the outbreak of the intifada also proved that it was still possible to negotiate and reach agreements—even after those traumatic events. From his experience, Beilin knows that in every negotiation it is impossible to ascertain the final positions of the sides until the actual signing of an agreement (because of the desire to achieve additional gains and in consideration of public opinion). This leads him to believe that the Taba talks could have led to an agreement. However, they concluded before the elections because it was clear the elections would bring an end to the Barak government.

After Sharon's victory, Beilin thought the Israeli representatives should continue the talks with the Palestinians unofficially as members of the opposition. In his mind, the wheels of the peace process needed to be continually oiled and kept in motion to prevent it from collapsing. While recognizing that the left would not return to power in the near future, Beilin believed that the opposition should work independently to advance an agreement in order to present both peoples with an option that could influence the leaderships and force them to consider it. This was the background to the contacts that led to the Geneva Accord in 2003.

# 10

# New Paths: Geneva, Meretz, Beilink

## 1

Ariel Sharon's election victory was expected; the only surprise was the magnitude of Barak's defeat. Only 37.6 percent of the votes went to Barak, compared to 62.4 percent for Sharon.

The defeat was not only due to the disillusionment felt by Jewish Israelis. It was also largely attributable to frustration that had accumulated in the Arab public in light of the Barak government's heavy-handed approach to the October 2000 disturbances. The Labor Party had assigned Beilin to mobilize the Arab vote, but despite his good relations with leaders of the Arab community, he felt helpless in the face of their justified complaints. One of these complaints was that even the government that had taken the furthest steps toward peace had refrained from appointing an Arab minister.

Soon after the elections, and after failing in an effort to stay on as defense minister in a unity government, Barak chose the American option that Netanyahu had introduced to the political culture in Israel: He left political life for the business world. The leaders of Israel were no longer the old-styled politicians who remained in the arena after defeat. Politics was now a personal career and no longer viewed as a lifelong calling.

Barak escalated his rhetoric against Arafat and the PA, and announced that since his government did not sign an agreement, the subsequent governments would not be bound by any of the unsigned understandings reached at Camp David and Taba. In this way, he wanted to deny the Palestinians a comfortable opening position in future negotiations.

The party, which dropped the One Israel brand and returned to its previous name as the Labor Party, prepared for the post-Barak period. Beilin hoped that one of three colleagues—Ben-Ami, Burg, or Ramon—would be chosen as party chairperson and would lead an energetic alternative to Sharon's right-wing government. But he was disappointed when Binyamin Ben-Eliezer defeated Burg in the race, and was again disappointed when the party's convention adopted a proposal by Peres and Ben-Eliezer to join a broad unity government in light of the security situation and to provide the necessary balance on the political-diplomatic front. Sharon sent his designated bureau chief, Dov Weisglass, to ask Beilin to serve as a minister in the unity government, but Beilin turned down the offer. He had resigned from the Knesset, at Barak's request, when he became justice minister, so now he was left without any formal position in the political arena. Ben-Eliezer was appointed defense minister in the unity government and Peres became foreign minister. But the government's policy was dictated by Sharon and the Likud, and the peace process gave way to armed conflict between Israel and the PA and the Palestinian terrorist organizations.

The personal case of Beilin, who lost his place as an elected official, was part of the general downfall of the liberal left, whose support eroded as the terror attacks continued. In March 2002 alone, 135 Israelis were killed. A particularly horrifying attack occurred on Passover eve at the Park Hotel in Netanya. The gruesome results of this attack—30 dead and about 150 injured, many of them elderly people—was the final catalyst for Operation Defensive Shield, launched on March 29. During the operation, the IDF reoccupied all of the cities of the West Bank, except for Hebron and Jericho, and dealt a heavy blow to the terrorist infrastructure. The PA was also damaged, but Israel refrained from toppling it. Arafat's compound in Ramallah was surrounded by IDF forces and was effectively isolated and under siege. The IDF's largest operation since the First Lebanon War succeeded in drastically reducing the number of attacks, though the construction of the separation barrier also played a key role in stopping the wave of terrorism. During the operation, Marwan Barghouti was arrested and later handed several life sentences for his involvement in terrorism. The overwhelming majority of Israelis supported this aggressive policy. The results of the operation reinforced the view that Israel should act with force vis-à-vis the Palestinians and maintain a Jabotinsky-esque iron wall until they opt again for the path of peace. Few Israelis made an effort to understand the Palestinian situation.

Sharon, who until a short time prior to the election had still been taboo to many Israelis, strengthened his standing as an accepted and valued leader. The fact that he had waited for a considerable while before launching Operation Defensive Shield helped him to establish his image as a level-headed, experienced, and cautious leader. He was now seen by most Israelis as a responsible leader who had become ripe for leadership after a long and profound process. As prime minister, Sharon pushed Arafat into a corner and international isolation—largely due to the change in American policy toward the PLO after the attacks of September 11, 2001. As noted, however, Sharon stopped short of toppling the PA. Since 2003, President George W. Bush and Sharon saw eye to eye on a future agreement in line with the "roadmap" the administration proposed—a plan based on the familiar formula of land for peace, but which conditioned a Palestinian state on progress in security arrangements and thus considerably slowed the peace process.

Sharon was the last representative of the generation that fought in the War of Independence, and since the Israeli-Palestinian conflict was now perceived, in light of the failure to reach an accord, as a confrontation that went back to the roots of the historical struggle between the two national movements, there was an advantage in being viewed by the public as a member of the founding generation.

On the other hand, Beilin, like others in the leftist camp, lost much of his public prestige. He of all people, who had fought most of his life against the anachronism reflected in the positions of the older generation within and outside of his party, was now seen by many as detached and irrelevant. He was viewed as someone who had gone astray, and his vision of peace was seen as a pipe dream. But Beilin continued to hold a contrary view and attacked the leaders of his party for sitting in the unity government. In July 2002, he announced the formation of the Shahar movement, designed to offer a new political framework for all members of leftist parties who supported the continuation of peace negotiations. (Shahar is a Hebrew acronym for peace, education, and social welfare.) At the movement's inaugural event, held at the Tel Aviv port, Beilin called for "a movement whose primary role is to unite the peace camp and keep Israel as a Jewish and democratic state based on peace and social justice." About one thousand people attended the opening event. But in the general public—and in the media, which echoed the emerging consensus—the reactions were mostly cynical. The fact that the event included pizza stands and a beverage bar was seen as Tel Aviv snootiness, the product of smugness and disconnection. Beilin now stood at the head of a movement for the first time in his political life. The movement was launched in a campaign featuring slogans such as "Taking responsibility, changing leadership" (a rhyme in Hebrew) and "Run, Yossi, Run."[1] But Beilin's call to unite the left went largely unanswered.

In the elections for the 16th Knesset on January 28, 2003, it was hard to attract votes with an agenda that supported the Oslo Accords with the Palestinian Authority. Israelis expressed skepticism about continuing the peace process and preferred Sharon's promises to achieve security and calm before any diplomatic moves. Amram Mitzna, the Labor Party's new chairperson, represented a dramatic contrast to Sharon, with a platform that included a clear call to partition the land and renew negotiations. But the alternative Mitzna offered crashed in the test of Israeli public opinion: For the first time in Israel's history, the Likud won twice as many Knesset seats as Labor. Within the Labor Party, too, the prominent representatives of the peace camp fell out of favor. Prior to the elections, Ramon—who had been mentioned as a potential candidate to head the Labor Party since the 1970s—decided to compete for the party's leadership, but won only 7 percent of the votes. This was a case of "high politics" (the debate over Oslo) dovetailing with "low politics" (personal vendettas). Beilin, who had won nearly a third of the votes when running for the party's leadership against Barak, was now unsuccessful in a bid to win a realistic slot on the Labor Party's Knesset list. His defeat was attributable in part to Ben-Eliezer's directive to his grassroots supporters to torpedo Beilin's career. (Ben-Eliezer had lost the party's leadership to Mitzna, but remained a power broker in the party.) Beilin tried to remain in the political picture in the framework of Meretz, which, upon his request, gave him the eleventh slot on the party's Knesset list (behind its ten incumbent MKs). But when the votes were tallied, Meretz, unsurprisingly, fell to only six Knesset seats. Beilin remained outside the Knesset.

Many Israelis who had voted for Labor or Meretz in the past opted this time for Tommy Lapid's Shinui party, which took from the left (in its Israeli version) only the secular white dimension—that is, the affiliation with Ashkenazi-bourgeois candidates. Shinui offered an activist stance on foreign affairs and security issues, and hawkish neoliberalism in economics. The success of the party, which soared from six to fifteen Knesset seats, unmasked many Israeli leftists and revealed their stark tribalism. Shinui voters could also have found themselves ideologically at home in Sharon's Likud, but it was more comfortable for them to remain in the "correct" camp. The votes for Shinui was a further blow to the left camp.

Let's return to the thesis of Danny Gutwein, who points to the connection between the left's abandonment of the socialist dimension and its electoral weakness, which, in turn, undermined the left's ability to promote its views on the peace process.[2] The main explanation for this is that without the social element in its platform, the left loses the moral justification for its diplomatic positions. That is, why care for the weak members of "the other" (that is, the Palestinians) when the weak members of Israeli society are not top-priority for the left? In this context, right-wing critics accuse the left of "hypocrisy." Underlying this accusation is the contention that the left's interest in peace accords is driven by the pursuit of economic gain. That is, the economic potential of an era of peace will primarily serve the wealthy, who will be able to expand their businesses and investments. This is part of the explanation for the phenomenon that distinguishes Israel from many states in the Western world: Members of the upper class in Europe tend to support the capitalist right, while the socialist left draws its support from the working class. In Israel, however, the right's constituency is mainly among the weaker socioeconomic segments of society, while the left is backed by wealthier voters.

Privatization in Israel, which continued and even accelerated under left-leaning governments after the upheaval of 1977, is another factor that reflected the abandonment of the local socialist dimension and led to the electoral weakness of the left. And the continuation of this privatization process contributed to the breakdown of solidarity in Israeli society and the widening of disparities, thus creating dependence on the Likud's ideology—an ideology that offered solidarity of a different sort, around support for a Jewish-traditional identity and an attachment to the Land of Israel.

2

Without a formal political position, Beilin chose to return to his home base, the Economic Cooperation Foundation (ECF). He hoped to use this platform to achieve what he had already envisioned at the conclusion of the Taba talks—an informal agreement with the Palestinian representatives. Contrary to his original inclination of instilling peace from the top down (through agreements between leaders and then to the general public), he sought to act from the bottom up this time (via an informal agreement). In other words, he hoped to convince the public of the feasibility of peace, and in this way prod the government to advance in the process.

The conversations that resulted in the Geneva Accords began in early 2002. The Palestinian side was led by Yasser Abbed Rabbo, whose resume included serving as communications minister in the PA government. (He later served as secretary-general of the PLO Executive Committee.) The talks were held in various places and reached fruition in October 2003, following marathon sessions between Israelis and Palestinians on the Jordanian side of the Dead Sea. The Israeli delegation was impressive in its academic credentials and intelligence, but again was quite homogeneous: Mitzna, Amnon Lipkin-Shahak, Burg, Pundak, Brig. Gen. (ret.) Giora Inbar, former Mossad and Foreign Ministry official David Kimche, Prof. Arie Arnon, Prof. Menachem Klein, former Center Party MK Nehama Ronen (and later a Likud member), Prof. Yuli Tamir (a Labor Party minister in the Barak and Olmert governments), Haim Oron of Meretz, the writer Amos Oz, Maj. Gen. (ret.) Shlomo Brom, Brig. Gen. (ret.) Shaul Arieli, and businessman Avi Shaked.

Arieli was the only Mizrahi in the Israeli delegation. The Arab citizens of Israel had no representative. There were only two women. The large majority of Israelis in the delegation belonged to the upper-middle class. It is also doubtful whether the Palestinian participants were authentic representatives of the population in the territories. Prominent among them were Nabil Qassis, who has a PhD in physics and served as tourism minister at the time; Samir Rantisi, a journalist and Abed Rabbo's former media adviser; Qadura Fares, a minister without portfolio; and Abdel Qader al-Husseini, the son of Faisal. This was quite an elite group.

Nonetheless, the Geneva Initiative, whose foundations were actually laid in the Beilin-Abu Mazen agreement, bridged many of the gaps between the positions of the Palestinians and the Israelis—though not all of them.[3]

The discussions were not easy, but several interesting bridging ideas were proposed that are still relevant today. For example, Netanyahu's current demand to recognize Israel as a Jewish state was resolved through a clause recognizing "Palestine and Israel as the national homelands of their respective peoples."

On the question of borders, the starting point was the lines of June 4, 1967, with land swaps of 1:1. Part of the settlement blocs was slated for annexation, which at the time meant that about 270,000 settlers would be included within Israel's borders. The Palestinians did not accept the annexation of Ariel to Israel, but agreed to leave Givat Ze'ev and Ma'alei Adumim under Israeli sovereignty, provided that the territory connecting these settlements to Israel is limited. Contrary to Beilin's original intention of leaving Jewish settlements under Palestinian sovereignty (with the settlers retaining Israeli citizenship), the Geneva Accords state that settlements that are not annexed to Israel will be dismantled and their residents will return to the Israeli side of the new border and receive compensation from an international fund to which Israel will contribute. Jerusalem, including the Jewish Quarter and the Western Wall, will be recognized as the capital of Israel. The Palestinians will receive sovereignty over the Arab neighborhoods and the Har Homa neighborhood built after 1967 on Palestinian lands in East Jerusalem. The Temple Mount will also come under Palestinian sovereignty, while ensuring access to Israelis. According to Prof. Menachem Klein, this allocation was based on the ritual importance of the holy sites, and not their theological sanctity. That is, the transfer of the Temple Mount to the Palestinians and the Western Wall to the Israelis stemmed from the fact that the Temple Mount has been a central place of ritual for Muslims for more than a millennium, while the Western Wall is a more active place of ritual for the Jews.[4]

In discussions on refugees, a problem arose when the Israelis sought to introduce a clause comparing the plight of Jewish refugees from Arab countries to the plight of Palestinian refugees. The Palestinian representatives objected.

It is interesting to note that until 2009, when Netanyahu's right-wing government launched a project to document the property left behind by Jews in Arab lands in order to prepare lawsuits for compensation, the Zionist establishment opposed labeling the Jews of Arab lands as refugees. The main reason for this opposition was that in the spirit of the original Zionist ethos, Israel absorbed immigrants who were returning after two thousand years of longing, not refugees who had unwillingly left Arab lands. Still, in many ways, the War of Independence created two types of refugees: Jews who were forced in the context of the Arab-Zionist struggle to leave Arab lands, and Palestinians who were forced to abandon Israel. The numbers are also comparable. About 800,000 came to Israel from Arab lands (by 1967); the UN estimated the number of Palestinian refugees after 1948 at 700,000.

Like the government of Israel, which later came to the same understanding, the Geneva Initiative participants realized that this comparison of refugees worked to Israel's favor. It was clear that Israel would come under international and Palestinian pressure to recognize its responsibility (at least in part) for the Palestinian refugee problem, and would face the demand for compensation even if it avoided absorbing most of the refugees. Against this background, the definition of the Jews of Arab lands as refugees could further two objectives: It could overshadow the Nakba narrative with the Jewish tragedy, and offset the monetary demand against Israel. According to calculations by several scholars, the Jews in Arab lands owned property of greater value than the property abandoned by the Palestinians. However, this comparison will not prevent judicial criticism. For example, if it can be proven that Israel unofficially collaborated with the Iraqi parliament's decision to seize the assets of Jews in exchange for allowing them to emigrate, the question will arise whether this constituted relinquishment of their property.

In any case, the Palestinian participants opposed drawing a parallel between the plight of the Jews and the Palestinians. In their view, the Palestinians were expelled from their homeland, while the Jews chose to leave and immediately became citizens in their new state. It was ultimately decided that the question of the right of return would be resolved by an Israeli declaration recognizing the suffering of the Palestinian refugees; however, except for thousands who would be permitted to return to the Israeli side of the Green Line, those wishing to return would resettle in the nascent Palestinian state or in other countries. Those remaining in their current country of residence would receive monetary compensation.

It was also agreed that the Palestinian state would be nonmilitarized, but would have an independent security force. Foreign forces would be deployed at the border crossings between Palestinian and Arab states to oversee the transfer of weapons.[5]

The agreement was signed in Geneva on December 1, 2003. The decision to hold the ceremony in Geneva was made in part because Switzerland provided sponsorship for the agreement. It would have been more natural to sign the agreement in the Middle East, and the Egyptians, who supported the initiative, indeed, wanted to hold the event at Taba. The Palestinians preferred Aqaba in Jordan in order to be closer to the West Bank, but this was unacceptable from Israel's perspective. Geneva was ultimately chosen for technical reasons as the most convenient venue, though the signing of the agreement in tranquil Geneva stirred criticism about the signers' detachment— physically and psychologically—from the weary and dusty Middle East.

The gallery of VIPs who came to the ceremony to give the agreement their blessing— including Mikhail Gorbachev, Jimmy Carter, and Frederik de Clerk, the former leaders of the Soviet Union, the United States, and South Africa—was truly impressive. Many world leaders voiced their support. At the signing ceremony, Jibril Rajoub read a letter from Arafat, who announced in retrospect that he did not intend to endorse the agreement, but welcomed in principle every effort for peace. His letter, and the presence of former leaders at the ceremony, seemed to underline one of the weaknesses of the agreement—the fact that it was not endorsed by the relevant leadership of the Israelis and Palestinians.

At around the same, a similar accord—though only a general statement of principles—was signed between Sari Nusseibeh, a Palestinian academic and one of the leaders of the first intifada, and Ami Ayalon, a former director of the Shin Bet. The fact that Nusseibeh and Ayalon chose to turn to the masses on both sides to add their signatures to their agreement only further reinforced the detached image of the Geneva negotiators, who seemingly skipped over their people and leaders.

Beilin tried hard to persuade Israelis who were not identified with the left to support the initiative. But the echoes of the intifada, which had yet to completely subside, made this difficult. All sorts of personal considerations also posed obstacles. For example, Uzi Dayan, a former IDF deputy chief of staff, who has since hopped from one political party to another (including the Likud), expressed support but said he was unwilling to sign because "that would burn me."[6] On the other hand, Colin Powell, the secretary of state under George W. Bush, met with Shahak, Beilin, and the heads of the Palestinian team immediately after the signing of the initiative and expressed his support. However, in a private letter to Beilin, he explained that he could not take action to promote it because the United States could not publicly encourage an agreement that was signed without the consent of the legally elected governments. "The United States remains committed to the president's vision of two states and the roadmap," Powell wrote. "But we also believe in projects like yours, which are important for preserving an atmosphere of hope, in which Israelis and Palestinians can conduct conversations on the issues that stand between them. This is critical, because the peoples are the ones who will shape the required consensus for achieving a two-state solution."[7]

Still, the agreement spurred the Israeli leadership to explore new paths for resolving the conflict. According to Dov Weisglass, who was kept abreast of the developments by Beilin, the initiative (and the support it received from the American administration) contributed to Sharon's decision to unilaterally disengage from the Gaza Strip.[8] Sharon realized that sooner or later, the agreement would become a threatening alternative to his policy. In an interview with *The New York Times* on April 16, 2004, Sharon explained that it was important for him to prevent the public and the international community from adopting initiatives like the Geneva Accords as a realistic option. He expressed a similar argument to fend off opponents of the disengagement plan within the Likud.[9] Sharon's subsequent decision to leave the Likud and form the Kadima party may also be attributable in part to his desire to offer an intermediate path between complete opposition to territorial compromise and the Geneva option.

3

In the wake of the Geneva Initiative, Beilin decided to cut his ties with the Labor Party. His decision was partly attributable to the hawkish stance many Labor members had adopted since the outbreak of the second intifada. Of course, he was also disappointed about his relegation on the party's Knesset list and recognized his weak position in the party. However, he did not intend to leave politics. His plan was to merge Shahar with Meretz, which was battered and leaderless after Sarid announced that he took personal responsibility for the party's decline in the 2003 elections (from ten to six seats) and would step down as party leader.

Beilin decided to compete for the leadership role. His opponent was Ran Cohen, who had emigrated from Iraq as a child and was a retired IDF colonel. Cohen, one of the long-time members of Meretz, was identified more with the social struggle than with diplomatic affairs. His great achievement was the Public Housing Law, intended to enable residents of public housing to purchase their apartments from the state at a significant discount, with the help of government grants.[10] The legislation, which Cohen shepherded in collaboration with members of the Mizrahi Democratic Rainbow Coalition, entered effect only in 2013, but it is hard to overstate its importance. Many saw Cohen's candidacy as an opportunity to open the party's ranks to weaker segments of the population.

Thus, in its time of distress, Meretz offered two fascinating alternatives, which is worth considering in light of the left's current situation: Cohen represented the social aspect, while Beilin represented the diplomatic aspect.

The two men also differed in their attitude toward refusal to serve in the army—a trend that had strengthened among young Israelis during the Al-Aqsa Intifada as the IDF escalated its use of force and the government offered no diplomatic alternative. Cohen and Beilin ostensibly stood together against those advocating the radical step of refusal among the party's youth. They shared a fidelity to the law and to the IDF, and rejected refusal in principle. However, there were differences in nuances. Cohen, who volunteered for reserve duty in the First Lebanon War, believed that even the discussion of refusal as an option alienates Meretz from broad segments of the population that could support its policies. Beilin rejected refusal as an illegal action, but expressed moral admiration for the motives of those who refused to serve in the IDF.

The debates between Cohen and Beilin were conducted, in the best Meretz tradition, in a businesslike manner, without making personal accusations in public. Behind the scenes, however, some of Beilin's supporters spoke of Cohen's narrow-mindedness. And in Cohen's camp, some pointed to Beilin as the epitome of why the public felt alienation toward the left.

Cohen proposed a new equation: investing the same amount of effort on social issues as on diplomatic issues. By focusing more on the former and less on the latter, the left could return to its socialist roots, he argued. Only by opening its ranks to a wider populace could the left mobilize the support needed for its diplomatic positions and succeed in elections. Beilin agreed on the importance of social issues, but claimed that a proper allocation of resources would not be possible without peace. For him, the Israeli left's primary banner should, indeed, be the diplomatic one, though this banner also has a social foundation because only a breakthrough toward peace will make it possible to remedy the ills of society. In any case, Beilin was less of a socialist than Cohen.

Beilin's opponent also spoke about the need to bring more Mizrahi Jews into a party whose character and image were so thoroughly Ashkenazi. He mentioned Moshe Katsav (long before his rape conviction, of course) and Meir Sheetrit as Mizrahi politicians with moderate views on diplomatic issues and a social orientation who would never join Meretz because of its blatantly Ashkenazi-bourgeois character. Beilin, who detests the politics of identity in principle, thought otherwise. He regarded Sheetrit as epitomizing the problematic nature of supporting a person because of his origin: Though born in Morocco and mistakenly identified with the weaker segments of society, Sheetrit supported Netanyahu's neoliberal policy and even justified it by pointing to himself as proof that any person, regardless of ethnic origin, could succeed in Israel.[11]

On March 16, 2004, Beilin won a majority of 53 percent of the votes. The Meretz rank and file, including many members of the kibbutz movement, preferred the Tel Avivian Beilin to Cohen, who found a home on Kibbutz Gan Shmuel after arriving in Israel.

For the first time in his life, Beilin became the leader of a political party. The most important thing he did in this position was to lead Meretz to support Ariel Sharon's disengagement plan. In principle, Beilin rejected unilateral arrangements and saw them as circumventing peace. He was also suspicious of Sharon's motives. But in light of the fierce opposition to the withdrawal within the Likud and the right-wing camp, Beilin thought it would be a mistake to hinder Sharon from carrying out the disengagement, and thus block the historic precedent of a Likud leader ordering a withdrawal from the Land of Israel. Therefore, though he had expressed opposition to the disengagement plan when it was first announced, the Meretz MKs provided Sharon with a "security net" for his initiative.

4

After defeating Ran Cohen, complaints about the Ashkenazi character of the Meretz party and its new leader continued to hound Beilin.

In a speech at a Meretz convention in April 2005, Beilin sought to focus, as usual, on diplomatic issues. He noted the danger of the Iranian nuclear program as another reason for the urgency of an accord with the Palestinians, because an accord would enable Israel to reach agreements with additional Sunni Arab states. "The Iranian problem is not artificial. It exists. There was already a prime minister here who believed in the need to reach a permanent accord with the Palestinians quickly, before there's a nuclear weapon in the hands of a hostile state," he declared, referring to one of Rabin's strategic reasons for pursuing the Oslo process.

To his surprise, there were shouts from the audience on a completely different subject: "What about the development towns, Yossi?" Beilin responded immediately. He asked the members to check whether there is an Israeli party that "is more democratic, more decent, and more open" and to tell him if they find such a party.[12]

Perhaps Beilin's response, which is basically correct, also illustrates the inability of Meretz to rehabilitate its image. Meretz is, indeed, open, decent and democratic relative to other parties in Israel's political arena. The leadership contest is open to all members and the party apparatus is not corrupt. But the fact is that the profile of its leaders has remained largely unchanged and the party has failed to make inroads in wider circles in Israeli society. This is a missed opportunity of enormous proportion: Among the grassroots populace, there are no fewer people ready for diplomatic compromise than in the wealthier classes. For example, the opposition to Sharon's disengagement initiative did not come from Likud bastions in the development towns, but primarily from religious Jews and settlers. The problem is that presenting Meretz as a democratic and decent party is not enough to attract support among the general populace, and Meretz does not invest enough in efforts to approach the weaker classes.

In any case, Beilin's standing continued to weaken. One of the reasons for this was the gradual strengthening of Hamas, especially after the death of Arafat in November 2004, which further eroded domestic support for Beilin's advocacy of negotiation with the Palestinians. In late January 2006, shortly before elections in Israel, Hamas was victorious in elections for the Palestinian legislature. Consequently, Beilin found himself—as in the case of the disengagement, when he ultimately supported the stance of his ideological rival, Sharon—aligned with the Likud vis-à-vis Hamas. Some in the political arena (including President Katsav) called for recognizing the new reality and engaging in dialogue with the Hamas government if the organization dropped its rejection of Israel's existence. But Beilin, like the Likud, argued strongly in favor of boycotting Hamas. It is true that Beilin's position was less simplistic than that of the Likud. He contended that Israel's policy of weakening the PLO and the lack of progress in the peace process were partly responsible for Hamas's ascendance. (The right, on the other hand, claimed that the victory of Hamas had unmasked the Palestinians who voted for it.) However, the developments in the Israeli-Palestinian conflict clearly made it difficult for Beilin to promote his traditional views.

Elections for the 17th Knesset were held on March 28, 2006, soon after Ariel Sharon's debilitating stroke. Kadima, led by Ehud Olmert, was the victor, emerging as the largest party. Beilin's Meretz party shed another Knesset seat, dropping from six to five. The disappointing results encouraged Zehava Galon and Ran Cohen to challenge his leadership.

Olmert's political platform as prime minister and his convergence plan—that is, a unilateral withdrawal from most of the West Bank if an accord was not reached—placed Beilin in an unusual and less comfortable position: On the one hand, he opposed the school of unilateralism; on the other hand, he saw how his basic stance on the need to divide the land was being adopted by the right.

Though Beilin doubted the ability of achieving lasting peace through unilateral arrangements, he recognized that another right-wing prime minister, who was raised in a Revisionist home (Olmert even abstained in the vote on the peace treaty with Egypt), was now affirming the judiciousness of Beilin's call for territorial compromise. "This is the moment I was waiting for," Beilin wrote after Olmert's convergence plan was published. "After long years in which he and his colleagues on the right scornfully dismissed the demographic problem or presented themselves as optimists, awaiting large-scale immigration from the West that would ensure a stable Jewish majority west of the Jordan [River], such a quintessential representative of the Likud had to admit that the problem exists and had to offer a solution of his own."[13]

However, the sense of victory that his view was finally adopted also carried a price. The blurring of the ideological gap made it difficult for Meretz and Beilin to find a clear and distinct place in the political field. The natural place for Meretz was in the opposition. But what was, indeed, different between its participation in the governments of Barak and Rabin in the 1990s and joining Olmert's government? In light of the developments, Meretz could have certainly found itself in an Olmert government at this stage, or at least merged again with the Labor Party and influenced it from within. But Beilin could not adopt either of these paths for reasons of conscience and personal reasons.

He found another solution: Prior to the elections for the 18th Knesset, Beilin announced in October 2008 that he had decided to leave political life. The reasons for his departure at a relatively young age (60), certainly relative to the customary practice of Israeli politicians, were complex: In terms of internal party politics, Beilin was ready to run against Galon and Cohen for the leadership of Meretz. However, when Haim Oron also announced his candidacy, Beilin understood that he had not only lost Oron's personal support, but also the support of many party members. Beilin had won the Meretz primaries thanks largely to supporters from the kibbutz movement, who were loyal to Oron.

A more substantial reason for Beilin's exit from the political stage was that his forte was in working in the shadow of the top leader. (Ironically, he was similar in this way to his first political patron, Peres.) Beilin was adept at driving processes when he functioned like adrenaline within the system, as an adviser and planner, and not when holding the top leadership post. Contrary to his image, Beilin is a person of simple ways, affable and inclined to speak openly and candidly; but he is not a people's person. He avoids contact with the masses, and almost never agrees to play the fool or act out of character to serve electoral needs. There are few politicians, even in Meretz, who are able to conduct themselves without compromising in these areas.

As noted, Beilin also quit politics when he understood that from a historical perspective his diplomatic path—dividing the land in an accord with the Palestinians—had won as an idea, though the idea proved unfeasible to implement at the current time.

Beilin will not be remembered as the most successful of Meretz's leaders, but it should be noted that Meretz also failed to soar after his departure. The weakness of Meretz in the early twenty-first century stems from more substantial reasons than the identity of its leader.

Though every party seeks to expand its base of voters in order to boost its influence (and in this sense, Meretz is in decline), the cumulative effectiveness of a party is not only measured by its electoral success. In this context, Meretz has enormous historical importance.

The core of Meretz, established prior to the 1992 elections, was the Ratz party, founded by Shulamit Aloni, a former Mapai member, and led primarily by Mapai dropouts like Aloni and Sarid. Two important parties, Mapam and Shinui, joined forces with Ratz. Despite their ideological differences, the alliance engendered a dozen Knesset seats. Meretz attracted many Israelis who were fed up with the establishment, but did not dare to break away from it. It was a Zionist left that was also well-versed in Judaism. (Both Aloni and Sarid had profound knowledge of the Bible, and Beilin is also knowledgeable about Jewish liturgy and the Talmud.) Meretz sought to refresh the discourse on peace, address relations between religion and state, and instill liberal values. In the social arena, due to the clear Ashkenazi-bourgeois roots of Ratz and Shinui, and the Ashkenazi roots of Mapam, Meretz has always had a problem of an elitist image, and it has not done much to change this image.

The decline of Meretz is clearly related to its nonconformity with a reality in which most of the Israeli public has become (largely because of the second intifada) more right-wing, with religious tradition playing a more salient role in Israeli society. But a deeper and broader look reveals that Meretz lost its attraction precisely because it succeeded. Many of its principles, which were once considered radical, are almost a consensus today, even if some of these principles are still far from being fully implemented. The central banner Meretz raised—two states for two peoples—is accepted by most of the public. When Aloni worked to overturn the law prohibiting homosexual activity, she was seen as a provocative extremist. Today, Israel's Foreign Ministry promotes Tel Aviv as the global capital of homosexuals. When Sarid protested against the Lebanon War and later quit the Labor Party over this issue, some viewed him as a traitor. Today, even Begin's loyalists recognize that the war was a mistake.

Many parties lose their relevance precisely when their values become acceptable. This happened to the General Zionists/Liberal Party, which waned as Israel became more bourgeois. This happened to the Tehiya party, whose mix of religious and secular Jews was a harbinger of the Jewish Home's approach today. This is also happening to Meretz. In recent years, Meretz has been at an ideological and political crossroads in terms of its place and contribution to Israeli society. Beilin, a Mapai man in essence and by his own definition, was not the right person to lead it in a new direction.

Beilin himself says that during his last months as chairman of Meretz, he realized that if he continued in this role he might unwittingly prove his doctoral thesis about the impact of intergenerational struggles in political parties. One of the conclusions of his dissertation was that at a particular stage, when the new generation that develops in the party seeks to spread its wings, the party's old guard fears it will lose its standing. Consequently, a personal struggle ensues that leads to stagnation instead of a search for new ideological paths. He felt this conclusion personally—for example, after one of his speeches at a Meretz gathering. On the way to his car, a young party activist approached and told him that she supported his stance on peace, "but I'll never vote for you." When Beilin asked why, she looked at his shoes and said in disgust: "You have leather shoes!"

This was the first time in his political life, in which he had become accustomed to accusations and slurs, that he had been castigated for wearing leather shoes. Since he was already thinking about stepping down, this anecdote was like the straw that broke the camel's back. He realized that a new, young generation was emerging in the left that was no longer focused, as it was during his day, on the pursuit of peace. The young left— in Israel and in the Western world—mobilizes around animal rights, environmental issues, LGBT rights, immigrants, the fight against globalization and neocapitalism, and so on. Beilin identifies with these issues, but they are not what impelled him to enter politics. As he pondered over his encounter with the young activist, he recognized that it was time for one of the most progressive and bold politicians in Israel to call it quits.

5

Since his departure from politics, Beilin has focused primarily on the company he formed—Beilink, a play on words designed to reflect the essence of the company: facilitating business initiatives in Israel and the world. The first investor in the company was Michael Steinhardt, an American businessman who also supported Beilin's efforts to create the Birthright project. Beilink helps its Israeli clients to promote business interests overseas via a network of contacts Beilin developed over the years, and similarly assists its foreign clients in conducting business in Israel. He surprised himself when he chose the independent business route. When he left politics, he thought he would land in a senior salaried position, but his sons, Gil and Ori, convinced him that he was still young enough to pursue a more challenging venture. Though his main advantage, as noted, is his web of global contacts, he does not see this as inappropriate exploitation of the political standing he acquired. In his view, he is making natural use of the assets and ability he accrued to benefit his company, which operates transparently and tends to promote social initiatives and Israeli interests.

Beilin also experienced a significant change in his personal life. After a divorce from his wife Helena in 2001, a romantic relationship developed with Daniela Raanan-Sielski, a long-time Labor Party activist. The couple live in Ramat Aviv. Beilin maintains good relations with Helena, who together with her partner, Yaakov Israeli, provided legal services for Beilink. They celebrate holidays and family occasions together with their children and grandchildren.

Beilin enjoys this new stage in his life. He believes that the many cases of divorce among those of his generation is an expression of an era in which people have options that were not available to previous generations. However, the norms and laws have not kept pace with the social developments. He is now thinking of a way to institutionalize divorce, in the same way that marriage is institutionalized, in order to avoid souring relations with family members and friends, and ruining the memories the couple shares. The social order should be adapted to reality, and thus prevent the rift that many still experience in the wake of divorce.

Beilin is close to his sons. Gil, formerly a television editor, and Ori, a musician, work together in an independent advertising agency. They also advise their father on marketing Beilink and have friendly relations with Daniela.

When he was in high school, Gil chaired the Labor Party's youth organization and later served as the party's representative in the student association at Tel Aviv University. However, the assassination of Rabin, and even more, Netanyahu's victory in 1996, convinced him to abandon the political path. (In 2016, Gil returned to political involvement, joining the Labor Party. Unlike his father, who raised the diplomatic banner as the focus of his political activity, Gil announced that he was primarily interested in domestic issues, especially road safety.) He is married to Ziv, an attorney, and the two are raising two daughters—who spend a lot of time with Grandfather Yossi and his wife. Ori is married to Mari, and they also have two children who enjoy their grandfather's babysitting care. Unlike his brother, Ori is completely uninvolved in politics.

Beilin, who serves as the honorary chairperson of the Geneva Initiative, has not abandoned the diplomatic arena, and stays in contact with senior PA officials and foreign statesmen. He also is involved in an initiative to locate and preserve ancient Jewish cemeteries in Eastern Europe, and recently took on a volunteer role as head of the Hillel organization in Israel. Hillel, the largest student organization in the Jewish world, operates at eight Israeli colleges and universities.

Though he is formally still a member of Meretz, he does not participate in any political forum. He presents his ideas in interviews and in articles that he writes for the *Israel Hayom* newspaper, where he enjoys communicating with a broad audience from a different political milieu than the one he is accustomed to addressing.

As a private citizen, Beilin allows himself to raise subjects that he refrained from addressing as a public official. He announced his decision to contribute his body to science, and also suggests changing the law so that the organs of every deceased person are automatically contributed to science and medicine—unless the person signs a refusal. He asks to cremate any of his organs that are not needed for transplants or science. Beilin does not believe in life after death and is confident that his loved ones will find a way to remember him without a grave to visit.

From time to time, he expresses opinions that challenge the consensus. For example, after Moshe Katsav, the former president, was convicted of rape and sentenced to prison, Beilin said that it would be best to release him after he acknowledges his guilt and apologizes, because Katsav was already sufficiently punished and there was no benefit in humiliating him and the state. He continued to express this view until Katsav was released in December 2016 after serving his sentence.

In September 2016, hours after the death of Binyamin Ben-Eliezer, Beilin surprised listeners by making blunt statements about the character of the deceased. For example, he said that Ben-Eliezer symbolized the lack of morality in Israeli politics. The interviews he granted stirred a fury because of the timing, but Beilin stuck to his words. His remarks naturally reflected the resentment Beilin harbored toward Ben-Eliezer, who was largely responsible for pushing him out of the Knesset. Primarily, however, they reflected his trait of speaking his mind on issues that he viewed as crucial. In a cold calculation, he concluded that his critique of Ben-Eliezer's ethics would not be effective unless it was expressed immediately on the day of his death. As happened throughout his career, many were disgusted by his words, while others admired his audacity.

Beilin's relations with Peres also suffered a near fatal blow after he quit politics. When Peres was the president, he updated Beilin about the talks he conducted with Abu Mazen, with Netanyahu's approval. But in 2011, when the talks reached the stage of fundamental understandings, the prime minister decided to put on the brakes. Beilin expected Peres to go public with this information, and even resign, and thus shake the political arena. In Beilin's eyes, Peres should have made this one last real contribution to the peace process. But Peres decided to refrain from speaking out, preferring to maintain correct relations with Netanyahu in the name of *mamlachtiyut* (statism). Beilin, disappointed, told Peres that he had taught him to be bold. The relations between the two chilled after this episode. Nonetheless, and though the two were never friends, Beilin still held deep and warm feelings toward Peres. After the latter completed his tenure as president, Beilin and Peres resumed their regular meetings.

# Epilogue to Peace

1

Beilin's public image was and remains the classic "leftist." Still, more than anything else, and despite the temptation to label him as Moshe Sharett's successor in his diplomatic orientation, Beilin is a Mapainik, a political dove close in spirit to Ben-Gurion in his later years.

His aspiration for a territorial compromise springs primarily from his view of Israel's security needs. Beilin recognizes the need to exercise force from time to time. He supported the First Lebanon War, though he preferred a limited operation, and even proposed directly attacking Syria to deter Hezbollah. Beilin has never crossed the fence toward supporting refusal to serve in the IDF, opposes the movements calling to impose a boycott on the State of Israel, and worries about the removal of the hyphen connecting Israel's Jewish and democratic character.

He articulated his views prior to the 2015 elections in a public debate conducted in the newspapers with Avrum Burg, his former partner in the Labor Party. The debate between the two was one of the most profound and principled discussions conducted in the twenty-first century by politicians representing the left, and it helps to locate Beilin on the ideology scale.

Under a headline "I feel for you, my brother Avrum," Beilin responded to Burg's decision to support the Hadash party:

Joining the Hadash council is not a crime, of course. It's a legitimate party, with democratic elements, and it has an interesting history—for example, support for the partition decision in 1947 and its pioneering stance on the two-state solution. On the other hand, it supported Stalin and saw the Soviet Union as a worthy governmental and social model. But Hadash is not a Zionist party, and if you will, it's an anti-Zionist party that views Zionism as coercion, occupation, abuse and theft—not as a project to rescue a people that was oppressed and persecuted in almost all of the countries in which it lived. It is certainly legitimate to maintain a non-Zionist party in Israel, and even an anti-Zionist one, like all of the ultra-Orthodox parties. However, your move—as a person born in the most Zionist home imaginable, who headed the World Zionist Organization (whose time has past, and which should be replaced by a new and representative institution) and headed the Jewish Agency (which since the creation of the state has no reason to exist)—to a party that rejects Zionism is a move that is hard to bear.[1]

Beilin explicitly placed himself on the other side of the popular trend among many young people in the Zionist left, who are looking for new solutions, including a state of all its citizens. Beilin's Zionism was and remains a national and moral idea designed—certainly in the wake of the Holocaust—to enable the Jewish people to exercise its self-determination in its own state. The Law of Return, which also was a point of dispute with Burg, is in his view a lofty expression of the essence of Zionism as a destination and place of refuge for the Jews of the world.

Burg responded in a dramatic article of his own, in which he called Beilin "the most important person in my political life" and "the person who went the furthest possible toward the limits of the Zionist genre." But Burg argued that Beilin's "ethical and ideological path has reached its end." According to Burg, Beilin was wrong in attributing the failure to realize the two-state model to a lack of political courage among Israeli and Palestinian leaders. Instead, he placed the blame on Beilin's "fundamental assumptions" that still identify the goal of Zionism as an ethnic nation-state:

Zionism has been an amazing success for Israel's Jewish citizens, but it has been a cause of despair for everyone else. The duty therefore is to continue ahead to the next stage in Israel's evolution, toward full equality and democracy. With Israel's establishment, the role of the Zionist movement came to an end and it should be succeeded and filled by a sense of Israeliness . . . the contemporary version of Zionism in Israel is the main system that creates discrimination between Jews and everyone else. This Zionism enables selective acceptance to towns and places of employment, the declaration of absolute monopolies for Jews over resources of land, nature, liberty, rights and identity. Tell me honestly: Isn't Zionism in Israel actually a type of racism?

I believe that the only way to save Israel from the threat of destruction from within is by exchanging nationalist discourse for civil discourse. It involves a transition from a terrible struggle between preferential rights for Jews and excessive distress for Arabs to creating a joint, fair civil space. The Zionist viewpoint, even the liberal and moderate one on which Beilin and I were raised, never seriously intended to transition from the Zionism of Jews to the citizenship of all . . . Beilin, the determined, courageous and sincere Zionist, is committed to paradigms of separation between the peoples and the communities, of physical and psychological walls between citizens. . . . Therefore, as strange as this may sound: My dear friend Beilin is not a leftist. Because left is not only a bold diplomatic accord, but also a complete system of values and principles. Two of the fundamental ones are equality and justice. And these, as the reality demonstrates, can no longer live under the Zionist umbrella. Not even that of Beilin.[2]

Burg is correct in arguing that Beilin and the ideological path he charted cannot be placed exactly in the left. Rather than ideology, Beilin was driven by pure Mapainik

Zionism, which sought to make the best of what was possible. Roughly speaking, there is no fundamental difference between Beilin's aspiration for a Jewish and democratic state and the stance of Netanyahu, who declared his readiness to partition the land in his famous Bar-Ilan speech in 2009. However, as Ben-Gurion claimed throughout his life, the differences between Zionist A and Zionist B lie first and foremost in the readiness to initiate, execute, and implement, and Beilin, indeed, identified and tried to contend with the curse of the occupation earlier and more effectively than many others. He was willing to pay the price for this, and not just the lip service that Netanyahu was prepared to pay.

The question is whether Burg is also right in the solution he offers to the young leftists who will replace Beilin and those of his generation. That is, should the vision of the Jewish-democratic state be abandoned in favor of a state of all its citizens, in which citizenship is the formative and unifying factor? In my view, there is little feasibility of a state of all its citizens, and its chances of surviving the Jewish-Arab conflict in the Middle East—which will persist even during a time of peace with the Palestinians (see, for example, the Islamic State organization) —are low. In an era of burgeoning nationalism, in Europe and in North America, and against the background of the volatile mix of religion and nationhood—contrary to the possibility raised here earlier, of mitigating nationalism via religion—a state of all its citizens is more dangerous than promising.

The way in which the oases of normality in Israel (Jaffa, for example) quickly erupted in September 2015 with the outbreak of the "intifada of knives," and the speed at which stabbings and executions in the streets became routine in Israel during that period, are stark warning signs regarding the notion of a state of all its citizens. When we think about Israel as a democratic Western state, which it actually is to a large extent, the expression "civil war" sounds far-fetched. But when you describe it as a Middle Eastern state, which, indeed, it is to a large extent, then the possibility of Israel experiencing a civil war as part of a "Palestinian Spring" within the Green Line would appear more tangible if it were a state of all its citizens.

From the moral perspective, too, it is doubtful whether a state of all its citizens is a justified idea, because the two sides would be forced to relinquish their respective Jewish and Palestinian identities in exchange for the new civic identity.

Therefore, the support of many leftists for the one-state option is today a greater threat to Beilin's path than the threat posed by the political right. The one-state formula has become a trend in recent years, particularly in academia, and from there it has reached the elites and the young generation of both nations. In the Jewish left and radical right, and among Palestinians on both sides of the Green Line, proponents of the two-state option are seen as archaic.

In light of the disappointment over the non-implementation of the Oslo Accords, and even more so after the events of October 2000, they view the "tension" between the Jewish and democratic components in Israel's definition as an irreconcilable contradiction, which can only be resolved if Israel becomes a state of all its citizens. The contention is that until there is complete equality—which requires eliminating the privileges accorded to Jews in Israel—there cannot be true coexistence. Of course, the political disappointment over the classic left's failed efforts to gain power has also contributed to the search for new horizons.

However, the one-state option's appealing fantasy of a shared and egalitarian life is unfeasible. It is nothing more than a theoretical formula. One state would not mitigate the conflict. On the contrary, it would intensify the outbursts of hostility between the communities, even if only instigated by an extremist minority.

The need for separation is also evident when considering the broader context. If it was possible to think that the world was marching toward a blurring of national identities after the establishment of the European Union, the first two decades of the twenty-first century illustrate that national identities, sometimes overlapping with religious identities, are only growing stronger. A state of all its citizens—though justification can be found for it if we choose to ignore the historical experience of the Jews—would meet the same fate as in Yugoslavia. Therefore, even if the evacuation of settlers becomes more problematic as time goes by, it is still an easier mission than contending with civil war.

The idea of partition as a possible solution was first proposed by the British in June 1937, when the Peel Commission's conclusions were published during the Palestinians' "Great Revolt." Nearly eighty years later, while the idea has gone out of fashion, it still offers the best prospects for coexistence.

## 2

Despite his adherence to the two-state model, Beilin cites two main failures in his path.

The first is personal. He failed to convince Rabin, and later Peres, to adopt the idea of trying to reach a final status accord at a time when he believed this was possible.

The second is more fundamental, and it pertains to the way the two-state idea was addressed. From the outset, the main goal of the peace process was separation, not coexistence. This was a mistake, Beilin believes. This was the key characteristic of the policies of Rabin, Peres, and Barak. The goal of separation is one of the paradoxes characterizing the difference between the left and the right in Israel: While the peace camp (the left) seeks to separate the two populations, the right is prepared to live alongside the Arabs in one state (albeit with lesser privileges for the latter). But peace will not be achieved when the Palestinians are treated as those to be separated from or subjected to discriminatory restrictions. Peace will be achieved only when the Israelis—and the Palestinians, too, of course—aspire to achieve an accord based on a recognition that the two peoples will be partners for life in the same space.

Against this background, Beilin wrote a retrospective article for the *New York Times*, published on May 14, 2015, to mark Israel's sixty-seventh Independence Day. The article made relatively few waves in Israel, but it included important soul-searching. He wrote that after the Oslo Accords were signed, "political leaders on both sides adopted the popular assumption that a final peace settlement must resemble a divorce—each side ridding itself of the other. Ehud Barak coined a campaign slogan:

'We are here and they are there.' And after a hurricane of violence began in 2000, too few of us in the Israeli peace camp opposed building a separation wall. In that way, even we contributed to fear and separation." The barrier of fear served the opponents of the peace process. Thus, Beilin concluded in hindsight: "It is clear that we should have been looking all along at confederation—cohabitation, not divorce."[3]

In this context, he recounts a conversation he had with Faisal al-Husseini in 1993, in the early days of the Rabin government, when Beilin was still seeking to bypass the PLO and before turning to the Oslo backchannel. Al-Husseini expressed hard-line views against Israel and its treatment of the Palestinians, but also asserted that the only option for a sustainable accord requires looking at the conflict through a lens of cooperation rather than separation. He acknowledged that he was bound by the PLO's positions and that after decades of conflict it would be difficult to convince public opinion on both sides to accept an accord that does not focus on separating into two states. However, he contended, a more farsighted perspective would clearly show the benefits of a confederative framework for the two states.[4] This approach was not adopted. The Oslo process was based on the motif of separation—between Israel and Palestine, and between the settlers in the territories and their Palestinian neighbors. Later, in the wake of the second intifada, the idea of separation found expression in a barrier constructed roughly along the Green Line, and the proliferation of bypass roads in the West Bank that protected the settlements as enclaves among Palestinian villages and cities.

According to Beilin, the next generation will be responsible for improving the Oslo formula in order to reach an accord based on two states, Israel and Palestine, linked in a way that will enable them to preserve their national identities, while sharing life in their common homeland.

## 3

Israel in 2018 does not offer great optimism about a peace agreement with the Palestinians. The last significant negotiations were conducted in 2008 between Olmert and Abu Mazen. Olmert presented a map of Palestine that stretched over 93.5 percent of the territories: Israel would annex the settlement blocs that account for 6.5 percent of the territories and, in return, would give the Palestinians land equal to 5.8 percent of the territories (east of the Gaza Strip and adjacent to the West Bank). In Jerusalem, Olmert proposed two separate municipalities for two capitals, and an "umbrella municipality" above them (that would reflect the Jewish majority). It was the most generous offer any Israeli prime minister has offered the Palestinians, and Olmert says he was ready to further accommodate them.[5] In principle, Olmert's proposal was based on the Beilin-Abu Mazen understandings from 1995, though it, too, was not put to a real test—in part, because Olmert was already immersed in criminal investigations and his political power was limited.

Since Netanyahu's return to power in 2009, the Israelis and Palestinians are quite distant in their opening positions, and with the exception of security coordination, there are essentially no contacts between them. The Middle East is still in the throes of the Arab Spring and, in light of the turmoil in the region, Israelis are satisfied with the stability of the Netanyahu era. The fact that a relative quiet has prevailed in the territories makes it easier to forget the question of Israel's future relations with the Palestinians. The election of Donald Trump as president of the United States has also lowered expectations that a new American initiative could restart the peace process and lead to a breakthrough.

Nonetheless, Beilin is far from despair. He is an optimist by nature. (He also believes there is a correlation between optimism and a leftist orientation, and between pessimism and a right-wing outlook on life.) And he still believes that the two-state model is the correct and feasible formula. In fact, he is so optimistic that his plans are aimed at the post-conflict era. In Beilin's view, achieving a lasting peace accord will be only one key chapter in the effort to instill meaning in Israel's existence. Moreover, and paradoxically, he believes that Jewish identity among Diaspora Jews is liable to wane in an era of peace. That is, when there is less concern for the security of Israel—which today serves as a focal point of Jewish identity—there will also be less interest in it, and Israel will lose its uniqueness.

Consequently, assimilation will increase, the connection with the Diaspora will weaken and the threat to the continuity of the Jewish people will grow stronger. As a person who is not religious and does not believe in God, Beilin has no profound philosophical answer to explain why the continued existence of the Jewish people is important. But it is important, even if the answer is teleological—just as continued self-existence is important, or in the same way that it is important for a person to ensure the existence of his offspring. Therefore, he proposes replacing the Jewish Agency with a new institution: a worldwide Jewish parliament that would position Israel as the cultural and spiritual center of the Jewish people.

The new parliament would not be defined as Zionist, since Zionism has already been realized and it no longer needs to contend with the Jewish alternatives that threatened it (ultra-Orthodoxy, which is developing its own connection to the State of Israel; or the Bund, which was wiped out with the destruction of East European Jewry in the Holocaust). The Jewish parliament, envisioned to exist alongside the Knesset and not above it, would address various Jewish issues, including encouraging Jewish immigration to Israel, assistance to communities in distress, and strengthening the connection to Israel, which is still the only option for Jewish life in the historical homeland, under a system of norms and laws that draw from Jewish history. To walk on the roads on Yom Kippur without a single car passing, even if you are not fasting; to smell the potatoes on Lag B'Omer, even if you are not participating in a bonfire; to know you are no longer a minority, not even a minority with equal rights—all this, from Beilin's perspective, is the essence of the State of Israel as the guardian of the embers of Judaism in an era of peace.

The Jewish parliament would represent the Jewish community and conduct regular discussions on issues of the day and questions of morality and values—including those that do not directly pertain to Jews. The parliament would be funded by membership dues collected from all of the Jews in the world, and from contributions that would still be collected by the United Jewish Appeal and Keren Hayesod; the Israel Bonds organization would be disbanded and become an investment fund in Israel. The fact that the parliament would not be funded by large donations would free it from dependence on philanthropists, thus facilitating the emergence of a generation of Jewish leaders that is not exclusively composed of millionaires. The Jewish parliament would be called Beit Yisrael (The House of Israel). In this way, the Jewish state would fully blend the political Zionism of Herzl with the cultural Zionism of Ahad Ha'am.

# Afterword

## 1

In June 1993, after Rabin had already taken over leadership of the talks with PLO representatives in Oslo, he surprised Peres and Beilin by deciding to halt the Oslo process. In a letter he sent to Peres, Rabin cited the dangers of direct contacts with the PLO and asked to renew the official talks with the Palestinian delegation in Washington.[1]

The revelation of the letter ostensibly supports the narrative claiming that Rabin was dragged by Peres and Beilin into the Oslo process unwillingly. Itamar Rabinovich, then Israel's ambassador in Washington and in charge of the talks with Syria, also stated that Rabin would have preferred to pursue the Syrian track rather than the Oslo track. There is no doubt that talking with the PLO was not Rabin's first choice. However, it is a fundamental error to say that he was "dragged" into pursuing this route. From the moment he was informed about the Oslo backchannel, Rabin was involved in every detail. His doubts along the way, until he concluded there was no realistic alternative, underline how deeply he recognized the significance of his decision to negotiate with the PLO.

Israel's leaders fully understood that the signing of an agreement with the PLO was a historic turning point in the state's relations with the Palestinian organization. However, the documents in Beilin's archives indicate how they failed to deeply examine the significance of the rapprochement and its repercussions on the two sides. The main reason for Israel's readiness to engage in dialogue with the PLO—which since 1988 had moderated its views, adopted the two-state formula, and recognized Israel's right to exist—was its assessment that the organization was at its very weakest in the wake of the Gulf War and that Israel should exploit this. This was the main reason for pursuing the Oslo talks, Peres explained to Secretary of State Warren Christopher immediately after the signing of the Declaration of Principles.[2] Indeed, the PLO was weak and isolated. The emergence of local leaders in the territories during the first intifada, the collapse of the Soviet Union that left the region under almost exclusive US patronage, the PLO's identification with Saddam Hussein during the First Gulf War— all contributed to weakening the PLO and compelled it to look for a new direction in direct talks with Israel.

In retrospect, it is apt to wonder whether it was, indeed, possible to overcome the hostility of more than a century through a paradigm of realpolitik, which sought to exploit the weakness of the other side, rather than through an approach in which both sides address the roots of the conflict and are prepared to recognize their wrongdoings. According to Col. (ret.) Ephraim Lavie, who represented the IDF intelligence branch in Israel's Camp David delegation in 2000: "The Oslo process failed because the decisions of the two sides to peacefully resolve the conflict were not complete and were not substantive and strategic."[3] In other words, both sides saw the negotiating process as a tactical move, enabling them to gain time and win international favor, while holding out for a more comfortable solution in the future. However, full reconciliation should be based on internal recognition of the value of the rival and his contentions. Thus, the dimension of "justice"—that is, an aspiration to redress historical grievances and not only achieve a concrete solution—turned out to be critical during the negotiations on a permanent accord at the Camp David summit in 2000. (The Palestinians insisted that Israel recognize the Palestinian right of return as an expression of the injustice they suffered, though they were willing to compromise on this right in practice.) In addition, conflict resolution studies have shown that disparities of power (and Israel has always demanded in negotiations to preserve its superior power) are an incentive for making conflicts violent.[4] That is, paradoxically, if Israel, indeed, wants peace, it should ultimately seek to establish a sustainable and democratic Palestinian state, with power of its own.

The breakthrough in Oslo was primarily on the symbolic level—the readiness to shake the hand of someone who was considered a bitter enemy of the Zionist movement and the State of Israel. The Oslo agreement was successful at the outset because the Israelis and the Palestinians skipped over the critical core issues, leaving them for later. For this very reason, the interim accords and arrangements that followed the Declaration of Principles were hollow in many ways. As we have seen, the sides refrained from seriously addressing the crucial issues in the Oslo Accords. There was no prohibition on settlement construction, though it came to a near halt during Rabin's term. Borders, sovereignty over the holy sites in Jerusalem, and the right of return were all postponed until final status negotiations. The problem is that Israel later continued to ignore the impact of the roots of the conflict on the Palestinians' positions; the various narratives were not given serious attention. In fact, except for the fact that the agreement was signed between Israel and the PLO (and not between Israel and Palestinian representatives from the territories, which Israel had sought since the 1970s), the Oslo Accords offered nothing new. They were only intended to add real content to the autonomy agreement Begin signed along with the Egypt-Israel peace treaty.[5] Rabin regarded the postponement of the core issues as an achievement that would allow him to gauge the seriousness and sincerity of the Palestinians during the years slated for autonomy. In other words, Rabin recognized the PLO, but he remained suspicious about its intentions. This made the Palestinian side no less suspicious of Israel's motives. Israel's proposals—regarded in the Israeli public as far-reaching, including those Ehud Olmert presented during his term as prime minister (2006–09) during the Annapolis negotiations and to Abu Mazen personally—are referred to by the Palestinians as *mu'amara*: a sophisticated conspiracy designed to create a limited state for them.[6]

Beilin feared that suspicions would only intensify with time, and tried to convince Rabin to build upon the momentum generated in public opinion on both sides in the wake of the Oslo Accords and immediately begin negotiating a final status accord. Rabin thought otherwise; he explained his preference for an agreement in stages by arguing that if the attempt to reach a permanent accord fails, it would be impossible to restart negotiations at the comfortable starting point that preceded the final status talks. The failure to bridge the gaps between the two sides would thus result in bloodshed (as, indeed, occurred after Barak's failed attempt to negotiate a permanent accord at Camp David in 2000.) Rabin feared that the Palestinians would balk at signing a permanent accord, but would use the Israeli promises they received during the final status talks as the starting point for future negotiations.

But herein lies the trap. If Israel is not ready in advance to pay the practical, symbolic, and narrative price required in exchange for full reconciliation, there is really no reason to embark on a process that aims toward such reconciliation. This only serves to increase Palestinian disappointment after building up expectations during the process, and the consequence is likely to be expressed in violence, which, in turn, convinces the Israelis that "there is no one to talk with"—no partner for peace.

Akram Haniyeh's Camp David diary illustrates that without Israel's readiness to relinquish sovereignty over the Temple Mount there will be no peace. Therefore, the question is not whether it is best to work immediately for a permanent accord, or to slow the pace of interim agreements. The question is: To what extent is Israel ready to make concessions when the moment of truth comes? This question was not discussed during the days of Rabin and Peres. The documents in Beilin's archives indicate that at no stage—from the time of Oslo until the collapse of Barak's government in 2001—was Israel ready or able to meet the Palestinians' demands. From the latter's perspective, the willingness to suffice with a state in the 1967 borders without fully exercising the right of return was already a major compromise. That is, even if they received 100 percent of the West Bank and Gaza Strip, they would remain with only 22 percent of the territory of Mandatory Palestine.

## 2

Beilin believes that the gradual and slow pace was detrimental to the process because it allowed the extremists on both sides plenty of time to undermine it. (We should recall that until the massacre executed by Baruch Goldstein in the Cave of the Patriarchs in February 1994, Hamas did not carry out suicide bombings within the Green Line.) However, even if Israel had tried to advance a permanent accord, the positions of the Rabin government would not have allowed true rapprochement.

"The absence of an honest effort among Palestinians and Israelis to confront the painful facts of history has seriously hindered reconciliation between Israel and eight Arab countries with which it is at peace or has commercial or diplomatic relations,"[7] the historian Rashid Khalidi wrote in a postmortem of the Oslo process. That is, the accord proposed in Oslo was mainly "functional," addressing territory and systems of governance, and failed to tackle the fundamental questions that brought Zionism into conflict with the Palestinians.

After all, the conflict was not (and is still not) only about the present and future; it was (and still is) about the past, too. However, Israel's leadership believed it would be easier to conduct negotiations as if it were a real estate deal.[8] With the exception of Rabin's statement (in his last Knesset speech in October 1995) that "we did not come here to an empty country," Israel refrained from addressing the narrative of the conflict, its responsibility for the plight of the Palestinians, and the significance of the agreement in terms of the historical path of Zionism. Yet these questions were critical for the Palestinians. Israel sought to put "an end to the story" of the conflict without attending to its narrative. However, unlike a story, a national narrative has no ending. Dealing with the past also has implications for the present and the future. Therefore, it is important. Without addressing the narratives of the conflict—that is, the questions pertaining not only to 1967 but also to 1948, and even to the early Zionist settlements in the late nineteenth century—there will be no real end to the conflict.

Shlomo Ben-Ami, who served as both foreign minister and public security minister during the twilight of the Barak government (a strange combination of ministerial portfolios, which also reflects Barak's manipulative approach to the peace process), wrote in retrospect that the main obstacle to achieving a final status accord was that the Palestinians were more concerned about "vindication and justice" than about a solution.[9] However, justice cannot be ignored because it is viewed by the Palestinians as an essential ingredient in the path toward a solution. Already in the 1920s, the Palestinians rejected various proposals for resolving the conflict with Zionism—not because they were blind to the possibilities, but because from their perspective the conflict was rooted in the inherent injustice of the Jewish drive for independence in the centuries-old homeland of the Palestinians. Thus, the conflict, in their eyes, stemmed from injustice. It is possible to accept their view, and it is possible to argue with it. (As a Zionist who believes in the justice of the basic argument of Zionism, and as a historian who is familiar with the many attempts by Zionists of various political stripes to offer the Palestinians formulas for peace since the 1920s, I am convinced that the Palestinians bear a considerable part of the responsibility for the lack of peace.) However, Israelis cannot deceive themselves into thinking that it is possible to achieve coexistence without addressing the negative impact of the Zionist project, however justified it might be, on the realization of Palestinian nationalism.

3

One of the reasons that Beilin failed to realize his vision is that the Israeli-Palestinian conflict is, indeed, complex, with various dimensions. The conflict has been an integral part of the historical reality of the Middle East at least since the late nineteenth century, and often reaches back to the biblical and pre-biblical periods. (In recent years, for example, some have claimed that the Palestinians are the descendants of the Canaanites.) And, indeed, despite the extensive discussion of this conflict in the media and in academic discourse in Israel and abroad, Beilin's archives show how blind we still are to some of its elements.

In many cases, public declarations on the issues in dispute are just cover for arguments that are only heard behind closed doors and express additional dimensions of the conflict. The city of Ariel is a case in point. In the eyes of most Israelis, Ariel must remain under Israeli sovereignty in any two-state solution. This demand has been accepted by all of the Israeli leaders who conducted negotiations after Oslo. (Only in the Geneva Initiative in 2003 did the Israeli team agree that Ariel would be part of the Palestinian state and its Israeli residents would be evacuated. Amnon Lipkin-Shahak, the former IDF chief of staff and a signatory of the Geneva Accords, advocated ceding Ariel to the Palestinians, arguing that Israel should not be burdened with sovereign responsibility for a city located far from its future border.)

The Palestinian demand for sovereignty over Ariel is interpreted in Israel as a territorial dispute that will require Israel to compensate the Palestinians with land swaps. However, the Palestinians' claim to Ariel, as expressed for example in the Annapolis talks in 2008, includes an additional dimension. One of the problems with Ariel, from their perspective, is that it was deliberately built in the area of a key aquifer in an effort to secure future water resources for Israel at the expense of the Palestinians.[10] Indeed, the battle of water resources is an important dimension in the conflict, though it is less often mentioned in public declarations by the two sides.

There is only one dimension that might change the state of affairs, but its impact is impossible to measure: the dimension of time. Another generation or two, or even more, may be needed for the Palestinians' foundational traumas to recede into oblivion. Thus, we return to one of the basic arguments Jabotinsky raised in *The Iron Wall*. Already in 1923, he saw that a compromise would not be reached until the Palestinians had time to come to terms with Zionism, because they could only understand the Jews' return to their biblical homeland as an invasion by settlers, displacing indigent people from their land—however justified the Jews' return to their historical homeland might be from the perspective of the Jewish historical and Zionist narrative. (He recognized that the viewpoint of each side was subjectively justified in the eyes of their beholders, but believed that the demands of Jewish justice outweighed those of the Palestinians because the Jews were "starving" while the Palestinians' "appetite" could be satisfied in one of the Arab states.) Since it was impossible to bridge the two conflicting positions, Jabotinsky accepted the need to live by the sword, to build an iron wall until both sides understand that it is impossible to defeat the other by force. What Jabotinsky could not have foreseen was that when the Palestinians finally agreed to divide the land and compromise, the Jews would need many more years before accepting the Palestinian demands as justified.

4

In the absence of a peace accord, and against the background of Israel's control of the 1967 territories, the filmmaker Udi Aloni defines Israel as an "apartheid state."[11] Aloni, the son of Shulamit Aloni, is a proponent of a binational state and believes the Oslo process failed because it was the continuation of the colonial project designed to rule over the Palestinians through more sophisticated means.

Aloni's thesis reflects a trend of radicalization that began in the left (and in the right) concerning the current situation and future solutions. He is wrong, in my opinion, in his analysis of the Oslo process, in his utopian vision, and in defining Israel as an apartheid state. A serious comparison of the characteristics of apartheid in South Africa and the situation in Israel cannot ignore the significant and salient differences.[12]

Although the Zionist project has characteristics that appear at first glance to be colonialist (if Zionists are seen as white Europeans who came from the West to the East under the patronage of the British Empire), other elements in this project contradict its definition as colonialist: the Jews of Europe were "the blacks" during the period of exile; the Zionist enterprise had no mother state, and relations between the British and the Jews descended into violence during the years of the British Mandate; the Zionists wanted to use the natural resources of Palestine for local development, not for export; the original Zionist aspiration for "Hebrew labor" is contrary to the colonialist inclination to exploit the local labor force; and it is difficult to deny the Jews' primeval connection to the Land of Israel.

It is true that since its establishment, the State of Israel (by its very definition as the state of the Jewish people) offers preference to Jews in certain areas, but there is no separation based on race in Israel and there is no legal hierarchy between Jews and Arabs. The restrictions imposed on the Palestinians in the territories, some of which (such as roads that Palestinians are prohibited from using), bring to mind the laws of apartheid, are ascribed to security needs, and in many ways the Palestinians live under an autonomous regime. Nonetheless, it should be noted that apartheid in South Africa developed, paradoxically, precisely as the white and black populations began to increasingly "mix" with one another. The history of South Africa shows that at a certain point in its history, the unifying dimension (in practice or in potential) grew stronger between whites and blacks in the context of a shared living space, and this stirred the desire for separation. That is, the racist mindset that sought to separate based on racial "superiority and purity" drew from a reality in which there was increasing interaction and partnership, which stirred fears among many of the whites. Consequently, they saw in apartheid a necessary form of government. The separation was also anchored in a "political theology" by whites who found justification for it in the Holy Scriptures.[13]

This is the danger that awaits Israel if we do not separate the two peoples. Therefore, the basic formula Beilin sought to promote—partitioning the land into two states—is still the best solution. However, what Aloni said jokingly to me one evening at a bar in Tel Aviv is worth serious attention: Aloni described himself as the most moderate person on the political scale in the Middle East, because his position is between that of the Islamic State organization and the extremists among the Jewish settlers.

# 5

In this context, perhaps the main problem plaguing the peace process is the fact that it is detached from those who are seen as representing the radical camps. In the Israeli-Palestinian context, there is a paradox: the two camps that are making it difficult to reach an accord—the settlers, on one side, and Hamas and the Islamic organizations, on the other side—are excluded from the process. At the same time, "moderates" on both sides reject the concessions required for peace. Jabotinsky wrote in 1938: "The root of the situation in the Land of Israel is the horrible fact that even the minimal demand of the moderate Arab and the minimal demand of the tiny Zionist are unbridgeable."[14] Correspondingly, Beilin, as a representative of the liberal camp, has warned during the past decade against an Israeli policy that "weakens the pragmatic Palestinian camp and strengthens Hamas,"[15] while PA officials make similar arguments.

But instead of trying in vain to moderate the moderates, perhaps it would be best to actually involve the "extremists" in the negotiations. In any case, as Israel's representatives have shown in the talks they have conducted with the Palestinians since 2001, the overriding Israeli focus in negotiations has shifted from security considerations to those pertaining to the settlers' positions and the need to evacuate as few settlers as possible in the framework of an accord.[16] So why not involve the settlers—whose number has grown fivefold since the Oslo process began—directly in the negotiations? (There are today about half a million settlers, including in East Jerusalem.) On the other hand, in this context, Hamas' decision in April 2017 to publish a document stating its readiness to accept a state in the 1967 borders is an important step in creating a new paradigm for the conflict. This document still rejected recognition of Israel, and the path to agreements with Hamas is long.[17] However, this was also the case in 1988, when the PLO declared its support for the two-state idea. It, too, was an initial and insufficient step (because the organization did not yet commit to refrain from terrorism), but five years later it provided a foundation for the accord between Israel and the PLO.

After all, against the background of their connection to religion, land, and absolute historical values, the radicals on both sides have a broader common denominator. One of the less-discussed conclusions of the peace process is that the exclusion of their representatives and views from the negotiations is the Achilles' heel of the process. We should actually be looking for peace between the positions of Hamas and the Israeli right, between Netanyahu's demand to compel the Palestinians to recognize Israel as a Jewish state and the Palestinians' demand for full sovereignty on the Temple Mount. On this issue, President Trump actually brings a far-reaching relativist approach that is willing to "tolerate" views, cultures, and patterns of government that are not acceptable in the liberal West in order to "close a deal." Perhaps the fact that his approach is not anchored in the liberal paradigm may surprisingly facilitate progress toward peace.

And if I am exaggerating in an effort to find a ray of light at a time when the facts, at least at first glance, do not offer many reasons for optimism, perhaps it is because there is no other way to conclude a book that revolves around the political biography of Yossi Beilin.

# Notes

## Introduction: The Left Wing Sorrow

1 See for example: "MK Miki Zohar: In the One State, Arabs Will Have Full Rights, Except Voting for the Knesset," *Walla!* March 6, 2017 [Hebrew].

2 Omar Zanany, *The Annapolis Process (2007-2008): Negotiation and Its Discontents*. Tel Aviv: Tami Steinmetz Center for Peace Research and Molad, 2015, p. 86.

3 In 2013, about 200,000 Jews lived in East Jerusalem, and this number has continued to grow in recent years.

4 Asher Susser, *Israel, Jordan and Palestine: The Two-State Imperative*. Brandeis University Press, 2011, pp. 213–15.

5 Ibid., pp. 213–30. Though support for the two-state idea has eroded over the years, it is still more popular than the other two alternatives—one state or a confederation. In a survey conducted in February 2017 by the Tami Steinmetz Center for Peace Research at Tel Aviv University and the Palestinian Center for Policy and Survey Research (PSR), 55 percent of the Israelis and 44 percent of the Palestinians supported a two-state solution. When the Oslo Accords were signed, over 66 percent of the Israelis and more than 70 percent of the Palestinians supported this idea.

6 Elie Holzer, "The Evolving Meaning of the 'Three Oaths' in Religious-Zionist Thought," *Daat: A Journal of Jewish Philosophy and Kabbalah*, Bar-Ilan University, 47, 2001, pp. 129–145 [Hebrew].

7 Alina Rocha Menocal and Kate Kilpatrick, "Toward More Effective Peace Building: A Conversation with Roland Paris," *Development in Practice* 15(6), 2005, p. 768.

8 Yossi Beilin's personal archives, Akram Haniyah's Camp David diary, July 2000.

9 Arie Dayan, "Barak Began Referring to the 'Holy of Holies,'" *Haaretz*, December 9, 2002.

10 Minxin Pei, "The Paradoxes of American Nationalism," *Foreign Policy* 136, 2003, p. 34.

11 Rashid Khalidi, "The Formation of Palestinian Identity: The Critical Years, 1917-1923," in James P. Jankowitz and Israel Gershoni (eds.), *Rethinking Nationalism in the Arab Middle East*. New York: Columbia University Press, 1997, pp. 171–90.

12 Yossi Beilin, *Touching Peace*. Tel Aviv: Yedioth Ahronoth, 2001, p. 170 [Hebrew].

13 Frantz Fanon, *The Wretched of the Earth*. Tel Aviv: Babel Publishers, 2006, p. 80 [Hebrew].

14 Michael Barnett, "Culture, Strategy and Foreign Policy Change: Israel's Road to Oslo," *European Journal of International Relations* 5(1), 1999, pp. 19–21.

15 On Shamir's attitude toward Judaism, see: Avi Shilon, "The Revisionist Movement Leaders' Attitudes Toward Jewish Religion, 1925-2005," PhD dissertation, Bar-Ilan University, 2014 [Hebrew].

16 José Casanova, *Public Religions in the Modern World*. Chicago, IL: University of Chicago, 1994.

17 Shmuel N. Eisenstadt, "The Transformation of the Religious Dimension and the Crystallization of New Civilizational Visions and Relations," in Gabriel Motzkin

and Yochi Fischer (eds.), *Religion and Democracy in Contemporary Europe*. London: Alliance Publishing Trust, 2008, pp. 21–35.

18  Paul Mendes-Flohr, *Divided Passions: Jewish Intellectuals and the Experience of Modernity*. Tel Aviv: Am Oved, 2010, p. 55 [Hebrew].

19  Yochi Fischer, "Secularization and Secularism: A Theoretical and Methodological Platform," in Yochi Fischer (ed.), *Secularization and Secularism: Interdisciplinary Perspectives*. Jerusalem: Van Leer Institute, 2016, p. 23 [Hebrew].

20  Guy Ziv, *Why Hawks Become Doves – Shimon Peres and Foreign Policy Change in Israel*. SUNY Press, 2015.

21  Baruch Kimmerling, *The End of Ashkenazi Hegemony*. Jerusalem: Keter, 2002, p. 11 [Hebrew].

22  Ziv Rubinovitz and Gerald Steinberg, "Menachem Begin's Autonomy Plan: Between Political Realism and Ideology," *The Public Sphere* 6, Tel Aviv: Tel Aviv University, 2012, pp. 75–95 [Hebrew].

23  Begin's official position was that there would be "full autonomy for the residents, but not for the territory," and he emphasized the "administrative nature of the self-rule." Menachem Begin, "The Autonomy Plan," *Maariv*, October 1, 1978 [Hebrew].

24  Begin's aide, Yehiel Kadishai, told me that Begin's long-range vision included readiness for a confederation with Jordan in which the Palestinians in the West Bank would be under joint Israeli-Jordanian patronage. Author's interview with Kadishai, May 20, 2014.

25  Gabriel Sheffer, "Moshe Sharett: His Moral Approach to the Israeli-Arab Conflict," in Ephraim Lavie (ed.), *Nationalism and Morality: Zionist Discourse and the Arab Question*. Jerusalem, Carmel, 2014, p. 189 [Hebrew].

26  Gabriel Sheffer, *Moshe Sharett: A Political Biography*. Jerusalem: Carmel Publishing House, 2015 [Hebrew].

27  Sheffer, "Moshe Sharett: His Moral Approach to the Israeli-Arab Conflict," pp. 177–97.

28  See for example: Avi Bareli, "The Partnership of Ben-Gurion and Sharett," a lecture at the Ben-Gurion House museum, February 6, 2015, and Benny Morris, *Israel's Border Wars: 1949-1956*. Oxford: Clarendon Press, 1997.

29  Zaki Shalom, "Ben-Gurion and Sharett's Opposition to Territorial Demands from Israel, 1949-1956," in *Iyunim Bitkumat Israel* 2, Sde Boker: Ben-Gurion Institute, 1992, pp. 197–213 [Hebrew].

30  Benny Morris, *The Birth of the Refugee Problem, 1947-1949*. Tel Aviv: Am Oved, 1991, p. 332 [Hebrew].

31  Sheffer, "Moshe Sharett: His Moral Approach to the Israeli-Arab Conflict," pp. 179–80.

32  See for example: Yehuda Shenhav, *In the Green Line Trap: A Jewish Political Treatise*. Tel Aviv: Am Oved, 2010 [Hebrew]; Atalia Omer, *When Peace Is Not Enough: How the Israeli Peace Camp Thinks about Religion, Nationalism and Justice*. Chicago: University of Chicago, 2013.

33  Uri Bialer, "The Road to the Capital: The Establishment of Jerusalem as the Official Seat of the Israeli Government in 1949," *Studies in Zionism* 5(2), 1984, pp. 273–96.

34  Moshe Sharett, "Israel and Arabia: War and Peace," parts of a lecture at Beit Berl, October 1957. The lecture was published in the Alignment's newspaper (*Ote*) in 1966 and appears on the website of the Moshe Sharett Heritage Society. Sharett's remarks came after he was relieved of his positions as prime minister and foreign minister in the wake of Ben-Gurion's return from his self-imposed hiatus in Sde Boker from 1953–1955. http://www.sharett.org.il/info/speeches/archive-002-israel-and-arabia-war-and-peace.htm

35 David Ben-Gurion, "Letter to Mapai Members," *Ben-Gurion Archives*, June 28, 1956 [Hebrew].

36 Avi Shlaim, *The Iron Wall: Israel and the Arab World*. New York: W. W. Norton & Co., 1999.

37 Ze'ev Jabotinsky, *Toward a State*. Jerusalem: Eri Jabotinsky, 1953, pp. 259–60 [Hebrew].

38 David Ben-Gurion, *The Renewed State of Israel*. Tel Aviv: Am Oved, 1975, p. 5. [Hebrew].

39 Benny Morris, *The Birth of the Refugee Problem, 1947-1949*, p. 325.

40 Moshe Sharett, "Israel and Arabia: War and Peace," p. 41.

41 Ibid.

42 Ibid.

43 For more on Ben-Gurion's views in later life, see: Avi Shilon, *Ben-Gurion: His Later Years in the Political Wilderness*. Lanham, MD: Rowman & Littlefield, 2016.

44 Binyamin Ze'ev Herzl, *The Jewish State [Der Judenstaat]*. Tel Aviv: Am Oved, 2008, p. 53 [Hebrew].

45 Isaac Epstein, "The Hidden Question," *HaShiloah*, August 1907, pp. 192–205 [Hebrew]. Ahad Ha'am, "Introduction to a New Edition," *At the Crossroads*, 1920.

46 On Golda Meir's rejection of the Rogers initiative and her preference for diplomatic stalemate rather than a land-for-peace deal with Egypt (as evident in her conversations with Henry Kissinger), see: Yigal Kipnis, "The Turning Point in Studying the Circumstances of the Outbreak of the Yom Kippur War," *Iyunim Bitkumat Israel* 26, Sde Boker: Ben-Gurion Institute, 2016, pp. 41–81 [Hebrew].

47 Cabinet meeting, June 19, 1967, article 561, Israel State Archives, A-8164/8 [Hebrew].

48 Dan Patir, "Rabin Dismisses Possibility of Negotiating with the Terrorists," *Davar*, July 14, 1974 [Hebrew].

49 Benny Morris, *One State, Two States: Israel and Palestine*. Tel Aviv: Am Oved, 2012, pp. 66–67 [Hebrew]. For more on Allon as a politician and his views, see: Udi Manor, *Yigal Allon: A Neglected Political Legacy, 1949–1980*. East Sussex: Sussex Academic Press, 2017; for the earlier Allon, see Anita Shapira, *Yigal Allon, Native Son*. Philadelphia: University of Pennsylvania Press, 2008.

50 Ephraim Ya'ar and Ze'ev Shavit (eds.), *Trends in Israeli Society*. Ra'anana: Open University, 2003, p. 1164 [Hebrew].

51 See note 5 above.

52 "*Baker's Five Points*, December 6, 1989," Knesset website: www.knesset.gov.il/process/asp/event_frame.asp?id=35 [Hebrew].

53 Dan Leon, "Israeli Public Opinion Polls on the Peace Process," *The Palestine-Israel Journal* 2(1), 1995, pp. 10–12. See: www.pij.org/details.php?id=676

54 Itamar Rabinovich, *Waging Peace: Israel and the Arabs, 1948-2003*. Or Yehuda: Dvir, 2004, p. 44 [Hebrew].

55 Benjamin Netanyahu, *A Place under the Sun*. Tel Aviv: Yedioth Ahronoth, 1993, p. 240 [Hebrew].

56 Nitzan Feldman, "Economic Peace: Theory vs. Reality," *Strategic Update* 12(3), Institute for National Security Studies, 2009, p. 17 [Hebrew].

57 Yossi Beilin, *Manual for a Wounded Dove*. Tel Aviv: Yedioth Ahronoth, 2001, p. 147 [Hebrew].

58 Nadim Khoury, "National Narratives and the Oslo Peace Process: How Peacebuilding Paradigms Address Conflicts over History," *Nations and Nationalism* 22(3), 2016, p. 476.

59  Ian Ward, "Democracy after Secularism," *The Good Society* 19(2), 2010, p. 34.
60  Olmert's speech at the Geneva Initiative conference, September 19, 2010.

# Chapter 1

1   Many articles and studies have been written about this episode. For a good summary, see: Shlomo Avineri, *Herzl*. Jerusalem: The Zalman Shazar Center, 2007, pp. 173–209 [Hebrew].

2   Elie Kedourie, *Nationalism*, Oxford: Blackwell Publishing, 1993, pp. 74–79. In Kedourie's view, there was a dichotomy between the nationalist era and the religious era. He saw an inherent contradiction between nationalism and religion because according to the ideology of nationalism, the nation creates its values— including the values of religion, which are relegated to an instrumental status of preserving the nation. On the other hand, most religions view themselves as having an absolute purpose, even if they are particular to a certain people, as in the Jewish case.

3   Many studies have been written on the relations between religion and nationhood in the Zionist movement. One of the most important of these is Yosef Salmon's study, which contradicts the view of Zionism as an alternative to the traditional world and identifies modern Jewish nationalism as a phenomenon that is not detached from the traditional religious past. Yosef Salmon, *Do Not Provoke Providence: Orthodoxy in the Grip of Nationalism*. Jerusalem: Zalman Shazar Center, 2006 [Hebrew]. In recent years, against the background of the "critique of secularization," more and more studies are challenging the dichotomy between the secular and religious components in Israeli society. See for example: Yaakov Yadgar, *Traditional Jews in Israel: Modernity Without Secularization*. Jerusalem: Keter, 2010 [Hebrew] and Guy Ben-Porat, *Between State and Synagogue: The Secularization of Modern Israel*. Cambridge University Press, 2013.

4   Casanova, *Public Religions in the Modern World*.

5   Eisenstadt, "The Transformation of the Religious Dimension and the Crystallization of New Civilizational Visions and Relations," pp. 21–35.

6   Fischer, "Secularization and Secularism: A Theoretical and Methodological Platform," p. 23 [Hebrew].

7   Amnon Raz-Krakotzkin, "There Is No God, But He Promised Us the Land," *Mitaʿam* 3, 2005, pp. 71–76 [Hebrew].

8   Amnon Raz-Krakotzkin, "The Return to the History of Redemption (Or, What is the 'History' to Which We 'Return' in the Phrase 'The Return to the History'?)" in Shmuel N. Eisenstadt and Moshe Lissak (eds.), *Zionism and the Return to History: A Reappraisal*. Jerusalem: Yad Ben-Zvi, 1999, p. 261 [Hebrew].

9   Lily Galili, "In the Yom Kippur War, I Tossed Away the Dairy Mess Kit," *Haaretz*, September 14, 1994 [Hebrew].

10  Moshe Shokeid, "The Religiosity of Middle Eastern Jews," in *Israeli Judaism: The Sociology of Religion in Israel*. New Brunswick, NJ: Transaction Publishers, 1995, pp. 255–84. The approach to religion by Jews from Arab lands—who are collectively referred to as "Mizrahi" (plural: "Mizrahim") in Israel—was usually moderate. They did not seek to rebel against religion, but also had no interest in taking religion to an extreme. In large part, this is attributable to the fact that contrary to what occurred among European Jewry from the eighteenth century, the winds of emancipation

and nationalism were not strongly felt in their communities and did not threaten their traditional ways of life. The question of the religious moderation of the majority of Jews from Arab lands and the way they related to the mix of religion and nationhood—a question that has occupied many scholars who have tried to decipher this phenomenon—does not directly concern us in this book. I will just note here another important and interesting reason offered by Bernard Lewis. He suggested that this religious moderation was also influenced by the Islamic environment in which they lived, where there was no clear-cut binary division between "secular" and "religious" in the Western sense of the word. Doubting the existence of God and legitimizing atheism were foreign to the Muslim society, even in the midst of modernization and secularization processes. These processes, indeed, weakened religious practice, but did not reject it. Therefore, those who led a secular lifestyle did not completely dismiss tradition and religious thinking; they did not become estranged from religious institutions. The centuries of interaction between Jews and Muslims bred a similarity between those conventionally described as "secular Muslims" and "traditional Jews"—that is, Jews whose secularity does not distance them from fundamental religious beliefs and does not alienate them from representatives of the religion, but only expresses distaste for meticulous observance of religion commandments. See: Bernard Lewis, *The Jews of Islam*. Princeton, NJ: Princeton University Press, 1987; and the comprehensive article: Nissim Leon, "Mizrahi Traditionalism as an Echo of Jewish Existence," *Akadamot* 23, Jerusalem, 2009, pp. 129–46 [Hebrew].

11  Yigal Elam, *What Happened Here*. Tel Aviv: Am Oved, 2012, pp. 18–19 [Hebrew]. David Ben-Gurion stated in the 1950s: "The Jews of Islamic lands say the verse 'May our eyes behold Your return to Zion in mercy' more than all of the literature of Zionism, which the overwhelming majority of them never heard." This realization was one of the reasons that led him to support a school curriculum designed to "strengthen Jewish consciousness." Ben-Gurion realized that he could not strengthen the connection to modern Jewish nationalism and social solidarity in Israel without a common bond to the religion and its symbols. The quote is from Haim Adler and Reuven Kahana (eds.), *Israel: A Society in Formation—A Sociological Analysis of Sources Vol. B (Religion and Culture)*. Jerusalem: Akademon, 1975, p. 14 [Hebrew].

12  Galili, "In the Yom Kippur War, I Tossed Away the Dairy Mess Kit."

13  "David Ben-Gurion's Diary," Ben-Gurion Archives, September 23, 1953, [Hebrew].

14  Hanna Yablonka, "Holocaust Survivors in Israel: Initial Conclusions," *On the Path of Remembrance* 27. Jerusalem: Yad Vashem, 1998, pp. 4–9 [Hebrew].

15  Tom Segev, *1967: The Year That Transformed Israel*. Jerusalem: Keter, 2005, pp. 111–12 [Hebrew].

16  Meeting of the committee of ministers for the economy, November 29, 1964, Israel State Archives, C-10345/1 [Hebrew].

17  Benny Morris, *Righteous Victims: The History of the Zionist-Arab Conflict, 1881-2001*. Tel Aviv: Am Oved, 2003, p. 293 [Hebrew].

18  Avi Shilon, *Ben-Gurion: Epilogue*. Tel Aviv: Am Oved, 2013, pp. 69–70 [Hebrew].

19  Davar, June 2, 1967. A Unity Government has been formed.

20  Benny Morris, *Righteous Victims: The History of the Zionist-Arab Conflict, 1881-2001*, pp. 286–327 [Hebrew].

21  Much has been written about the religious excitement stirred by the conquest of the territories. See for example: Segev, *1967: The Year That Transformed Israel* [Hebrew].

22  Contrary to the father of the Revisionist movement, Ze'ev Jabotinsky, whose demand for both sides of the Jordan River was based on historical, political, and legal grounds, Begin made a point of linking the demand for Greater Israel to the divine promise and theology. For example, see his inauguration speech in June 1977, where he stated: "We received our right to our homeland from the God of our fathers. . . . The Land of Israel is the beloved fatherland, our only land, we clung to it throughout the generations. We never severed the connection with it. We prayed about it. We longed for it. We loved it with all our heart and all our soul. Our holy ancestors carried its name on their lips when dragged by the brutal enemy to all sorts of deaths. We were exiled from its land and we returned to it in faith." Knesset Proceedings, June 20, 1977, Vol. 80, p. 15 [Hebrew].

23  Anita Shapira, *Israel: A History*. London: Weidenfeld & Nicolson, 2012, pp. 307–10.

24  interview with Beilin, September 3, 2016.

25  Gideon Rahat, "The Election System 1948-1959: From Default to an Entrenched System," *Iyunim Bitkumat Israel* 11, Sde Boker: Ben-Gurion Institute, 2001, p. 375 [Hebrew].

26  Yossi Beilin, "Intergenerational Friction in Three Parties in Israel," PhD dissertation, Tel Aviv University, 1980, p. 54 [Hebrew].

27  Kipnis, "The Turning Point in Studying the Circumstances of the Outbreak of the Yom Kippur War," p. 47 [Hebrew].

28  In September 1971, Ben-Gurion said: "Already at the end of Nasser's rule, he had come to the conclusion that the sole idea of destroying Israel was absurd, and that the major, true problem is how to improve the lives of the Arab people. Now, the entire world is advancing. There is no longer any country in Europe where there is a majority of people working the land, impoverished, uneducated, whose situation is deteriorating from year to year. . . . The chances of peace depend on the Arabs sobering up, and this is a process I believe in." Rafael Bashan, "A Day with B.G.," *Bamahane* 14, September 1971, p. 27 [Hebrew].

29  Many books and studies have been written about the Yom Kippur War and the events that preceded it. As essential background, see for example: Uri Bar-Yosef, *The Watchman Fell Asleep: The Surprise of Yom Kippur and Its Sources*. Albany, NY: SUNY Press, 2012; Yigal Kipnis, *The Road to War*. Charlottesville, VA: Just World Books, 2013.

30  Naama Azoulai, "We Are the Secular Jews? Definition of Identity in the Jewish Renewal Movement in the Secular Space," in Yochi Fischer (ed.), *Secularization and Secularism: Interdisciplinary Perspectives*. Jerusalem: Van Leer Institute, 2016, p. 322 [Hebrew].

# Chapter 2

1  Haim Israeli, *Scroll of Life*. Tel Aviv: Yedioth Ahronoth, 2005, p. 124 [Hebrew].

2  Yigal Allon, "After the Pupils' Assembly," *Lemerhav* 16, June 2, 1954 [Hebrew].

3  On this subject, see: Uri Cohen and Nissim Leon, *The Herut Movement's Central Committee and the Mizrahim, 1965-1977: From Patronizing Partnership to Competitive Partnership*, Jerusalem: Israel Democracy Institute, 2011 [Hebrew].

4  Udi Manor, *Yigal Allon: A Political Biography*, 1949-1980. Or Yehuda: Zemora Beitan Dvir, 2016, p. 383 [Hebrew].

5    The sources of the disagreement over the meaning of Resolution 242 lies in the fact that the English wording of the resolution, approved in November 1967, speaks of a withdrawal from "territories." This allows the resolution to be interpreted as not requiring a withdrawal from all of the territories. The French wording of the resolution, however, refers to a withdrawal from "the territories"—that is, all of them.

6    For more on Tabenkin's attitude toward the territories, see: Avi Shilon, "Ben-Gurion's Approach to Borders," *Zion* 83, Jerusalem, 2016, pp. 407–33 [Hebrew].

7    Patir, "Rabin Dismisses Possibility of Negotiating with the Terrorists."

8    The Allon Plan was submitted to Prime Minister Levi Eshkol on July 26, 1967, shortly after the Six-Day War. Though it was not submitted for discussion and approval by the government, it became the basis of the territorial stance of Labor Party leaders. According to the plan, which views peace with the Arab states as essential for ensuring Israel's security, Israel must maintain defensible borders and a Jewish majority for it to exist as a Jewish and democratic state. The Palestinians, who are not recognized in the plan as a nation with a right of political self-determination, are slated to receive autonomy after Israel's withdrawal and choose between a political attachment to Jordan or to Israel—to be negotiated between Israel, the Palestinians, and Jordan. According to the plan, Israel's eastern border would be the Jordan River and the line that bisects the Dead Sea, continuing along the Mandatory border in the Arava; west of the Jordan River, a strip of land 15 kilometers wide would be annexed to Israel; in the Judean Desert region, including Kiryat Arba, the strip would reach 25 kilometers wide and serve as a link connecting the Negev to the Jordan Valley; in the Jericho area, there would be a transit corridor from the East Bank of the Jordan to the West Bank; a transit corridor would also connect the West Bank and Gaza Strip; and Jerusalem would be under Israeli sovereignty. Morris, *One State, Two States: Israel and Palestine*, pp. 66–67 [Hebrew]. Regarding Allon as a politician and his views, see: Manor, *Yigal Allon: A Neglected Political Legacy, 1949–1980*. For the early Allon, see: Shapira, *Yigal Allon, Native Son*.

9    Yitzhak Tabenkin, *Chapters of Life: The Man and His Work—Friends and Pupils Recount His Teachings*. Ramat Efal, 1984, p. 27 [Hebrew].

10   See: Ya'akov Tsur, "Between Land and State: The Complete Land in the Approach of Tabenkin and Hakibbutz Hameuchad," PhD dissertation, University of Haifa, 2012 [Hebrew].

11   Yitzhak Tabenkin, *Devarim [Collected Speeches]*. Vol. B, Tel Aviv: Hakibbutz Hameuchad, 1967, p. 293 [Hebrew].

12   See Anita Shapira, *The Army Controversy, 1948: Ben-Gurion's Struggle for Control*. Tel Aviv: Hakibbutz Hameuchad, 1985, pp. 9–59 [Hebrew].

13   Anita Shapira, *Yigal Allon, Native Son*. Tel Aviv: Hakibbutz Hameuchad, 2003, p. 445 [Hebrew].

14   David Ben-Gurion, *War Diary*, Vol. B. Tel Aviv: Am Oved, 1982, p. 605 [Hebrew].

15   Yigal Allon to Ben-Gurion, March 27, 1949, Correspondence Division, Ben-Gurion Archives [Hebrew].

16   See the film "Rabin, in His Own Words." Directed by Erez Laufer, 2016.

17   Protocol of the Labor Party's secretariat, November 9, 1972, 2-24-1972-B100, Labor Party Archives. Quoted in Yitzhak Greenberg, "Buried His Head in the Sand," *Israel* 10, 2006, p. 252 [Hebrew].

18   Ibid.

19   "Moked," *Israeli Television*, May 1, 1970, Protocols Division, Ben-Gurion Archives [Hebrew]

20 *Davar*, "The Government Must Maintain the Law But No Less Important – The Unity of the Nation," December 12, 1975 [Hebrew].

21 *Haaretz*, "The Big Debate," May 16, 1977 [Hebrew].

22 Asher Arian, *The Elections in Israel 1977*. Jerusalem: Academic Press, 1980, pp. 277–80.

23 Asher Arian, *Security Threatened: Surveying Israeli Opinion on Peace and War*. Cambridge University Press, 1995, pp. 149–51.

24 Yonathan Shapiro, *The Road to Power: Herut Party in Israel*. Albany, NY: SUNY Press, 1991, p. 4.

25 Dani Filc, *The Political Right in Israel: The Many Faces of Jewish Populism*. London: Routledge, 2010.

26 It is important to note that Filc distinguishes between the Likud's inclusive populism under Begin and the Likud's populism under Netanyahu. He defines the latter as an old-new form of "post-populism" in light of Netanyahu's neoliberal economic policy, which excludes the weaker segments of society, and because the relations between the leader and masses during his tenure are based on electronic and internet communication. Dani Filc, "Post-Populism in Israel: The South American Model of Netanyahu '96," *Theory and Criticism* 9, Winter 1996, p. 229 [Hebrew].

27 Pierre Bourdieu, "Structures, Habitus, Practices," in *The Logic of Practice* (transl. Richard Nice), Stanford University Press, 1990, pp. 52–65.

28 See: Avi Pikar, *Selective Immigration: Israel's Policy toward the Immigration of North African Jews, 1951-1956*. Sde Boker: Ben-Gurion Institute, 2013 [Hebrew].

29 Ze'ev Yafet, "Lessons Weren't Learned, Nothing was Done," *Haaretz*, October 15, 1982 [Hebrew].

30 Ben-Gurion to Haim Gouri, May 15, 1963, Correspondence Division, Ben-Gurion Archives [Hebrew].

31 Avi Shlaim, *The Iron Wall: Israel and the Arab World*. Tel Aviv: Yedioth Ahronoth, 2005, p. 344 [Hebrew].

32 Teddy Preuss, *Begin in Power*. Jerusalem: Keter, 1984, p. 40 [Hebrew].

33 On the change in Peres's views on defense and foreign affairs, see: Ziv, *Why Hawks Become Doves—Shimon Peres and Foreign Policy Change in Israel*.

34 "To Be Shimon Peres," *Channel Two*, January 16, 2014. Director: Naftaly Gliksberg [Hebrew].

35 Netanyahu's remarks came in response to a report by the state comptroller on the cost of living and housing. See: *Haaretz*, February 26, 2015 [Hebrew].

# Chapter 3

1 "Main points from the meeting of Moshe Dayan, the foreign minister, with the deputy prime minister of Egypt, Hassan Touhami, in Rabat," September 17, 1977, Israel State Archives [Hebrew].

2 Ibid.

3 "Memo of the Foreign Ministry's Center for Political Research and Planning on Sadat's speech, November 10, 1977," Israel State Archives, File 4172/13 [Hebrew].

4 "Protocol of Cabinet Meeting," November 24, 1977, Israel State Archives, 4269/6-A [Hebrew].

5 "Protocol of Cabinet Meeting," November 20, 1977, Israel State Archives [Hebrew].

6 Rubinovitz and Steinberg, "Menachem Begin's Autonomy Plan: Between Political Realism and Ideology," pp. 75–95 [Hebrew].

7   Begin's official position was that there would be "full autonomy for the residents, but not for the territory," and he emphasized the "administrative nature of the self-rule." Menachem Begin, "The Autonomy Plan," *Maariv*, October 1, 1978 [Hebrew].

8   Moshe Foxman Shaal (ed.), *The Camp David Accords: Collection of Articles and Lectures*. Jerusalem: Carmel and the Begin Heritage Center, 2010, p. 65 [Hebrew].

9   Yossi Beilin's personal archives.

10  Ibid.

11  Ibid.

12  Ibid.

13  Ibid.

14  Author's interview with Yariv Ben-Eliezer on June 9, 2011. "Ben-Gurion liked Yitzhak and always gave him credit for remaining in the army after the dismantling of the Palmach, even if he participated in its final gathering."

15  Zaki Shalom, *Like Fire in His Bones: Ben-Gurion and His Struggles over the Character of the State and Its Leadership, 1963-1967*. Sde Boker: Ben-Gurion Institute, 2004, p. 37 [Hebrew].

16  Yitzhak Rabin with Dov Goldstein, *Pinkas Sherut*. Tel Aviv: Maariv, 1979, p. 86 [Hebrew] [published in English as *The Rabin Memoirs*].

17  Shaul Webber, *Yitzhak Rabin: The Growth of a Leader*. Tel Aviv: Maariv, 2010, pp. 230–34 [Hebrew].

18  Rabin with Goldstein, *Pinkas Sherut*, p. 86 [Hebrew].

19  Ben-Gurion's diary, July 23, 1970 [Hebrew].

20  Yossi Almogi, May 30, 1978, Testimonies Division, Ben-Gurion Archives [Hebrew].

21  Enzo Sereni (1905-1944) was from a Jewish family in Italy and emigrated in 1927. He was one of the founders of Givat Brenner and prominent for his literary skills and pugnacious personality. Despite opposition from the Yishuv's leaders, including Ben-Gurion, he joined the group of Jewish parachutists from Palestine who were dispatched to Nazi-occupied territory in Europe to assist in the Allied war effort and help European Jews. Sereni was captured by the Nazis and executed at the Dachau concentration camp. The quote is from Ze'ev Tzahor, *Vision and Reckoning: Ben-Gurion—Ideology and Politics*. Tel Aviv: Yedioth Ahronoth and Sifriyat Poalim, 2004, p. 253 [Hebrew].

22  Michael Bar-Zohar, *Like a Phoenix: Shimon Peres—Biography*. Tel Aviv: Yedioth Ahronoth, 2006, pp. 492–93 [Hebrew].

23  For more on Begin's leadership style, see: Avi Shilon, "I'm Responsible, You Decide: Menachem Begin's Detached Leadership Pattern in the Etzel," *Iyunim Bitkumat Israel* 26, Sde Boker: Ben-Gurion University, 2016, pp. 249–80 [Hebrew].

24  See for example the well-known study by the sociologist Yonathan Shapiro, *Chosen to Command: The Road to Power of the Herut Party—A Sociopolitical Interpretation*. Tel Aviv: Am Oved, 1989 [Hebrew].

25  See: Amos Shifris, *Israel Galili: A Man of Words and Deeds*. Tel Aviv: Yad Tabenkin, 2010 [Hebrew].

26  Arye Naor, *Begin in Power*. Tel Aviv: Yedioth Ahronoth, 1993, p. 233 [Hebrew].

27  Yossi Beilin's personal archives.

28  "The Chosen," director and presenter Haim Yavin, June 1981, Israel Television Archives.

29  Kimmerling, *The End of Ashkenazi Hegemony*, p. 11 [Hebrew].

30  Israel Television Archives, June 27, 1981, Dudu Topaz: "It's a pleasure to see this audience. It's a pleasure to see there aren't *tchachachim* who spoil election rallies . . . the *tchachachim* are at Metzudat Ze'ev [Likud headquarters]. They're barely sentries, if

they go to the army at all. The soldiers and commanders of the combat units are here"
    [Hebrew].

31  Not all members of the Liberal Party supported the union with Herut. A minority,
    members of the Progressive faction, formed the Independent Liberal party, which
    later merged with the Labor Party.

32  Yossi Beilin, "Toward a Social-Liberal Alignment," *Haaretz*, May 10, 1982 [Hebrew].

33  It is important to note that while many of the General Zionists saw Chaim Weizmann
    as their leader and ideologue, Weizmann himself sought to distance himself from
    party affiliation and establish his political power within the Zionist institutions.
    See: Jehuda Reinharz, "Chaim Weizmann's Leadership: Statecraft as the Art of the
    Possible," Introduction chapter in Yemima Rosenthal (ed.), *Chaim Weizmann—The
    First President: Selected Letters and Speeches*. Jerusalem: Israel State Archives, 1995
    [Hebrew].

34  Amir Goldstein, "The Decline of the General Zionists and the Failure of the Liberal
    Alternative, 1959-1961," *Iyunim Bitkumat Israel* 16, Sde Boker: Ben-Gurion Institute,
    2006, p. 339 [Hebrew].

35  Colin Shindler, *The Rise of the Israeli Right*. Cambridge University Press, 2014, p. 266.

36  The Peace Process, Settlements and National Priorities—2013, Molad survey,
    http://www.molad.org/researches/%D7%A1%D7%A7%D7%A8-
    %D7%9E%D7%95%D7%9C%D7%93-2013-%D7%97%D7%9C%D7%A7-%D7%91

37  See: Shlomit Levy, Hanna Levinson and Elihu Katz, *Beliefs, Observances and Social
    Interactions Among Jews in Israel*. Jerusalem: Louis Guttman Institute of Applied
    Social Research, 1994 [Hebrew]; Shlomit Levy, Hanna Levinson and Elihu Katz,
    *A Portrait of Israeli Jewry*. Jerusalem: Avi Chai Foundation and Israel Democracy
    Institute, 2002; Asher Arian (head of research team), *A Portrait of Israeli Jewry: Beliefs,
    Observances and Values among Israeli Jews*. Jerusalem: Israel Democracy Institute and
    Guttman Center for Public Opinion and Policy Research, 2009. According to these
    surveys, there is a broad consensus in the Jewish public on the commitment to Jewish
    identity, Jewish culture, and the continued selective preservation of traditional Jewish
    life (without accepting Jewish law as a system of binding commandments and without
    accepting what is regarded as religious coercion.) A study conducted by the Israel
    Democracy Institute in October 2013 found that Israeli Jews gave higher priority
    to Israel's Jewish component than its democratic component when asked: "Israel is
    defined as both a Jewish and democratic state. Personally, which part of the definition
    is more important to you?" A total of 37 percent of the respondents said that both
    components are equally important; 32.3 percent said the Jewish component is more
    important; while 29.2 percent said the democratic component is more important. In
    Tamar Hermann (ed.), *The Israel Democracy Index 2013*. Jerusalem: Israel Democracy
    Institute, 2013, pp. 184 and 207. For additional information, see "Chapter 3: Source of
    Authority: Religion or State?" pp. 84–106.

38  Gidi Weitz, "A Reunion of the Labor Party's Octet," *Haaretz*, May 14, 2015 [Hebrew].

# Chapter 4

1   Ze'ev Schiff and Ehud Ya'ari, *War of Deception*. Tel Aviv: Schocken, 1984, pp. 118–19
    [Hebrew] [published in English as *Israel's Lebanon War*].

2   Arye Naor, *Cabinet at War*. Tel Aviv: Yedioth Ahronoth, 1986, p. 35 [Hebrew].

3 Author's interview with Maj. Gen. (ret.) Yanush Ben-Gal, December 17, 2006.

4 "How to End It," *Haaretz*, June 16, 1982 [Hebrew].

5 Bar-Zohar, *Like a Phoenix: Shimon Peres—Biography*, p. 507 [Hebrew].

6 Yitzhak Rabin, "Against Capturing West Beirut," *Yedioth Ahronoth*, June 25, 1982 [Hebrew].

7 Thomas L. Friedman, *From Beirut to Jerusalem*. Tel Aviv: Maariv, 1990, p. 139 [Hebrew].

8 Weitz, "A Reunion of the Labor Party's Octet."

9 Ben-Porat, *Conversations with Yossi Beilin*, p. 66 [Hebrew].

10 "Unprecedented Demonstration in Tel Aviv," *Haaretz*, September 26, 1982 [Hebrew].

11 Yitzhak Navon, Begin Heritage Center archives, Testimonies Division, December 18, 2000: "After Sabra and Shatila, I asked to see Begin and I said to him that it is inconceivable that something awful like this will occur without examining the matter. We need to form a state commission of inquiry. He said: 'If we form a commission of inquiry, it means an admission of guilt.' I said to him: 'On the contrary, people in the world are already saying that we're guilty. The only way to get out of this and refute this is to form a commission.' Again, he said he'd think about it. He thought and said that we'll assign a general in the army to check the matter. I said to him: 'Don't assign this to any general. Only a judge. Otherwise, there will be no confidence in his conclusions.' I called him on the telephone and informed him that I was going to publicly state my view, and I issued a statement on television and on radio in support of establishing a judicial commission of inquiry. In the NRP, they told me that this tipped the scales in favor of establishing the commission."

12 Speaking to IDF officers at the National Security College in August 1982, Begin explicitly defined the war as a "war of choice." He argued that a leader is morally obligated to launch wars of choice in order to save lives that might be lost when no alternative remains, because the state will ultimately need to go to war when the good cards are not in its hands. Begin illustrated this by arguing that if France had launched a war in March 1936, after Hitler announced the abrogation of the Treaty of Versailles, it could have defeated the German army and prevented the Second World War. An abridged version of the speech appeared in the *Maariv* newspaper on August 20, 1982 [Hebrew].

13 Aluf Benn, "The Irreplaceable Man," *Haaretz*, January 6, 2006 [Hebrew].

14 Reuven Y. Hazan, "Party System Change in Israel, 1948–98: A Conceptual and Typological Border-Stretching of Europe?" in Paul Pennings and Jan-Erik Lane (eds.), *Comparing Party System Change*. London: Routledge, 1998, pp. 151–66.

15 Yitzhak Reiter (ed.), *The Arab Society in Israel*. Jerusalem: Abraham Fund, 2013, chapter 2, "The National-Historical Aspect," p. 12 [Hebrew].

16 Avishai Ben-Haim, *Man of Vision: The Ultra-Orthodox Ideology of Rabbi Shach*. Jerusalem: Mosaica, 2004, pp. 151–56 [Hebrew].

17 On Sharon's attitude toward Judaism, see: Shilon, "The Revisionist Movement Leaders' Attitudes toward Jewish Religion, 1925-2005."

18 See: Shilon, "Ben-Gurion's Approach to Borders," pp. 407–33 [Hebrew]. In regard to the desire to settle in southern Lebanon, it is interesting to note that on the eve of the Arab Revolt in 1936, Ben-Gurion met with Chaim Weizmann, Yehoshua Hankin, and Moshe Sharett to discuss Hankin's proposal to purchase land in Lebanon. The proposal called for establishing a Zionist company that would be authorized to buy lands in Lebanon under a ten-year concession; every year, 7,500 Jews would settle there and develop 100,000 dunams of land. (In an effort to convince the Arabs to

support the plan, it stipulated that half of the workforce in all of the professions required for developing Jewish settlement in Lebanon would be Lebanese.) In the wake of the Arab Revolt, however, the plan was shelved; the Zionist leadership decided that the time was not ripe for settlement in an Arab country. See: Arthur Ruppin to Chaim Weizmann, June 1, 1936, Central Zionist Archives, z4/17024/B [Hebrew].

19  Asher Kaufman, "Borders, Identities and Territorialism in the Middle East: Seven Shi'ite Villages as Case Studies," *Jama'a* 14, 2005, p. 71 [Hebrew].

20  Knesset Proceedings, session 57 of the 11th Knesset, February 12, 1985 [Hebrew].

21  Yossi Beilin, "Unilateral Withdrawal of the IDF from Southern Lebanon" in Yaacov Bar-Siman-Tov (ed.), *The Security Zone in Lebanon: A Reconsideration.* Jerusalem: The Leonard Davis Institute and the Hebrew University, 1997, pp. 47–53 [Hebrew].

22  Ben-Porat, *Conversations with Yossi Beilin,* p. 78 [Hebrew].

23  Knesset Proceedings, session 235 of the 11th Knesset, August 5, 1986 [Hebrew].

24  Fatah was founded in 1959 and initiated operations against Israel in 1965. Arafat became the PLO's chairman in 1969 and held this role until his death in 2004.

25  On the negotiations between the sides, see: Menachem Klein, *Antagonistic Collaboration: PLO-Jordanian Dialogue, 1985-1988.* Jerusalem: The Leonard Davis Institute, 1988, pp. 23–26 [Hebrew].

26  Gabriel Sheffer, "Principles of Pragmatism: A Reevaluation of British Policies toward Palestine in the 1930s," *Cathedra* 29, September 1983, pp. 113–44 [Hebrew].

27  David Ben-Gurion, *Meetings with Arab Leaders.* Tel Aviv: Am Oved, 1967, p. 20 [Hebrew].

28  Ibid.; Shabtai Tevet, *Ben-Gurion and the Arabs of Israel,* Jerusalem and Tel Aviv: Schocken, 1985, pp. 221–43 [Hebrew].

29  Gurion, *Meetings with Arab Leaders,* p. 47 [Hebrew].

30  See: Moshe Zak, *King Hussein Makes Peace: Thirty Years of Secret Talks.* Ramat Gan: Bar-Ilan University Press, 1996, pp. 200–10 [Hebrew].

31  Yossi Beilin's personal archives.

32  Ibid.

33  Ibid.

34  Ibid.

35  Ibid.

36  Theodor Herzl, *Old New Land [Altneuland].* Createspace Independent Publishing Platform, 2012, p. 113.

37  For a fascinating discussion of Zionism and Africa, see: Eitan Bar-Yosef, *A Villa in the Jungle: Africa in Israeli Culture.* Jerusalem: Van Leer Institute and Hakibbutz Hameuchad, 2014 [Hebrew].

38  David Ben-Gurion, *East and West: We and Our Neighbors.* Tel Aviv: Davar, 1931, pp. 246–48 [Hebrew].

39  See: Aaron Klein, *The Master of Operations: The Story of Mike Harari.* Jerusalem: Keter, 2014 [Hebrew].

40  Yossi Beilin's personal archives.

41  Ibid.

42  Bar-Zohar, *Like a Phoenix: Shimon Peres—Biography,* p. 555 [Hebrew].

43  Ibid., p. 577.

44  "Text of the memorandum of understanding between the government of Jordan and the foreign minister of Israel," April 11, 1987, File 5152/8-A, Israel State Archives [Hebrew].

45  George P. Shultz, *Turmoil and Triumph: My Years as Secretary of State*. New York: Scribner's Sons, 1993, pp. 936–45.

46  Author's online conversation with Charles Hill, April 1, 2016.

47  George P. Shultz, *Turmoil and Triumph: My Years as Secretary of State*, pp. 936–45.

48  Author's online conversation with Charles Hill, April 1, 2016.

49  The Iran-Contra affair entailed a secret connection conducted in the mid-1980s: Israeli business and intelligence agents sold weapons to Iran, and the United States supplied other weaponry to Israel in return. Some of the money received from Iran was transferred to the US government "off the books" and diverted to fund the Contras (rebels fighting the Sandinista government in Nicaragua) without congressional knowledge. This arrangement circumvented the prohibition imposed by President Reagan on the sale of weapons to states that support terrorism and violated a congressional embargo on assistance to the Contras. According to Peres and senior Israeli officials, the plan was devised by an American intelligence official who proposed the sale of weapons to Iran to facilitate the release of American hostages held by Hezbollah in Lebanon and to foster relations with moderates in Iran. Peres agreed to the arrangement, unaware that it had not been approved by all of the relevant decision makers in the US administration. Some accused Israel of initiating the plan, but Israeli officials insisted that the idea came from close associates of President Reagan. In any case, it turned out that the promises to release all of the hostages were not fulfilled. The hope of forging a backchannel to moderates in Iran was also dashed. In addition, a considerable amount of the money from the arms deals "disappeared." The full story of the affair has yet to be revealed. For Peres's role in the affair, see: Bar-Zohar, *Like a Phoenix: Shimon Peres—Biography*, pp. 545–50 [Hebrew].

50  Menachem Klein, *Antagonistic Collaboration: PLO-Jordanian Dialogue, 1985-1988*, p. 13 [Hebrew].

51  "Prime Minister Shamir to Secretary of State George Shultz," May 13, 1987, File 443/1-A, Israel State Archives [Hebrew].

52  Ben-Porat, *Conversations with Yossi Beilin*, p. 94 [Hebrew].

53  Yossi Beilin's personal archives.

54  Ibid.

55  Moshe Shemesh, "PLO: The Path to Oslo—1988 as the Turning Point in the History of the Palestinian National Movement," *Iyunim Bitkumat Israel* 9, Sde Boker: Ben-Gurion Institute, 2009, p. 201 [Hebrew].

56  Author's conversation with Dr. Raef Zreik, Tel Aviv University, May 21, 2015.

57  Yossi Beilin's personal archives.

58  On the sense of power of young Palestinians vis-à-vis Israel as one of the factors that sparked the intifada, see" Moshe Shemesh: "PLO: The Path to Oslo—1988 as the Turning Point in the History of the Palestinian National Movement," p. 202 [Hebrew].

59  For more on Kastner and his controversial efforts to save the Jews of Hungary, see: Yechiam Weitz, *The Man Who Was Murdered Twice: The Life, Trial and Death of Israel Kastner*. Jerusalem: Keter, 1995 [Hebrew].

60  Yitzhak Shamir, *Summing Up: An Autobiography*. Tel Aviv: Yedioth Ahronoth, 1994, p. 251 [Hebrew].

61  Baron Salo, *Modern Nationalism and Religion*. Philadelphia, PA: Jewish Publication Society of America, 1960, pp. 4–6.

# Chapter 5

1   Ofer Kenig, "Primaries in Israel after 20 Years: An Interim Balance Sheet," *The Public Sphere* 7, Tel Aviv: Tel Aviv University, 2012, pp. 139–50 [Hebrew].

2   Yonathan Shapiro, *An Elite without Successors*. Tel Aviv: Am Oved, 1984 [Hebrew].

3   Theodor Herzl, *The Jewish State* [*Der Judenstaat*] (transl. Sylvie D'Avigdor), p. 42, www.mideastweb.org/jewishstate.pdf

4   Akiva Eldar, "Under Pressure from His Aide, Peres Decides Not to Resign," *Haaretz*, November 21, 1988 [Hebrew].

5   Moshe Halevi (ed.), *Ze'ev Jabotinsky: Letters, 1935*. Tel Aviv: Jabotinsky Institute, 2009, Letter 90: May 2, 1935, pp. 102–13 [Hebrew].

6   Ben-Porat, *Conversations with Yossi Beilin*, p. 96 [Hebrew].

7   Ibid. 97.

8   Uzi Rebhun and Gilad Malach, *Demographic Trends in Israel*. Jerusalem: Metzilah Center, 2009, p. 23 [Hebrew].

9   On recent trends in Mizrahi ultra-Orthodoxy, see: Nissim Leon, *Soft Ultra-Orthodoxy: Religious Renewal in Oriental Jewry in Israel*. Jerusalem: Yad Ben-Zvi, 2010 [Hebrew]; on new trends in ultra-Orthodox society in general, see: Kimmy Kaplan, *Internal Popular Discourse in Israeli Haredi Society*. Jerusalem: Zalman Shazar Center, 2007 [Hebrew].

10  Yehudit Winkler, "Kaiser attacks Beilin for call to accept 6-7% inflation," *Haaretz*, August 29, 1989 [Hebrew].

11  Ben-Porat, *Conversations with Yossi Beilin*, p. 98 [Hebrew].

12  Uri Bahral, *The Effect of Mass Immigration on Wages in Israel*. Jerusalem: Falk Project for Economic Research in Israel, 1965, p. 18.

13  Avi Bareli and Uri Cohen, "The Revolt of the Intellectuals" [forthcoming], p. 13.

14  Gil Horev and Shmulik Shelah, "Indictment against the Government," *Maariv*, August 8, 2005 [Hebrew].

15  The GINI index measures inequality in the allocation of income, on a scale of zero (absolute equality) to one (absolute inequality). In Bareli and Cohen, "The Revolt of the Intellectuals," p. 14.

16  Danny Gutwein, "The Israeli Left: Alive or Dead?" *Eretz Acheret* 27, April 28, 2005 [Hebrew].

17  Shemesh, "PLO: The Path to Oslo—1988 as the Turning Point in the History of the Palestinian National Movement," pp. 188–89 [Hebrew].

18  "*Baker's Five Points*, December 6, 1989," Knesset website: www.knesset.gov.il/process/asp/event_frame.asp?id=35 [Hebrew].

19  Itamar Rabinovich, *Yitzhak Rabin: Soldier, Leader, Statesman*. Modi'in: Kineret Zmora-Bitan Dvir, 2017, p. 185 [Hebrew].

20  Shemesh, "PLO: The Path to Oslo—1988 as the Turning Point in the History of the Palestinian National Movement," pp. 228–40 [Hebrew].

21  "*Mubarak's Ten Points*, September 19, 1989," Knesset website: www.knesset.gov.il/process/asp/event_frame.asp?id=34 [Hebrew].

22  Ben-Porat, *Conversations with Yossi Beilin*, p. 102 [Hebrew].

23  Eliezer Shach, *Letters and Articles*. Bnei Brak, 1989, Vol. D, p. 157 [Hebrew].

24  Ibid., Vol. A-B, p. 15.

25  Ibid., Vol. E, p. 105.

26  Ibid.

27  Rabbi Shach's "*Rabbits Speech*," March 26, 1990, www.youtube.com/
    watch?v=GSi7MbP4Pp0&t=17m10s

28  Joseph Ringel, "The Construction and De-construction of the Ashkenazi vs.
    Sephardic/Mizrahi Dichotomy in Israeli Culture: Rabbi Eliyahou Zini vs. Rabbi
    Ovadia Yosef," *Israel Studies* 21 (2), Summer 2016, pp. 155–82.

29  Bar-Zohar, *Like a Phoenix: Shimon Peres—Biography*, p. 595 [Hebrew].

30  Ben-Porat, *Conversations with Yossi Beilin*, p. 104 [Hebrew].

31  Shimon Shiffer, "And There's No Peace," *Yedioth Ahronoth*, September 29, 2016,
    [Hebrew].

32  Bar-Zohar, *Like a Phoenix: Shimon Peres—Biography*, p. 594 [Hebrew].

33  Shayke Ben-Porat, *Conversations with Yossi Beilin*, p. 104 [Hebrew].

34  Ofer Kenig, "Twenty Years Later: The Stinking Maneuver in the Mirror of Time," *Israel
    Democracy Institute Website*, www.idi.org.il/articles/1629, March 13, 2010 [Hebrew].

35  Beilin, *Touching Peace*, p. 48 [Hebrew].

36  Ibid., p. 46.

37  Yitzhak Laor, "The Left's Chance," *Walla!* September 12, 2009 [Hebrew].

38  Rabinovich, *Waging Peace: Israel and the Arabs, 1948-2003*, p. 35 [Hebrew].

39  On the Madrid Conference, see: Eytan Bentsur, *The Road to Peace Crosses Madrid*. Tel
    Aviv: Yedioth Ahronoth, 1997 [Hebrew].

40  Itamar Rabinovich, *Waging Peace: Israel and the Arabs, 1948-2003*, p. 44 [Hebrew].

41  Yossi Beilin, "Gaza Now," *Haaretz*, January 2, 1991 [Hebrew].

42  Yossi Beilin's personal archives.

43  Ibid.

44  Ibid.

45  Dmitri Slivniak, "Neither a Badge of Courage, Nor a Mark of Cain," *Eretz Acheret*,
    March 10, 2002 [Hebrew].

# Chapter 6

1  Beilin, *Touching Peace*, pp. 58–59 [Hebrew].

2  Bar-Zohar, *Like a Phoenix: Shimon Peres—Biography*, p. 601 [Hebrew].

3  On the importance of the basic laws and how they constitute a "constitutional
   revolution," see: Ruth Gavison, *The Constitutional Revolution: Reality or Self-Fulfilling
   Prophecy?* Jerusalem: Israel Democracy Institute, 1998 [Hebrew].

4  Gideon Sapir, *The Constitutional Revolution: Past, Present and Future*. Tel Aviv:
   Yedioth Ahronoth, Bar-Ilan University and University of Haifa, 2010, p. 15 [Hebrew].

5  According to Meridor, "Shamir did not take much interest in enacting the basic
   laws"—and thanks to the prime minister's lack of involvement, Meridor was able to
   push forward this legislation. Author's interview with Dan Meridor, Tel Aviv, May 9,
   2007. See also similar remarks by Amnon Rubinstein in his article "Why I Wept in the
   Knesset Plenum," *Israel Hayom*, March 30, 2012 [Hebrew].

6  Sapir, *The Constitutional Revolution: Past, Present and Future*, p. 18 [Hebrew].

7  Moshe Berent, *A Nation Like All Nations: Towards the Establishment of an Israeli
   Republic*. Jerusalem: Carmel, 2009, pp. 34-35 [Hebrew].

8  Eliezer Don-Yehiya, *Politics of Accommodation: Settling Conflicts of State and Religion
   in Israel*. Jerusalem: Floersheimer Institute for Policy Studies, 1997, pp. 20–30
   [Hebrew].

9   Ibid., pp. 118–22.

10  Ran Hirschl, "The Struggle for Hegemony: Explaining the Expansion of Judicial Power through the Constitutionalization of Rights in Culturally-Divided Polities," *Stanford Journal of International Law* 36, 2000, pp. 73–118.

11  Even without the Tehiya votes that were cast in vain because the party failed to reach the threshold percentage, the leftist camp (Labor, Meretz, Hadash, Arab Democratic Party) received just 48.3 percent of the votes. Furthermore, the fact that Shas joined the coalition ran contrary to the right-wing inclinations of most of its voters. See the Knesset website, Elections to the Thirteenth Knesset: www.knesset.gov.il/description/ eng/eng_mimshal_res13.htm

12  On the impressions of Palestinian delegation members vis-à-vis the negotiations in Washington, see: "Reflections on the Peace Process: An Interview with Haydar Abd al-Shafi," *Journal of Palestine* 22(1), Autumn 1992, pp. 57–69; "Reflections on the Peace Process: An Interview with Nabil Shaath," *Journal of Palestine* 22(1), Autumn 1992, pp. 70–77.

13  Beilin, *Touching Peace*, p. 59 [Hebrew].

14  Avi Shlaim, *The Iron Wall: Israel and the Arab World*. New York: W. W. Norton & Company, 2001, pp. 511–12.

15  Yossi Beilin's personal archives.

16  Yair Hirschfeld, *Oslo: Formula for Peace*. Tel Aviv: Rabin Center and Am Oved, 2000, pp. 92–95 [Hebrew].

17  Yossi Beilin's personal archives.

18  Beilin, *Touching Peace*, p. 83 [Hebrew].

19  Yossi Beilin's personal archives.

20  Ibid.

21  Ibid.

22  Ibid.

23  Shimon Peres (with David Landau), *Battling for Peace*. London: Weidenfeld and Nicholson, 1995, p. 385.

24  Yossi Beilin's personal archives.

25  Beilin, *Touching Peace*, p. 108 [Hebrew].

26  Bar-Zohar, *Like a Phoenix: Shimon Peres—Biography*, p. 620 [Hebrew].

27  "From Rabin to Peres: Top Secret," *Maariv*, September 12, 2003 [Hebrew].

28  Beilin, *Touching Peace*, pp. 111–12 [Hebrew].

29  The historian Adam Raz, who wrote a fascinating article in an attempt to understand Rabin's attitude toward Oslo, thinks that Rabin's letter to Peres was designed to exert pressure on the PLO's Tunis-based leadership to soften their stance because he assumed the letter would be leaked from Peres's office to Arafat's associates. Raz's main thesis is that Rabin was compelled to accept Oslo because he feared the political threat posed by Peres within the party and primarily because Peres and Beilin had succeeded, through Arafat, in preventing progress in the talks with the territories-based Palestinian delegation; Oslo thus became the only alternative, despite Rabin's lingering reservations about it. However, the documents in Beilin's archive, as reflected in this book, do not support Raz's thesis. See: Adam Raz, "Divided Fronts—The 'Strange' Anatomy of Rabin's Oslo Decision," *Israelis* 4, Ben-Gurion University, 2012, pp. 97–132 [Hebrew].

30  Uri Sagi, *Lights in the Fog*. Tel Aviv: Yedioth Ahronoth, 1998, p. 187 [Hebrew].

31  Martin Indyk, *Pax Americana*. Tel Aviv: Am Oved, 2009, pp. 87–100 [Hebrew]. [published in English as *Innocent Abroad: An Intimate Account of American Peace Diplomacy in the Middle East*].

32  Ephraim Sneh, *Navigating Perilous Waters*. Tel Aviv: Yedioth Ahronoth, 2002, pp. 22–24 [Hebrew].

33  Bar-Zohar, *Like a Phoenix: Shimon Peres—Biography*, p. 638 [Hebrew].

34  Yossi Beilin's personal archives.

35  Ibid.

36  See: Efraim Halevy, *Man in the Shadows: Inside the Middle East Crisis with a Man Who Led the Mossad*. Tel Aviv: Matar, 2006, p. 67 [Hebrew].

37  Yossi Beilin's personal archives.

38  Beilin, *Touching Peace*, pp. 114–15 [Hebrew].

39  Yossi Beilin's personal archives.

40  Ibid.

41  Bar-Zohar, *Like a Phoenix: Shimon Peres—Biography*, p. 624 [Hebrew].

42  On American policy, see: Dennis Ross, *The Missing Peace: The Inside Story of the Fight for Middle East Peace*. New York: Farrar, Straus and Giroux, 2004, pp. 90–121.

43  Beilin, *Touching Peace*, p. 126 [Hebrew].

44  Yoram Peri, "The Political–Military Complex: The IDF's Influence over Policy towards the Palestinians since 1987," *Israel Affairs* 11(2), 2005, pp. 324–44.

45  "The Iranian problem is not artificial. It exists. There was already a prime minister here who believed in the need to reach a permanent accord with the Palestinians quickly, before there's a nuclear weapon in the hands of a hostile state," Beilin declared at the Meretz convention on December 4, 2005. Yossi Beilin's personal archives.

46  Author's interview with Yossi Beilin, May 18, 2005.

47  Shlomo Aronson, *Nuclear Weapons in the Middle East, 1948-2013: Israel's Nuclear Option in the Region and in Israeli Politics*. Jerusalem: Akademon, 2014, pp. 108–19 [Hebrew].

48  Ibid., p. 337.

49  Yossi Beilin's personal archives.

50  Peri, "The Political–Military Complex," pp. 324–44.

51  Itamar Rabinovich, *Yitzhak Rabin: Soldier, Leader, Statesman*, pp. 212–17 [Hebrew].

52  Indyk, *Pax Americana*, p. 99 [Hebrew].

53  Bar-Zohar, *Like a Phoenix: Shimon Peres—Biography*, p. 628 [Hebrew].

54  Ibid., p. 631.

55  Yossi Beilin's personal archives.

56  Ibid.

57  Ofer Aderet, "Beilin: I Don't Know What Rabin's Vision Was," *Haaretz*, October 23, 2015 [Hebrew].

58  Shimon Shiffer, *Yedioth Ahronoth*, August 24, 1993 [Hebrew].

59  "Enough Tears and Blood," *Maariv*, September 14, 1993 [Hebrew].

60  Beilin, *Touching Peace*, p. 144 [Hebrew].

61  Yossi Beilin's personal archives.

62  Nissim Mishal interviewing Yossi Beilin and Yitzhak Shamir, February 1995: https://www.youtube.com/watch?v=ev71dFJpnfM [Hebrew].

63  Knesset Proceedings, September 23, 1993 [Hebrew].

# Chapter 7

1  Beilin, *Touching Peace*, p. 170 [Hebrew].

2  Ibid.

3  Ibid., p. 174.

4  In this context, it should be noted that according to Israel's Central Bureau of Statistics, there were only 110,000 settlers in the West Bank on the eve of the Oslo Accords in 1993. (There were also about 6,000 settlers in the Gaza Strip.) This number tripled by 2016, and some estimate the number is even higher. This makes evacuation more difficult. Nonetheless, it is important to note that half of the growth was in three settlements: Modiin Ilit, Beitar Ilit (both primarily ultra-Orthodox), and Ma'alei Adumim. According to the Israeli proposals raised at Camp David in 2000 and in the Geneva Initiative, all three would remain within Israel as part of the settlement blocs after the creation of a Palestinian state.

5  Beilin, *Touching Peace*, p. 182 [Hebrew].

6  Yossi Beilin's personal archives.

7  Rafael Bashan, "The Great Moments in My Life: Interview of the Week with David Ben-Gurion," *Maariv*, May 22, 1970, p. 16 [Hebrew].

8  Moshe Pearlman, *David Ben-Gurion*. Tel Aviv: Zmora Bitan, 1987, p. 159 [Hebrew].

9  Michael Bar-Zohar, *Ben-Gurion*. Tel Aviv: Am Oved, 1977, Vol. 3, p. 1526 [Hebrew].

10  Arnon Sofer and Gila Shalev, "The De-Facto Implementation of the Palestinian Demand for Return," *Ensemble*, National Security College and University of Haifa, July 2004, pp. 5–6 [Hebrew].

11  Michal Ben-Josef Hirsch, "From Taboo to the Negotiable: The Israeli New Historians and the Changing Representation of the Palestinian Refugee Problem," *Perspectives on Politics* 5.02, 2007, pp. 241–58.

12  Yoav Gelber, *Independence and Nakba: Israel, the Palestinians and the Arab States, 1948*. Or Yehuda: Dvir, 2003, p. 357 [Hebrew].

13  Mark R. Amstutz, *The Healing of Nations: The Promise and Limits of Political Forgiveness*. London: Rowman & Littlefield, 2004.

14  Daniel de-Malach, "Where Is the Occupation, the Discrimination and the Imperialism? Notes on the Discussion of the Repercussions of Globalism in Israel," *Theory and Criticism* 35, 2009, pp. 111–40 [Hebrew].

15  Yossi Beilin's personal archives.

16  *Yedioth Ahronoth*, December 6, 1994 [Hebrew].

17  Knesset Proceedings, Session 285 of the 13th Knesset, December 14, 1994 [Hebrew].

18  Erez Tadmor, "The Blood Test of the Peace Formula," *Mida*, Septemner 15, 2014 [Hebrew].

19  Yossi Beilin's personal archives.

20  I owe this insight to Prof. Amnon Raz-Krakotzkin.

21  Aviva Lori, "The PLO Was Weakened, and We Were Weakened," *Haaretz*, December 13, 1993 [Hebrew].

22  Yossi Beilin's personal archives.

23  Ibid.

24  Ibid.

25  Ibid.

26  Ibid.

27  Ibid.

28  Ibid.

29  Ibid.

30  See Itamar Rabinovich, *The Brink of Peace: The Israeli-Syrian Negotiations*. Princeton, NJ: Princeton University Press, 1999.

31  Yossi Beilin's personal archives.

32  Hadar Horesh, "Economically, the Agreements Succeeded," *Walla!* October 22, 2015 [Hebrew].

33  Yossi Beilin's personal archives.

34  Abigail Jacobson and Moshe Naor, *Oriental Neighbors: Middle Eastern Jews and Arabs in Mandatory Palestine*. Waltham, MA: Brandeis University Press, 2016.

35  Yossi Beilin's personal archives.

36  Ibid.

37  Dror Ze'evi, "ISIS: The Rise of Baathist Salafism," *The Forum for Regional Thinking*, December 14, 2015, https://www.regthink.org/articles/%D7%93%D7%90% D7%A2%D7%A9-%D7%A2%D7%9C%D7%99%D7%99%D7%AA%D7%94- %D7%A9%D7%9C-%D7%94%D7%A1%D7%9C%D7%A4%D7%99%D7%94-%D7% 94%D7%91%D7%A2%D7%AA%D7%99%D7%A1%D7%98%D7%99%D7%AA [Hebrew].

38  Yossi Beilin's personal archives.

39  Ibid.

40  Ibid. Kabariti: "Elections are also expected in Jordan in about two years and I'll run in my voting district. Don't be surprised if you hear me saying things that I don't believe. There is nothing further from me than pan-Arabism or pro-Palestinianism. I don't believe in them. I don't wish to deliberate with them. But I have no choice. We want no part in the current arrangement with the Palestinians. We Jordanians just want to know where we're heading. We're convinced that if there's an accord, the Arab world will change toward Jordan too, and this will directly affect the Palestinians living in Jordan. Today, we don't want a federation of confederation. If in the future the PA wants to create this type of connection, we'll think about it. From Jordan's perspective, the dangers of federation outweigh its advantages."

41  Yossi Beilin's personal archives.

42  Weitz, "A Reunion of the Labor Party's Octet."

43  Yossi Beilin, *Birthright: The True Story*. Tel Aviv: Hakibbutz Hameuchad, 2009, p. 100 [Hebrew].

44  Galili, "In the Yom Kippur War, I Tossed Away the Dairy Mess Kit."

45  Yossi Shain and Sarah Fainberg, "The Israelization of Judaism and the Jews of France," *Jewish Review of Books*, Fall 2015, https://jewishreviewofbooks.com/articles/1771/the-israelization-of-judaism-and-the-jews-of-france/

46  Yossi Beilin, *Birthright: The True Story*, p. 35 [Hebrew].

47  Shayke Ben-Porat, *Conversations with Yossi Beilin*, p. 140 [Hebrew].

48  "*Israeli-Palestinian Interim Agreement*, September 28, 1995," *Ministry of Foreign Affairs website*: www.mfa.gov.il/mfa/foreignpolicy/peace/guide/pages/the%20israeli-palestinian%20interim%20agreement.aspx

49  Knesset Proceedings, Session 357 of the 13th Knesset, June 28, 1995. "Motion for the Agenda—Toward Implementation of Stage 2 of the Oslo Accords" [Hebrew].

50  See for example "The Hidden Question," an article by the educator Isaac Epstein (*HaShiloah*, August 1907, pp. 192–205 [Hebrew]). Ahad Ha'am also addressed the Palestinian question, already in his early writings. For example: "A people's historical right to a land inhabited by others means nothing other than this: the right to return and settle in the ancestral land, to work it and develop its capacity without hindrance. . . . However, this historical right does not deny the right of the other

inhabitants of the land, who come with the real right of residence and labor in the land for generations. This land is also their national home in the present, and they also have a right to develop their national capacity to the extent they can. This situation, therefore, makes the Land of Israel a place shared by different peoples, each trying to build their national home there." Ahad Ha'am, "Introduction to a New Edition," *At the Crossroads*, 1920.

51  The document appears on the website of the Institute for National Security Studies: http://heb.inss.org.il/index.aspx?id=4662. Yossi Beilin's personal archives.

52  From the TV program "The Way It Was" with Yossi Beilin, Channel 1, May 2015, http://www.iba.org.il/schedule/program.aspx?scode=2062805 [Hebrew].

# Chapter 8

1  Binyamin Ze'ev Begin, *A Sad Story*. Tel Aviv: Yedioth Ahronoth, 2000, p. 214 [Hebrew].

2  See Noam Yuran, *Channel 2: The New Etatism*. Tel Aviv: Resling, 2001 [Hebrew].

3  Michael Feige, "Rabin's Murder and the Ethnic Margins of Religious Zionism," *Theory and Criticism* 45, 2015, p. 32 [Hebrew]. Sadly, Feige, who studied the sociology of Israel, was killed in a terror attack in Tel Aviv on June 8, 2016.

4  Aluf Benn, Barak Ravid and Avi Issacharoff, "The Prime Minister Is Interested in the Beilin-Abu Mazen Document of 1995," *Haaretz*, September 11, 2007 [Hebrew].

5  Lior Lehrs, *Peace Talks over Jerusalem: A Review of the Israeli-Palestinian Negotiations Concerning Jerusalem, 1993-2011*. Jerusalem: Jerusalem Institute for Israel Studies, 2011, p. 94 [Hebrew].

6  Beilin, *Birthright: The True Story*, p. 138 [Hebrew].

7  Ibid., p. 139.

8  Yossi Beilin's personal archives.

9  Ibid.

10  Ibid.

11  Shapira, *Israel: A History*, pp. 195–96.

12  Shapiro, *The Road to Power: Herut Party in Israel*, p. 4.

13  Filc, "Post-Populism in Israel: The South American Model of Netanyahu '96," pp. 217–32 [Hebrew].

14  Yossi Beilin's personal archives.

15  Ibid.

16  Ibid.

17  Efrat Ben-Ze'ev, "Hidden Scripts: The Social Evolution of Alterman's 'Don't You Give Them Guns,'" *Israel Studies Review* 29(1), 2014, pp. 1–17.

18  Beilin, *Manual for a Wounded Dove*, p. 37 [Hebrew].

19  Ibid., p. 41.

20  Ibid., p. 19.

21  Ibid., p. 19.

22  "The Wye River Memorandum, October 23, 1998," *Ministry of Foreign Affairs website*: https://archive.is/20121218170902/www.mfa.gov.il/NR/exeres/EE54A289-8F0A-4CDC-93C9-71BD631109AB.htm

23  Ze'ev Jabotinsky, "Man Is Wolf to Man," in *Nation and Society*. Jerusalem: Eri Jabotinsky, 1950, p. 256 [Hebrew].

# Chapter 9

1  Yossi Verter, "Don't Eulogize Me, Fuad Asks," *Haaretz*, June 20, 2005 [Hebrew].
2  Yossi Beilin's personal archives.
3  Ibid.
4  Ibid.
5  Yossi Beilin, *Manual for a Wounded Dove*, p. 86 [Hebrew].
6  Ibid., p. 75.
7  Ibid., p. 93.
8  Yossi Beilin, *A Guide to Leaving Lebanon*. Tel Aviv: Hakibbutz Hameuchad, 1998 [Hebrew].
9  Avraham Sela, "The Security Zone: Lebanese and Regional Aspects," in Yaacov Bar-Siman-Tov (ed.), *The Security Zone in Lebanon: A Reconsideration*. Jerusalem: The Leonard Davis Institute, 2001, pp. 35–45 [Hebrew].
10  Tzipi Israeli and Yehudit Orbach, "'Rags' and VIPs Looking to Make Headlines: Protest, Media and National Security," *Kesher* 47, Tel Aviv University, Winter 2015, p. 65 [Hebrew].
11  See for example: Yossi Beilin, "*Moom Shmoom*" [loosely translated: "Worthless Talks"], Yedioth Ahronoth, April 5, 1998 [Hebrew]; "Disengaging from Lebanon," *Yedioth Ahronoth*, September 15, 1997 [Hebrew].
12  Shlomo Ben-Ami, "So Close and Yet So Far: Lessons from the Israeli-Palestinian Peace Process," *Israel Studies* 10(2), Summer 2005, p. 73.
13  Yossi Beilin's personal archives.
14  On the changes that occurred among the settlers, see the special edition of *Theory and Criticism*—"The Settlements: New Perspectives," 47, Winter 2016 [Hebrew].
15  Barak Zino, "Barak Legitimizes the Legal Bubble in the Territories," *Ynet*, September 14, 2006 [Hebrew].
16  Yair Auron, *Reflections on the Inconceivable: Theoretical Aspects in Genocide Studies*. Ra'anana: The Open University of Israel, 2006, pp. 47–48 [Hebrew].
17  Galili, "In the Yom Kippur War, I Tossed Away the Dairy Mess Kit."
18  Yossi Beilin, "Beilin-Abu Mazen in full responsibility," *Haaretz*, November 9, 2001 [Hebrew].
19  Beilin, *Manual for a Wounded Dove*, pp. 120–27 [Hebrew].
20  Shlomo Ben-Ami, "So Close and Yet So Far: Lessons from the Israeli-Palestinian Peace Process," pp. 73–74.
21  The State of Israel, as stipulated in the UN partition resolution of 1947, included the coastal strip, eastern Galilee, northern valleys, Arava, southern Negev, and coast of the Gulf of Eilat; it did not include the central and western Galilee, a strip in the western Negev along the Egyptian border (the Nitzana area), the eastern part of the Negev including Beersheba, the hills of Samaria, and the Jordan Valley. Jaffa was to be an Arab enclave inside the Jewish state, while Jerusalem and Bethlehem were slated to be demilitarized areas under UN supervision. In total, 14,900 square kilometers were allocated for the Jewish state.
22  Gilad Sher, *Within Reach: The Israeli-Palestinian Peace Negotiations, 1999-2001*. Tel Aviv: Yedioth Ahronoth, 2001, p. 21 [Hebrew].
23  Yossi Beilin, *Manual for a Wounded Dove*, p. 249 [Hebrew].
24  Shlomo Aronson, *Nuclear Weapons in the Middle East, 1948-2013: Israel's Nuclear Option in the Region and in Israeli Politics*, p. 349 [Hebrew].

25  Yossi Beilin's personal archives.
26  Yossi Beilin, *Manual for a Wounded Dove*, p. 148 [Hebrew].
27  Zanany, *The Annapolis Process (2007-2008): Negotiation and Its Discontents*, p. 86.
28  Beilin, *Manual for a Wounded Dove*, p. 156 [Hebrew].
29  Uriya Shavit's review of Meir Hatina, "Martyrdom in Modern Islam: Piety, Power and Politics," *History* 35, Summer 2015, p. 111 [Hebrew].
30  Beilin, *Manual for a Wounded Dove*, p. 157 [Hebrew].
31  Ibid., p. 147.
32  Ari Shavit, "The Ice Man," *Haaretz*, June 13, 2001 [Hebrew].
33  Yossi Beilin's personal archives.
34  Ibid.
35  Ibid.
36  Ibid.
37  Ibid.
38  Raviv Drocker, *Harakiri—Ehud Barak, The Failure*. Tel Aviv: Yedioth Ahroonoth Books, 2002, pp. 349–60 [Hebrew].
39  Zanany, *The Annapolis Process (2007-2008): Negotiation and Its Discontents*, p. 86.
40  Yossi Beilin's personal archives.
41  Shaul Arieli, *A Border Between Us and You: The Israeli-Palestinian Conflict and Ways to Resolve It*. Tel Aviv: Aliyat Hagag Books and Miskal, 2013 [Hebrew].
42  Author's interview with Beilin, June 2017.
43  Yossi Beilin's personal archives.
44  Zanany, *The Annapolis Process (2007-2008): Negotiation and Its Discontents*, p. 86.
45  Ibid., p. 20.
46  Ibid., p. 21.
47  Yossi Beilin's personal archives.
48  Yasser Arafat, "The Palestinian Vision of Peace," *The New York Times Magazine*, February 3, 2002.
49  Yossi Beilin's personal archives.
50  Akiva Eldar, "A First Look at the Taba document," *Haaretz*, February 13, 2002 [Hebrew].

# Chapter 10

1  Attila Somfalvi, "Beilin Forming One Peace Movement for the Entire Left," *Ynet*, June 3, 2002 [Hebrew].
2  The left's role in dismantling the welfare state, starting with the economic stabilization plan of 1985, continued with the privatization policy of the second Rabin government, which sought to weaken the Histadrut and privatize the health system and labor market. The Barak government contributed to this trend when it sought to privatize prisons during Ben-Ami's term as minister of public security.
3  The full text of the agreement can be found on the Geneva Initiative website: http://www.geneva-accord.org/mainmenu/english
4  Menachem Klein, "A Response to Critics of the Geneva Accord," *Strategic Update* 7(2), July 2004, p. 41 [Hebrew].
5  "The Geneva Initiative," *Institute for National Security Studies website*, October 13, 2003.

6   Yossi Beilin's personal archives.

7   Ibid.

8   Weisglass responded to a question about what precipitated the disengagement plan: "In fall 2003, we understood that everything was stuck. Though the Americans held the Palestinians responsible and not us, Arik realized that this reality would not last. That they wouldn't leave us alone. They wouldn't let up on us. Time was working against us. And there was international erosion; there was domestic erosion. In Israel, meanwhile, everything was falling apart. The economy was on the ropes. And when the Geneva Initiative appeared, there was broad support for it." In Ari Shavit, "The Plan behind the Disengagement Plan," *Haaretz*, October 8, 2004 [Hebrew].

9   Sharon: "If the Disengagement Isn't Approved, We'll Adopt the Geneva Initiative," *Nana*, April 30, 2004 [Hebrew].

10  See: Ran Cohen, *The Battle for the Home: The Public Housing Law*. Tel Aviv: Yedioth Ahronoth-Hemed, 2008 [Hebrew].

11  Nachman Gilboa, "A Polite Confrontation," *Hadaf Hayarok*, February 26, 2004 [Hebrew].

12  Yossi Beilin's personal archives.

13  Yossi Beilin, *The Path to Geneva: The Quest for a Permanent Agreement, 1996—2004*. Tel Aviv: Yedioth Ahronoth, 2004, p. 48 [Hebrew].

# Chapter 11

1   Yossi Beilin, "I Feel for You, My Brother Avrum," *Israel Hayom*, January 4, 2015 [Hebrew].

2   Avraham Burg, "Beilin, It's Time for Hadash," *Haaretz*, January 8, 2015 [Hebrew]. (The title can also be translated "Beilin, a new time has come": *hadash* means "new" but is also an acronym in Hebrew for the Democratic Front for Peace and Equality.)

3   Yossi Beilin, "Confederation Is the Key to Mideast Peace," *The New York Times*, May 14, 2015.

4   Ibid.

5   Condoleezza Rice, *No Higher Honor: A Memoir of My Years in Washington*. New York: Cron Publishers, 2011, p. 723.

# Chapter 12

1   The letter was published by *Maariv* on September 12, 2003.

2   Yossi Beilin's personal archives.

3   Henry Fishman and Ephraim Lavie, *The Peace Process: Seventeen Plans in Ten Years*. Tel Aviv: Peres Center for Peace and the Palestine Center for Strategic Studies, 2010, p. 364.

4   Ze'ev Maoz and Bruce Russett, "Normative and Structural Causes of Democratic Peace, 1946-1986," *Politics* 26, Jerusalem: The Leonard Davis Institute, Hebrew University, 2017, p. 25 [Hebrew].

5   Knesset Proceedings, Session 357 of the 13th Knesset, June 28, 1995. "Motion for the Agenda—Toward Implementation of Stage 2 of the Oslo Accords" [Hebrew].

6   Omar Zanany, *The Annapolis Process (2007-2008): Negotiation and Its Discontents*,
    p. 44. Olmert was the last prime minister to try to propose an agreement to the
    Palestinians.

7   Rashid Khalidi, "Truth, Justice and Reconciliation: Elements of a Solution to the
    Palestinian Refugee Issue," in Ghada Karmi and Eugene Cotran (eds.), *The Palestinian
    Exodus, 1948-1998*. Reading: Ithaca Press, 1999, p. 224.

8   Amos Oz, *In the Land of Israel*, New York: Harcourt and Brace, 1993, p. 248.

9   Ben-Ami, "So Close and Yet So Far: Lessons from the Israeli-Palestinian Peace
    Process," p. 85.

10  Omar Zanany, *The Annapolis Process (2007-2008): Negotiation and Its Discontents*,
    p. 96.

11  Udi Alon, "Out of Loyalty to Our Common Past," *Haaretz*, April 7, 2016 [Hebrew].

12  In a fascinating article, Raef Zreik and Azar Dakwar compare Israel and apartheid-era
    South Africa. They argue that apartheid is a separation regime created from a unifying
    national framework according to the following elements: relations in the labor market;
    political theology; the embracing state framework; and the role of languages in the
    state. These components, they contend, were agents of unity in South Africa in the
    twentieth century (that is, creating a unifying framework for apartheid). In their view,
    these elements play a different role in Israel and this makes it harder to recognize the
    Israeli reality as apartheid. However, they claim, the separation in Israel is comparable
    in some situations to what was practiced in South Africa. See: "On South Africa
    Then and Palestine/Israel: Apartheid and Ways of Conceptualizing It," in Hunaida
    Ghanem and Azar Dakwar (eds.), *The Analogy of Apartheid for Palestine/Israel and Its
    Boundaries: A View from Palestine*, pp. 187–88.

13  Ibid.

14  Ze'ev Jabotinsky, "Vanity of Vanities," *Hayarden* 12, February 1938 [Hebrew].

15  "Netanyahu's Mistakes," *Maariv*, November 17, 2007 [Hebrew].

16  This is the assessment of Dr. Shaul Arieli. As a colonel in the IDF, Arieli headed the
    Interim Agreement Administration during the Rabin government and the Peace
    Administration under the Barak government. See: Zanany, *The Annapolis Process
    (2007-2008): Negotiation and Its Discontents*, p. 91.

17  Mati Steinberg, "What's New in Hamas' New Document," *Haaretz*, May 3, 2017
    [Hebrew].

# Bibliography

*Some of the Hebrew sources cited in this book are also available in English. Most of the page references below are to the Hebrew version.*

## Archives

Ben-Gurion Archives
Central Zionist Archives
Israel State Archives
Labor Party Archives
Yad Tabenkin Archives
Yossi Beilin's archives

## Lectures

Bareli, Avi. "The Partnership of Ben-Gurion and Sharett," a lecture at the Ben-Gurion House museum, February 6, 2015.
Sharett, Moshe. "Israel and Arabia: War and Peace," parts of a lecture at Beit Berl, October 1957.

## Diaries

Yossi Beilin
Akram Haniyah

## Articles (Hebrew)

Azoulai, Naama. "We Are the Secular Jews? Definition of Identity in the Jewish Renewal Movement in the Secular Space." In Yochi Fischer (ed.), *Secularization and Secularism: Interdisciplinary Perspectives*, 314–40. Jerusalem: Van Leer Institute, 2016.
Beilin, Yossi. "Unilateral Withdrawal of the IDF from Southern Lebanon." In Yaacov Bar-Siman-Tov (ed.), *The Security Zone in Lebanon: A Reconsideration*, 47–53. Jerusalem: The Leonard Davis Institute and the Hebrew University, 1997.
Ben-Gurion, David. *East and West: We and Our Neighbors*, 246–8. Tel Aviv: Davar, 1931.
De-Malach, Daniel. "Where is the Occupation, the Discrimination and the Imperialism? Notes on the Discussion of the Repercussions of Globalism in Israel." *Theory and Criticism* 35 (2009): 111–40.

Epstein, Isaac. "The Hidden Question." *HaShiloah*, August 1907, 192–205.

Feige, Michael. "Rabin's Murder and the Ethnic Margins of Religious Zionism." *Theory and Criticism* 45 (2015): 31–56.

Feldman, Nitzan. "Economic Peace: Theory vs. Reality." *Strategic Update* 12, no. 3, Institute for National Security Studies (2009): 17–25.

Filc, Dani. "Post-Populism in Israel: The South American Model of Netanyahu '96," *Theory and Criticism* 9 (Winter 1996): 217–32.

Goldstein, Amir. "The Decline of the General Zionists and the Failure of the Liberal Alternative, 1959–1961." *Iyunim Bitkumat Israel* 16, Sde Boker: Ben-Gurion Institute (2006): 203–343.

Greenberg, Yitzhak. "Buried his Head in the Sand." *Israel* 10 (2006): 247–53.

Gutwein, Danny. "The Israeli Left: Alive or Dead?" *Eretz Acheret* 27 (April 28, 2005).

Holzer, Elie. "The Evolving Meaning of the 'Three Oaths' in Religious-Zionist Thought." *Daat: A Journal of Jewish Philosophy and Kabbalah* 47, Bar-Ilan University (2001): 129–45.

Israeli, Tzipi and Yehudit Orbach. "'Rags' and VIPs Looking to Make Headlines: Protest, Media and National Security." *Kesher* 47, Tel Aviv University (Winter 2015): 61–75.

Kaufman, Asher. "Borders, Identities and Territorialism in the Middle East: Seven Shi'ite Villages as Case Studies." *Jama'a* 14 (2005): 65–89.

Kenig, Ofer. "Primaries in Israel after 20 Years: An Interim Balance Sheet." *The Public Sphere* 7 (2012): 139–50.

Kenig, Ofer. "Twenty Years Later: The Stinking Maneuver in the Mirror of Time." Jerusalem: Israel Democracy Institute, 2010. Available at: www.idi.org.il/articles/1629 (March 13, 2010).

Kipnis, Yigal. "The Turning Point in Studying the Circumstances of the Outbreak of the Yom Kippur War." *Iyunim Bitkumat Israel* 26, Sde Boker: Ben-Gurion Institute (2016): 41–81.

Klein, Menachem. "A Response to Critics of the Geneva Accord." *Strategic Update* 7, no. 2 (July 2004): 38–43.

Leon, Nissim. "Mizrahi Traditionalism as an Echo of Jewish Existence." *Akadamot* 23, Jerusalem (2009): 129–46.

Maoz, Ze'ev and Bruce Russett. "Normative and Structural Causes of Democratic Peace, 1946–1986." *Politics* 26, Jerusalem: The Leonard Davis Institute, Hebrew University (2017): 1–41.

Rahat, Gideon. "The Election System 1948–1959: From Default to an Entrenched System." *Iyunim Bitkumat Israel* 11, Sde Boker: Ben-Gurion Institute (2001): 369–447.

Raz, Adam. "Divided Fronts – The 'Strange' Anatomy of Rabin's Oslo Decision." *Israelis* 4, Ben-Gurion University (2012): 97–132.

Raz-Krakotzkin, Amnon. "The Return to the History of Redemption (Or, What is the 'History' to Which We 'Return' in the Phrase 'The Return to the History'?)" In Shmuel N. Eisenstadt and Moshe Lissak (eds.), *Zionism and the Return to History: A Reappraisal*, 249–76. Jerusalem: Yad Ben-Zvi, 1999.

Raz-Krakotzkin, Amnon. "There is No God, But He Promised Us the Land." *Mita'am* 3 (2005): 71–76.

Rubinovitz, Ziv and Gerald Steinberg. "Menachem Begin's Autonomy Plan: Between Political Realism and Ideology." *The Public Sphere* 6, Tel Aviv: Tel Aviv University (2012): 75–95.

Sela, Avraham. "The Security Zone: Lebanese and Regional Aspects." In Yaacov Bar-Siman-Tov (ed.), *The Security Zone in Lebanon: A Reconsideration*, 35–45. Jerusalem: The Leonard Davis Institute, 2001.

Shalom, Zaki. "Ben-Gurion and Sharett's Opposition to Territorial Demands from Israel, 1949–1956." *Iyunim Bitkumat Israel* 2, Sde Boker: Ben-Gurion Institute (1992): 197–213.

Shavit, Uriya. Review of Meir Hatina, "Martyrdom in Modern Islam: Piety, Power and Politics." *History* 35 (Summer 2015): 111–19.

Sheffer, Gabriel. "Moshe Sharett: His Moral Approach to the Israeli-Arab Conflict." In Ephraim Lavie (ed.), *Nationalism and Morality: Zionist Discourse and the Arab Question*, 177–97. Jerusalem: Carmel, 2014.

Sheffer, Gabriel. "Principles of Pragmatism: a Reevaluation of British Policies Toward Palestine in the 1930s." *Cathedra* 29 (September 1983): 113–44.

Shemesh, Moshe. "PLO: The Path to Oslo – 1988 as the Turning Point in the History of the Palestinian National Movement." *Iyunim Bitkumat Israel* 9, Sde Boker: Ben-Gurion Institute (2009): 186–245.

Shilon, Avi. "Ben-Gurion's Approach to Borders." *Zion* 83, Jerusalem (2016): 407–33.

Shilon, Avi. "I'm Responsible, You Decide: Menachem Begin's Detached Leadership Pattern in the Etzel." *Iyunim Bitkumat Israel* 26, Sde Boker: Ben-Gurion University (2016): 249–80.

Slivniak, Dmitri. "Neither a badge of courage, nor a mark of Cain." *Eretz Acheret*, March 10, 2002.

Sofer, Arnon and Gila Shalev. "The De-Facto Implementation of the Palestinian Demand for Return." *Ensemble*, National Security College and University of Haifa (July 2004): 4–7.

Yablonka, Hanna. "Holocaust Survivors in Israel: Initial Conclusions." *On the Path of Remembrance* 27, Jerusalem: Yad Vashem (1998): 4–9.

Ze'evi, Dror. "ISIS: The Rise of Baathist Salafism." *The Forum for Regional Thinking*, December 14, 2015, www.regthink.org/articles

Zreik, Raef and Azar Dakwa. "On South Africa Then and Palestine/Israel: Apartheid and Ways of Conceptualizing It." In Hunaida Ghanem and Azar Dakwar (eds.), *The Analogy of Apartheid for Palestine/Israel and its Boundaries: A View from Palestine* (forthcoming).

## Books by Yossi Beilin

*A Guide to Leaving Lebanon*. Tel Aviv: Hakibbutz Hameuchad, 1998.

*Manual for a Wounded Dov*. Tel Aviv: Yedioth Ahronoth, 2001.

*The Path to Geneva: The Quest for a Permanent Agreement, 1996–2004*. Tel Aviv: Yedioth Ahronoth, 2004.

*Touching Peace*. Tel Aviv: Yedioth Ahronoth, 2001.

## Books (Hebrew)

Adler, Haim and Reuven Kahana (eds.). *Israel: A Society in Formation – A Sociological Analysis of Sources Vol. B (Religion and Culture)*. Jerusalem: Akademon, 1975.

Arian, Asher (head of research team). *A Portrait of Israeli Jewry: Beliefs, Observances and Values Among Israeli Jews*. Jerusalem: Israel Democracy Institute and Guttman Center for Public Opinion and Policy Research, 2009.

Arieli, Shaul. *A Border Between Us and You: The Israeli-Palestinian Conflict and Ways to Resolve It*. Tel Aviv: Aliyat Hagag Books and Miskal, 2013.

Aronson, Shlomo. *Nuclear Weapons in the Middle East, 1948–2013: Israel's Nuclear Option in the Region and in Israeli Politics*. Jerusalem: Akademon, 2014.

Auron, Yair. *Reflections on the Inconceivable: Theoretical Aspects in Genocide Studies*. Ra'anana: The Open University of Israel, 2006.

Avineri, Shlomo. *Herzl*. Jerusalem: The Zalman Shazar Center, 2007.

Bar-Yosef, Eitan. *A Villa in the Jungle: Africa in Israeli Culture*. Jerusalem: Van Leer Institute and Hakibbutz Hameuchad, 2014.

Bar-Zohar, Michael. *Ben-Gurion*. Tel Aviv: Am Oved, 1977.

Bar-Zohar, Michael. *Like a Phoenix: Shimon Peres – Biography*. Tel Aviv, Yedioth Ahronoth, 2006.

Begin, Binyamin Ze'ev. *A Sad Story*. Tel Aviv: Yedioth Ahronoth, 2000.

Ben-Gurion, David. *Meetings with Arab Leaders*. Tel Aviv: Am Oved, 1967.

Ben-Gurion, David. *The Renewed State of Israel*. Tel Aviv: Am Oved, 1975.

Ben-Gurion, David. *War Diary*, Vol. B. Tel Aviv: Am Oved, 1982.

Ben-Haim, Avishai. *Man of Vision: The Ultra-Orthodox Ideology of Rabbi Shach*. Jerusalem: Mosaica, 2004.

Ben-Porat, Shayke. *Conversations with Yossi Beilin*. Tel Aviv: Hakibbutz Hameuchad, 1996.

Bentsur, Eytan. *The Road to Peace Crosses Madrid*. Tel Aviv: Yedioth Ahronoth, 1997.

Berent, Moshe. *A Nation Like All Nations: Towards the Establishment of an Israeli Republic*. Jerusalem: Carmel, 2009.

*Birthright: The True Story*. Tel Aviv: Hakibbutz Hameuchad, 2009.

Cohen, Ran. *The Battle for the Home: The Public Housing Law*. Tel Aviv: Yedioth Ahronoth-Hemed, 2008.

Cohen, Uri and Nissim Leon. *The Herut Movement's Central Committee and the Mizrahim, 1965–1977: From Patronizing Partnership to Competitive Partnership*. Jerusalem: Israel Democracy Institute, 2011.

Don-Yehiya, Eliezer. *Politics of Accommodation: Settling Conflicts of State and Religion in Israel*. Jerusalem: Floersheimer Institute for Policy Studies, 1997.

Elam, Yigal. *What Happened Here*. Tel Aviv: Am Oved, 2012.

Fanon, Frantz. *The Wretched of the Earth*. Tel Aviv: Babel, 2006.

Fischer, Yochi (ed.). *Secularization and Secularism: Interdisciplinary Perspectives*. Jerusalem: Van Leer Institute, 2016.

Fishman, Henry and Ephraim Lavie. *The Peace Process: Seventeen Plans in Ten Years*. Tel Aviv: Peres Center for Peace and the Palestine Center for Strategic Studies, 2010.

Foxman Shaal, Moshe (ed.). *The Camp David Accords: Collection of Articles and Lectures*. Jerusalem: Carmel and the Begin Heritage Center, 2010.

Friedman, Thomas L. *From Beirut to Jerusalem*. Tel Aviv: Maariv, 1990.

Gavison, Ruth. *The Constitutional Revolution: Reality or Self-Fulfilling Prophecy?* Jerusalem: Israel Democracy Institute, 1998.

Halevi, Moshe (ed.). *Ze'ev Jabotinsky: Letters, 1935*. Tel Aviv: Jabotinsky Institute, 2009.

Halevy, Efraim. *Man in the Shadows: Inside the Middle East Crisis with a Man Who Led the Mossad*. Tel Aviv: Matar, 2006.

Hermann, Tamar (ed.). *The Israel Democracy Index 2013*. Jerusalem: Israel Democracy Institute, 2013.

Herzl, Binyamin Ze'ev. *The Jewish State [Der Judenstaat]*. Tel Aviv: Am Oved, 2008.

Hirschfeld, Yair. *Oslo: Formula for Peace*. Tel Aviv: Rabin Center and Am Oved, 2000.

Indyk, Martin. *Pax Americana*. Tel Aviv: Am Oved, 2009.

Israeli, Haim. *Scroll of Life*. Tel Aviv: Yedioth Ahronoth, 2005.

Jabotinsky, Ze'ev. *Toward a State*. Jerusalem: Eri Jabotinsky, 1953.

Kaplan, Kimmy. *Internal Popular Discourse in Israeli Haredi Society*. Jerusalem: Zalman Shazar Center, 2007.

Kimmerling, Baruch. *The End of Ashkenazi Hegemony*. Jerusalem: Keter, 2002.

Kipnis, Yigal. *The Road to War*. Charlottesville: Just World Books, 2013.

Klein, Aaron. *The Master of Operations: The Story of Mike Harari*. Jerusalem: Keter, 2014.

Klein, Menachem. *Antagonistic Collaboration: PLO-Jordanian Dialogue, 1985–1988*. Jerusalem: The Leonard Davis Institute, 1988.

Lehrs, Lior. *Peace Talks over Jerusalem: A Review of the Israeli-Palestinian Negotiations Concerning Jerusalem, 1993–2011*. Jerusalem: Jerusalem Institute for Israel Studies, 2011.

Leon, Nissim. *Soft Ultra-Orthodoxy: Religious Renewal in Oriental Jewry in Israel*. Jerusalem: Yad Ben-Zvi, 2010.

Lewis, Bernard. *The Jews of Islam*. Princeton, NJ: Princeton University Press, 1987.

Mendes-Flohr, Paul. *Divided Passions: Jewish Intellectuals and the Experience of Modernity*. Tel Aviv: Am Oved, 2010.

Morris, Benny. *The Birth of the Refugee Problem, 1947–1949*. Tel Aviv: Am Oved, 1991.

Morris, Benny. *One State, Two States: Israel and Palestine*. Tel Aviv: Am Oved, 2012.

Morris, Benny. *Righteous Victims: The History of the Zionist-Arab Conflict, 1881–2001*. Tel Aviv: Am Oved, 2003.

Naor, Arye. *Begin in Power*. Tel Aviv: Yedioth Ahronoth, 1993.

Naor, Arye. *Cabinet at War*. Tel Aviv: Yedioth Ahronoth, 1986.

Netanyahu, Benjamin. *A Place Under the Sun*. Tel Aviv: Yedioth Ahronoth, 1993.

Pearlman, Moshe. *David Ben-Gurion*. Tel Aviv: Zmora Bitan, 1987.

Pikar, Avi. *Selective Immigration: Israel's Policy toward the Immigration of North African Jews, 1951–1956*. Sde Boker: Ben-Gurion Institute, 2013.

Preuss, Teddy. *Begin in Power*. Jerusalem: Keter, 1984.

Rabin, Yitzhak with Dov Goldstein, *Pinkas Sherut*. Tel Aviv: Maariv, 1979. [*published in English as The Rabin Memoirs*].

Rabinovich, Itamar. *Waging Peace: Israel and the Arabs, 1948–2003*. Or Yehuda: Dvir, 2004.

Rabinovich, Itamar. *Yitzhak Rabin: Soldier, Leader, Statesman*. Modi'in: Kineret Zmora-Bitan Dvir, 2017.

Rebhun, Uzi and Gilad Malach. *Demographic Trends in Israel*. Jerusalem: Metzilah Center, 2009.

Reiter, Yitzhak (ed.). *The Arab Society in Israel*. Jerusalem: Abraham Fund, 2013.

Sagi, Uri. *Lights in the Fog*. Tel Aviv: Yedioth Ahronoth, 1998.

Salmon, Yosef. *Do Not Provoke Providence: Orthodoxy in the Grip of Nationalism*. Jerusalem, Zalman Shazar Center, 2006.

Sapir, Gideon. *The Constitutional Revolution: Past, Present and Future*. Tel Aviv: Yedioth Ahronoth, Bar-Ilan University and University of Haifa, 2010.

Schiff, Ze'ev and Ehud Ya'ari, *War of Deception*. Tel Aviv: Schocken, 1984. [*published in English as Israel's Lebanon War*].

Segev, Tom. *1967: The Year that Transformed Israel*. Jerusalem: Keter, 2005.

Shach, Eliezer. *Letters and Articles*. Bnei Brak, 1989.

Shalom, Zaki. *Like Fire in his Bones: Ben-Gurion and his Struggles over the Character of the State and its Leadership, 1963–1967*. Sde Boker: Ben-Gurion Institute, 2004.

Shamir, Yitzhak. *Summing Up: An Autobiography*. Tel Aviv: Yedioth Ahronoth, 1994.

Shapira, Anita. *The Army Controversy, 1948: Ben-Gurion's Struggle for Control*. Tel Aviv: Hakibbutz Hameuchad, 1985.

Shapiro, Yonathan. *Chosen to Command: The Road to Power of the Herut Party – A Sociopolitical Interpretation*. Tel Aviv: Am Oved, 1989.

Shapiro, Yonathan. *An Elite without Successors*. Tel Aviv: Am Oved, 1984.

Sheffer, Gabriel. *Moshe Sharett: A Political Biography*. Jerusalem: Carmel, 2015.

Shenhav, Yehuda. *In the Green Line Trap: A Jewish Political Treatise*. Tel Aviv: Am Oved, 2010.

Sher, Gilad. *Within Reach: The Israeli-Palestinian Peace Negotiations, 1999–2001*: Tel Aviv: Yedioth Ahronoth, 2001.

Shifris, Amos. *Israel Galili: A Man of Words and Deeds*. Tel Aviv: Yad Tabenkin, 2010.

Shilon, Avi. *Ben-Gurion: Epilogue*. Tel Aviv: Am Oved, 2013.

Shlaim, Avi. *The Iron Wall: Israel and the Arab World*. Tel Aviv: Yedioth Ahronoth, 2005.

Sneh, Ephraim. *Navigating Perilous Waters*. Tel Aviv: Yedioth Ahronoth, 2002.

Tabenkin, Yitzhak. *Chapters of Life: The Man and His Work – Friends and Pupils Recount his Teachings*. Ramat Efal: Ha'kibutz Hameuhad, 1984.

Tabenkin, Yitzhak. *Devarim* [Collected Speeches]. Tel Aviv: Hakibbutz Hameuchad, 1967.

Tevet, Shabtai. *Ben-Gurion and the Arabs of Israel*. Jerusalem and Tel Aviv: Schocken, 1985.

Tzahor, Ze'ev, *Vision and Reckoning: Ben-Gurion – Ideology and Politics*. Tel Aviv: Yedioth Ahronoth and Sifriyat Poalim, 2004.

Webber, Shaul. *Yitzhak Rabin: The Growth of a Leader*. Tel Aviv: Maariv, 2010.

Weitz, Yechiam. *The Man Who was Murdered Twice: The Life, Trial and Death of Israel Kastner*. Jerusalem: Keter, 1995.

Ya'ar, Ephraim and Ze'ev Shavit (eds.). *Trends in Israeli Society*. Ra'anana: Open University, 2003.

Yadgar, Yaakov. *Traditional Jews in Israel: Modernity Without Secularization*. Jerusalem: Keter, 2010.

Yuran, Noam. *Channel 2: The New Etatism*. Tel Aviv: Resling, 2001.

Zak, Moshe. *King Hussein Makes Peace: Thirty Years of Secret Talks*. Ramat Gan: Bar-Ilan University Press, 1996.

# Films

"To Be Shimon Peres," director: Naftaly Gliksberg, 2014.

"The Chosen," director and presenter: Haim Yavin, 1981.

"Rabin, in His Own Words," director: Erez Laufer, 2016.

# PhD dissertations

Beilin, Yossi. "Intergenerational Friction in Three Parties in Israel." Tel Aviv University, 1980.

Shilon, Avi. "The Revisionist Movement Leaders' Attitudes Toward Jewish Religion, 1925–2005." Bar-Ilan University, 2014.

Tsur, Ya'akov. "Between Land and State: The Complete Land in the Approach of Tabenkin and Hakibbutz Hameuchad." University of Haifa, 2012.

# Newspapers, journals and websites

*Bamahane*
*Davar*
*Haaretz*
*Hadaf Hayarok*
*Israel Hayom*
*Maariv*
*The New York Times*
*Walla!*
*Ynet*

# Protocols

Knesset Proceedings

# Books (English)

Amstutz, Mark R. *The Healing of Nations: The Promise and Limits of Political Forgiveness.* Lanham, MD: Rowman & Littlefield, 2004.

Arian, Asher. *The Elections in Israel 1977.* Jerusalem: Academic Press, 1980.

Arian, Asher. *Security Threatened: Surveying Israeli Opinion on Peace and War.* Cambridge: Cambridge University Press, 1995.

Baron, Salo. *Modern Nationalism and Religion.* Philadelphia, PA: Jewish Publication Society of America, 1960.

Bar-Yosef, Uri. *The Watchman Fell Asleep: The Surprise of Yom Kippur and its Sources.* Albany, NY: SUNY Press, 2012.

Ben-Porat, Guy. *Between State and Synagogue: The Secularization of Modern Israel.* Cambridge: Cambridge University Press, 2013.

Casanova, José. *Public Religions in the Modern World.* Chicago, IL: University of Chicago Press, 1994.

Filc, Dani. *The Political Right in Israel: The Many Faces of Jewish Populism.* New York: Routledge, 2010.

Herzl, Theodor. *Old New Land [Altneuland].* Stanford, CA: Createspace Independent Publishing Platform, 2012.

Kedourie, Elie. *Nationalism.* Oxford: Blackwell, 1993.

Manor, Udi. *Yigal Allon: A Neglected Political Legacy, 1949–1980.* Eastbourne, East Sussex, UK: Sussex Academic Press, 2017.

Morris, Benny. *Israel's Border Wars: 1949–1956.* Oxford: Clarendon Press, 1997.

Omer, Atalia. *When Peace is Not Enough: How the Israeli Peace Camp Thinks About Religion, Nationalism and Justice.* Chicago, IL: University of Chicago Press, 2013.

Oz, Amos. *In the Land of Israel.* New York: Harcourt and Brace, 1993.

Peres, Shimon (with David Landau). *Battling for Peace: Memoirs.* London: Weidenfeld and Nicholson, 1995.

Peri, Yoram, Telepopulism: *Media and Politics in Israel*, Stanford, CA: Stanford University Press, 2004.

Rabinovich, Itamar. *The Brink of Peace: The Israeli-Syrian Negotiations*. Princeton, NJ: Princeton University Press, 1999.

Rice, Condoleezza. *No Higher Honor: A Memoir of My Years in Washington*. New York: Crown, 2011.

Ross, Dennis. *The Missing Peace: The Inside Story of the Fight for Middle East Peace*. New York: Farrar, Straus and Giroux, 2004.

Shapira, Anita. *Israel: A History*. London: Weidenfeld & Nicolson, 2012.

Shapira, Anita. *Yigal Allon, Native Son*. Philadelphia, PA: University of Pennsylvania Press, 2008.

Shapiro, Yonathan. *The Road to Power: Herut Party in Israel*. Albany, NY: SUNY Press, 1991.

Shilon, Avi. *Ben-Gurion: His Later Years in the Political Wilderness*. Lanham, MD: Rowman & Littlefield, 2016.

Shilon, Avi. *Menachem Begin: A Life*. New Haven, CT: Yale University Press, 2012.

Shindler, Colin. *The Rise of the Israeli Right: From Odessa to Hebron*. Cambridge, MA: Cambridge University Press, 2014.

Shlaim, Avi. *The Iron Wall: Israel and the Arab World*. New York: W. W. Norton, 2001.

Shultz, P. George. *Turmoil and Triumph: My Years as Secretary of State*. New York: Scribner's Sons, 1993.

Susser, Asher. *Israel, Jordan and Palestine: The Two-State Imperative*. Walheim, MA: Brandeis University Press, 2011.

Zanany, Omar. *The Annapolis Process (2007–2008): Negotiation and Its Discontents*. Tel Aviv: Tami Steinmetz Center for Peace Research and Molad, 2015.

Ziv, Guy. *Why Hawks Become Doves: Shimon Peres and Foreign Policy Change in Israel*. Albany: State University of New York Press, 2015.

## Articles and Chapters (English)

Abd Al-Shafi, Haydar. "Reflections on the Peace Process: An Interview with Haydar Abd Al-Shafi." *Journal of Palestine Studies* 22, no. 1 (Autumn 1992): 57–69.

Arafat, Yasser. "The Palestinian Vision of Peace." *The New York Times Magazine*, February 3, 2002.

Bahral, Uri. *The Effect of Mass Immigration on Wages in Israel*. Jerusalem: Falk Project for Economic Research in Israel, 1965.

Barnett, Michael. "Culture, Strategy and Foreign Policy Change: Israel's Road to Oslo." *European Journal of International Relations* 5, no. 1 (1999): 5–36.

Beilin, Yossi. "Confederation Is the Key to Mideast Peace." *The New York Times*, May 14, 2015.

Ben-Ami, Shlomo. "So Close and Yet So Far: Lessons from the Israeli-Palestinian Peace Process." *Israel Studies* 10, no. 2 (Summer 2005): 72–90.

Ben-Ze'ev, Efrat. "Hidden Scripts: The Social Evolution of Alterman's 'Don't You Give Them Guns.'" *Israel Studies Review* 29, no. 1 (2014): 1–17.

Bialer, Uri. "The Road to the Capital: The Establishment of Jerusalem as the Official Seat of the Israeli Government in 1949." *Studies in Zionism* 5, no. 2 (1984): 273–96.

Bourdieu, Pierre. "Structures, Habitus, Practices." In *The Logic of Practice*, trans. Richard Nice, 52–65. Stanford: Stanford University Press, 1990.

Eisenstadt, Shmuel N. "The Transformation of the Religious Dimension and the Crystallization of New Civilizational Visions and Relations." In Gabriel Motzkin and

Yochi Fischer (eds.), *Religion and Democracy in Contemporary Europe*, 21–35. London: Alliance Publishing Trust, 2008.

Hazan, Reuven Y. "Party System Change in Israel, 1948–98: A Conceptual and Typological Border-Stretching of Europe?" In Paul Pennings and Jan-Erik Lane (eds.), *Comparing Party System Change*, 151–66. London: Routledge, 1998.

Hirsch, Michal Ben-Josef. "From Taboo to the Negotiable: The Israeli New Historians and the Changing Representation of the Palestinian Refugee Problem." *Perspectives on Politics* 5, no. 2 (2007): 241–58.

Hirschl, Ran. "The Struggle for Hegemony: Explaining the Expansion of Judicial Power through the Constitutionalization of Rights in Culturally-Divided Polities." *Stanford Journal of International Law* 36 (2000): 73–118.

Katz, Gideon. "Beyond the Religious-Secular Dichotomy." *Israel Studies Review* 30, no. 2 (2015): 92–112.

Khalidi, Rashid. "The Formation of Palestinian Identity: The Critical Years, 1917–1923." In James P. Jankowitz and Israel Gershoni (eds.), *Rethinking Nationalism in the Arab Middle East*, 171–90. New York: Columbia University Press, 1997.

Khalidi, Rashid. "Truth, Justice and Reconciliation: Elements of a Solution to the Palestinian Refugee Issue." In Ghada Karmi and Eugene Cotran (eds.), *The Palestinian Exodus, 1948–1998*, 221–41. Reading, UK: Ithaca Press, 1999.

Khoury, Nadim. "National Narratives and the Oslo Peace Process: How Peacebuilding Paradigms Address Conflicts over History." *Nations and Nationalism* 22, no. 3 (2016): 465–83.

Leon, Dan. "Israeli Public Opinion Polls on the Peace Process." *The Palestine-Israel Journal* 2, no. 1 (1995): 10–12.

Menocal, Rocha Alina and Kate Kilpatrick. "Toward More Effective Peace Building: A Conversation with Roland Paris." *Development in Practice* 15, no. 6 (2005): 767–77.

Pei, Minxin. "The Paradoxes of American Nationalism." *Foreign Policy* 136 (2003): 31–37.

Peri, Yoram. "The Political–Military Complex: The IDF's Influence Over Policy Towards the Palestinians Since 1987." *Israel Affairs* 11, no. 2 (2005): 324–44.

Ringel, Joseph. "The Construction and De-construction of the Ashkenazi vs. Sephardic/Mizrahi Dichotomy in Israeli Culture: Rabbi Eliyahou Zini vs. Rabbi Ovadia Yosef." *Israel Studies* 21, no. 2 (Summer 2016): 155–82.

Shaath, Nabil. "Reflections on the Peace Process: An Interview with Nabil Shaath." *Journal of Palestine Studies* 22, no. 1 (Autumn 1992): 70–77.

Shain, Yossi and Sarah Fainberg. "The Israelization of Judaism and the Jews of France." *Jewish Review of Books*, Fall 2015. Available at: https://jewishreviewofbooks.com/articles/1771/the-israelization-of-judaism-and-the-jews-of-france/

Shokeid, Moshe. "The Religiosity of Middle Eastern Jews." In *Israeli Judaism: The Sociology of Religion in Israel*, 255–84. New Brunswick: Transaction, 1995.

Ward, Ian. "Democracy after Secularism." *The Good Society* 19, no. 2 (2010): 30–36.

# Index